Interdisciplinary Approaches to Human Rights

Interdisciplinary Approaches to Human Rights: History, Politics, Practice is an edited collection that brings together analyses of human rights work from multiple disciplines. Within the academic sphere, this book will garner interest from scholars who are invested in human rights as a field of study, as well as those who research, and are engaged in, the praxis of human rights.

Referring to the historical and cross-cultural study of human rights, the volume engages with disciplinary debates in political philosophy, gender and women's studies, Global South/Third World studies, international relations, psychology, and anthropology. At the same time, the authors employ diverse methodologies including oral history, theoretical and discourse analysis, ethnography, and literary and cinema studies. Within the field of human rights studies, this book attends to the critical academic gap on interdisciplinary and praxis-based approaches to the field, as opposed to a predominantly legalistic focus, drawing from case studies from a wide range of contexts in the Global South, including Bangladesh, Colombia, Haiti, India, Mexico, Palestine, and Sudan, as well as from Australia and the United States in the Global North.

For students who will go on to become researchers, practitioners, policy makers, and activists, this collection of essays will demonstrate the multi-faceted landscape of human rights and the multiple forces (philosophical, political, cultural, economic, historical) that affect it.

Rajini Srikanth is Professor of English and Dean of the Honors College at the University of Massachusetts Boston, USA. Her research interests include the intersection between literature and human rights, post-apartheid South Africa, comparative race and ethnic studies, and Asian American literature. Her recent publications include *Constructing the Enemy: Empathy/Antipathy in US Literature and Law* (2012) and *The Cambridge History of Asian American Literature* (2016).

Elora Halim Chowdhury is Professor and Chair of Women's, Gender and Sexuality Studies at the University of Massachusetts Boston, USA. Her research interests include transnational feminisms, film and culture, and human rights narrative with an emphasis on South Asia. H[...]
*Transnationalism Reversed: Women Organizing aga[...]
desh* (2011) and *Dissident Friendships: Feminism, h[...]
darity* (2016).

D1410019

Interdisciplinary Approaches to Human Rights

History, Politics, Practice

Edited by
Rajini Srikanth and Elora Halim
Chowdhury

Routledge
Taylor & Francis Group

LONDON AND NEW YORK

First published 2019
by Routledge
2 Park Square, Milton Park, Abingdon, Oxon OX14 4RN

and by Routledge
711 Third Avenue, New York, NY 10017

Routledge is an imprint of the Taylor & Francis Group, an informa business

British Library Cataloguing in Publication Data
A catalogue record for this book is available from the British Library

Library of Congress Cataloging-in-Publication Data
Names: Chowdhury, Elora Halim, editor. | Srikanth, Rajini, editor.
Title: Interdisciplinary approaches to human rights : history, politics, practice / edited by Elora Halim Chowdhury and Rajini Srikanth.
Description: First edition. | London ; New York : Routledge, 2019. | Includes bibliographical references and index.
Identifiers: LCCN 2018028642 |
ISBN 9781138482050 (hardback : alk. paper) |
ISBN 9781138482265 (pbk. : alk. paper) |
ISBN 9781351058438 (ebook)
Subjects: LCSH: Human rights.
Classification: LCC JC571 .I574 2019 | DDC 323--dc23
LC record available at https://lccn.loc.gov/2018028642

ISBN: 978-1-138-48205-0 (hbk)
ISBN: 978-1-138-48226-5 (pbk)
ISBN: 978-1-351-05843-8 (ebk)

Typeset in Goudy
by Taylor & Francis Books

Contents

List of tables   viii
List of contributors   ix
Acknowledgments   xvi

Introduction   1
RAJINI SRIKANTH AND ELORA HALIM CHOWDHURY

PART I
Human rights discourse: context and history   17

 1 Imaginary and real strangers: Constructing and reconstructing
    the human in human rights discourse and instruments   19
    MICKAELLA PERINA

 2 Rise of the global human rights regime: Challenging power with
    humanity   34
    DARREN KEW, MALCOLM RUSSELL-EINHORN AND
    ADRIANA RINCÓN VILLEGAS

 3 Between nothingness and infinity: Settlement and anti-blackness
    as the overdetermination of human rights   50
    ANDRÉS FABIÁN HENAO CASTRO

 4 Human rights, Latin America, and left internationalism during
    the Cold War   65
    STEVE STRIFFLER

 5 Women, gender, and human rights   79
    NADA MUSTAFA ALI

 6 The United States–Mexico border and human rights   98
    LUIS F. JIMÉNEZ

7 Unintended consequences in the postcolonies: When struggling
   South Africans experience rights discourse as disempowering   111
   SINDISO MNISI WEEKS

PART II
Critical areas in human rights   129

8 The mysterious disappearance of human rights in the 2030
   Development Agenda   131
   GILLIAN MACNAUGHTON

9 Addressing General Recommendation no. 35 from an
   intersectional perspective on violence, gender, and disability in
   Mexico   148
   ANA MARÍA SÁNCHEZ RODRÍGUEZ

10 Global LGBTQ politics and human rights   165
   JAMIE J. HAGEN

11 Refugee camps and the (educational) rights of the child   180
   RAJINI SRIKANTH

12 Persistent voices: A history of indigenous people and human
   rights in Australia, 1950s–2000s   196
   MARIA JOHN

PART III
Praxis and human rights   213

13 So, you want to work in human rights?   215
   JEAN-PHILIPPE BELLEAU

14 Migrant workers in the Gulf: Theoretical and human rights
   dilemmas   228
   AMANI EL JACK

15 Ethical reckoning: Theorizing gender, vulnerability, and agency
   in Bangladeshi *Muktijuddho* film   243
   ELORA HALIM CHOWDHURY

16 Right now in no place with strangers: Eudora Welty's queer love   261
   AVAK HASRATIAN

17 On the human right to peace in times of contemporary colonial
power   285
ADRIANA RINCÓN VILLEGAS

18 Beyond dignity: A case study of the mis/use of human rights
discourse in development campaigns   297
CHRIS BOBEL

19 Teaching health and human rights in a psychology capstone:
Cultivating connections between rights, personal wellness, and
social justice   312
ESTER SHAPIRO, FERNANDO ANDINO VALDEZ, YASMIN BAILEY,
GRACE FURTADO, DIANA LAMOTHE, KOSAR MOHAMMAD, MARDIA PIERRE
AND NICK WOOD

Appendix   331
BRYAN GANGEMI AND RITA ARDITTI
Index   335

Tables

8.1 The Millennium Development Goals (2001–2015)   134
8.2 Sustainable Development Goals (2015)   140

Contributors

Nada Mustafa Ali is a scholar, practitioner, and an activist whose scholarship spans the fields of comparative politics: women's, gender, and feminist studies, development studies, and African and Middle Eastern studies. A visiting associate professor in the Women's and Gender Studies Department, Nada has worked as a researcher or consultant at a number of international and grassroots organizations and United Nations (UN) agencies. She has worked as the Women's Program Coordinator at the Cairo Institute for Human Rights Studies in Egypt, and as the Africa Women's Rights Researcher at Human Rights Watch. She has consulted for a range of organizations and agencies including UN Women, UN Development Programme, UN Population Fund, USAID, US Institute of Peace, the Small Arms Survey, Almanar, and the South Sudan Women's Empowerment Network. She is the author of the book, *Gender, Race and Sudan's Exile Politics: Do We All Belong to This Country?*

Rita Arditti was a founding member of the Human Rights Working Group at UMass Boston. A PhD in biology, Rita spent three decades of her career teaching doctoral students in an interdisciplinary program at the Union Institute and university. Always an activist, she co-founded three political projects – Science for the People, New Words Bookstore, and the Women's Community Cancer Project. She wrote *Searching for Life: The Grandmothers of Plaza de Mayo and the Disappeared Children of Argentina* (1999) and co-edited two other books: *Science and Liberation*, with Pat Brennan and Steve Cavrak (1980); and *Test Tube Women: What Future for Motherhood?* with Renate Klein and Shelley Minden (1984). Rita died in 2009 after living with metastatic breast cancer for over 30 years.

Yasmin Bailey, University of Massachusetts Boston (UMass Boston) BA December 2017, majored in psychology with a minor in human rights, where she was president of the award-winning Poetry Slam Club. A daughter of Afro-Caribbean immigrants, she is a strong voice for local, global, and coalitional multi-racial and gender justice activism through her work on campus, with Beacon Leadership for Service, and with community non-profits. She is currently Lead Organizer of Campaigns and

Operations at the Youth Justice and Power Union while she prepares for graduate studies focused on human rights and social justice.

Jean-Philippe Belleau is Associate Professor of Anthropology. His areas of expertise are lowland indigenous societies, hunters-gatherers, human rights, anthropology of becoming, Amerindian perspectivism, mass violence, Brazilian cinema, and raw art. His books include *Ethnophilie. L'amour des autres nations* (Ethnophilia: Loving Other Cultures). Prior to joining UMass Boston, he worked for a decade in human rights and development with the Organization of American States, the UN, ADF International, UN Development Programme and various non-governmental organizations, including Viva Rio and the International Foundation for Electoral Systems. He directed the Human Rights Education Fund in Haiti and was the political adviser to the Organization of American States chief of mission in Haiti.

Chris Bobel is Associate Professor of Women's and Gender Studies and focuses her research most broadly on the relationships between gender, embodiment, and resistance through an intersectional feminist lens. She is the author of numerous books including *New Blood: Third Wave Feminism and the Politics of Menstruation*. Her two current major projects include writing a book that explores the framing of menstrual health campaigns in the Global South and co-editing (with Samantha Kwan) the second volume of their collection *Embodied Resistance: Challenging the Norms, Breaking the Rules.*

Elora Halim Chowdhury is Professor and Chair of Women's, Gender and Sexuality Studies at UMass Boston. Her research interests include transnational feminisms, film and culture, and human rights narrative with an emphasis on South Asia. Her recent publications include *Transnationalism Reversed: Women Organizing against Gendered Violence in Bangladesh* (2011) and *Dissident Friendships: Feminism, Imperialism and Transnational Solidarity* (2016).

Amani El Jack is Associate Professor of Women's and Gender Studies. She specializes in gender, globalization, transnational migration, conflict resolution, Islam, and international relations. Currently, she is researching social movements and uprisings in the Middle East and investigating gender dimensions of Islamic revivalism. She is the author of the forthcoming book, *Militarized Commerce: Gender Dimensions of Transnational Migration in South Sudan*. She teaches courses on forced migration, war and gender, and development and militarism in Africa.

Grace Furtado, UMass Boston BA Spring 2017 and Latino Leadership Opportunity Program 2017, majored in psychology. She is completing the UMass Boston ms program in transnational, cultural, and community studies, focusing her work on Latinx and Puerto Rican students' educational success. She has worked in community-based organizations as advocate/ organizer in health, mental health, and housing. At UMass Boston, she has worked at the Gaston Institute, Office of Community Partnerships, and Dana Farber/Center for Excellence in Cancer Health Disparities. Her presentations and publications include research on Latina/women of color coalitional organizing, Latinx student leadership, and pregnant women's risk assessment regarding Zika virus exposure.

Bryan Gangemi is the former chairperson of the University of Massachusetts Human Rights Working Group. He served as an executive committee member for the Ignacio Martin Baró Fund for Health and Human Rights and is currently on the board of directors for Justice at Work, a workers' rights organization based in Boston. Bryan has worked in roles ranging from organizing to policy analysis for the Service Employees International Union and the Massachusetts Teachers Association. He holds a BA in psychology and Spanish literature from UMass Boston and a master's of industrial and labor relations from Cornell University.

Jamie J. Hagen is a doctoral candidate at UMass Boston in the Global Governance and Human Security program. Her work at the intersection of gender, security studies, and LGBTQ communities appears in a number of peer-reviewed journals including *International Affairs* (2016) and *Critical Studies in Security* (2017). Jamie also published the working paper "Sexual Orientation and Gender Identity as Part of the WPS Project" (2016) with the London School of Economics Center for Women, Peace and Security. She is currently a graduate member of the Feminist Theory and Gender Studies executive committee of the International Studies Association.

Avak Hasratian received his PhD from Brown University and began teaching at UMass Boston in 2008. He teaches in the English Department, Honors College, and Composition Program. He studies 20th-century and contemporary American and transnational literature's response to and modifications of changing definitions of the human and its others. His commitment to students outside the classroom is in team leading an Honors College book club and in directing master's and undergraduate honors theses and final projects. Such projects have been about the aesthetics and ethics of Danzy Senna, Tayeb Salih, Cormac McCarthy, Nathaniel Hawthorne, William Faulkner, Carson McCullers, Dennis Cooper, and Franz Kafka.

Andrés Fabián Henao Castro is Assistant Professor of Political Science at the University of Massachusetts Boston. Before joining UMB, he was the Karl Lowenstein Fellow at Amherst College, and currently holds a Post-Doctoral Fellowship at the Academy of Global Humanities and Critical Theory at the University of Bologna. His current book manuscript criticizes the theoretical reception of Sophocles' tragedy, *Antigone*, in democratic theory, queer theory, and the theory of biopolitics, by foregrounding the settler colonial logics of capitalist accumulation by which subject-positions are aesthetically distributed in the play and its reception. His research has been published in *Theory & Event*, *La Deleuziana*, *Theatre Survey*, *Contemporary Political Theory*, *Hypatia: A Journal of Feminist Philosophy*, among others.

Luis F. Jiménez is Assistant Professor of Political Science. His main research interests are Latin American politics and social remittances, particularly the way that immigrant networks spread ideas about democracy to their home countries. Currently he's working on a book that explores the impact of immigrants in the internal politics of Mexico, Colombia, and Ecuador. He received his PhD from the University of Pittsburgh in December and is originally from Guadalajara, Mexico.

Maria John received her PhD in History from Columbia University. Before joining UMass Boston as Assistant Professor of Native American History, she was indigenous studies Mellon Postdoctoral Fellow in the American Studies Department at Wesleyan University. Her research interests include 20th-century urban indigenous histories, comparative histories of settler colonialism, social and political histories of health and healthcare, histories of health activism, and the history of indigenous sovereignty. Her book-in-progress compares health struggles and indigenous health activism among urban indigenous communities in Australia and the United States in the mid–late 20th century. At UMass Boston, she teaches undergraduate and graduate classes on Native American history, indigenous studies, comparative colonialisms and decolonization, Native American health, and oral history.

Darren Kew (Ph.D. in International Relations, Tufts University, 2002) is Associate Professor and Chair of the Department of Conflict Resolution, Human Security, and Global Governance, and Executive Director of the Center for Peace, Democracy, and Development at the University of Massachusetts, Boston. He studies the relationship between conflict resolution methods – particularly interfaith and inter-ethnic peacebuilding – and democratic development in Africa. He has been a consultant on democracy and peace initiatives to the United Nations, USAID, the US State Department, and to a number of NGOs, including the Carter Center. He is author of numerous works on African politics, religion and ethnicity, and conflict resolution, including the book *Civil Society, Conflict Resolution, and Democracy in Nigeria* (Syracuse UP, 2016).

Diana Lamothe, UMass Boston graduate Spring 2017 and Latino Leadership Opportunity Program 2017, majored in psychology. Daughter of Mexican and French immigrant parents, she focuses her research and activism on access and success for disadvantaged groups. She is currently Fair Housing Coordinator at the Mayor's Office of Fair Housing and Equity, and previously worked in the Mayor's Office of Immigrant Advancement. Her presentations and workshops include participatory action research on Latina/women of color social identities, Latinx student leadership, impacts of mixed-race status, and coalitional organizing. She is preparing for graduate studies in a public policy/social justice field.

Gillian MacNaughton is Assistant Professor of Public Policy of Excluded Populations, School for Global Inclusion and Social Development. Mac-Naughton is an international human rights lawyer who works on economic and social rights, particularly the rights to health, education, and decent work, and their relationship to equality rights. She is also involved in developing human rights-based methodology and tools, including human rights impact assessment and indicators. In addition, MacNaughton has consulted on human rights projects for the World Health Organization, UNICEF, the World Bank, and the UN Special Rapporteur on the right to health, governments, and non-governmental organizations. She is a member of the Vermont Bar.

Sindiso Mnisi Weeks is Assistant Professor in Public Policy of Excluded Populations at UMass Boston, and Adjunct Associate Professor in Public Law at the University of Cape Town. Mnisi Weeks received her DPhil from the University of Oxford's Centre for Socio-Legal Studies, as a Rhodes Scholar, and previously clerked for then Deputy Chief Justice of the Constitutional Court of South Africa, Dikgang Moseneke. Mnisi Weeks has authored *Access to Justice and Human Security: Cultural Contradictions in Rural South Africa (Routledge, 2018) and co-authored African Customary Law in South Africa: Post-Apartheid and Living Law Perspectives* (OUPSA, 2015).

Kosar Mohammad, UMass Boston graduate Spring 2017, majored in psychology with minors in women and gender studies and human rights. A refugee and resilient survivor of Somalian civil wars, child bride, and proud mother of a college-enrolled son, she applies global gender equity/human rights perspectives towards achieving justice for Somalian refugees and other disadvantaged groups. At UMass Boston, Mohammad was awarded a merit-based scholarship and the 2017 Beacon Leadership "Unsung Hero" award for 2017, well describing her generous preferred activism as a member of communities on campus, locally, and globally. She is preparing for graduate studies in global gender justice.

Mickaella Perina is Associate Professor of Philosophy at UMass Boston. She specializes in philosophy of law, social and political philosophy, contemporary French philosophy Caribbean philosophy and critical philosophy of race. She has published widely on rethinking the links between race and political membership in general and citizenship. Her research interests include rights, autonomy and sovereignty, the relations between individuals, communities and states, and human rights in transnational contexts.

Mardia Pierre, UMass Boston graduate Spring 2017, majored in psychology. Daughter of Haitian immigrants who struggled with barriers to educational and economic opportunities, survivor of sexual assault, she is passionate about educating and empowering diverse, low-income, and under-represented individuals by promoting positive mental health and wellbeing and mobilizing cultural strengths and creative arts supporting recovery and resilience. She is Co-Founder and Volunteer Coordinator for *More than This*, a project affiliated with Boston Area Rape Crisis Center using creative arts to create communities of solidary, support, and recovery from gender-based violence. She is preparing for graduate studies in a social justice field.

Malcolm Russell-Einhorn is an international and comparative law and public administration specialist with over two decades of experience in international development and graduate-level teaching, including work in international legal and regulatory reform, public administration capacity building, administrative justice, decentralization, and legislative development. He is currently a lecturer in International Relations and Comparative Public Administration and a senior fellow at the Center for Peace, Democracy, and Development in the McCormack Graduate School of Policy and Global Studies. He is the author of several articles on comparative governance and administrative justice. Mr. Russell-Einhorn received bachelor's and master's degrees from Yale University and a law degree from Harvard Law School.

Ana María Sánchez Rodríguez is currently an Irish Research Council and a Marie Skłodowska-Curie Actions' fellow at Maynooth University, working in partnership with Humanity and Inclusion. She holds a PhD in Public Policy from the University of Massachusetts Boston and an MSc in NGO Management from the London School of Economics and Political Science. She was selected as an Inter-American Grassroots Development fellow for the 2015–16 cycles and a COFUND–Collaborative Research Fellow for a Responsive and Innovative Europe (CAROLINE) 2017. She has worked in human rights and social development at the federal and local governmental levels in Mexico.

Ester Shapiro is Associate Professor of Psychology, Research Associate for the Mauricio Gastón Institute for Latino Community Development and Public Policy, and Director of the Community Engagement Core at UMass Boston's HORIZON Center, a center of excellence in reducing minority health disparities. She wrote *Grief as a Family Process: A Developmental Approach to Clinical Practice* (1994; 2nd edition forthcoming) and was coordinating editor of *Nuestros Cuerpos Nuestras Vidas* (2000), the Spanish transcultural adaptation of *Our Bodies, Ourselves*. Current projects include the impact of intensified immigration enforcement and anti-immigrant attitudes on mental health and resource use by immigrants; mental health resources for success for diverse students at UMass Boston; and community engagement in community-based participatory research.

Rajini Srikanth is Professor of English and Dean of the Honors College at UMass Boston. Her research interests include the intersection between literature and human rights, post-apartheid South Africa, comparative race and ethnic studies, and Asian American literature. Her recent publications include *Constructing the Enemy: Empathy/ Antipathy in US Literature and Law* (2012) and *The Cambridge History of Asian American Literature* (2016).

Steve Striffler is Professor of Anthropology and Director of the Labor Resource Center. He writes and teaches about labor, migration, and the left in relation to Latin America and the United States. He is currently working on a book, *Solidarity: Latin America, Human Rights, Labor, and the American Left*. He is the author of numerous books including *Chicken: The Dangerous Transformation of America's Favorite Food*.

Fernando Andino Valdez, UMass Boston graduate Spring 2017 and Latino Leadership Opportunity Program 2017, majored in social psychology and received the Psychology Department's JFK Award nomination and the Social Psychology Book award for outstanding graduating senior. He is a Puerto Rican disabilities activist interested in cultivating knowledge and communications for solidarity promoting inclusion and social change. His presentations include a Photovoice project on Latino students with disabilities, and the opening statement for the September 2017 Human Rights Education Panel, *Why Human Rights Education Matters*. He plans to apply for graduate studies in rehabilitation counseling.

Adriana Rincón Villegas is a doctoral candidate in the Global Governance and Human Security PhD program at UMass Boston. She currently works as an Individualized Study Tutor at Athabasca University (Canada), and also holds a Visiting Fellow position in the Latin American Research Centre at University of Calgary. Adriana has a law degree from Universidad Jorge Tadeo Lozano, Bogotá, Colombia. She earned her MA in geography from the University of Georgia. Using decolonial feminism and critical approaches to law and peace, her research explores the gender assumptions, roles, and identities of multiple notions of peace in the Colombian legal system.

Nick Wood, UMass Boston graduate Spring 2017, majored in English and is currently enrolled in the Simmons College master's in social work program, where he is preparing for school-based work with adolescents and young adults. Growing up as a poor black woman in the south, Nick has dedicated his life to intersectional social justice through community organizing, particularly focused on gender, race, diverse sexualities, and poverty. He has worked extensively with community-based organizations, and with social justice through writing and communications.

Acknowledgments

This book emerged from the unique terrain of the campus where we both teach. The eclectic, collaborative ethos of the University of Massachusetts Boston (UMass Boston) made possible the conversations and actions that resulted in this publication. Our journey began in 2000 with the Human Rights Working Group. Our first thanks, therefore, are to the students, faculty, staff, and community activists who comprised the Human Rights Working Group at UMass Boston and gave the spark to vibrant discussions of human rights at both local and global levels. The energy and vision of this group set the framework for critical engagement with the subject of human rights. Our students, for whom human rights is not just a theoretical construct, remind us every day of our responsibility to help them make sense of their lived realities. Refugees, immigrants, working-class, and undocumented students on our majority-minority campus battle circumstances every day that motivate us to infuse our pedagogy with urgency.

We thank our faculty colleagues for their willingness to join in this interdisciplinary endeavor of research, pedagogy, and scholarship. They trusted us to make visible the unusual ties that exist among faculty from disparate disciplinary areas. They trusted us to convey the extraordinary attributes of our students and to show that an urban public university like UMass Boston has something worthwhile to share with researchers, practitioners, and educators all over the world.

Our thanks to Alexandra McGregor of Routledge for believing in the project and encouraging us to submit the proposal, and Kitty Imbert for her patient shepherding of us through all the stages of the process.

Each of us – the two co-editors – draws her inspiration from the particular areas in which we ground our teaching and scholarship. Rajini Srikanth wishes to thank the numerous community activists in South Africa who have been on the frontline for the struggle for free anti-retrovirals, tuberculosis treatment, housing, sanitation, and safety from gender-based violence. With meager resources, these activists successfully challenge their government, using the framework of human rights discourse, but employing the strategies of grassroots organizing and mass protest. She is awed by their resolve and their long view. Her South African activist friends show her that commitment to struggles for justice must be sustained over the long term. Similarly, she wishes to thank her colleagues in the United States who are engaged in the fight for Palestinian rights. Deriving their inspiration from the anti-apartheid campaign of the 1980s, these researchers, educators, and activists for Palestinian rights keep hope alive despite the intimidation tactics and obstacles launched continuously by Zionist forces. Elora Halim Chowdhury learned the vicissitudes of transnational human rights advocacy and draws inspiration from survivor-activists of gender violence in her native country, Bangladesh, and wishes to thank them for their visionary and courageous work and solidarity. She is also grateful for the steadfast support of her family who always encourages her to dream big and act conscientiously.

Lastly, we wish to thank Riva Pearson, our research assistant, whose meticulous and diligent editorial work made the manuscript submission process smoother and efficient. We are so grateful for her sincere commitment to this project.

Rajini Srikanth and Elora Halim Chowdhury

Introduction

Rajini Srikanth and Elora Halim Chowdhury

This introductory chapter examines the concept of human rights and presents the history of how it became established as a global imperative. It traces the trajectories of history, thought, and practice leading up to the Universal Declaration of Human Rights (UDHR), adopted in 1948 by the United Nations, and focuses on the primary articles from it that have animated human rights efforts since that time. We introduce the primary tensions in the study and practice of human rights: universal versus culture-specific; global governance versus the sovereignty of states; legal/juridical versus ethical; aspirational versus practical. The chapter shows how human rights work requires insights from multiple areas of knowledge, and we provide an overview of the book's essays as they collectively illustrate the rich interactions among multiple disciplines. Human rights work is ongoing, its legal protocols and geopolitical realities continually shifting, and its interventional value regularly contested. This chapter engages the profound impact of human rights discourse and practice in certain locations as well as its problematic disruptive and destabilizing consequence in others. The central thrust of this chapter is to foreground the complexity of human rights work, while engaging critically human rights discourse. We do not necessarily embrace human rights discourse as benign, but one that has inherited the "racial grammar" (Philipose, 2008) of colonial divisions and global hierarchies. Yet, we want to acknowledge the use of this discourse, its instruments, and legal platforms that enable struggles for justice for oppressed populations in the North and the South. At the same time, we argue for informed caution in unquestioningly adopting human rights discourse given its problematic and selective enforcements.

In the international realm of human rights scholarship, there is tentative consensus on when the idea of human rights first emerged. There is the generally accepted understanding that in the West the contemporary proclamation of human rights is the UDHR that was ratified in 1948. The sentiments contained in this document could be viewed as existing in embryonic form in the Magna Carta of 1215[1], the Renaissance-era (14th–17th centuries) recognition of the value of the "human" (as opposed to an exclusive focus on the divine),[2] the United States' (US) Declaration of Independence in

1776 and the French Revolution ideals of 1789. Thus, the trajectory of human rights thinking in the West could be said to reside in that sequence of changes, culminating in the 1948 declaration.

However, human rights scholars have identified far earlier traditions that reveal a commitment to the *idea* of human rights, though these articulations may not resemble the recognized discourse of the past 60 years as to what constitutes a commitment to human rights. Among the early instances is the text located on the Cyrus Cylinder, which was originally found in the area that today constitutes Iran. Cyrus was a Persian monarch of the 6th century BCE, a conqueror who expanded his empire to span the landmass from the "Hellespont to the Indies" and brought large numbers of people under his rule. His decree, which was inscribed on a clay cylinder measuring "21.9 centimetres [in length] and 10 centimetres [in diameter]" (British Museum), was officially blessed by the United Nations in 1971 as being the first declaration of a concern for rights. The text on the cylinder, known as the "Edict of Cyrus," is in the Babylonian language and in cuneiform script. The original cylinder is in the British Museum, and a replica of it is in the United Nations headquarters in New York.[3]

We devote attention to the Cyrus Cylinder because it enables analysis of the contested terrain of human rights, in which dictators can champion declarations of tolerance and freedom, and regimes that colonize can enthusiastically embrace the desire for self-determination. The drama of the Cyrus Cylinder's elevation to being considered the first charter of human rights is replete with these contradictions and tensions.

In 1971, the Shah of Iran, Reza Pahlavi, held an elaborate ceremony to mark 2,500 years of the Persian Empire, established by Cyrus the Great. The Shah used this grand occasion to present the United Nations with a replica of the Cyrus Cylinder, as marking the first extant articulation of human rights. That the Shah was a highly repressive ruler was perhaps an irony that did not escape many, though it was not publicly articulated. The then secretary-general of the United Nations, U Thant, sent the Shah a congratulatory message to mark the significant anniversary and recognized the unique contribution of the Cyrus Cylinder to the cause of human rights.

The 1971 enshrining of the Shah's gift of a replica of the Cyrus Cylinder to the United Nations is recorded in a press release issued by the United Nations Office of Public Information. The press release declares: "Cyrus the Great overthrew Babylon in 539 B.C. and pronounced the 'edict' to protect the populace of Babylon and other cities." The English translation of the text of the "Edict," which is considered by Iran to be the first representation of human rights, reads as follows:

> I am Cyrus, King of the World, Great King, mighty King, King of Babylon, King of the Four Quarters… I, well disposed, entered Babylon and amidst public jubilation sat on the royal throne…

My numerous troops took over Babylon without molestation. I
allowed no one to harass or terrorize the peoples of Sumer or Akkad.

I concerned myself with the needs of the Babylonians and their sanc-
tuaries to promote their well being.

I freed the citizens of Babylon from the yoke of servitude. I restored
their dilapidated dwellings and redressed their grievances.[4]

Not only is it ironic that the Shah of Iran in 1971 proudly claimed the "Edict
of Cyrus" as his heritage, given the many human rights violations of his
regime, but it is also equally ironic that in 2010 the Iranian president
Mahmoud Ahmadinejad proclaimed the "pre-Islamic" Cyrus Cylinder as
symbolic of the benevolent power of the rulers of the Islamic Republic
(Sanadjian, 2011).

The relationship between the power of rulers (or states) and a commitment to human rights has and continues to be a contested and volatile area
of interaction. Those who hold the power over the citizens and residents in
their domain are also those who have the responsibility of ensuring that
these denizens are protected from unjust and inhumane practices. International bodies like the United Nations, which are charged with being watch-
dog organizations overseeing the implementation of human rights, in reality
have very little power to ensure enforcement. Before the establishment of
the United Nations as an aspirational global governance body, states were
entirely free to act in ways that those in power saw as advantageous to them.
Thus, there appeared to be no contradiction in the minds of the framers of
the US Declaration of Independence that their mighty proclamations of liberty and the pursuit of happiness were simply unavailable to all the slaves in
the new republic; likewise the lofty French rights of man (*des droits de
l'homme*) assertions of the 1789 revolution did not prevent the colonization
of Algeria and Morocco. Indeed, the framers of the Declaration of Independence and the French rights of man may not have considered slaves and
colonized peoples to be fully human at all, or would likely have considered
them to be partially human.[5] In the 18th century, the free African American
Benjamin Banneker wrote to Thomas Jefferson and brought this contradiction between the document that Jefferson helped author and the condition of slaves to his attention (Banneker, 1791). Even in 1948, when the
UDHR was proclaimed, there were colonized nations in Africa that were
still under French and British rule to whom the principles of the UDHR did
not apply.

Crystal Parikh's examination of the "political imaginaries of writers of
color" draws attention to the shortcomings even into the 21st century of the
robust application of the ideals enshrined in the Declaration of Independence and the American Bill of Rights. She writes, "freedom, justice, and
self-determination for persons of color in the United States [is] an ongoing
and incomplete political project" (Parikh, 2017, p. 3). She goes on to echo
historian Gary Okihiro's sentiment that groups on the margins in the US

have moved the country toward fulfilling its articulated ideals.[6] Parikh argues, "the social and historical location of these particular minor subjects proves an indispensable fulcrum for reading the possibilities of human rights against the mandates of possessive individualism, multicultural neoliberalism, and modern state sovereignty" (p. 3).

It is crucial, therefore, to consider human rights documents and proclamations as aspirational rather than realized! The sphere of human rights law, policy, and practice is replete with contradictions. One of the many tensions is between the hegemony of Western modes of thinking and longstanding religious and cultural traditions like Buddhism. The canonical texts of Buddhism, as Perry Schmidt-Leukel argues, even as early as the 3rd century BCE, had specific ideas about the duty of the monarch to rule his kingdom "according to the moral principles of the Dharma" (Schmidt-Leukel, 2006, p. 37). The ten virtues of the Dharma king that Schmidt-Leukel recounts from the scriptures include "generosity, morality, spirit of sacrifice, integrity, mildness, spiritual discipline, peaceableness, non-violence, forbearance, and non-offensiveness" (p. 37). It was therefore the obligation of the monarch to ensure that his subjects did not feel the pain of poverty or experience other forms of suffering. Damien Keown goes one step further in stating the direct connection between the Buddhist monarch's obligations or duties and the subjects' rights: "If under Dharma it is the duty of a king (or political authority) to dispense justice impartially, then subjects (citizens) may be said to have a 'right' to just and impartial treatment before the law" (quoted in Schmidt-Leukel, 2006, p. 38). He applies this connection to the "whole of Buddhist morality so that, in his view, different rights emerge from the various moral precepts of Buddhism: for example, the right to life from the precept not to kill, the right to property from the precept not to steal" (p. 38).

Schmidt-Leukel observes that in Buddhism there is "no contradiction between responsibility for oneself and responsibility for one's fellow humans or beings [sentient beings]... Protecting oneself, one protects others; protecting others, one protects oneself (Samyutta-Nikaya)" (p. 40). The dialectical relationship between the individual and the collective is a facet of human rights that manifests itself in the late 20th and 21st centuries in discussions of the rights of indigenous peoples. Scholars of Buddhism remind us that the tension between the individual and the collective is not one that can or should be resolved always in favor of the individual (as is the case with rights as they are construed in Western traditions). For many Buddhist thinkers, the Western human rights emphasis on the individual elevates the ego and leads to egoism and selfishness and the valorization of individual greed over the public good:

> Human responsibilities and human rights should complement rather than supersede each other. Emphasizing moral and social responsibility must not lead to a removal of that basic intuition of human rights that

seeks legal protection for the individual's freedom of self-determination. On the other hand, this right cannot prevail without any limitations.

(Schmidt-Leukel, 2006, p. 43)

Many religious traditions, including Islam and Catholicism, echo this sentiment. Thus the relationship between religiosity and human rights is complicated, and those who are observant and faithful to the core beliefs of their religion are not necessarily giving up their individual rights.

The essays in this collection do not subscribe, without interrogation, to the sacredness of any human rights articulations. They recognize the necessity of human rights work even as they acknowledge the deep self-reflection and examination of cultural stereotypes that must accompany this effort. We would argue that human rights work also requires us to examine species stereotypes and to question anthropocentrism (Weitzenfeld and Joy, 2014). Humans have inflicted the most horrific cruelties on fellow humans, typically resorting to animalistic images to cast fellow humans as being outside the ambit of ethical considerations. In conceiving of fellow humans as "cockroaches," for example (as was the case in the Rwandan genocide of 1994), and in treating Iraqi prisoners as dogs, controlled with leashes (Hatzfeld, 2005; Puar, 2004, p. 527) by soldiers of the US army, human rights violators demean both humans and animals and give the lie to the belief that humans have an exclusive claim on questions of "morality."

The contributors and their institutional context

The contributors to this volume come from the University of Massachusetts Boston (UMass Boston), where they are engaged in human rights teaching and research. The range of disciplinary locations is expansive, and the regions of the world that are the focus of the contributors' teaching and/or research span Australia, Bangladesh, Colombia, Haiti, India, Mexico, Nigeria, Palestine, Qatar, South Africa, Sudan, and the US. UMass Boston is a highly diverse campus (48 percent students of color) with many students being the first in their family to attend college. Our students also bring with them complex life experiences of being refugees or the children of refugees, veterans, working-class, and undocumented persons. Their lived knowledge of the impact of local and global laws and policies, wars and natural disasters makes them exacting interlocutors of the courses we offer. They understand that complex challenges can only be addressed by bringing in insights from multiple disciplines. As a result, UMass Boston values interdisciplinary collaboration among faculty members and actively promotes an inter-disciplinary pedagogy. Our enriching experiences with collaboration lead us to offer this collection to scholars, activists, and educators in the realm of human rights. The volume's approach to the field of human rights is less about navigating the organizational structures of particular institutions than it is about transcending the disciplinary boundaries that prevail in all institutions. We recognize that the UMass Boston framework of cross-disciplinary curricular collaboration and pedagogy is one of many available models to emulate. Contextual particularities will dictate the extent to and form in which our efforts can be adopted. We hope that this collection might stimulate approaches that emerge from and are related to specific institutional realities and constraints.

At UMass Boston, faculty, students, staff, and community activists who are committed to the study and practice of human rights formed a working group in 2000 that over a period of several years birthed a human rights minor. The faculty come from diverse disciplines, as do the students, who major in fields as diverse as anthropology, biology, history, philosophy, women's and gender studies, political science, psychology, economics, and English. That the human rights minor coheres across disciplinary boundaries is, we believe, evidence of the feasibility of structurally innovative academic endeavors. The appendix includes the essay "Human Rights at a Public University," by Rita Arditti and Bryan Gangemi (2005), that traces this history of the development of the minor from its beginnings in the working group. Gangemi and Arditti were part of the original founding group of the Human Rights Working Group (HRWG) at UMass Boston, which was convened in 2000. Their essay captures those early years and describes the impulses and motivations of a group of faculty, students, and community activists who felt compelled to begin discussion of human rights as both a domestic and global set of issues. In fact, at the outset, the HRWG insisted on the inseparability of the local and the global, emphasizing that US foreign policy drew on and had implications for domestic policy. Gangemi and Arditti's essay describes the first events organized by the HRWG – hosting the grandmothers of the Plaza de Mayo, organizing a forum on the USA Patriot Act, convening a symposium on efforts within Massachusetts to eviscerate bilingual education in the public schools – and tells the story of how the momentum of these early public discussions led to the creation of a unique introductory course on human rights. This course then became the first step in the creation of the human rights minor. Their essay provides a crucial context for understanding a sustainable process that combines intellectual rigor, community activism, theory, practice, and pedagogy. We recognize that the exigencies, opportunities, obstacles, and possibilities vary significantly across institutions. Thus, Gangemi and Arditti's essay should not be construed as a blueprint. Rather, their essay should be seen as encouraging analysis of specific institutional structures to assess the readiness of any institution to embark on cross-departmental curricular collaborations. Even if an institution is not contemplating any kind of cross-departmental collaboration, Gangemi and Arditti present a narrative of effective mobilizing in the realm of human rights education.

This co-edited collection of essays on human rights scholarship and praxis brings together analyses of human rights work from multiple disciplinary perspectives so that both scholars and students (but especially students) can appreciate the complexity and interdisciplinary nature of this field. At the same time, methodological and conceptual approaches in this volume encompass the ethnographic, literary, filmic, archival, discourse analysis, feminist, historical, postcolonial, and decolonial. Contributors who straddle varied geographic and professional spaces are sensitive to the multiplicity of the scholarly and applied terrains of human rights and are deeply reflective and self-reflective of the power dynamic infusing knowledge production and circulation. Given that students go on to become future researchers, practitioners, policy makers, and activists, we believe that it is crucial to demonstrate the multifaceted landscape of human rights and the multiple forces (philosophical, political, cultural, economic, historical) that affect it.

Human rights work is methodologically "messy"

Human rights work is knotty, multidimensional, and involves players from diverse institutional and geographical locations. Consider the case of securing the human rights of Indonesian (and other Southeast and South Asian) migrant workers in Saudi Arabia. The migrant workers suffered horrific abuses at the hands of their Saudi employers, with no protections granted them by the Saudi government. Human Rights Watch collected testimonials from the workers, and these testimonials galvanized the Indonesian government to intervene and place a ban in 2010 on migrant workers going to Saudi Arabia. In 2014, the two governments signed an agreement to protect the rights of the 1 million Indonesian workers who were still in Saudi Arabia. However, despite the official agreement, there were many steps that needed to occur to ensure implementation: workers had to be educated about their rights, they had to be encouraged to come forward when their rights were violated, and supported once they did so; enforcement mechanisms had to be put in place, along with the continued monitoring of the Saudi government by Human Rights Watch. We thus see the many state and non-state agencies, the various types of political, psychological, and infrastructure interventions that have to be set up in order to protect the migrant workers' rights.

Migrant workers' rights underscore the human body as a basic site and focus of human rights. Labor rights, reproductive rights, healthcare rights, protection against torture and arbitrary imprisonment, and the right to shelter are all articulations designed to preserve the integrity of the body so that it does not become a utilitarian tool and an object of abuse. In Toni Morrison's novel *Beloved* (1987) a slave mother kills her child rather than allow the infant to be raised in slavery; in doing so, Sethe actively rejects her participation in the economic foundation of slavery where the body of the slave and her offspring become assets that can be counted and traded. A recent literary work, *Temporary People* (2017), reveals modern-day conditions of near slavery in the United Arab Emirates. The author, Deepak Unnikrishnan, draws on the techniques of magical realism to foreground the physical and emotional realities within which humans work under inhuman conditions. Unnikrishnan grew up in the United Arab Emirates, a region that, in the last 30 years, has seen tremendous growth and construction, made possible by the labor of South and Southeast Asian men and women (primarily Bangladeshis, Filipinas, Indians, Indonesians, Malaysians, Pakistanis, and Sri Lankans). These men and women endure extremely harsh treatment by their employers in the construction industry as well as in the domestic work sector. Unnikrishnan's skillful narration, which includes an abundance of fantasy, underscores how the workers seek to transcend their unbearable environment by imagining alternative realities and indulging in speculations that take them outside their own brutalized bodies.

For instance, he writes, "In a labor camp, somewhere in the Persian Gulf, a laborer swallowed his passport and turned into a passport. His roommate swallowed his suitcase and turned into a little suitcase" (Unnikrishnan, 2017, p. 5). These objects of travel that the laborers metamorphose into signify both the hope with which they journey to the Emirates to make money and the despair they experience when they are unable to escape from their brutal working conditions because their employers have taken control of and sequestered their passports. We meet the character

> Anna Varghese [who]… taped construction workers who fell from incomplete buildings… Anna, working the night shift, found these injured men, then put them back together with duct tape or some good glue, or if stitches were required, patched them up with a needle and horse hair, before sending them on their way.
>
> (p. 9)

Unnikrishnan describes how release for these hurriedly repaired workers comes only when they fall from a great height when, in their descent, moments before they crash, they feel the liberation of birds. We reference these fantastical literary representations to draw attention to the multiple modalities of knowing that we encourage readers to be open to in order to comprehend the affective depth of human rights work beyond its legalistic and governmental frameworks.

Through our endeavor to present human rights issues within a complex analytical framework, we hope that students, scholars, and practitioners come to appreciate the multiple players and forces that intersect in this deeply fissured and textured landscape. Specifically, we envision this volume to be useful to scholars who research and teach human rights; undergraduate and graduate students who are interested in learning about human rights to prepare for careers in the field; organizations that document, monitor, and assess human rights implementation in locations around the world; and readers in the policy world who seek to engage the full dimension of human rights concerns in order to shape and craft responsive policy.

We hope *Interdisciplinary Approaches to Human Rights: History, Politics, Practice* will appeal to readers both within and outside the academic realm.

Within the academic sphere, this book will garner interest from scholars who are invested in human rights as a field of study as well as those who research and are engaged in the praxis of human rights. This volume is an interdisciplinary project that refers to historical and cross-cultural study of human rights, and engages with disciplinary debates in political philosophy, gender and women's studies, literary studies, Global South/Third World studies, international relations, psychology, and anthropology. At the same time, the authors employ diverse methodologies including interdisciplinary comparisons, oral history, discourse analysis, ethnography, and literary and cinema studies. Within the field of human rights studies, *this book* attends to the critical academic gap on interdisciplinary and praxis-based approaches to the field, as opposed to a predominantly legalistic focus, drawing from case studies from the Global South.

In this way, the book will be of interest to scholars who center on a critical and transnational approach to human rights discourse as well as those individuals who bring in questions of geopolitics, and cross-border collaborations in their research and pedagogy. The book's contribution to human rights is essential to the ongoing debates on the North–South dynamic in humanitarian intervention by incorporating important research conducted by theorists and practitioners and by contributing a nuanced analysis of place-based and site-specific issues. Furthermore, the book's extensive use of field research as well as content analysis will also appeal to those invested in the field from a pedagogical perspective and those interested in learning more about narratives of resistance, solidarity, and struggles for justice. Although predominately an academic text, *Interdisciplinary Approaches to Human Rights: History, Politics, Practice* is stylistically accessible to all readers and its engaging subject matter will be of interest to readers committed to the politics, histories, legacies, and enactment of human rights in contemporary world politics.

Organizational structure of the book

The book is divided in three sections: the first unit on human rights context and history provides an overview of the emergence of the field and the multiple historical trajectories that gave shape to it. Unlike predominant thinking that positions human rights discourse as established in the post-World War II era with the codification of the UDHR, the essays in this section put this modern European emergence in historical context, shedding light on the conceptualization of the human in earlier trajectories of that indelibly marked moment of who counts as human within terrains of colonial power. The articulation of the UDHR, and its many platforms and treaties, on the one hand continued the exclusionary practices and solidified a global morality platform, but on the other opened up various infrastructure for marginalized populations to claim their vision of justice, and collective notion of rights. Alongside the hegemonic rights discourse, this section integrates contrary, contested, and context-specific emergence of rights. The second unit emphasizes critical areas within the field of human rights, and the international instruments that provide protection to specific "vulnerable" communities. Chapters in this section interrogate how "gender," "child rights," "disability," "indigenous," and "development" come to represent areas of concern and intervention within human rights policy domains and how these categories unwittingly reproduce and entrench power dynamics between the Global North and South. The third unit offers examples of topics and cases that engage a human rights lens or framework to meet the challenges of oppression and resistance. The chapters pay attention to how a human rights consciousness, or praxis, informs engagement, whether at the individual level or at the collective, whether through an engagement with film and literature as vehicles of advocacy, or codification through legal texts, and approaches deployed in grassroots or transnational campaigns, and pedagogical innovations within classrooms. All three areas employ an interdisciplinary and cross-cultural lens, and are cognizant of multiple and overlapping traditions and geopolitical realities of the field of human rights.

Part I. Human rights discourse: context and history

Collectively, the first seven chapters in Part I probe the tension between the norms of universal justice established by the UDHR and the principle of independent and sovereign nations defined by controlled borders and established cultures. In "Imaginary and real strangers: constructing and reconstructing the human in human rights discourse and instruments," Mickaella Perina demonstrates processes through which this tension is sustained to examine unfulfilled ambitions of universal human rights in a world that foregrounds nation-state systems of governmentality. She argues that the state-centric approach to international human rights discourse and instrument is an inherent limit to the universal enjoyment of these rights, and a more significant obstacle than cultural differences to the universality of human rights.

In "Rise of the global human rights regime: challenging power with humanity," Darren Kew, Malcolm Russell-Einhorn, and Adriana Rincón Villegas provide an overview of international human rights law and its affiliated system for the management of violations developed in the post-1945 era. Their chapter provides a thorough review of the UDHR and subsequent covenants and treaties and United Nations bodies that constitute the current global human rights system. At the same time, the authors pay special attention to the roles of power politics and non-governmental organizations (NGO)-based activism shaping the global human rights system and how these processes affect activist- and state government-driven advocacy and policy, and how a global morality platform gets shaped at the intersection of legal and cultural priorities.

Andrés Fabian Henao Castro's essay, "Between nothingness and infinity: settlement and anti-blackness as the overdetermination of human rights," demystifies the post-1945 inception of human rights discourse as formative. Specifically, he engages theoretical traditions like decolonial theory, afro-pessimism, and settler colonial critique to emphasize the ways in which anti-blackness and settlements remain the structural forms of oppression by which the universality of the human is historically constructed. Contrasting the French Declaration and the Haitian Constitution, he exposes the limits of the universal, when it comes to confront the discourse of human rights in the context of disciplining black and indigenous bodies, as the original "others" through whose abjection "the human" becomes coherent. Henao Castro's critique of the universality of the human rights discourse illuminates how the category "human" becomes political, racialized, and unevenly worthy.

Also in the postcolonial vein, Nada Mustafa Ali's essay, "Women, gender, and human rights" takes a critical look at the shaping of key tenets of international human rights conventions, resolutions, and instruments devoted to women's human rights and to gender equality, namely the Convention on the Elimination of All Forms of Discrimination against Women (1979), the United Nations Resolution 1325 on Women, Peace and Security (2000), and the Protocol to the African Charter on Human and People's Rights on the Rights of Women in Africa (2003). In so doing, she sheds light on how advocacy for women's human rights and gender equality, especially in Global South settings, can reproduce what postcolonial Nigerian writer Chimamanda Ngozi Adichie calls the "single story" about Other women and communities, and thereby inadvertently elevate the cultural superiority of the North.

Several chapters in this section engage the influences of geopolitics and historical conflict in shaping the domain of human rights in locations ranging from the US–Mexico border, South Africa, and Latin America. Steve Striffler's essay, "Human rights, Latin America, and left internationalism during the Cold War," explores how human rights became a dominant way of framing and mobilizing international solidarity during the 1970s and 1980s in the Americas, eclipsing other more longstanding internationalisms, notably socialism, anti-imperialism, anti-colonialism, labor solidarity, and pan-Africanism. Striffler argues that the emergence of human rights as a dominant way to think about and practice internationalism served to detach international solidarity from an identifiably left politics (focused on economic redistribution and equity of resources), thereby undermining structural transformation and elevating depoliticized forms of internationalisms like NGO-type politics.

In "The US–Mexico border and human rights," Luis Jiménez examines the historical dynamic of the US–Mexico border, one mired in a tremendous power differential, where the experienced reality and the expectations of its "denizens" clash with the state institutions and control on both sides of the border, but especially the one emanating from the US state authority. He traces this dynamic across human rights abuses occurring at the creation of the border and subsequent conquest and subjugation of its inhabitants; the establishment of border patrol and its myriad forms of control; and the transformation of regulation at the boundary between the two countries. Drawing from international relations and human rights approaches to questions of borders and security, Jiménez looks at the *longue durée* of surveillance, exclusion, and oppression of the Mexican population by its northern neighbor.

Sindiso Mnisi Weeks' chapter titled "Unintended consequences in the postcolonies: struggling South Africans experiencing rights discourse as disempowering" explores how the concept of "rights" as protected by the constitution in South Africa has not led to the empowerment of or ensuring of true citizenship to all South Africans. Weeks looks to the inability of the rights discourse to deliver its promised equality, and whether its limited definition of rights has failed to adequately "vernacularize" it so as to have meaning for ordinary peoples. What would "rights" look like or encompass, she asks, if its content and parameters were to draw from the needs of those who struggle from below? The task of vernacularizing rights she posits ought to recognize the country's diverse history and populations.

Part II. Critical areas in human rights

The collection of five essays in this section looks at critical areas formative of human rights conventions and instruments, their emergence, enactments, limits, and sphere of possibilities. In "The mysterious disappearance of human rights in the 2030 development agenda," Gillian MacNaughton examines the 2030 Agenda for Sustainable Development Goals, which, even if seemingly grounded in the principles of the UDHR, demonstrates a striking absence of references to human rights in its proposed targets and implementation plan. The failure to fully integrate human rights into the global development plan, MacNaughton posits, reinforces the separate but parallel tracks of development and human rights and the troubling implication of this formative disparity in policy, law, and planning.

Ana María Sánchez Rodríguez's essay, "Addressing general recommendation no. 35 from an intersectional perspective on violence, gender, and disability in Mexico," sheds light on the gaps in the vitally important Convention on the Elimination of All Forms of Discrimination against Women in its failure to integrate a critical consideration to disability. Utilizing an intersectional approach, Sánchez Rodríguez shows what this absence might mean for the conceptualization of policy geared to protect vulnerable social groups.

Jamie Hagen and Maria John write about the use of human rights instruments by LGBTQ communities and indigenous communities, using a transnational and historical lens, respectively. International relations scholar Hagen's chapter, "Global LGBTQ politics and human rights," provides an overview of human rights organizing around LGBTQ identity and inequality, and she critiques the ways in which agendas are set and proliferated at the domestic level as well as in transnational contexts. She assesses which concerns are highlighted and by whom, the asymmetrical plane of North–South mobilizations, and the instrumental use of the human rights paradigm across regions.

In "Refugee camps and the (educational) rights of the child," Rajini Srikanth calls attention to the efforts undertaken by United Nations agencies to educate children in refugee camps by focusing on recent camps set up for Syrian refugees, longstanding camps in Kenya populated by displaced Sudanese and Somali populations, and Palestinian camps under Israeli occupation in the West Bank and Gaza. She looks at extant policies with regard to children's education, drawing attention to the types of education that are offered in camps and their relation to the kinds of futures envisioned by the camps' inhabitants. She concludes with thoughts on citizenship within and without national borders and how the refugee status might offer a particular vision for conceptualizing a global humanity.

Historian Maria John, in her essay titled "Persistent voices: a history of indigenous people and human rights in Australia, 1950s–2000s," seeks to evaluate if and how a human rights framework may appeal to indigenous peoples in the postwar era. She explores how indigenous communities have pushed the boundaries of this framework to envision a more expansive and deeper conceptualization of questions of sovereignty and justice for Aboriginal Australian communities.

Part III. Praxis and human rights

This section offers perspectives, cases, and pedagogies of praxis that grapple with human rights as a field of inquiry, sphere of advocacy, reflexive practice and consciousness raising, and innovative pedagogy. Jean-Philippe Belleau's essay, "So you want to work in human rights?" offers a cautionary note to prospective human rights workers about what this occupation/expertise encompasses and the often unexpected ambiguities and predicaments of the job. Demystifying the field as a "career" and not a "calling," he draws on his own personal experiences in Haiti in conducting interviews, investigating cases, data gathering, and working with the judicial system to address human rights violations.

Amani El Jack's chapter, "Migrant workers in the Gulf: theoretical and human rights dilemmas," takes stock of national and international policy with regard to the rights of migrant workers in the Arabian Gulf region. She shows that the United Nations Convention and International Labour Organization Declaration both advocate for the rights of migrant workers, which include wage protection, the provision of social security, and employment benefits. However, in reality these international measures tend to be symbolic in nature and lack the power to protect migrant workers' rights. She draws on her field research on Qataris' attitudes towards migrant workers to highlight the shortcomings of the existing system of migrant sponsorship (*Kafala*) in the Gulf, which enables migrant labor to enter the Gulf region legally with a work permit as temporary workers but simultaneously undermines their basic human rights.

Engaging with the question of gender justice, Elora Halim Chowdhury's article, "Ethical reckoning: theorizing gender, vulnerability, and agency in Bangladeshi *Muktijuddho* film," shows how as a genre human rights cinema serves to mobilize awareness, raise critical consciousness, and political action with regard to the Bangladesh Liberation War of 1971. Her chapter makes the case for a central role for national cinema in portraying the role of women as protagonists of liberation struggles and in illuminating the human rights issues surrounding their cinematic figurations.

Avak Hasratian's essay, "Right now in no place with strangers: Eudora Welty's queer love," is a meditation on critical human rights literacy as he performs a queer examination of Eudora Welty's fiction and its depiction of the relationship between rights, humans, and sexuality. He finds in Welty's writings an ethical engagement with the human in its development of desire, intimacy, and kindness between strangers.

In her essay titled, "On the human right to peace in times of contemporary colonial power," Adriana Rincón Villegas examines the Colombian Constitution's article 22 where peace is outlined as a human right. "What does it mean for a country to categorize peace as a human right?" she asks as she explores the scope of this right through a textual analysis of the constitution from a critical legal, feminist, and decolonial methodology. She reveals that this article makes selective inclusion/exclusion of certain bodies including peasant women, women of color, and the LGBT community.

Chris Bobel's essay, "Beyond dignity: a case study of the mis/use of human rights discourse in development campaigns," traces how contemporary campaigns in the Global South, namely the Menstrual Hygiene Management movement, articulate a vision for girls' and women's empowerment through narratives of efficiency and consumption as opposed to valuing women as women, their liberation and agency. The language of rights is championed in these neoliberal campaigns through the use of tropes such as dignity and privacy that construct female bodies as dirty and in need of containment. In both Villegas' and Bobel's essays we see a cooptation of the language of human rights – namely, concepts such as dignity and peace – to serve the political agendas of powerful institutions.

Finally, Ester Shapiro and her students Fernando Andino Valdez, Yasmin Bailey, Grace Furtado, Diana Lamothe, Kosar Mohammad, Mardia Pierre, and Nick Wood take readers through a journey of their course on gender, culture, and health in their co-authored chapter, "Teaching health and human rights in a psychology capstone: cultivating connections between rights, personal wellness, and social justice." This chapter offers a framework for teaching health and human rights linking personal health and social justice. A gendered health and human rights perspective on citizenship and activist methods of inquiry supports the students in making connections between personal lived experiences as members of marginalized communities, impacts on personal/family/community health, and their educational and professional trajectories. The contributors offer a vision for potential pathways for enhancing access to resources and thereby contributing to personal healing and social change. An example of student learning that is based in a human rights-centered pedagogical model, the module serves as the catalyst for transformative education and shifting frameworks from struggle to resistance and resilience.

In conclusion, *Interdisciplinary Approaches to Human Rights: History, Politics, Practice* builds on existing scholarship on human rights, but also offers a unique, critical transnational approach and methodology on this field of inquiry. The principal areas that we intervene in encompass: a genuinely inter and multidisciplinary approach, rich and deeply engaged case studies, a comprehensive coverage of geographical regions and cultural contexts, pedagogies of human rights, and scholar-activist approaches to the study of human rights. In addition, we have a unique story to tell – how we thought about and implemented the human rights curriculum on this campus, a public university with a diverse student body whose life trajectories, we believe, encompass lived experiences of transnational migration, oppression, and social justice. Community voices and experiences have and continue to be the bedrock of our vision, curriculum, and commitment from the outset and are reflected in the range of perspectives offered in these pages. Readers, we hope, will appreciate the political and cultural terrain and debates upon which human rights issues play out in this interdisciplinary book of essays.

Notes

1 The Magna Carta was a "charter" – or written agreement – by King John of England that all free men in the kingdom would have certain liberties, which were spelled out by him. See the British Library's translation of the full text of the Magna Carta.
2 See John Jeffries Martin, The Renaissance: a world in motion, and Samuel K. Cohn, Jr., The Black Death, tragedy and transformation; both essays are in Jeffries Martin, 2007. See also Olsen, 2004.
3 See the Dag Hammarskjöld Library. Hammarskjöld was the second secretary-general (1953–1961) of the United Nations.
4 See "UN Archives File related to Cylinder of Cyrus" and "Cylinder of Cyrus Press Release" in the Dag Hammarskjöld Library.
5 Lynn Hunt observes that liberty and rights were qualified by "individual autonomy. To have human rights, people had to be perceived as separate individuals who were capable of exercising independent moral judgment" (2007, p. 27). Clearly, there were populations in 1776 and 1789, among them women and children, slaves, and American Indians, who were perceived as lacking individual autonomy.
6 Okihiro, 1994, p. ix. Okihiro says that marginalized populations in the US have, "in their struggles for equality… helped preserve and advance the principles and ideals of democracy and have thereby made America a freer place for all."

References

Arditti, R. and Gangemi, B. (2005). Human rights at a public urban university: The case of UMass Boston. *TwelveTen: US Human Rights Network Semi Annual Newsletter*, 1, pp. 5–6.

Banneker, B. (1791). To Thomas Jefferson. *Founders Online*. Available at: https://founders.archives.gov/documents/Jefferson/01-22-02-0049 [Accessed May 1, 2018].

British Library (n.d.). English translation of the Magna Carta. Available at: www.bl.uk/magna-carta/articles/magna-carta-english-translation [Accessed May 1, 2018].

British Museum (n.d.). The Cyrus Cylinder. Available at: www.britishmuseum.org/research/collection_online/collection_object_details.aspx?objectId=327188&partId=1 [Accessed May 1, 2018].

Cylinder of Cyrus press releases (1971). Available at: http://ask.un.org/loader.php?fid=8500&type=1&key=517c22dc0833d0e1aed9ca958d30fc4c [Accessed May 1, 2018].

Dag Hammarskjöld Library (2017). Where can I find UN information on the "Cylinder or Cyrus" aka "Edict of Cyrus?" Available at: http://ask.un.org/faq/194027 [Accessed May 1, 2018].

Hatzfeld, J. (2005). *Machete season: The killers in Rwanda speak*. Translated by L. Coverdale. New York: Farrar, Straus, and Giroux.

Hunt, L. (2007). *Inventing human rights: A history*. New York: W.W. Norton & Company.

Jeffries Martin, J., ed. (2007). *The Renaissance world*. New York: Routledge.

Okihiro, G. (1994). *Margins and mainstreams: Asians in American history and culture*. Seattle, WA: University of Washington Press.

Olsen, G.W. (2004). Humanism: The struggle to possess a word. *Logos: A Journal of Catholic Thought and Culture*, 7(1), pp. 97–116.

Parikh, C. (2017). *Writing human rights: The political imaginaries of writers of color*. Minneapolis, MN: University of Minnesota Press.

Philipose, E. (2008). Decolonizing the racial grammar of international law. In: R.L. Riley, C.T. Mohanty, and M.B. Pratt, eds, *Feminism and war: Confronting US imperialism*. London: Zed Press, pp. 103–116.

Puar, J. (2004). Abu-Ghraib: Arguing against exceptionalism. *Feminist Studies*, 30(2), pp. 522–534.

Sanadjian, M. (2011). Islamic rule and pre-Islamic blessing, the "homecoming" of the Cyrus Cylinder. *Dialectical Anthropology*, 35(4), pp. 459–474.

Schmidt-Leukel, P. (2006). Buddhism and the idea of human rights: Resonances and dissonances. *Buddhist-Christian Studies*, 26, pp. 33–49.

UN Archives File Related to Cylinder of Cyrus. Available at: https://search.archives.un.org/uploads/r/united-nations-archives/6/0/e/60e01378f4efade1353c642dc378bc55 44138ce0ce2f3f4cab3a7ad37905a49a/S-0882-0002-02-00001.pdf [Accessed May 1, 2018].

Unnikrishnan, D. (2017). *Temporary people*. New York: Restless Books.

Weitzenfeld, A. and Joy, M. (2014). An overview of anthropocentrism, humanism, and speciesism in critical animal theory. *Counterpoints*, 448, pp. 3–27.

Part I

Human rights discourse: context and history

1 Imaginary and real strangers

Constructing and reconstructing the human in human rights discourse and instruments

Mickaella Perina

Introduction

As I reflect upon my experience teaching the introduction to human rights course at the University of Massachusetts Boston, I appreciate the various ways students' questions and their engagement with class materials have impacted my own approach to human rights discourse and instruments. Consequently, I find it important to include in this essay relevant classroom experiences.[1]

As they cautiously review human rights instruments (Universal Declaration of Human Rights (UDHR), Convention on the Elimination of All Forms of Discrimination against Women, Office of the United Nations High Commissioner for Human Rights, etc.) at the beginning of the semester, students often ask how there can be so many human rights violations in the world if all humans have the rights asserted in these documents simply by virtue of being human. In doing so they point to the tension between the universality of the rights and the particular humans who have them but may not enjoy or exercise them at any given time. I suspect that what puzzles them is the intersection of universal human rights claims with the particularities of human experiences and the unequal responses to human rights violations and neglect across the globe.

The understanding of both "human" and "rights" in the phrase human rights has changed over time. The expression "universal human rights" has its roots in the UDHR proclaimed by the United Nations General Assembly on December 10, 1948, a declaration conceived of as "a common standard of achievement for all people and all nations" (UDHR, General Assembly resolution 217A). Human rights legal instruments, such as the UDHR, were often developed in response to gross human rights violations or human rights struggles where individuals and groups fought for the recognition of their rights as human rights and challenged established standards and understandings of human interests. The recognition of these rights often faced significant opposition and resistance from sovereign states, groups, or individuals with authority and power. As Paul Gordon Lauren rightly noted, visions of human rights "raised profoundly disturbing issues about what it means to be truly human, thereby directly threatening traditional patterns of authority and privilege, vested interests, and the claims of national sovereignty"(Lauren, 2003).

The tension between the universal standards created by the UDHR and the principle of independent and sovereign nations defined by controlled borders and recognized cultures is pervasive in human rights scholarship. While there seems to be widespread agreement about the validity of universal human rights, there has been significant disagreement about the categorization of particular conducts as human rights violations on the ground of cultural differences. As Abdullahi Ahmed An-Na'im argued, one of the main reasons behind such disagreements is the lack of cultural legitimacy of human rights standards as when insiders see a conduct sanctioned by the norms of a particular culture as legitimate, and outsiders see it as cruel, inhuman, or degrading (An-Na'im, 1992). How does one make sense of such disagreement and how can these standards gain cross-cultural legitimacy? How universal can human rights be? How universally can human rights be claimed?

Multiple articles and books, positing the need for universal agreement about human rights, have pointed to ways in which disagreements can be resolved or at least mitigated (An-Na'im, 1992; Donnelly, 2007; Sen, 2005). While I do not question the merit of such analysis, in this essay I explore different aspects of disagreements about the universal legitimacy of human rights standards. I distinguish between processes through which disagreements manifest themselves but do not preclude consensus building and processes through which disagreements are used as an excuse to sustain limits to the exercise and enjoyment of universal human rights in a world of states associated with borders and membership. First I make a case against the idea that the diversity of cultural values across the world is the paradigmatic obstacle to universally claimed and enjoyed human rights; in my view this diversity creates disagreements but does not necessarily prevent consensus building. Second, I argue that the creation of strangers (real and imagined) central to the current conception of citizenship, coupled with the assumption that all members of a citizenry have, and organize their lives around, shared values constitute a crucial obstacle to the universal enjoyment of human rights. Here, cultural disagreements are presupposed and used to justify differences in the exercise and enjoyment of human rights. Since the diversity of cultural values, real or assumed, is not the ultimate barrier to universal human rights claims and enjoyments, notwithstanding existing beliefs in insurmountable barriers between cultural values, we need to examine other, perhaps more effective, obstacles. Through a brief analysis of the experience of migrants, I argue last that the state-centric approach to international human rights discourse and instruments is an inherent limit to the universal enjoyment of these rights. State-centrism and the strong drive to identify who belongs and deserves to have her human rights protected and who is a stranger to the state and has no protection constitute major obstacles to the realization of universal human rights.

Universal human rights, cultural diversity, and cross-cultural legitimacy

The validity of universal human rights claims and international human rights instruments is often questioned on the basis of the world diversity of cultures and values. The argument takes various forms but can be roughly restated as follows: given the diversity of cultures, cultural practices, and values in the world, any given human right claim that is valid in one culture may be invalid in another; likewise the identification of a human rights violation may in fact be the condemnation of a cultural practice.[2] The cultural divide may be conceived of as a divide between the West and the rest of the world thereby making universal human rights Western and non-Western cultural practices potential violations. It can also be conceived of as a divide between universal rights and universal aspirations justifying the absence of enjoyment of said universal rights (and not their violations) in some communities and not in others. Consequently, fundamental cultural differences make it inherently impossible to have and protect universal human rights everywhere at all times. I propose that this claim is grounded in two deeply problematic assumptions, namely that a) cultural differences are necessarily incompatible differences between cultures and do not exist within cultures and b) cultures are constant, invariable, unchanging, or homogeneous.

Questioning assumption 1: different cultures necessarily have irreducible incompatible norms and values

In a divided world where universalism has historically been used to mask forms of cultural imperialism and where cultural autonomy and cultural appropriation are often in conflict, it is not unreasonable to apply special scrutiny to universal human rights claims and claims about human rights violations. After all, human rights talks have in various cases promoted a Eurocentric or Western notion of culture. However, to take the diversity of cultures and values seriously is one thing, to conclude that cultural values are inherently and necessarily incompatible or that universal human rights claims are invalid is another. One can be committed to both the autonomy of cultures and the universality of claims about human rights. In other words, the idea of universal human rights can cover and protect a range of differences, interests, and moral principles.

Disagreements about universal human rights and about human rights violations are often moral and political disagreements. International human rights law provides valuable legal instruments to protect human rights, but most disagreements concern practices or conducts that appear illegitimate to some and legitimate to others; often the ground for this conflict about legitimacy is morality,[3] a code of conduct or set of standards of good and bad, right and wrong. In fact, the broad category of universal human rights includes both claims that are recognized as valid because of a set of legal rules, and claims that owe their validity to a set of moral principles. The latter claims can be challenged when the interests being protected by them, such as life, education, or bodily integrity, are not universally recognized as valuable or are understood differently.

Philosophers often distinguish between thin and thick moral concepts; on such account thin universal moral concepts or principles become thicker when adapted to historical contexts. For instance while we all have a general concept of the good, at different times and in different spaces different conducts will be regarded as good. But do moral concepts start thick or thin? Do we start with the general or with the particular? Michael Walzer offers a useful conception of the relationship between thick and thin concepts: "Morality is thick from the beginning, culturally integrated, fully resonant, and [it] reveals itself thinly only on special occasions, when moral language is turned to specific purposes" (Walzer, 1994). If Walzer is right, we start with thick moral concepts and it is through moral deliberations that the thin concept is uncovered. Is it through moral deliberation that we can all agree that "everyone has a right to life, liberty and security of persons" (UDHR, article 3) or that "No one shall be held in slavery or servitude" (UDHR, article 4)? Do all people agree that humans have a right to autonomy and self-determination over one's own body, and against potential abuses of such right by states and government through forced labor, torture, or cruel punishment? How have these principles been historically integrated in particular societies and cultures to become a universal moral rule?

Disagreements and conflicts do exist but they are not necessarily signs of fundamental incompatibility; they may be only prima facie conflicts. Appiah suggests that instead of dismissing values that are foreign to us as primitive and irrational, one can try and hope to understand how this value might motivate someone (2006). It may seem difficult to take other people's interests seriously, especially when such interests are unfamiliar, but it is possible to use our imagination to understand why they hold these interests. And it is easier to do so when the apparent unfamiliar practice happens to be shared by someone we know. I think for example of my student X, who, in the context of a class discussion on the right to bodily integrity, explained why scarification was valued in the community she originally came from, why it was valuable to her despite the fact that her parents made the choice for her when she was very little and unable to choose, and why she did not conceive of it as a violation of her right to bodily integrity. X was a conscientious and well-regarded member of the class who had migrated to the US from West Africa with her parents when she was a young child, something most of her classmates ignored until she mentioned it that day. X sharing her interest in scarification made the practice less foreign to other students, allowing for new ways of seeing this practice while making it possible to discuss different practices of body modification within and outside the United States. Students were able to examine how conceptions of the right to bodily integrity and cultural body modification practices could differ even when there was agreement on the value of a right to bodily integrity. They were able and willing to see scarification through the eyes of their classmate and to see their own practices and other practices familiar to them as other people might see them. They were able to understand what might motivate someone to have an interest in scarification and more broadly to examine why some practices are more scrutinized than others in different contexts. Consequently, they were able to question the assumed opposition between universality and cultural specificity, to understand that universality should not be constructed as historical or anthropological since "claims to historical or anthropological universality confuses values such as justice, fairness, and humanity with practices that aim to realize those values" (Donnelly, 2007). The point here is that understanding the universality of human rights implies understanding the diversity of human values and practices, the possibility of cross-cultural legitimacy, overlap or consensus, and the ongoing struggle to ensure protection to all; universal human rights do not require universal practices.

Questioning assumption 2: cultures are constant, invariable, unchanging, or homogeneous

One correlated questionable assumption is that insurmountable differences exist across cultures but not within cultures. It is often wrongly assumed that there is agreement about fundamental moral standards and social norms within cultures that simply does not exist across cultures. But cultures are not homogeneous or static; they are dynamic and made of both continuity and change. Different norms and principles get defended and dropped at different times within any given culture; cultures are subjected to internal debate and internal contradictions. Moreover, it is widely accepted that cultures often experience some level of cultural alteration, although there is debate about the value of such alteration. It would be difficult today to find cultures that would be completely immune to any external or foreign influence. Consequently, it is mistaken to assume that disagreements about practices occur mainly across cultures and not within cultures. Agreements about the type of human interests that qualify as human rights and the type of conducts that qualify as human rights violations require cross-cultural legitimacy.

Here again An-Na'im's account (1992, p. 21) can be helpful: "Having achieved an adequate level of legitimacy *within* each tradition, through this internal stage, Human rights scholars and advocates should work for *cross-cultural* legitimacy, so that people of diverse cultural traditions can agree on the meaning, scope, and methods of implementing these rights." In his view people are more likely to observe normative propositions if they are sanctioned by their own cultural traditions, and observance of human rights standards can be improved by enhancing the cultural legitimacy of these standards. Fostering understanding and recognizing that agreement about practices is not a necessary condition to the validity and force of universal standards can enhance such cultural legitimacy. To say that is not to suggest that all practices are acceptable or permissible; the very concept of toleration requires the intolerable. There is a fundamental difference between objectionable, wrong, or bad practices that can be tolerated and the intolerably wrong or intolerably bad practices that must be rejected. To recognize the possibility of cross-cultural legitimacy in matters of international human rights is to be committed to both the universality of what is owed to humans and the pluralism of the cultures in which they are situated. The idea that some cultures have definitively reached a satisfactory level of legitimacy and others have not and must be demonized needs to be scrutinized. The plurality of cultures, norms, and principles both within and across cultures is not the paradigmatic obstacle to the enjoyment of universal human rights; the assumption that differences are necessarily insurmountable and need to be questioned and overcome for cross-cultural legitimacy to be achieved is the obstacle. How human rights are conceived and protected is an ongoing process that is partly contingent upon cultures' dynamics. Next, I consider conceptions of the *human* that may be inherently more damaging to the protection of universal human rights than different cultural norms and values.

Universal human rights, citizens and strangers

International human rights instruments are intended to protect humans from violations and abuses. But who are the humans whose human rights are being violated and who are the rights violators? Human rights scholars typically defend one of two views: the institutional account (Pogge, 2008; Risse, 2008; Nickel, 2007; Beitz, 2011) and the interactional account (Caney, 2005; Nagel, 2002; Tasioulas, 2012). Pogge first introduced the distinction in 2002:

> We should conceive human rights primarily as claims on coercive social institutions and secondarily as claims against those who uphold such institutions. Such an *institutional* understanding contrasts with an *interactional* one... On the interactional understanding of human rights, governments and individuals have a responsibility not to violate human rights. On my institutional understanding, by contrast, their responsibility is to work for an institutional order and public culture that ensure that all members of society have secure access to the objects of their human rights.
>
> (Pogge, 2002: pp. 46, 65)

On the institutional view, only governments or those acting as representatives of governments can violate human rights; on the interactional account, individuals of their own accord are equally capable of violations of human rights and have the duty to ensure that a person's human rights are not violated. To better understand this distinction let's assume that there is a human right to freedom from extreme poverty. If so, who can be held responsible and who has a duty to ensure that this human right is not violated? On the institutional account only co-nationals or other members of what Pogge called the "institutional scheme" (a system of interdependence such as trade, production, consumption, law, etc.) will have a duty to ensure that the human right not to suffer from extreme poverty be enjoyed. On the interactional account this duty will fall on all other persons who can help regardless of their membership. In addition, on the institutional account cases such as domestic violence involving individual violators do not constitute a violation of the human right to physical security, only states and government officials can violate human rights and protect human rights. Are human rights political norms regulating how governments should treat their people, or are they moral norms guiding interpersonal conducts? Are human rights defined by current practices and norms regulating the relations between states and their citizens, or are they claims against the conducts of all individuals regardless of a shared institutional background? I will not attempt to settle the issue here or to argue for a combined account; for the purpose of my inquiry I will in what follows focus only on the institutional account and return to the interactional account in the last section of this essay.

The humans protected by human rights instruments are not simply humans who happened to be culturally situated; they are primarily citizens, since the world as we experience it today is a world of states. The individuals recognized by states and towards whom states have obligations are not humans qua humans but citizens. States enter international treaties and agree to duties and obligations to respect, protect, and fulfill human rights; these treaties require that states put in place domestic legislation consistent with international treaties, obligations, and duties. As a result, domestic legal systems become de facto the primary legal protection of the human rights guaranteed by international law. If and when domestic legal legislation fails to protect human rights, to take positive action to facilitate the enjoyment of human rights or to address human rights abuses and violations, procedures are available at the regional and at the international level for individuals and groups to complain. Since the protection of human rights depends on state legislation and since states have obligations primarily to their citizens and not to humans qua humans, it appears unlikely that the human rights of non-citizens will be fully protected by states.

The very nature of international human rights instruments presupposes a tension between the protections guaranteed to humans by international human rights law and the fact that these protections are expected to be guaranteed by domestic law. This makes non-citizens the paradigmatic example of vulnerable persons more likely to have their human rights neglected or violated. Unlike other groups whose historical exclusion from citizenship is now generally regarded as unjust, as in the case of African Americans in the US, indigenous peoples or women, the exclusion of non-citizens is often regarded as legitimate. The demarcation between citizens – deserving of protection – and non-citizens is grounded in a long tradition that distinguishes between citizens and persons. In this framework, citizenship is conceived of as a form of national belonging associated with rights while personhood is associated with the rights of individuals independently of their political membership. The rights people have independently of their political membership often have moral force but do not have the legal force required to assure real, as opposed to simply formal, protection. As paradoxical as it may seem, in the absence of recognized political membership it becomes extremely difficult to have one's rights, including one's human rights, protected. The paradigmatic example of such human experience is statelessness; as Hannah Arendt argued in 1951, "the stateless person is not a citizen and consequently, in situations of crisis, is not even a human being" (Arendt, 1951).

Undoubtedly, membership in a bounded community remains crucial today; political membership remains a distinctive feature of the world, and it seems that without such membership human rights claims have no recognized validity. Nevertheless the value assigned to citizenship should not be overstated. As Balibar pointed out,

> there exists a double tendency to elevate a given definition or conversely to consider citizenship a mere "legal fiction" which expresses nothing but the mask of domination. In both cases one loses sight of the differential change and the essential mobility of the "citizen" (or of its relation to the state).
>
> (Balibar, 1988)

Between the idea of a promised democratic fulfillment and the idea of a mere legal fiction, citizenship marks humans and their relation to the state and influences how the human is being explicitly and implicitly constructed and reconstructed in human rights discourse and instruments. I contend that immigrants' experiences offer opportunities to rethink the distinction between legitimate citizens and other precarious residents (or candidates to such residency) as well as the obligations states have to their own citizens to the detriment of non-citizens. The contemporary experience of migrants has the potential to significantly impact our conceptions of what it means to be humans and to have human rights.

Migration has a very concrete institutional dimension – migrants tend to move from one institutional or legal category to another (illegal, asylum seeker, internally displaced, refugees, undocumented, etc.), sometimes with no prospect of ever finding adequate recognition. I propose that to conceive of migrations as a challenge to citizenship theory is grounds for reconstructing the "human" in human rights to include non-citizens and to extend the obligation of states beyond their own citizens. While in theory, citizenship is associated with equality between individuals independent of their social condition, in practice citizenship depends upon the terms of the relation between the individual and a collectivity, whether such collectivity is a given state associated with her citizenship, other states, or the world broadly constructed. While progress is occurring within states open to incorporating principles of human rights into domestic law, such progress remains unequal and fragile. It may become easier in some liberal democracies to become a citizen when one is a permanent resident or to acquire the right to vote in local elections when one is a permanent resident, as in the case of European Union (EU) members in various states of the union, but it remains extremely difficult for migrants from certain countries to obtain the right to enter other states and in particular for foreigners to migrate to Western liberal democracies. For instance, controls of the EU southern border have increased significantly creating a proliferation of clandestine ways to arrive to Europe and casualties involving migrants. "The main outcome of increased controls seems thus to be the differentiation and diversification of migration routes, rather than the reduction of irregular migration and the defeat of criminal organisations" (Cuttitta, 2008). Moreover, "the real aim of the current Italian and EU border regime seems not to be to arrest mobility but to tame it" (Walters, 2004, p. 248) through the selection of both regular and irregular immigrants (Cuttitta, 2008). States, as moral and legal persons, appear to share the common belief that a sovereign state is always justified in expelling migrants on national security, peace, or stability grounds; they often cooperate to fight international migrations. The ethical view that all individuals are of equal worth, or that all human beings are citizens of the world, does not have bearing on this understanding of state sovereignty or states' coercive power. States exercise their power of coercion justified by national interests to strengthen borders that have gradually become control and management zones with an increasing involvement of neighboring states. The conventional view that basic national interests must determine immigration and refugee policy is constantly implemented in direct or indirect violation of fundamental principles of international law, such as the principle of non-refoulement, or of other rights such as the rights of unaccompanied children.

In this context, political membership becomes a necessary condition to have one's human rights protected. Strangers to the polity do not have valid claims against the state, and their human rights can easily be infringed upon or overridden. Here the divide is not between cultural practices deemed irreconcilable but between those who have human rights that are legally protected and those whose human rights are merely moral claims. I contend that this divide is as much an obstacle to the universality of human rights as the assumed incompatibility between conflicting cultural practices. From the perspective of a human rights practitioner, violators of human rights are states and government actors when they do not respect or fulfill the rights of their own citizens. This makes stateless persons and migrants attempting to gain entry to a foreign state de facto vulnerable to abuses that may never be recognized as human rights violations. Interestingly, while the right to a nationality (the right to acquire, change, and retain a nationality) is recognized as a fundamental human right by various human rights international documents including the UDHR, statelessness remains a reality for many humans. Likewise, having their human rights fulfilled remains very difficult for undocumented immigrants, refugees, or asylum seekers. Here again the obstacle is not their cultural practices per se but the complete lack of political membership, in the case of stateless persons, or the absence of obligations on the part of foreign states in the case of migrants. How can human rights be regarded as universal if their very exercise or enjoyment depends upon state membership or nationality and therefore presupposes a principle of exclusion? The institutional understanding of human rights makes noncitizens de jure strangers to the polity, vulnerable humans whose human rights do not have legal force in the face of states in which they have no recognized membership. This understanding provides the right type of protection in case of genocide, crime against humanity, and, to a lesser extent, torture understood as violations orchestrated by states against their own citizens, but does not appear sufficient in the face of phenomena such as the European migrant crisis or any form of population displacement.

Beyond a state-centric approach to universal human rights?

As discussed in the previous section, the institutional approach to human rights emphasizes a very specific form of vulnerability experienced by human beings, namely the vulnerability experienced by a person facing her own state, or its representatives, exercising its power of coercion over her. In that view, international treaties signed between states appear to be the appropriate instrument to protect humans qua citizens from possible violations orchestrated by states. Moreover, efforts to integrate human rights norms into domestic laws appear as adequate protections and guarantees. But why limit human rights to the rights one has against one's own state? Can't human rights be conceived of as claims against all and any state, against all and any fellow human? I believe the answer to this question lies partly in a version of the interactional account of human rights and partly in the correlativity of rights and duties. If people other than state officials can violate human rights, then these people also have a duty to protect rights.

Here again I am reminded of how my students responded to the issue of statelessness. As we were examining the legal definition of a stateless person, "a person who is not considered as a national by any State under the operation of its law" and discussing testimonies of stateless individuals, one student expressed her bewilderment asking how such experience could be possible in a world essentially composed of states. Another student offered that perhaps we should first ask whether every human is assigned a nationality or citizenship at birth and if so whether nationality could be taken away. A third student described how children born in refugee camps are often born without papers and at risk of becoming stateless. And a fourth one pointed to the possibility of gendered citizenship laws asking whether in some states the transmission of nationality was not limited to male citizens, thereby making it impossible for women to transfer their nationality to their children. This exchange made possible by a diverse group of students provided a remarkable opportunity for the class to collectively explore various ways in which individuals can become stateless and to uncover that statelessness is often the product of state policies and regulations aiming to exclude persons regarded as outsiders or non-legitimate members. How can this experience be reconciled with article 15 of the UDHR that stipulates: "Everyone has the right to a nationality" and "No one shall be arbitrarily deprived of his nationality nor denied the right to change his nationality"? Students were prompt to underline not the issue of the validity of human rights claims, a problem that can be understood as a matter of cultural legitimacy as discussed in the first section of this paper, but rather an inherent tension, if not a contradiction, in the right to a nationality recognized by states that reserve the authority to deny nationality to some. Arguably, in the world as we experience it today, nationality is a necessary condition for the enjoyment of many other rights, and yet being able to exercise and enjoy this right is a real challenge for a significant number of people. Is it that the right of sovereign states to select their members trumps the rights of humans to have a national identity? Why are these violations seemingly accepted by states?

In the aftermaths of World War II, Hannah Arendt made the following observation: "We became aware of the existence of a right to have rights... and a right to belong to some kind of organized community, only when millions of people emerged who had lost and could not regain these rights because of the new global situation" (Arendt, 1973). It is only in a world of states that one can be deprived of the rights recognized and protected by states and consequently left only with the moral right to have rights. If Arendt was right to categorize this situation as "humanity naked" and if this ultimate right is a moral right, it seems that the institutional account must be supplemented with a version of the interactional account. If when people have lost their political membership no other state has any obligation to protect their rights, then who else other than fellow humans could have the duty to protect the right to have rights? To focus on violations of human rights as violations perpetrated by states and state officials on their own citizens is to limit the grounds for human rights justification and the scope of human rights application. On the institutional account, there is something eminently political about human rights that is in fact damaging to the rights of non-citizens and, I would argue, to the universality of human rights. If the recent migrant crisis in Europe has taught us anything it is that through various forms of border surveillance, migrants are forced into alternative routes and innovative techniques to attempt to enter territories that are closed to them and that they cannot hope to enter legally. This mechanism is made more efficient with the improvement of technology and with the development of agreements between states. Gradually the control of population movements has been globalized, and asylum seeking and, more generally, border crossing are often regarded as a burden of world misery if not as a threat. Migrants and refugees are often described as undesirable, illegal, clandestine, and possibly dangerous persons as opposed to rights holders. Various forms of waiting zones or camps have been developed to keep them at the border of national territories, making migrants in a vulnerable position lose all forms of political membership and become de facto stateless. The experience of refugees in general and the recent European migrant crisis in particular illustrate the limits of the institutional conception of human rights and the significance of the interactional account. On the interactional account refugees have valid claims against all other persons who can help regardless of their state membership and all other persons who can help have a duty to ensure that these human rights are not violated. In practice, these duties might be fulfilled by individuals who provide food, clothing, and shelter to migrants or by individuals and grassroots organizations rescuing them at sea. Of course these individuals and groups may or may not act to uphold human rights per se, they may understand their duties to have different grounds, but to recognize that refugees have human rights on the interactional account makes it possible to understand that they have valid claims against all other persons able to help and that they deserve to have these human rights met.

Taking the refugee experience seriously suggests that we should rethink the correlativity of rights and duties in the context of human rights. If we conceive of rights as not correlated to single duties[4] but to many, it becomes clear that their protection may involve a variety of duty bearers and that at times, when all duties associated with rights cannot be fulfilled, at least some of them may be fulfilled, preventing a complete violation or a full neglect of the right in question. On this account both states and individuals have a variety of duties grounded in the human rights of others. This view is compatible with the interactional account of human rights, augments the institutional account, and proposes a less state-centric, more satisfactory understanding of universal human rights allowing for a more satisfactory conception of humans as equal rights holders despite the necessary difference in situations, experiences, and values.

Conclusion

Conceptions of human rights and experiences of human rights violations continue to generate reflections on what it means to be human and what type of protections humans deserve. Numerous treaties and conventions have followed the very first iteration of the human rights instrument in 1948, the UDHR, in a continuous attempt to guarantee that individuals and groups are treated with the respect they deserve. While our conception of the "human" has been reconstructed over time to become more inclusive, significant exclusions remain, in part, I have argued, due to the persistence of a state-centric and institutional approach to human rights. On my account the institutional approach is insufficient and must be supplemented with an interactional approach to guarantee the universality of human rights; such an account requires that the sovereignty and the power of coercion of states be scrutinized when human rights violations are experienced by humans, including by non-citizens. In other words, I recommend distinguishing humans from citizens when considering the state's obligations grounded in human rights claims in order to make the protection of humans less formal and more real. As I have argued, in the current state of affairs only citizens are really in a position to make valid human rights claims against their states, which makes strict human rights claims at best formal and potentially valid but certainly not actual.

Discussion questions

1   Considering what you know of the rights listed in the UDHR, the International Covenant on Economic, Social and Cultural Rights, or the International Covenant on Civil and Political Rights, what are the rights that you think might be less likely to be exercised and enjoyed universally? Why? Can you think of cultural practices that may conflict with these rights? When you think of experiences of human rights violations, what images come to mind? What do these images have in common and what distinguish them from one another? What is their cultural content?

2   Human rights practice and discourse have evolved significantly over the past 70 years but how we ought to conceive of human rights and what it means to say that humans have them remains a controversial terrain. On the institutional account, only government and government actors can violate human rights, and on the interactional account both government and non-government actors can violate human rights. Reviewing the arguments in favor of both views, explain what is in your view the best approach and why.

3   Consider article 15 of the UDHR (Everyone has the right to a nationality. No one shall be arbitrarily deprived of his nationality, nor denied the right to change his nationality) and the experience of statelessness. How would you define statelessness and when was the first time you were exposed to it? What was the context of this exposure? Do you believe article 15 should be interpreted to support a basic human right to nationality, making statelessness a human rights violation, or do you think being "stateless" should be regarded as a status that is conducive to human rights violations? On what do you base your beliefs? Can you think of possible counter-arguments and how would you respond to them?

Notes

1   This essay owes much to my experience teaching an introductory course on human rights and an upper-level philosophy course on the nature and value of rights, to class discussions and to individual conversations with my students

before and after classes. I thank my students for their engagement with the material and the issues.

2 This is not a strict relativist argument. It is not that *all* rights claims valid in one culture are invalid in another but rather that, while there are some agreed upon objective standards, there exist some other claims that will be valid in one culture and invalid in another; this range has led to justifying that scrutiny and suspicion be applied to all claims.

3 I use morality and ethics, moral and ethical, interchangeably in this essay – as it is generally, although not always, done in philosophy. I do not distinguish between ethics understood as a set of standards of good and bad imposed by some external group or profession (as in business ethics or legal ethics) and morality understood as one's own personal sense of good and bad or right and wrong; this distinction is often made outside the discipline of philosophy.

   Philosophers raise various issues about definitions of morality and often distinguish between two main usages of the term, a descriptive use and a normative use. Descriptively, morality denotes codes of conduct imposed by society or by a group and/or accepted by individuals. In this sense morality is to be distinguished from other codes of conduct such as religion, law, or etiquette. Normatively, the term is used to characterize a code of conduct that would be accepted by any individual who meets specific intellectual conditions such as being rational.

4 I borrowed the conception of rights as correlated to multiple duties to Waldron, 1989. In this piece Waldron was concerned with rights and not with human rights per se; however I think his account of waves of duty is helpful in the context of human rights.

References

An-Na'im, A., ed. (1992). *Human rights in cross-cultural perspectives: A quest for consensus*. Philadelphia, PA: University of Pennsylvania Press.

Appiah, A. (2006). *Cosmopolitanism: Ethics in a world of strangers*. New York: W.W. Norton & Company.

Arendt, H. (1951). *The burden of our time*. London: Secker & Warburg.

Arendt, H. (1973). *The origins of totalitarianism*. San Diego, CA: Harvest Book/Harcourt.

BalibarE. (1988). Propositions on citizenship. *Ethics*, 98(4), p. 724.

Beitz, C. (2011). *The idea of human rights*. Oxford: Oxford University Press.

Caney, S. (2005). *Justice beyond borders: A global political theory*. Oxford: Oxford University Press.

Cuttitta, P. (2008). The case of the Italian southern sea borders: Cooperation across the Mediterranean. In: D. Godenau, V. Zapata Hernández, P. Cuttitta, A. Triandafyllidou, T. Maroukis, and G. Pinyol, eds, *Immigration flows and the management of the EU's southern borders*. Barcelona: Documentos CIDOB, pp. 45–62.

Donnelly, J. (2007). The relative universality of human rights. *Human Rights Quarterly*, 29(2), pp. 281–306.

Lauren, P.G. (2003). *The evolution of international human rights: visions seen*. 2nd ed. Philadelphia, PA: University of Pennsylvania.

Nagel, T. (2002). Personal rights and public space. In: T. Nagel, ed., *Concealment and exposure: And other essays*. Oxford: Oxford University Press, pp. 31–52.

Nickel, J. (2007). *Making sense of human rights*. 2nd ed. Oxford: Blackwell.

Pogge, T. (2002). *World poverty and human rights: Cosmopolitan responsibilities and reforms*. Cambridge: Polity Press.

Pogge, T. (2008). *World poverty and human rights: Cosmopolitan responsibilities and reforms*. 2nd ed. Cambridge: Polity Press.

Risse, M. (2008). What are human rights? Human rights as membership rights in the global order. Harvard University Kennedy School of Government Working Paper no. RWP 08-006, February.

Sen, A. (2005). Human rights and capabilities. *Journal of Human Development*, 6(2), pp. 151–166.

Tasioulas, J. (2012). Towards a philosophy of human rights. *Current Legal Problems*, 65 (1), pp. 1–30.

Waldron, J. (1989). Rights in conflict. *Ethics*, 99(3), pp. 503–519.

Walters, W. (2004). Secure borders, safe haven, domopolitics. *Citizenship Studies*, 8(3), pp. 237–260.

Walzer, M. (1994). *Thick and thin: Moral argument at home and abroad*. Notre-Dame, IL: University of Notre-Dame Press.

Further reading

Abusharaf, R.M., ed. (2007). *Female circumcision: Multicultural perspectives*. Philadelphia, PA: Pennsylvania Press University.

Agier, M. (2008). *On the margins of the world: The refugee experience today*. Cambridge: Polity Press.

Agier, M. (2011). *Managing the undesirables: Refugee camps and humanitarian government*. Cambridge: Polity Press.

Hayden, P., ed. (2001). *The philosophy of human rights: Readings in context*. St Paul, MN: Paragon House.

Ntarangwi, M. (2007). "I've changed my mind now": US students' responses to female genital cutting in Africa. *Africa Today*, 53(4), pp. 87–108.

Schotel, B. (2012). *On the right of exclusion: Law, ethics and immigration policy*. New York: Routledge.United Nations (2006). *Human rights: A compilation of international instruments*. Volumes I and II. New York: United Nations.

United Nations (2006). *The rights of non-citizens*. New York: United Nations.

United Nations (2015). *Behind closed doors: Protecting and promoting the human rights of migrant domestic workers in an irregular situation*. New York: United Nations.

Wellman, C.H. and Cole, P. (2011). *Debating the ethics of immigration: Is there a right to exclude?* Oxford: Oxford University Press.

2 Rise of the global human rights regime

Challenging power with humanity

Darren Kew, Malcolm Russell-Einhorn and Adriana Rincón Villegas

Introduction

The global human rights system, much like international law and organization themselves, developed organically over time through a process of constant negotiation, advocacy, and political horse trading. Nonetheless, the resulting patchwork of human rights conventions, treaties, commissions, and United Nations (UN) bodies that have grown over time still form a system that remarkably is far more coherent than one might expect after a century of development. Supporting this system is a massive global network of civil society organizations and movements engaging with government and intergovernmental institutions on a regular basis, and pushing them to expand human rights protections in a number of new directions.

Over the course of this history of the global human rights system, several trends are apparent, during which efforts to develop the system tended to cluster around specific themes for defined periods of time. Activists in the field often refer to these trends as "generations" of human rights treaties and architecture, during which the general focus was on a specific type of human rights protection. Four such generations appear discernable since the foundation of the UN in 1945, beginning with an initial focus on civil and political rights, the first generation, and followed thereafter by second-generation socioeconomic rights, and third-generation rights focusing on specific groups or sectors, such as women, indigenous communities, and minorities. Recent years have seen discussion of a fourth generation of human rights, focusing on the environment and/or cultural rights.

With the first-generation rights, and to some extent the second generation as well, state governments initially took the lead in pushing for their adoption and enforcement. As this period also coincided with the early years of the Cold War, the first- and second-generation rights also tended to divide between the Western and Eastern blocs, with the United States (US) and its allies generally taking the lead in advocating civil and political rights, and the Soviet Union stressing socioeconomic ones. By the 1970s, however, much of the initiative began to shift to civil society groups worldwide, whose advocacy and enforcement efforts pushed governments much further than many had originally intended, such that a host of new rights treaties were developed and new protection mechanisms envisioned.

Consequently, both power politics and civil society activism played key roles in shaping the global human rights system. The result has been a vast patchwork of compromises and incomplete protections, such that international human rights law and its enforcement system are not the same as legal protections within most advanced states, nor do they conform with most people's sense of morality. Activists driven by a sense of moral justice, however, have been critical to extending human rights protections under international law in the face of often stiff resistance from state governments. A review of the development of the four generations of human rights protections will show that this creative tension between the law as states define it and the moral advocacy of civil society groups have been essential in pushing the expansion of the limits of what states have been willing to accept over time. Critical legal perspectives also demonstrate some of the cultural influences and problems with the law, and suggest directions in which the system may develop in the future.

Origins of fundamental United Nations bodies

Although several important human rights treaties predate the foundation of the UN in 1945, particularly in regard to humanitarian issues like the treatment of prisoners, the UN Charter is without a doubt the foundational document for the human rights system, much as it is for public international law overall. The charter includes multiple references to human rights as a key principle to inform the work of the UN, and also tasks its key organs with their promotion, particularly the General Assembly and the Economic and Social Council. Notably, the passages creating the powerful Security Council do not explicitly mention human rights.

From the beginning, several of the major powers and many of the smaller states feared that a robust international human rights system would lead to unwanted scrutiny of their domestic policies and infringe their sovereignty. As one of the American lawyers who assisted the US State Department in drafting the charter later explained, in

> the preliminary working draft of the Charter... relatively little attention was given to the question of human rights... We were told... that to inject this subject into the Charter would cause the Soviet Union to fear intervention in its domestic affairs [and] that the British would fear that reference to fundamental freedom would somehow have serious complications for their colonial relationships.
>
> (Cohen, 1949)

The Americans, however, persisted, and succeeded in getting the references inserted. In this effort, the US government was both assisted and pressured by American humanitarian, public interest, and religious organizations, as well as members of the legal community, who felt that the horrors of the 1914–1945 period demanded greater international protections of human rights in the face of massive state failures worldwide.

This impressive coalition of human rights proponents within the US government and across American civil society groups continued through the 1940s, spearheaded by US ambassador to the UN Eleanor Roosevelt. Although the intention was to create an international convention on human rights, stiff resistance from state governments forced the coalition to compromise and settle for a resolution passed by the General Assembly: the 1948 Universal Declaration of Human Rights (UDHR). General Assembly resolutions are not legally binding on the state members of the UN, but the UDHR has over the years been so frequently cited in treaties, judicial decisions, UN business, and the official correspondence of governments worldwide that it is now seen by some as having greater influence than even the binding treaties that followed it (Glendon, 2004). The UDHR encompassed most of the fundamental rights that are now recognized worldwide: life, liberty, privacy, equality before the law, and others, as well as prohibitions against slavery and torture and freedoms of religion, assembly, opinion, and expression. Social, economic, and cultural rights were also included in the UDHR, as well as basic democratic rights such as participation in government and choice of representatives. Its fundamental characteristics – universal, inalienable, indivisible, interrelated, and interdependent – would provide the framework for a multitude of human rights treaties and bodies that followed. In 1993, governments as diverse as Iran and China affirmed that the UDHR is indeed universal, such that no cultural variation or exception can be claimed anywhere.

The UN Charter also created the Economic and Social Council (ECOSOC) in 1945 and tasked it with "making recommendations for the purpose of promoting respect for, and observance of, human rights and fundamental freedoms for all" (article 62). As one of its earliest acts, ECOSOC created the UN Commission on Human Rights in 1946, which was the body that drafted the UDHR. Structurally, however, the commission was hobbled from the beginning by the fact that its members were all representatives of state governments, many of whom had poor human rights records themselves, thus frequently preventing comprehensive action. Nonetheless, non-governmental organizations (NGOs) and human rights activists in the 1960s began sending unsolicited information on human rights abuses to the commission (and its Subcommission on the Prevention of Discrimination and the Protection of Minorities) that began to appear in commission and subcommission reports. Beginning in 1967, the commission created a series of new procedures that allowed for public consideration of specific country situations, such as apartheid South Africa or Cambodia under the Khmer Rouge, and allowed NGOs an opportunity to submit "communications" to the commission on countries that demonstrate a consistent pattern of massive human rights violations to be "dealt with in closed sessions of the Commission and Subcommission" (Rodley, 1992). Special rapporteurs named by the commission to investigate and report on specific countries and themes, such as torture, followed later. In order to coordinate the work of the growing number of these rapporteurs, and to create a single office responsible for overseeing the work of human rights at the UN, the General Assembly created a High Commissioner for Human Rights in 1993.

The commission's fundamental structural problem of having governments with massive human rights violations sitting and voting on its business – and thus hindering or preventing its actions – continued to be a source of frustration well after the end of the Cold War. Consequently, the commission was replaced in 2006 with the UN Human Rights Council, which features a vehicle for the removal of government members accused of persistent human rights violations. The council also absorbed and expanded the commission's mechanisms for receiving complaints from NGOs and individuals on systematic rights abuses worldwide, and instituted a Universal Periodic Review of protection of human rights in the entire membership of the UN.

Together with the High Commissioner for Human Rights, the UN Human Rights Council offers an important vehicle for providing UN-level scrutiny of systematic human rights violations by governments worldwide. Yet as UN bodies, these vehicles remain limited by the fact that they are beholden to the member states, such that many countries, especially powerful ones and their allies, are still able to prevent or delay scrutiny of their actions. In addition, both the Human Rights Council and the high commissioner can at best only bring global attention to systematic human rights problems – they have no enforcement authority. They can, however, bring such concerns to the attention of the UN Security Council, which can impose enforceable decisions on the entire UN membership if it chooses, and which has utilized the work of the high commissioner and the council in recent years on specific cases.

The first generation: civil and political rights

Building on the framework of the 1948 UDHR, the UN General Assembly adopted the two foundational International Human Rights Covenants in December 1966. They formed, along with the UDHR, the "International Bill of Rights" so fervently sought by many advocates at the time of the San Francisco Conference that created the UN in 1945. While it took 18 years for the General Assembly to adopt and open for signature the Covenant on Civil and Political Rights (ICCPR), the Covenant on Economic, Social, and Cultural Rights (ICESCR), and the First Optional Protocol to the ICCPR – and another decade before 35 states ratified both instruments to bring them into force[1] – the two treaties gave additional impetus to the notion that the UDHR was more than a mere hortatory pronouncement. Instead, as the preamble to the UDHR noted, it serves "as a common standard of achieve-ment for all peoples and all nations." While the delay in the drafting of the covenants actually enhanced the authoritative nature of the UDHR during a period of little stasis, only with the ratification of the two covenants did the special moral and normative character of the UDHR become manifest.[2]

It is not an exaggeration to say that the modern machinery of the interna-tional human rights system took root following the ratification of the two covenants, and especially following the establishment of the Human Rights Committee under the ICCPR.[3] The committee established not only a reporting system by states parties, but the "soft" (non-binding) jurisprudence of treaty interpretations (so-called "General Comments" on the ICCPR) and the ability of individuals to petition the committee concerning alleged viola-tions of the covenant. As will be discussed below, these reporting mechan-isms, interpretive functions, and quasi-judicial petitioning procedures have evolved considerably in the four succeeding decades with regard to both the ICCPR and the ICESCR, and have provided an influential foundation for the wide range of other human rights treaties that have followed in their wake.

The ICCPR recapitulates most of the key civil and political rights men-tioned in the UDHR, but adds a number of additional ones. For example, the covenant addresses rights to life, liberty, privacy, political participation, fair civil and criminal trials (including the right to attorney and protection against self-incrimination), the presumption of innocence in the latter, and security of the person. It also recognizes freedom of speech, association, religion, assembly, and movement, while enshrining prohibitions against slavery, torture, cruel, inhuman or degrading treatment, or arbitrary arrest, detention, or exile. Other rights in the ICCPR that are not mentioned in the UDHR include freedom from imprisonment for non-payment of debt; the right to be treated with humanity and respect for the inherent dignity of the human person while detained or imprisoned; and the right of every child to "acquire a nationality" and to be accorded "such measures of protection as are required by his status as a minor."[4]

While article 4 of the ICCPR permits certain rights to be "derogated" (suspended) in case of public emergency (such as acute civil unrest or war), some rights (notably those dealing with life, civil liberties, and discrimina-tion) may not be so abridged (roughly a quarter of the 46 articulated rights in the covenant).[5] At the same time, the covenant permits states parties to limit or restrict the exercise of some rights, but these limitations are themselves circumscribed in particular ways, such as limitations placed on the free exercise of religion only where "necessary to protect public safety, order, health or morals or the fundamental rights and freedom of others" (article 18, para. 3) (Kiss, 1981). Meanwhile, all rights are to be given full and immediate effect by virtue of article 2(2), which requires the states parties "to adopt such legislative or other measures as may be necessary to give effect to the rights" in the covenant where they do not already exist in the domestic legal system. This is contrasted with the ICESCR, discussed below, which calls for the progressive implementation of economic, social, and cultural rights based on available resources (Schachter, 1981).

The pioneering impact of the covenant as an action-oriented mechanism derives from the work of the Human Rights Committee established under the treaty, and certain functions provided for under the (First) Optional Protocol to the ICCPR. The committee's central purpose is to examine reports on human rights compliance by states parties that address measures taken to effect the rights recognized in the covenant and "progress made in the enjoyment of these rights" (article 40(1)). The 18 members of the committee utilize all information at their disposal – including reports by UN agencies and special rapporteurs as well as national and international NGOs – to question state representatives and demand further information. In this manner, the committee can identify serious compliance problems and bring them to the attention of both the General Assembly and the general public and press.[6] While the reports have typically been submitted every four to seven years, in 2009 the committee adopted an optional simplified reporting procedure whereby the committee proactively submits a list of targeted issues to states parties before a periodic report is due; the state can provide written responses to the issues raised, in lieu of submitting a report (Young, 2002).[7] Ultimately, the committee holds open hearings (webcast live) and transmits published concluding observations, some of which require "follow-up" by the state in question within one year. Based on the follow-up efforts, the committee issues a grade of A, B, C, D, or E on the country's compliance and may request further action (Schmidt, 2000).

The other major feature of the covenant furthering compliance is the petition system established by the First Optional Protocol. It allows private parties alleging violations of the covenant to file "communications" (individual complaints) with the Human Rights Committee, so long as they have exhausted available – and "effective" – domestic remedies. On the basis of such communications, a state party is given six months to respond on the merits. Decisions ("views" in committee parlance) are issued by the committee with majority and minority (dissenting) opinions (Committee Rules of Procedure 91, 86). While a special rapporteur for the follow-up of views is responsible for ensuring that violations of the covenant are remedied and both the state party and victim(s) are heard from, ultimately compliance is effected through meetings with state representatives and even through meetings with the heads of diplomatic missions to the UN. See Committee Rules of Procedure 101.

While the ICCPR has been criticized in some quarters for being ineffective (Keith, 1999), the foundation it has created has paved the way for significant progress in both treaty compliance[8] and "naming and shaming" activities both by, and outside, the committee. In particular, the "grades" handed out to states parties by the committee and the information assembled by the committee and various civil society organizations and international NGOs have trained a light on violations in particular countries that have amplified pressure for compliance. At the same time, the collective jurisprudence of the "views' rendered by the committee in individual cases (communications) has created a valuable body of legal interpretation and decision making that has influence far beyond the ICCPR and the committee, affecting the work of many other regional treaty bodies and human rights practitioners.[9] While overarching UN bodies like the General Assembly, the UN Commission on Human Rights, and the Human Rights Council have fallen prey to significant politicization, the Human Rights Committee has attained a reputation for integrity and impartiality (perhaps due to the legal qualifications of its members). It has generally won praise for its technocratic work.

Perhaps most important, the ICCPR created a model that gave rise to a number of other treaties and compliance bodies.[10] The most notable treaties – later designated by the UN as "core" treaties – have been the Convention on the Elimination of All Forms of Discrimination against Women (adopted 1979; entered into force 1981); the Convention against Torture and Other Cruel, Inhuman or Degrading Treatment or Punishment (adopted 1984; entered into force 1987); the Convention on the Rights of Persons with Disabilities (adopted 2006; entered into force 2008); and the International Convention for the Protection of All Persons from Enforced Disappearance (adopted 2006; entered into force 2010).

As evidence of the emergence of a coordinated human rights treaty compliance "system," chairpersons of the various treaty bodies met in 2006 under the aegis of the UN High Commissioner for Human Rights and adopted harmonized guidelines on reporting, including a common basic framework for review and for the adoption of concluding observations. All bodies seek "constructive dialogue" with state party representatives, are increasingly more transparent and sophisticated about their work (with increased publicity and use of statistical information), and most have adopted the simplified and more targeted procedure recommended by the General Assembly in 2014.

Second generation: economic, social, and cultural rights

The ICESCR, while adopted contemporaneously with the ICCPR, is often viewed as ushering in a "second generation" of human rights – ones that are complementary to civil and political rights, that often seek to protect groups, and that require progressive implementation over time, based on available resources. Indeed, many of the key treaties falling under this rubric went into force only in the past few decades. At the same time, while early commentators posited that civil and political rights were "negative" in nature – merely requiring the state to forbear from certain actions – most observers today would agree that the dichotomy is exaggerated; not only do economic and social rights require certain positive steps to be taken with regard to individual rights (most notably formation of courts and other state-sanctioned dispute-resolution mechanisms, as well as freedoms necessary for social and cultural life to prosper), but civil and political rights require property rights and the right to work to be well protected in order to be effectively exercised.

In fact, the covenant contains a very comprehensive inventory of economic, social, and cultural rights, including the right to work, the right to the enjoyment of just and favorable conditions of work, the right to form and join trade unions, the right to social security (including social insurance), the right to the protection of the family, the right to an adequate standard of living, the right to education, and the right to take part in cultural life. The covenant also defines these rights and lays out key steps to attain their realization. Unlike the ICCPR, the ICESCR specifically urges states parties not only to take progressive steps individually, but "through international assistance and cooperation" (article 2(1)). In light of this understanding of "progressive realization," as well as the unique set of resources available to any given country, it is recognized that different criteria may govern how they can meet their treaty obligations. At the same time, as elaborated in general comments by the ICESCR, some obligations have immediate effect – e.g., non-discrimination in the exercise of economic and social rights, and the need to in fact "take steps" toward their realization (General Comment No 3 (1990)).

While the reporting and complaints machinery of the ICESCR is based on the ICCPR, there are some notable differences. First, communications – which only became possible after a protocol went into force in 2013 – can be submitted by groups as well as individuals (article 2). Second, there are specific provisions to encourage a "friendly settlement" of petitions" (article 7). Third, the committee is charged with considering the "reasonableness" of the steps taken by the state party toward compliance, and should acknowledge the range of possible policy measures that the state can employ to affect implementation of the rights at issue.

Based on the general purview of the ICESCR, a number of specialized treaties have come into existence, including the Convention on the Rights of the Child (adopted 1989; entered into force 1990); the International Convention on the Protection of the Rights of All Migrant Workers and Their Families (adopted 1990; entered into force 2003); the Convention Concerning Indigenous and Tribal Peoples in Independent Countries (adopted 1989; entered into force 1991); and the Convention for the Safeguarding of Intangible Cultural Heritage (adopted 2003; entered into force 2006). In addition, there have been a host of treaties adopted under the aegis of the International Labour Organization and a plethora of specialized declarations by the General Assembly – from a Declaration of Commitment on HIV/AIDS to the Millennium Declaration in 2000. There have also been numerous compacts directed at the private sector and corporate social responsibility, from the UN Global Compact, adopted by the General Assembly in 2000, to Guiding Principles on Business and Human Rights, endorsed by the Human Rights Council in 2011.

The growth of regional human rights mechanisms

While a global framework for the enforcement of the UDHR took several decades to emerge, regional precedents for binding treaty enforcement of human rights took shape considerably earlier, and today form a vital complementary arena for human rights compliance. In 1953, the European Convention on Human Rights entered into force, protecting most of the rights articulated by the UDHR. In the decades that followed, additional protocols have added a number of other important rights, including those to property, education, free and secret elections, and to equality of spousal rights. To ensure observance of the treaty undertakings, both the European Commission of Human Rights and the European Court of Human Rights were established (both were superseded by a full-time Court of Human Rights in 1998) (Haas, 2014). The court (both the present court and its original predecessor) has generated the most effective regional enforcement mechanism and jurisprudence in the world, delivering nearly 2,500 judgments as recently as 2015 and adopting procedural innovations to address the most serious and urgent cases in priority fashion (Bates, 2011). Enforcement, carried out through the Committee of Ministers, has been generally very effective, even in cases involving states such as Russia and Ukraine with spotty human rights records.

Another important regional framework exists through the Organization of American States and specifically its charter, and the American Declaration of the Rights and Duties of Man, both adopted in 1948. While the latter was originally viewed as non-binding, it subsequently took on a fully normative character. In 1959, the Inter-American Commission on Human Rights was established, creating a working body that examined and issued reports and recommendations and (as of 1965) heard individual petitions. The body's overall status and powers were enhanced in 1970, in conjunction with a new American Convention on Human Rights (which was promulgated in 1969 and eventually entered into force in 1978). Pursuant to the creation of the Inter-American Court of Human Rights at the same time, the commission or states parties can refer cases to the court for decision (there is no individual right to petition the court directly). Despite this limitation, large numbers of important human rights cases have been referred to the court, including critical judgments on forced disappearances, arbitrary executions, denials of due process, and even the rights of indigenous peoples to land and resources (Haas, 2014),

A later regional treaty framework – the African Charter on Human and Peoples' Rights, which entered into force in 1986 – is another significant regional rights forum. It differs from the European and American Conventions on Human Rights by virtue of its focus on duties, as well as rights, its codification of peoples' collective rights as well as individual rights, and its equal emphasis on economic, social, and cultural rights (particularly the right to development) alongside civil and political rights (Haas, 2014). To some, the emphasis on duties may endanger individual rights if states are in a position to determine that rights are limited by the rights of others or in relation to collective security considerations. The charter's compliance body – the African Commission on Human and Peoples' Rights – has both quasi-judicial and reporting/advisory/educational functions. The former permits the commission to address individual complaints and to authoritatively interpret the charter by broadly incorporating normative sources of law from the UN system and individual African countries. While the commission has taken a strong stand on a variety of cases ranging from fair trial procedure to detention and imprisonment, the lack of a prescribed enforcement mechanism has often prevented its recommendations from being adopted by member governments (Viljoen, 2012).

Third- and fourth-generation rights

Third-generation rights, or solidarity rights, emerged in the late 1970s and were developed by scholars in the 1980s. In 1977, UNESCO legal advisor Karel Vasak coined the term *third-generation human rights* to refer to an emergent set of collective rights whose preponderance became relevant in the international arena, such as peace, development, and a healthy environment. Interestingly, Vasak pointed out that the three generations of human rights corresponded to the three ideals of the French Revolution: liberty (first generation), equality (second generation), fraternity (third generation) (Wellman, 2000, p. 639), which strengthened the argument of the need for a third generation of rights.

Alston (1982) argues that third-generation rights depart from the core assumption that the other two generations of rights do not adequately respond to a set of demands based on solidarity for their realization. For Marks (1981), this human rights generation encompasses rights that, "belong neither to the individualistic tradition of the first generation nor to the socialist tradition of the second" (p. 441). As Vasak (1984) observes, third-generation human rights

> seek to infuse the human dimension into areas where it has all too often been missing, having been left to the State, or States... [T]hey are new in that they may both be invoked against the state and demanded of it; but above all (and herein lies their essential characteristic) they can be realized only through the concerted efforts of all actors on the social scene: the individual, the State, public and private bodies and the international community.
>
> (Vasak, 1984, p. 838)

Advocates of third-generation rights challenge the idea of human rights as changeless and static, and they argue that it is possible to understand the nature and relevance of human rights by understanding the historical context in which they have emerged. Under that logic, Wellman (2000, p. 640) and Rich (2002) observe, the relevance of third-generation rights derives from the urgency of securing peace and food, preserving the environment, and generating economic development, as well as from the new global logics of the postcolonial world. In sum,

> first-generation rights were designed to protect the individual from mistreatment by the state, and second-generation rights were intended to enable the individual to demand that the state create and maintain governmental programs to benefit himself. However, this neglects the fact that the individual cannot thrive without participation in the life of the community and that any life worthy of human beings requires fraternity as well as liberty and equality.
>
> (Wellman, 2000, p. 642)

Third-generation rights have received criticism, especially concerning the massive proliferation of rights in the last decades, which poses the risk of creating spaces for rhetoric instead of effective protection of tangible rights. Also, the disparity in the capacity and willingness of states to cooperate in the protection of these rights, along with the lack of enforceable international measures to ensure their protection, make it difficult to guarantee these rights in practice.

There is little agreement on which generation of rights indigenous and women rights belong. An additional generation of rights (fourth-generation rights) emerged in the literature in the early 1990s. It arose based on the need of acknowledging certain claims of specific communities such as indigenous peoples and women. The idea of a fourth generation of human rights was borrowed from Manuel and Posluns' (1974) *The Fourth World: An Indian Reality*, where they propose the "fourth world" as a site for respect and coexistence between white and non-white – specially indigenous – peoples (in Bailey, 1975, pp. 251–253). Fourth-generation rights have generated certain debates on cultural relativity (Otto, 1997), as well as critiques to the claimed universality of human rights.

Challenges for international human rights law

The human rights system has countless advocates, both in policy and academia. However, it also has its critics. Two core ideas are salient in critical human rights literature. One is about the human rights system and its pretension of universality. This critique refers to the fact that the universalization of human rights faces the risk of ignoring the specific context and harming local practices, expectations, and realities. Freeman observes that the concept of human rights is "Western in origin, and some would say that the West remains hegemonic in the production, interpretation, and implementation of human-rights norms" (2011, p. 121). Otto (1997) observes, "in the post-Cold War environment the knowledges of modernity, including the liberal discourse of universal human rights, have the potential to serve a set of powerful political agendas which have little to do with fundamental human dignity" (p. 2) *The Vienna Declaration and Programme of Action* adopted by the World Conference on Human Rights in 1993 reiterates former international human rights declarations that define human rights as "universal, indivisible and interdependent and interrelated" (1993, num. 5) Thus, states are compelled to promote these universal rights, both in "nations large and small," Western and non-Western.

The critics of the universalism of human rights come especially from multiple expressions of dissent, from groups historically marginalized from global debates, those who come "from the 'margins' of modernity" (Otto 1997, p. 4), such as feminist, postcolonial, decolonial, and subaltern theorists, as well as activists and indigenous groups. An-Na'im (1991) argues that one of the main causes of human rights violence is precisely the imposition and lack of cultural legitimacy of human rights standards, thus he proposes that the "internal and cross-cultural legitimacy for human rights standards needs to be developed" (1991, p. 19). For Mutua (2001), the human rights narrative is imprecise and raises several questions.

> For example, the UN Charter describes its mandate to "reaffirm faith in fundamental human rights, in the dignity and worth of the human person, in the equal rights of men and women and of nations large and small." This phraseology conceals more than it reveals. What, for example, are fundamental human rights, and how are they determined? … Is there any essentialized human being that the corpus imagines? Is the individual found in the streets of Nairobi, the slums of Boston, the deserts of Iraq, or the rainforests in Brazil?
>
> (Mutua, 2001, p. 206)

According to authors such as Mutua (2001) and Mignolo (2009), the liberal discourse of human rights is based on the logics of civilization narratives that are characteristic of colonialism. Mutua (2001) proposes a metaphor to illustrate this point,

> The human rights movement is marked by a damning metaphor. The grand narrative of human rights contains a subtext that depicts an epochal contest pitting savages, on the one hand, against victims and saviors, on the other. The savages-victims-saviors (SVS) construction is a three-dimensional compound metaphor in which each dimension is a metaphor in itself.
>
> (2001, pp. 201–202)

The SVS metaphor departs from the assumption of "victims" in need of salvation, "savages" in need of redemption, and "saviors" in debt of intervening and solving violence by introducing Western values (economic development, liberal democracy, and human rights law) to non-Western spaces. Freeman (2011) and Mutua (2001) agree in the fact that their goal is not to suggest that human rights are bad per se. "Rather, it suggests that the globalization of human rights fits a historical pattern in which all high morality comes from the West as a civilizing agent against lower forms of civilization in the rest of the world" (Mutua, 2001, p. 201).

Finally, the human rights system receives criticism for its practical effectiveness. For Freeman (2011), the human rights system is far from being neutral, universal, and effective. "Law appears to provide 'objective' standards that 'protect' the concept of human rights from moral and political controversy. This appearance is, however, illusory, for the meaning and application of human-rights standards is legally and politically very controversial. International human-rights law is made by governments that act from political motives" (p. 8). This criticism raises questions on the real impact of the liberal discourse of human rights.

Pushing the envelope further

Despite these important criticisms, the international human rights system remains an important vehicle for, in the least, bringing violations to the attention of the global community and, on occasion, the possibility of redress and reform. Since the end of the Cold War in 1989 revived the UN, however, the international human rights system has continued to show that it is no substitute for domestic human rights legislation and enforcement, which, when fully enabled, remain the surest path to the protection of fundamental freedoms. Nonetheless, in circumstances where governments are negligent or predatory, the global system of human rights protections has provided an important oversight function that has on occasion scrutinized massive violations and helped to empower local activists in pressing for reform.

Over the years, the efforts of civil society actors have been essential in overcoming the resistance of states to improving human rights protections and expanding the system. From the beginning with the insertion of human rights language into the UN Charter, civil society groups have been instrumental in pressing governments to extend protections and shame perpetrators. Since the 1970s, the sophistication of the civil society advocacy networks have come to dwarf the effectiveness of the formal, UN-based human rights system. Nonetheless, during periods when these activists had visionary leadership as allies in office, especially in the governments of more influential states, the system expanded greatly with new mechanisms, treaties, and initiatives set in place. The US played a particularly important role in the early years of this development and at several important junctures after the Cold War. If similar coalitions with civil society groups can be developed in the future and expanded outside the US and European areas, the international human rights system could again move forward and improve protections worldwide.

Discussion questions

1 Why is it important to have in place a global human rights system in addition to domestic human rights systems?
2 What are the main mechanisms by which international and/or regional human rights commissions address allegations of abuse? How effective are they?
3 What is the importance of third- and fourth-generation rights?
4 Could the flaws of the human rights system be solved by expanding its generational system?

Notes

1 The covenants were ratified and went into force in 1976. As of 2017, the number had grown to 168 states parties to the ICCPR and 164 to the ICESCR.
2 This normative character is heightened not only by the adoption of the language of the UDHR into the two covenants, but by the explicit reference to the UDHR in all regional human rights treaties and even many national constitutions around the world (van der Heijden and Tahzib-Lie, 1998; Hannum, 1995).
3 As of 2016, of the 168 countries that have ratified the ICCPR, 115 have ratified the Optional Protocol. The Second Optional Protocol to the ICCPR, meanwhile, requires the abolition of the death penalty by any ratifying state. The protocol was open for signature on December 15, 1989 and came into force on July 11, 1991.
4 Meanwhile, a few rights in the UDHR were not included in the ICCPR, such as the right to own property, the right to asylum, and the right to a nationality (Lillich, 1984).
5 A state that invokes the right of derogation is supposed to inform the UN secretary-general of the specific rights being temporarily abridged, so that, among other things, other countries can then notify their citizens in that country about the source of the dangers and the suspension of certain civil and political rights.
6 Typically, a report is examined by a country rapporteur and a country task force composed of four to six members.
7 The streamlined procedure was adopted in large measure due to poor compliance by states parties, particularly poorer countries with fewer staff or other resources.
8 See, e.g., Simmons, 2009. This author contends that countries that ratify human rights treaties are more likely to adopt implementing legislation and to experience a reduction in human rights violations, although this is less pronounced, as might be expected, in certain dictatorships or in countries with more historically negative human rights records.
9 Also influential in this regard are the more foundational "general comments" (guidance) adopted by the committee as authoritative interpretation of the obligations of states parties under the covenant (Donnelly, 2013; Shelton, 2000).
10 Certain other important conventions do predate the ICCPR, such as the Convention on the Prevention and Punishment of the Crime of Genocide (adopted 1948; entered into force 1951) and the International Convention on the Elimination of All Forms of Racial Discrimination (adopted 1965; entered into force 1969), but the modern operational machinery subsequently taken up by most UN compliance bodies originated with the work of the ICCPR's Human Rights Committee.

References

Alston, P. (1982). A third generation of solidarity rights: Progressive development or obfuscation of international human rights law? *Netherlands International Law Review*, 29(3), pp. 307–322.

An-Na'im, A. (1991). Toward a cross-cultural approach to defining international standards of human rights. In: A. An-Na'im, ed., *Human rights in cross-cultural perspectives: A quest for consensus*. Philadelphia, PA: University of Pennsylvania Press, pp. 19–43.

Bailey, J.W. (1975). Review: the fourth world: An Indian reality by George Manuel and Michael Posluns. *American Indian Quarterly*, 2(3), pp. 251–253.

Bates, E. (2011). *The evolution of the European convention on human rights*. Oxford: Oxford University Press.

Cohen, B. (1949). Human rights under the United Nations Charter. *Law and Contemporary Problems*, pp. 430–437.

Donnelly, J. (2013). *Universal human rights in theory and practice*. Ithaca, NY: Cornell University Press.

Freeman, M. (2011). *Human rights: An interdisciplinary approach*. Boston, MA: Polity.

Glendon, M.A. (2004). The rule of law in the Universal Declaration of Human Rights. *Northwestern Journal of International Human Rights*, 2(1), pp. 2–19.

Haas, M. (2014). *International human rights: A comprehensive introduction*. London: Routledge.

Hannum, H. (1995). The UDHR in national and international law. *Georgia Journal of International and Comparative Law*, 25, p. 287.

Keith, L. (1999). The United Nations Covenant on Civil and Political Rights: Does it make a difference in human rights behavior? *Journal of Peace Research*, 38(1), pp. 95–118.

Kiss, A. (1981). Permissible limitations on rights. In: L. Henkin, ed., *The International Bill of Human Rights: The Covenant on Civil and Political Rights*. New York: Columbia University Press, pp. 290–300.

Lillich, T. (1984). Civil rights. In: T. Meron, ed., *Human rights in international law: Legal and policy issues*. Vol. 1. Oxford: Clarendon Press.

Manuel, G. and Posluns, M. (1974). *The fourth world: An Indian reality*. Minneapolis, MN: University of Minnesota Press.

Marks, S.P. (1981). Emerging human rights: A new generation for the 1980s?, *Rutgers Law Review*, 33, pp. 435–452.

Mignolo, W. (2009). Who speaks for the "human" in human rights? *Hispanic Issues On Line*, 5(1), pp. 7–24.

Mutua, M. (2001). Savages, victims, and saviors: The metaphor of human rights. *Harvard International Law Journal*, 42, pp. 201–245.

Otto, D. (1997). Rethinking the universality of human rights law. *Columbia Human Rights Law Review*, 29(1), pp. 1–46.

Rich, R. (2002). Solidarity rights give way to solidifying rights. *Dialogue*, 21(3), pp. 24–33.

Rodley, N. (1992). United Nations non-treaty procedures for dealing with human rights violations. In H. Hannum, ed., *Guide to international human rights practice*. Philadelphia, PA: University of Pennsylvania Press.

Schachter, O. (1981). The obligation to implement the covenant in domestic law. In: L. Henken, ed., *The International Bill of Human Rights: The Covenant on Civil and Political Rights*. New York: Columbia University Press, pp. 311–331.

Schmidt, M. (2000). Follow-up mechanisms before UN human rights treaty bodies and the UN mechanisms beyond. In: A. Bayefsky, ed., *The UN Human Rights Treaty System in the 21st Century*. Boston, MA: Kluwer Law International, pp. 233, 244.

Shelton, D. (2000). Commitment and compliance: The role of non-binding norms in the international legal system. *Oxford Scholarship Online*, pp. 449–464.

Simmons, B. (2009). *Mobilizing for human rights: International law in domestic politics*. New York: Cambridge University Press.

Van der Heijden, B. and Tahzib-Lie, B. (1998). *Reflections on the Universal Declaration of Human Rights*. Leiden: Brill and Nijhoff.

Vasak, K. (1984). Pour une troisième génération des droits de l'homme. In: C. Swinarski, ed., *Studies and essays on international humanitarian law and Red Cross principles*. Leiden: Martinus Nijhoff, pp. 837, 839.

Vasak, K. (1977). Human rights: A thirty-year struggle: the sustained efforts to give force of law to the Universal Declaration of Human Rights. *UNESCO Courier*, 30(11).

Viljoen, F. (2012). *International human rights law in Africa*. 2nd ed. Oxford: Oxford University Press.

Wellman, C. (2000). Solidarity, the individual and human rights. *Human Rights Quarterly*, 22(3), pp. 639–657.

World Conference of Human Rights (25 June 1993), Vienna Declaration and Programme of Action.

Further reading

Forsythe, D. (2000). *Human rights in international relations*. Cambridge: Cambridge University Press.

Goodhart, M. (2013). *Human rights: Politics and practice*, 2nd ed. Oxford: Oxford University Press.

Risse-Kappen, T., Risse, T., Ropp, S.C., and Sikkink, K., eds (1999). *The power of human rights: International norms and domestic change*. Vol. 66. Cambridge: Cambridge University Press.

Steiner, H.J., Alston, P., and Goodman, R. (2008). *International human rights in context: Law, politics, morals: Text and materials*. New York: Oxford University Press.

3 Between nothingness and infinity

Settlement and anti-blackness as the overdetermination of human rights

Andrés Fabián Henao Castro

Inspired by Broeck's (2013, p. 102) call to connect critical theory to the episte-mology of the middle passage, in this chapter I argue that settlement and anti-blackness function historically as the overdetermination of the human rights discourse. Drawing from afro-pessimism, black studies, indigenous studies, and decolonial theory, here I argue that what connects the relative autonomy of the superstructure to the determination in the last instance by the economy is the racialized and gendered modern/colonial system that has in settlements and anti-blackness its historical foundation. The social death that settler colonialism produced supplements Althusser's anti-humanist thesis, by explaining how the human order of the subject of rights historically asserts itself through the ontological denial of indigenous and black people, whose erasure gives to the social order its coherence and integrity. I thus trace the historical birth of the human back to the racialized and gendered modes of settler colonial dehu-manization, in order to properly understand the expulsion of indigenous and black people from the human condition in modernity. This historical back-ground allows me to demonstrate the disciplinary function that human rights acquire when faced with those displaced to the conditions of social death; a disciplinary function that explains why the French Revolution continues to be legible as the site of the universal, while the universality of the Haitian Revolu-tion remains in question. It is against the asymmetrical reception of that his-torical background that it is worth revisiting the most progressive Western critiques of the human rights discourse (Marx, Arendt, and Rancière), and hold them accountable for their inability to fully theorize the overdetermining roles that settler colonialism and anti-blackness play in the construction of the human. Such a foundation, I conclude, calls not for the verification of the rights of the human but, as Fanon claims, for the radical decolonization of the social order the human rights discourse ultimately seeks to protect.

Settlement and anti-blackness as the overdetermination of human rights

In his famous anti-humanist rewriting of the base-superstructure theoretical tradition in Marxism, Louis Althusser (1962, pp. 87–128) proposed the concept of *overdetermination* as a materialist principle that, although dialectic,

would be neither teleological, nor articulate a simple notion of contradiction. According to Althusser (p. 111), Marx's new terms – "on the one
hand, determination in the last instance by the (economic) mode of production; on the other, the relative autonomy of the superstructures and their
specific effectivity" – did not merely "invert" Hegel but overcome speculative philosophy by giving up on the ahistorical concept of the subject.
From the humanist subject to the anti-humanist structure, articulated
around multiple contradictions, the relationality of Marx's new terms posed
a new problem for Althusser: how to understand the specific effectivity of
the superstructures and other "circumstances," given that the economic
dialectic is, as Althusser (p. 113) claimed against the very economic deter-
minism that some would mistakenly raise against him, "never active *in the
pure state*" (emphasis in the original)?

Conspicuously referring to the lack of theoretical elaboration on this area
as an outline, "like the map of Africa before the great explorations,"
Althusser (1962, p. 114) claimed that he could only think of Antonio
Gramsci as following up Marx and Engels on the exploration of this effectivity, primarily through the development of the concept of hegemony.
Gramsci's hegemony is, arguably, the most important political concept of
contemporary Marxism, moreover after its re-elaboration by Laclau and
Mouffe (1985). Supplying a political theory of ideology as the contingent and
conflictive sedimentation of social consensus, the Gramscian concept of
hegemony has nevertheless been rightly criticized by the postcolonial tradition of the subaltern studies, the critical tradition of indigenous studies, and
that of afro-pessimism, all of them invested in rethinking that specific effectivity. The first by claiming that coercion (domination), rather than consensus (hegemony), was the political formula of colonialism (Guha, 1997).
The second by claiming that it is the settler claim to territorial indigeneity
that fuels the compulsive erasure of its prior inhabitants in an ongoing
repetition of that foundational violence, and one by which the myth of civil
society is perpetuated through the continuous erasure of the native (Byrd,
2011, pp. 130–132). The third by troubling the most brutal history of coercion in the modern/colonial production of the slave as socially dead, out of
which the consensual capacities of civil society were ultimately defined
(Hartman, 1997, p. 65; Wilderson, 2007, pp. 27–28). Historically prior to the
subaltern, however, it is the native and the black who occupy the position-
alities that must be fully "othered" for the "properly" subjective position
that is both civil and social, that is, consensually capable, to cohere and
acquire integrity in the modern figure of the human.

It is my claim, in this chapter, that in the racialized and gendered differences produced since the original accumulation of capital through ongoing
processes of settler colonization, we have a solution to the mystery that
Althusser (1962, p. 112) recognized, his notion of an "overdetermined contradiction" merely gestured towards clarifying how "History 'asserts itself'
through the multiform world of the superstructures." History, I claim,

asserts itself through the settler colonial reproduction of absolute differences that cannot be asserted within the superstructural order of human rights. Not unless consensus immediately turns into its opposite, into the very violence the social order links to blackness in the form of an already imputed criminality; not unless the civic turns into the opposite, the brutality the social order links to the native in the form of an already imputed savagery.

The birth of the human

Afro-pessimism, black studies, indigenous studies, and decolonial theory converge today in tracing the historical birth of the human beyond the spatial-temporal boundaries of European modernity, where poststructuralism traced its origins only to demarcate its end, as Foucault (1994, p. 387) did under the Nietzschean-inspired image of "a face drawn in sand at the edge of the sea."[1] Seeking a broader spatial-temporal genealogy of the human, these theories looked not for the imaginary face drawn at the edge of the sea – and about to be erased in the 20th century by the new European epistemic shift away from the subject and towards subjectless structures – but for the real faces drowned at the bottom of the ocean by the intersecting structures of oppression that settler colonial capitalism set in motion. If Foucault (1961, p. 8) first sought in the ship of fools a history of the "other," per opposition to the anti-humanist archeology of the human sciences that he eventually offered as "the history of the order imposed on things" (Foucault 1994: xxiv), afro-pessimism and decolonial theory were interested in the slave ship, where the "other" was turned into the very thing to be ordered. "Colonization = 'thingification,'" Aimé Césaire (1955, p. 42) summarized, linking the humanist formation of the European Subject, on one side of the Atlantic, to the inhuman formation of the Colonial Object on the other side. Following Césaire's insights, decolonial theory traced the discursive formation of European humanism back to the Valladolid Conference (1550–1551), most famously in the debates between Bartolomé de las Casas and Ginés de Sepúlveda, which first articulated the separation of the properly human from the "almost the same, but not quite" (emphasis in the original, Bhabha, 1994, p. 122), through the Christian iconography of sin, giving to the humanism of the Renaissance its first racial/ethnic/gendered rationale.[2] According to Wynter (2003) the rationale changed as a consequence of the industrial and scientific revolutions of the Enlightenment, which turned the gaze from the spirituality of the sky to the mechanics of the earth. During what she called the overrepresentation of the human by man, European imperialism looked no longer for a new order among celestial bodies but among terrestrial ones, replacing the religious preoccupation with the soul with the scientific examination of the body, and the iconography of sin with the hereditary phenotypical norm as the new racial/ethnic/gendered rationale governing the hierarchical separation of the human from the less-than-human.

Missing from decolonial theory's historicization of the racial-ethnic-modern-colonial gender system of social classification (Quijano, 2000; Lugones, 2007), out of which the human was overdetermined, was a more rigorous investigation of the different settler colonial logics that made possible what Marx (1976, pp. 873–940) first theorized as the "original accumulation of capital." As Day (2016, p. 27) has persuasively argued, settler colonialism made of land the primary relationship between settler colonizers and indigenous peoples, and labor that between settlers and enslaved Africans transported to the Americas. Drawing from Wolfe's (2001) distinction between a settler colonial logic of elimination and one of exclusion, Day argues that while the primary objective of settlers, vis-à-vis natives was elimination – through either genocide or their biopolitical absorption via miscegenation policies – their primary objective vis-à-vis enslaved blacks "was not to eliminate that population but to *increase* it and, by extension, increase the property value of that exclusive labor force" (emphasis in the original, Day, 2016, p. 27). What such a distinction otherwise misses, and the reason I argue that both settlement and anti-blackness function as the overdetermination of the discourse of human rights, is that racial exclusion, in the case of enslaved Africans, already incorporated its own logic of elimination. In other words, the labor force that settlers were interested in increasing was socially dead labor, a term first coined by Orlando Patterson (1982, p. 13) to characterize various systems of slavery structured by gratuitous violence, general dishonor, and natal alienation. This explains the otherwise contradictory fact that death outpaced births in the colonies, that "each year, between 5 and 10 percent of the slave population succumbed to overwork and disease," a stunning number that could have been easily reduced by merely allowing a few weeks of rest from plantation work to pregnant black women, yet never tried because "it was cheaper to let slaves die and buy more from Africa" (Dubois, 2012, p. 21).[3]

Social death

Black and indigenous peoples never reached the status of human subjectivity that they helped to constitute, because their constitutive role made them into the negative bearers of absolute difference, that is, difference outside of the play of ontological difference. Indigenous peoples and enslaved Africans were the first populations to have been subjected to the absolute difference that is social death, thus equally subjected to an eliminatory logic. This condition is best clarified when contrasted with the ontological question that distinguishes the human condition of the modern *Dasein* (Heidegger, 2010, pp. 11–12), as the being that questions the finitude of her/his own being by being-towards-death. Like indigenous peoples under the brutal conditions of settler colonialism, enslaved black people's ontological questioning indicated not the existence of a being-towards-death, for whom death was a contingent event displaced into a real future – a sort of existential horizon defining being's awareness of freedom in the contingency of human action – but social death.[4]

Slavery, to which both indigenous peoples and enslaved Africans were systematically subjected, it is worth stressing, was the substitute for death, servitude in exchange for the deferral of the death penalty. The enslaved were forced to choose between real death and symbolic death, that is, between the physical termination of their life and the continuity of their living in conditions of social death. Despite their differences, real or symbolic death's leftovers never resulted in a recognizable subject but in a de-animated object: the former leaving a desecrated corpse, the latter a commodity to be sold in the marketplace. Death, in other words, was not a future possibility, as death was the overall condition of the present and that of the past too, given that slavery was inherited, for black people, and through biopolitical absorption, resulted in the symbolic erasure of indigenous people when they were no longer enslaved. Natality, in short, did not mark the beginning of a human condition (à la Arendt, 1998, p. 9), but the first event in the endless animation of the end, as any affirmation of subjectivity immediately threatened the slave and the native with the physical termination of that which could no longer be properly called a life.[5]

Under such conditions of elimination, to which black people in the US would be continuously subjected, death was ultimately lost as a category of being. Death, as David Marriot (2007, p. 231) rightly concludes, "emerges as a transcendental fact of black existence but without transcendence... [t]his is no longer death but a deathliness that cannot be spiritualized or brought into meaning." This explains why slaves' physical deaths were equally brutalized, denied proper burials, if not further violated/instrumentalized through the spectacle of lynching. In short, displaced to the zone of non-being, there is not an abyss or a void that serves in this case as the groundless ground for the play of Being, there is only the infinite confinement in the underground: from the mines, the dungeons, the belly of the ship, and the plantation system, all the way to the concentration archipelago of today, inclusive of the prison industrial complex, inclusive of the misnamed as detention centers for immigrants, and the offshore concentration camps.[6]

The human rights

The specific effectivity of settler colonialism and anti-blackness asserts itself through the post-emancipatory inclusion of the slave and the native into the social order of the human, where rights "never quite" work in the noun form of a subjective entitlement. This is, in part, because at the heart of the contractarian figure of the "free subject" lies the continuous reinscription of colonial "thingification." Essential to the noun form of rights, thus, is the proprietorial history of contractual subjectivity, where self-ownership distinguishes the "free" from the unfree, the worker who can sell her/his labor power as a commodity in the marketplace, from the enslaved one who is sold as the commodity itself in the marketplace. The "free" worker, however abstract and devoid of substance that freedom is under the alienated conditions of modern/colonial capitalism, sells her/his labor power in the marketplace. To have something to sell, however precarious and coerced such a selling is, denotes the extent to which the modern/colonial notion of freedom is tethered to appropriation, even when such proprietorial notion of personhood takes the minimal and always alienated form of self-ownership. Property, thus, distinguishes *having* a commodity to sell, one's labor power, from *being* the commodity that is sold in the market. Hence the useful distinction introduced by afro-pessimism between alienation and fungibility. By having a commodity – however precarious and alienated such a commodity is when it is only one's own cheapened labor power what one possesses – workers temporarily stand in the same ground with the owners of the means of production, as potential buyers of other commodities in the market. What grounds the fetishization of such abstract and quite minimal equality, and one that Wilderson (2010: 13) characterizes as the "intramural exchange" of civil society, is thus the "mutual, possessive possibilities" that structures it, in which all "free" workers can "own either a piece of Black flesh or a loaf of white bread or both." Hence, the worker can be exploited, and such overexploitation can and often reaches conditions whose violence and brutality border on those of slavery. But the condition of being owned and traded, of *being* the object that others can *have*, ontologically separates the temporally marked exploitation of the socially alienated being, from the temporally endless fungibility of the natally alienated non-being. As Hartman argues, "the slave is thus the object that must be de-animated in order to be exchanged and that which, by contrast, defined the meaning of labor" (Hartman and Wilderson, 2003, p. 199, n. 2).

As entitlements, that is, as something that you can "possess," rights do not work in "quite the same" way for black and indigenous people, as they continue to figure as the embodiments of dispossession. Possessive possibilities, after all, always already presuppose the colonial remaking of territory, that is, the expropriation of land that tethers freedom to property, and civil society with national-state sovereignty. It is, in other words, the human who rights the dehumanized, and such "righting" describes a different economy of power, the one that Foucault (1975) explored at the micro-physical level of various disciplinary technologies of power, and that he nevertheless historically and geographically misplaced in 17th-century Europe.[7] "Not quite" human yet, rights take the verb form of a disciplinary regulation, one charged with the metamorphosis function of humanizing the dehumanized, rather than the noun form of a protective entitlement.[8] The two functions are related, and colonial modernity establishes a racialized and gendered relationship between the noun form of rights, seeking to defend society, and the verb form of rights, forever keeping the human – to be defended – outside of the socially dead's reach – in need of discipline and regulation.[9] And it is the linear-progressive desirability of moving from death to life that both sustains human rights as an emancipatory goal, and perpetuates the temporally oppressive structure of that deferral.

The illegible universality of the Haitian Revolution

The (dis)encounter between the French soldiers that Napoleon had sent to suppress the Haitian Revolution and the black army of self-liberated slaves represents an iconic historical scene of this perpetual deferral. According to Žižek (2009, p. 112), when the French soldiers heard that the Haitians were singing the *Marseillaise*, "they started to wonder out loud whether they were not fighting on the wrong side." Inspired by Buck-Morss' (2009, p. 151) idea that "universal humanity is visible at the edges," Žižek then added that such a singing of the *Marseillaise* should be taken neither as an index of colonial subordination nor as one of national assimilation, but as the declaration of universal humanity at the edges, when the other says that: "in this battle, we are more French than you, the Frenchmen, are – we stand for the innermost consequences of your revolutionary ideology, the very consequences you were not able to assume." According to this formulation, universal humanity rests in the revolutionary enactment of this excess, where the not "quite the same" becomes "more French than the Frenchmen," to the extent that they take the radically egalitarian principle of the Revolution to the innermost consequences of decolonizing the Republic, a consequence that not even the French Jacobins were able to assume (Benot, 1987; Vergès, 2001).

Žižek (2009, p. 115) is wrong, however, when he claims that "when colonial countries demand independence and enact a 'return to roots,' the very form of this return (that of an independent nation-state) is Western," or that "in its very defeat (losing the colonies), the West thus wins, by imposing its social form on the other." What I believe Žižek wants to say is that a radically egalitarian revolutionary France, hence one that would have necessarily included the end of colonial domination in Haiti and all the other colonies, was the real communist horizon. Thus, when he claims that the foundation of Haiti as an independent nation-state was, in the end, a Western imposition, I think that what he means is that such a foundation was the inevitable outcome of France's failure to stand for the innermost consequences of its revolutionary ideology, when it denied full equality to the ex-slaves in St Domingue, and forced them to fight for their own nation-state as the only political alternative that could secure their freedom. It is not, however, by losing the colonies that the West won, nor is it true that when colonized countries demand independence and enact a "return to roots," the very form of that return is inevitably Western. Moreover, if one takes into account that *Ayití*, instead of St Domingue, was the name that the Taínos gave to the island, prior to European colonization, and the one honored by the Black Jacobins. What the criticism of a "return to the roots" fails to see, in what it otherwise misreads as a giving up on the universal, is the universality that is enacted through what is misread as a "return," that is, the revolutionary unsettling of European colonialism in the decolonization of the *polis*. Radicalizing the universality of the egalitarian principle as an attempt to undo the settler colonial logic of European accumulation, the Black Jacobins restituted to the land its original name. And here Wolfe's (2013, p. 266) definition of settler colonialism as "being continuous across time, as structure rather than event," gives to this otherwise misunderstood "return to the roots" its future-oriented emancipatory drive.

But if the historically circumscribed signifier "French" failed to reach the true universality of its *Déclaration des droits de l'homme et du citoyen*, first by delaying the abolition of slavery until February 4, 1794, while restricting its geopolitical scope, and then by failing to decolonize the Republic until slavery was restored by Napoleon; Haiti was constitutionally founded on the radical affirmation of that universal equality. This was the aim of ending white mastery and property (article 12), as well as that of declaring that irrespective of their race, all Haitians "shall hence forward be known only by the generic appellation of Blacks" (article 14) in the 1805 Constitution of Haiti.[10] That it was easier for Žižek, as well as for Buck-Morss (2009, pp. 145–148), to see the universality of "French" and not that of "Black," is not inconsequential. It is the other side of the failure to hear universal humanity when it is black people who sing the *Marseillaise* on the other side of the Atlantic. It is true that the Haitian Revolution also failed in its emancipatory efforts at undoing settler colonial capitalism. Like the French Revolution, it failed to fully recognize gender equality, and then it imposed "agrarian militarism," while keeping the plantation system intact. Such a failure, however, cannot be understood outside of the horrifying debt that was imposed on Haiti, and of the constant threat to Haiti's sovereignty that all European empires continued to pose.[11] In other words, it cannot be understood outside of the white supremacist capitalist patriarchy that continues to dominate the universal order of the human, and structure the continuousness of settler colonial capitalism.

The limits of the Western critique of the right to have rights

There are two famous critiques of human rights in the Western tradition, both of which completely erase the Haitian Revolution from their record. The first one was formulated by the early Karl Marx in "On the Jewish question," originally published in 1844; the second one by Hannah Arendt in her most often quoted chapter on the decline of the nation-state, with which she concluded the second volume of *The origins of totalitarianism* in 1951.

According to Marx (1978), political emancipation, or the abstract recognition of equality before the law exercised an ideological role to the extent that real emancipation was displaced from its concrete site of realization in the material world of social production, and depoliticized through a legal form of recognition that made symbolic equality compatible with real inequality. In other words, human rights depoliticized the struggle for real equality by solving that struggle in ideological terms. The ideological neutralization of real equality through symbolic emancipation meant, for the late Marx, a crucial change in the modalities of power. In a sentence that Chakrabarty (2000, p. 56) is right in highlighting, anticipating the basic theme of Foucault's *Discipline and punish*, apropos the move from sovereign power to disciplinary power, Marx claimed that the "overseer's book of penalties replaces the slave-driver's lash [in capitalist management]." What Marx, Foucault, and Chakrabarty himself missed, however, is the ways in which, as Wilderson (2010, p. 37) argues, the slave continues to establish the grounds by which the discourse of freedom becomes intelligible without ever entering its frame. After providing the grammar that makes legible civil society's ethical dilemmas, that is after being figuratively appropriated by the worker, the slave must retreat to the background of the picture, must be replaced with the "free" worker as the subject of history; just as the "pre-modern" plantation system of the colony must be replaced with the "modern" industrial factory of the metropole, as the real site of social alienation; and just like the "backward" maroon must be replaced with the avant-garde commune, as the concrete site of freedom and emancipation.[12]

Arendt, as Rancière (2004) rightly suggests, inverts Marx's formulation. Thus, in Arendt's framework, it is not the citizen who masks the human but the opposite, a fact proven by the impossibility of refugees and the stateless, who could only claim their equal belonging to humanity, to see their human rights recognized after World War I. Or, as Arendt puts it:

> The Rights of Man, after all, had been defined "inalienable" because they were supposed to be independent of all governments; but it turned out that the moment human beings lacked their own government and had to fall back upon their minimum rights, no authority was left to protect them and no institution was willing to guarantee them.
>
> (Arendt, 2004, p. 370)

Like Marx, who traced the formation of modern capitalism back to the colonization of the Americas and the enslavement of Africans, Arendt also traced European imperialism and the crisis of the nation-state after World War I back to the colonization of Africa, if not all the way to the Conquest. Like Marx, the enslaved "other" also makes her/his appearance to be accumulated, that is, to provide the grammar for the wrong in order to immediately retreat into oblivion. Arendt's formulation is, however, considerably more problematic, when she claims that "the danger in the existence of such people" – "such people" being the old colonized and the new stateless – "is twofold: first and more obviously, *their* ever-increasing numbers threaten *our* political life, *our* human artifice, the world which is the result of *our* common and co-ordinate effort in much the same, perhaps even more terrifying, way as the *wild elements of nature* once threatened the existence of man-made cities and countrysides" (my emphasis, Arendt, 2004, p. 383). "*Their* ever-increasing numbers" and "*our* political life," Arendt concludes her second volume on imperialism with an all too familiar imperialistic language, in which the separation of the human from the less-than-human is coded as that between the civilized and the wild savage. One could argue that when Arendt (2004, p. 363) described "statelessness" as a global malady that "spread like a contagious disease," she was only describing a political condition of dispossession her own description did not contribute to reproduce. It is the institutional and political framework of the nation-state within the horizon of imperialism and capitalism, in other words, that she makes politically responsible for creating the conditions by which non-citizens lose their significance and "belong to the human race in much the same way as animals belong to a specific animal species" (Arendt, 2004, p. 383). But one could also be more attentive to the problematic terms Arendt chooses when describing a condition that the stateless themselves articulated in very different ways when they contested their various forms of exclusion. A right to have rights Arendt considered necessary when an international system of sovereign nation-states produced humans outside of a recognizable *polis*, failing to notice that this was the very outside that indigenous peoples and enslaved blacks structurally occupied vis-à-vis the settler colonial *polis*, even prior to mass statelessness after World War I. To be in the condition of natives and enslaved blacks was, in other words, the "global danger" European imperialism had extended to the stateless of the 20th century, and one that for Arendt required a critique of imperialism, and perhaps an overcoming of the nation-state formation, but not the revolutionary undoing of the settler colonial logics of elimination and exclusion that made the existence of "such people" "dangerous" in the first place.

When Rancière (2004, p. 302) reformulates Arendt's notion of the "right to have rights" outside of its vicious circularity and calls instead for "the rights of those who have not the rights that they have and have the rights that they have not," the positionality of the black and that of the native completely disappear from the record. According to Rancière (p. 303), the politics of human rights results from bringing together i) the written right, not just as an ideal but as "part of the configuration of the given," and ii) its verifiable form, in which some "make something of that inscription... a case for the verification of the power of the inscription." Rancière's politics of verification – arguably the most democratic articulation of the idea of human rights in the contemporary Marxist tradition – gives up on a foundation and places the temporal location of the event of authorization as following the claim, rather than grounding it in advance. What Rancière misses, however, is that for indigenous and black people under settler colonial nation-states, an "improper standing" to make claims is not the contingent result of a political event of verification, but a structural reality of ongoing dispossession. In other words, when racially undifferentiated stateless, refugees, undocumented immigrants, and the new subaltern make claims to the state on the basis of putting to test the facticity of the written inscription, they do not just authorize themselves, they also relegitimize the authorial validity of the settler colonial *polis* as the primary addressee of that claim. The temporal gap of political *dissensus* is only traveled on the condition that another transit accompanies that travel, what Byrd has called the "transit of empire." Such a transit is not merely a traveling to the foundational event of colonization in the past (i.e., the Conquest of the Americas), but a different political verification of the ongoing reproduction of imperialism that, as Byrd (2011, p. xxxix) claims, forces both "settlers and arrivants to cathect the space of the native as their home."[13] When the emancipatory character of the temporal gap is figured in the linear-progressive movement that leads from death to life, from savage to civilized, the afro-pessimist embrace of death, and the radical indigenous reclamation of savagery, are not just uncritical accommodations to the dictates of white supremacy, but the ultimate refusal to turn real loss into meaningful profit in the symbolic order of rights.

Between nothingness and infinity

Such a refusal was exemplary articulated in Fanon's (1952) phenomenological analysis of the lived experience of the black man. After having been rejected by the settler colonial universality of white supremacy in the iconic double misinterpellation: i) "Look! A Negro!," and its proto-neoliberal soft version, ii) "Look how handsome that Negro is," Fanon (p. 94) was forced to counter-assert himself as a "BLACK MAN" (capitals in the original). "The handsome Negro says, 'Fuck you,' madame," Fanon (p. 94) replied, thus refusing to valorize the "minor differences that [would have brought him] closer to health, to life, to sociality" (Sexton, 2011, p. 27), and revolutionary embodying the "existential danger" to the civilized that a full immersion into the particularity of social death implies for the social order. It is only after acknowledging the complementary forms of the xenophobic deficit ("almost the same, but not quite"), and the xenophilic excess ("more French than the Frenchman"), enacted through the complementary racist statements of the "Negro [who is] going to eat me," of the white child, and the "handsome Negro" with which his mother tries to acquiesce this future inheritor of the social order, that Fanon characterizes anti-blackness as a form of overdetermination from the outside.

"At the crossroads between Nothingness and Infinity" (Fanon, 1952, p. 119) when, after refusing to accept the amputation of his soul Fanon was prescribed "humility," he began to weep the tears of the wretched. But what followed the weeping was not an insistence on the human rights of the wretched of the earth, and one by which the coherence and the integrity of the settler colonial order of the human would be forever extended. No, Fanon's weeping expands to the Infinity of a different cry, which cries for decolonization from the underground of that Nothingness, that is, through the subversive organization of militant action oriented towards collective liberation. Fanon's (2004: 239) call to decolonize the human, as Wynter

(2003, p. 331) rightly interprets, consists in making the reintroduction of "invention into existence" inseparable from the revolutionary unsettling of the coloniality of being. In other words, and to borrow from the anti-humanist thesis of queer theorist Lee Edelman (2004, p. 29), yet decolonially modifying it with a necessary supplement, that wretched cry of Fanon says what the settler colonial order hears anyway, in any affirmative expression of black and indigenous organizing in which it continues to hear the death that haunts the reproduction of the settler colonial social order. It says: Fuck the social order that human rights seek to protect, and the white "innocent Child in whose name [black and indigenous people are] collectively terrorized."

Discussion questions

1   In what ways do settler colonialism and anti-blackness trouble the emancipatory horizon of human rights?
2   What political forms does the speech of the socially dead take within the discourse of human rights? Or is the claim of indigenous and black people speechless within that discourse?
3   After following the claims on settler colonialism as a structure, rather than an event, what is the relationship between decolonization and the order of human rights? Are these two political projects ultimately antagonistic?
4   Does decolonization entail an undoing of the settler colonial order of the human? Is that undoing the condition of a new humanism?

Notes

1   On afro-pessimism see Wilderson (2010, pp. 35–53), on black studies see Barrett (2014, pp. 1–43), on indigenous studies see Moreton-Robinson (2015, pp. 47–65), on decolonial theory see Dussel (2007, pp. 3–35).
2   It is in this radical sense that one should interpret Bhabha's formulation, a difference that indicates, in the impossible resemblance, the reminder of the colonial history of modernity. For an analysis of the Valladolid Conference as representative of Europe's first colonial modernity, see Wynter (2003), Dussel (2007), and Mignolo (2009).
3   Day (2016, p. 27) is right when, following Sean Coulthard, Annette Jaimes, and especially Katherine Ellinghaus, she inscribes intermarriage policies within the settler colonial biopolitical logic of elimination. Too fast, however, she contrasts the eliminatory logic of miscegenation with the exclusionary one of the "one-drop-rule" that "relegated to blackness a biological permanence that would survive any amount of interracial mixing," moreover after the wonderful investigation of Sexton (2008) on the anti-blackness that also fuels miscegenation and the discourse of multiracialism.
4   For an excellent development of the coloniality of being in critical conversation with Heidegger's work see Maldonado-Torres (2007).
5   In the US context black people are ultimately made equivalent to criminality (Hartman 1997, pp. 145–163), a history that explains why in the US criminal activity continues to be "*unrecognizable* without a black body" (emphasis in the original, Cacho 2012, p. 2).

6 Equally sensitive to the connection between the ship of fools and the slave ship, Rodríguez (2007) traces the disciplinary power of the "Great Confinement," characteristic of the prison system back to the slave ship, as does Browne (2015).

7 A critique perhaps first raised by Stoler (1995), and most recently restated by Weheliye (2014).

8 On the disciplinary power of rights in the US see the wonderful work of Hartman (1997), on their disciplinary role in South Africa see that of Comaroff (1997).

9 As Hartman (1997, pp. 116–124) argues, emancipation, the inclusion of the slave into the human order of rights, does not constitute a radical break with the systematic subjugation of the racialized and gendered bodies that were forced to embody devalued "otherness" under chattel slavery. The socially dead do not experience freedom post-emancipation but slavery's aftermath, when racialized and gendered systems of subjugation adapt to the performative aspects of what Hartman describes as "burdened individuality" (p. 117).

10 On the debiologization and inseparable politicization of race in the context of the Haitian Revolution, see Fischer (2004, pp. 231–232). On the different universalism enacted by the Haitian Revolution, see Getachew's (2016) wonderful article.

11 According to Dubois (2012, p. 8), "by 1892, fully half of Haiti's government budget went to paying France and the French banks. By 1914, that proportion had climbed to 80 percent."

12 For an alternative reading of freedom as maroonage see Roberts (2015).

13 "Arrivant" is a term Byrd (2011, p. xix) borrows from the Afro-Caribbean poet Kamau Brathwaite "to signify those people forced into the Americas through the violence of European and Anglo-American colonialism and imperialism around the globe."

References

Althusser, L. (1962). *For Marx*. New York: Verso, 2005.

Arendt, H. (1998). *The human condition*. Chicago, IL: Chicago University Press.

Arendt, H. (2004). *The origins of totalitarianism*. New York: Schocken Books.

Barrett, L. (2014). *Racial blackness and the discontinuity of western modernity*. Edited by J. Joyce, D. McBride, and J. C. Rowe. Urbana, IL: University of Illinois Press.

Benot, Y. (1987). *La Révolution française et la fin des colonies 1789–1794*. Paris: La Découverte.

Bhabha, H. (1994). *The location of culture*. New York: Routledge.

Broeck, S. (2013). The legacy of slavery: White humanities and its subject. A manifesto. In: J. Barreto, ed., *Human rights from a third world perspective: Critique, history and international law*. Cambridge: Cambridge Scholars Publishing, pp. 102–116.

Browne, S. (2015). *Dark matters: On the surveillance of blackness*. Durham, NC: Duke University Press.

Buck-Morss, S. (2009). *Hegel, Haiti, and universal history*. Pittsburgh, PA: University of Pittsburgh Press.

Byrd, J. (2011). *The transit of empire: Indigenous critiques of colonialism*. Minneapolis, MN: University of Minnesota Press.

Cacho, L.M. (2012). *Racialized rightlessness and the criminalization of the unprotected*. New York: New York University Press.

Césaire, A. (1955). *Discourse on colonialism*. New York: Monthly Review Press, 2001.

Chakrabarty, D. (2000). *Provincializing Europe: Post-colonial thought and historical difference*. Princeton, NJ: Princeton University Press.

Comaroff, J. (1997). The discourse of rights in colonial South Africa: Subjectivity, sovereignty, modernity. In: A. Sarat and T. Kearns, eds, *Identities, politics and rights*. Ann Arbor, MI: University of Michigan Press, pp. 193–237.

Day, I. (2016). *Alien capital: Asian racialization and the logic of settler colonial capitalism*. Durham, NC: Duke University Press.

Dubois, L. (2012). *Haiti: The aftershocks of history*. New York: Picador.

Dussel, E. (2007). Alterity and modernity (Las Casas, Vitoria, and Suárez: 1514–1617). In: N. Persram, ed., *Postcolonialism and political theory*. New York: Lexington Books, pp. 3–35.

Edelman, L. (2004). *No future: Queer theory and the death drive*. Durham, NC: Duke University Press.

Fanon, F. (1952). *Black skin white masks*. New York: Grove Press, 2008.

Fanon, F. (2004). *Wretched of the Earth*. New York: Grove Press.

Fischer, S. (2004). *Modernity disavowed: Haiti and the cultures of slavery in the age of revolution*. Durham, NC: Duke University Press.

Foucault, M. (1961). *History of madness*. New York: Routledge, 2004.

Foucault, M. (1975). *Discipline and punish*. New York: Vintage, 1995.

Foucault, M. (1994). *The order of things: An archeology of the human sciences*. New York: Vintage Books.

Getachew, A. (2016). Universalism after the post-colonial turn: Interpreting the Haitian revolution. *Political Theory*, 44(6), pp. 821–845.

Guha, R. (1997). *Dominance without hegemony: History and power in colonial India*. Cambridge, MA: Harvard University Press.

Hartman, S. (1997). *Scenes of subjection: Terror, slavery, and self-making in nineteenth-century America*. Oxford: Oxford University Press.

Hartman, S. and Wilderson, F. (2003). The position of the unthought. *Qui Parle*, 13 (2), pp. 183–201.

Heidegger, M. (2010). *Being and time*. Albany, NY: State University of New York.

Laclau, E. and Mouffe, C. (1985). *Hegemony and socialist strategy*. New York: Verso.

Lugones, M. (2007). Heterosexualism and the colonial/modern gender system. *Hypatia*, 22(1), pp. 186–209.

Marx, K. (1976). *Capital*. Volume I. New York: Penguin.

Marx, K. (1978). On the Jewish question. In: R. Tucker, ed. *The Marx-Engels reader*. New York: W.W. Norton & Company, pp. 26–52.

Maldonado-Torres, N. (2007). On the coloniality of being. *Cultural Studies*, 21(2–3), pp. 240–270.

Marriot, D. (2007). *Haunted life: Visual culture and black modernity*. Camden, NJ: Rutgers University Press.

Mignolo, W. (2009). Who speaks for the "human" in human rights? *Hispanic Issues On Line*, 5(1), pp. 7–24.

Moreton-Robinson, A. (2015). *The white possessive: Property, power, and indigenous sovereignty*. Minneapolis, MN: University of Minnesota Press.

Patterson, O. (1982). *Slavery and social death*. Cambridge, MA: Harvard College.

Quijano, A. (2000). Colonialidad del poder y clasificación social. *Journal of World-Systems Research (Festschrift for Immanuel Wallerstein: Special Issue)*, 11(2), pp. 345–386.

Rancière, J. (2004). Who is the subject of the rights of man? *South Atlantic Quarterly*, 103(2–3), pp. 297–310.

Roberts, N. (2015). *Freedom as maroonage*. Chicago, IL: University of Chicago Press.

Rodríguez, D. (2007). Forced passages. In: J. James, ed. *Warfare in the American Homeland*. Durham, NC: Duke University Press, pp. 23–34.

Sexton, J. (2008). *Amalgamation schemes: Antiblackness and the critique of multiracialism.* Minneapolis, MN: University of Minnesota Press.

Sexton, J. (2011). The social life of social death: On afro-pessimism and black optimism. *InTensions* 5(1), pp. 1–47.

Stoler, A.L. (1995). *Race and the education of desire: Foucault's history of sexuality and the colonial order of things.* Durham, NC: Duke University Press.

Vergès, F. (2001). *Abolir l'esclavage: une utopie colonial. Les ambigüités d'une politique humanitaire.* Paris: Albin Michel.

Weheliye, A.G. (2014). *Habeas viscus: racializing assemblages, biopolitics, and black feminist theories of the human.* Durham, NC: Duke University Press.

Wilderson, F.B. (2007). The prison slave as hegemony's (silent) scandal. In: J. James, ed., *Warfare in the American homeland*. Durham, NC: Duke University Press, pp. 23–34.

Wilderson, F.B. (2010). *Red, white and black.* Durham, NC: Duke University Press.

Wolfe, P. (2001). Land, labor, and difference: Elementary structures of race. *American Historical Review*, 106(3), pp. 866–905.

Wolfe, P. (2013). Recuperating binarism: A heretical introduction. *Settler Colonial Studies*, 3(3–4), pp. 257–279.

Wynter, S. (2003). Unsettling the coloniality of being/power/truth/freedom: Towards the human, after man, its overrepresentation – an argument. *New Centennial Review*, 3(3), pp. 257–337.

Žižek, S. (2009). *First as tragedy, then as farce.* New York: Verso.

Further reading

Jackson, Z. (2016). Losing manhood: Animality and plasticity in the (neo)slave narrative. *Qui Parle*, 25(1–2), pp. 95–136.

Simpson, A. (2014). *Mohawk interruptus: Political life across the borders of settler states.* Durham, NC: Duke University Press.

Tuck, E. and Wayne Yang, K. (2012). Decolonization is not a metaphor. *Decolonization: Indigeneity, Education, Society*, 1(1), pp. 1–40.

Warren, C. (2018). *Ontological terror: Blackness, nihilism, and emancipation.* Durham, NC: Duke University Press.

4 Human rights, Latin America, and left internationalism during the Cold War

Steve Striffler

United States (US)-based solidarity with Latin America came of age during the Cold War through the human rights and peace movements of the 1970s and 1980s. It tentatively emerged around the Dominican Republic and Brazil in the 1960s following US interventions, gathered steam during the 1970s in response to US support for South American dictatorships, and reached its apogee during the 1980s when Ronald Reagan's aggressive backing of military regimes in Central America drew tens of thousands of people into the peace movement.

The following essay situates this Cold War solidarity boom within a longer history of international solidarity, and asks a straightforward, but complex, question: Why human rights? Why did activists turn to human rights in the 1970s and 1980s as a way of framing, confronting, imagining, and mobilizing solidarity? Why were human rights, as opposed to other currents of internationalism, the vehicle through which US–Latin American solidarity emerged as an identifiable political project? And, perhaps most importantly, what did it matter that US-based solidarity developed (primarily) through a particular form of internationalism? What is the legacy of human rights for the US left?

In retrospect, the close association between international solidarity and human rights appears almost inevitable. By the 1980s, the two were increasingly synonymous as many activists simply saw human rights as *the* way to engage in progressive internationalism. Yet, as late as 1970, the capture of internationalism by human rights was far from assured. Human rights were barely on the map and not part of mainstream discourse. More than this, there were other, more prominent and longstanding internationalisms from which people could (and did) draw upon in order to understand and organize solidarity in the Americas, including most notably socialism, anti-imperialism, anti-colonialism, labor solidarity, and pan-Africanism. What needed to happen, in a sense, was that human rights had to replace other better travelled internationalisms in the marketplace of ideas. Human rights had to become established, in relation to already existing projects, as a compelling and useful vision, cause, and form of advocacy and engagement.

The following traces the interrelated histories of two broad (and internally differentiated) currents within US-based international solidarity, one defined by human rights and the other by left internationalism, arguing that the dramatic ascent of human rights not only profoundly shaped US–Latin American solidarity during its formative period, but assumed and facilitated the marginalization of other forms of internationalism. Human rights became the dominant way to think about and practice internationalism, a process that drew unprecedented human and financial resources to international activism, while at the same time largely detaching such solidarity from an identifiably left politics.

In a broader sense, then, this chapter explores the relationship between human rights activism and forms of (left) internationalism that seek to not only secure basic civil and democratic rights, but look to build fundamentally more equitable worlds through collective action. How does the human rights project facilitate, neutralize, or marginalize left internationalisms that struggle to advance an openly left politics with the aim of capturing state power and restructuring the political economy?

* * *

Solidarity with Latin America has tended to follow US aggression. The US war against Mexico in the mid-1800s generated considerable dissent from mainstream politicians, peace groups, anti-imperialists, and others. Similarly, when the US flirted with becoming an overseas colonial power in the late 1800s, the American Anti-Imperialist League was formed (1898) to oppose US annexations of the Philippines, Cuba, and other territories after the Spanish–American War. Although it put limits on US imperial designs, its perspective was more isolationist than internationalist and offered little in the way of cross-border solidarity. Some anti-imperialists were even opposed to the establishment of US colonies because they did not want to incorporate so-called inferior peoples from tropical regions into the US.

The deepest example of international solidarity during the pre-World War II era occurred around the Mexican Revolution in the 1910s. US-based actors participated in the first truly trans-border solidarity with Mexican rebels who rose against the US-supported dictatorship of Porfirio Díaz. Drawing on the left internationalism of the period, this was a radical and working-class solidarity that went beyond anti-imperialism (Foner, 1988; MacLachlan, 1991). Finally, when the US occupied the Dominican Republic, Haiti, and Nicaragua during the 1910s and 1920s, a vibrant anti-imperialism re-emerged.

The point here is not that pre-war solidarity was deep or wide, evolving in any particular direction, or somehow more ideologically pure or radical than what came later. In all these cases, we are talking about very few people in the US, acting for brief moments, sometimes for nationalist and even racist motives, and rarely in active/direct solidarity with Latin Americans themselves. Yet, not only did these efforts draw and develop from a wide range of existing internationalisms (not just peace/pacifism but pan-Africanism, anti-imperialism, and labor) but they all contained and promoted political projects, visions, and agendas. Such projects were, to be sure, incomplete, inconsistent, and muddled on a number of levels, but they nonetheless assumed that the world should be ordered in fundamentally different ways. They were political not simply in the sense of being partisan, or in the recognition that power and wealth were unequally distributed, but in that they were implicitly or explicitly grounded in collective notions of liberation that would usher in a fundamentally different world.

World War II and the Cold War deeply disrupted this uneven development of international solidarity by bringing about the near complete destruction of all forms of US-based left internationalism. During World War II, much of the US, and especially the liberal left, set aside concerns about US empire and participated in the anti-fascist struggle. This was reasonable enough given the importance of the fight and the fact that the US government itself was preoccupied with Europe, and hence not intervening as aggressively in Latin America.

Moreover, because anti-fascism quickly gave way to anti-communism following the war as the US sought to contain the Soviet Union and engineer a global capitalism under its own control, left internationalism within the US was slow to rebound. The US emerged a superpower, its imperialism turbocharged by anti-communism, and there was very little in the way of domestic opposition to empire. Opponents either acquiesced to, or were silenced by, imperial power. Some within the liberal left joined the fight against communism, seeing it as part of a broader struggle against "totalitarianism," while others stayed the course and found themselves under attack (Gosse, 2005, pp. 10–15).

What this ultimately suggests is that when US-backed Cold War violence swept over Latin America, the very forms of left internationalism that might have been expected to offer a challenge were either absent or severely debilitated. Few within the US paid much attention to Bolivia during the 1950s, the violence surrounding Stroessner's Paraguay in 1954, the overthrow of Arbenz in Guatemala in the same year, military rule in Brazil during the mid-1960s, or the US invasion of the Dominican Republic in 1965. More to the point, when Latin Americans sought foreign allies they had few places to turn. Human rights networks had not yet developed, leaving Latin Americans to appeal for solidarity through the most familiar of internationalisms, as socialists reaching out to fellow socialists. Their calls were not completely ignored, especially in the Soviet Union and Europe, but there was not much to connect to in the US.

There is probably no clearer evidence of both the poverty of US-based internationalism during this period, as well as the energy, promise, and tensions embodied in early solidarity efforts, than in Brazil during the mid-1960s. When the Brazilian military, with the full blessing of the US government, staged a coup in 1964 with the goal of restoring the domestic political order by eliminating all forms of dissent, there was little in the way of opposition from groups within the US. Vietnam had not sufficiently unraveled to allow for the broader questioning of US foreign policy, and few Americans were interested in, let alone challenged, US policies toward Latin America.

However, as James Green charts, by 1968 when the Brazilian military regime renewed its commitment to violence, the political winds had shifted sufficiently to produce a small, but energetic, solidarity campaign between Brazilians, made up largely of exiles, and Americans, made up largely of academics, clergy, and other progressives with experience and expertise in Brazil. The campaign, which would eventually expand to include leaders within the World Council of Churches and the Catholic Church, a wide range of academics, prominent civil rights activists such as Ralph Abernathy and Andrew Young, and Amnesty International (AI) (which launched one its first widely publicized campaigns regarding torture) succeeded in shaming the Brazilian regime internationally (Green, 2003, 2010).

Its emergence, moreover, was due in part to the fact that activists began to unevenly and tentatively frame the Brazilian cause in the language and practices of human rights. In what would become routine within a decade, Latin Americans asked international allies to publicize the crimes of the Brazilian military government. Human rights – which had emerged unevenly after the United Nation's Universal Declaration in 1948 – would prove to be a particularly effective way of doing this, in part by separating the violence itself from the messiness of political agendas, and doing so in a way that the "international community" could understand, connect with, and rally around. Although this shaming strategy would not prove particularly effective in lessening the repression or removing Brazil's military government, the campaign did succeed in turning the Brazilian government into an international pariah defined by human rights violations. This "success" ensured that the tactic of shaming military governments by exposing human rights abuses would become a central part of the solidarity toolkit.

It is important to note, however, that the small number of activists who were most actively involved in the initial efforts, including both Brazilians and their US allies, tried to articulate and use a (left) version of human rights that made connections between repression and the broader political projects of both the military regime and its opposition. It was by no means common sense during this period to understand repression as "human rights violations," or to disconnect such violations from a larger politics of oppression or emancipation. These efforts at education, at making connections, met with some success as the mainstream media in the US caught on to some of the themes and issues, especially as they resonated with the war in Vietnam. Yet, torture and brutal prison conditions, particularly when disconnected from politics, were always an easier sell than economic inequality, especially in a climate where such discussions could quickly be labelled communist (Green, 2003, 2010).

Moreover, the broader effort to link the "human rights" cause to leftist programs for social change, to understand and support the political projects of those being targeted by state violence, did not find much traction in the US. Not only was there not much to connect to in the US, but what there was tended to focus narrowly on torture, leaving aside the question of broader collective political projects and solidarity. James Green captures the complex nature of this "solidarity":

> The campaigns against torture won international support and linked the Brazilian government to repressive actions but did not seem to have a palpable effect on the military's policies. In the United States, torture in Brazil had been denounced, and then men and women of good will had moved on. Even the phrase Brazilian solidarity group, has a clumsy, inauthentic ring to it, because many signatories of petitions against Brazilian torture and repression were reacting against an inhumane situation and not necessarily in favor of a program or political current in Brazil.
>
> (Green, 2010, p. 3)

Even as late as the 1973 coup in Uruguay, where intense repression seemed ideally suited for a human rights framing, Uruguayan activists were slow and reluctant to adopt the language, instead understanding "torture and death as part of the risks of leading a proper revolutionary life." This was no doubt common sense to many Latin American leftists who had long struggled with how to combat state violence while simultaneously fighting for socialism. Many activists assumed that occasional arrests, brief stays in prison, periodic exile, and certain levels of state violence were fundamental features of being active in the left (Markarian, 2005, pp. 99). Even with respect to political prisoners (the very issue that would animate the human rights movement for the rest of the decade), Uruguayan leftists felt the problem "should be confronted politically, positioned in terms of class struggle" (ibid.).

Nevertheless, if Latin Americans were skeptical about human rights as a form of engagement, by the early to mid-1970s the emerging international movement was difficult to ignore. The level of repression in many countries had intensified so dramatically that it made it increasingly difficult to even be a leftist. The struggle for socialism, many reasoned, could not be advanced without first securing basic civil and political rights. More than this, initial indications suggested that human rights possessed the potential for attracting a wider range of allies both at home and abroad, in part because even people who agreed on little, who shared no political project, could agree that governments should not falsely imprison and torture their citizens. Human rights were also difficult for Latin Americans to ignore because other internationalisms were bringing relatively few allies (especially from the US) to the table at a time when they were so desperately needed. And, as the growing presence of organizations like AI suggested, the international human rights movement seemed poised to provide support from around the world at a time when allies were scarce. It was a potentially useful tool.

Amnesty International and the rise of human rights

The rise of AI captures the sudden and powerful emergence of human rights during the 1960s and early 1970s, as well as the long-term impact of its brand of solidarity. Founded in 1961, AI barely survived the 1960s. It almost collapsed in 1967 due to internal disputes, and the US section (AIUSA), which emerged in 1965, nearly folded under financial pressure in 1970 (Cmiel, 1999, p. 1234). The organization's fortunes then changed dramatically in the 1970s:

> Between 1970 and 1976, the number of dues-paying members in the US went from 6,000 to 35,000. AIUSA had one paid, half-time staff member in 1970. The organization, such as it was, was run by a volunteer board of directors. A decade later, however, there were fourteen paid staffers with offices in New York City, San Francisco, California, Chicago, Illinois, Colorado, and Washington, D.C. The international organization grew similarly in those years. In 1977, it was awarded the Nobel peace prize.
>
> (Cmiel, 1999, p. 1235)

Timing was clearly part of its success. Human rights activism exploded during the 1970s. Organizations formed, governments took note, and the term itself became part of mainstream public discourse. The Ford Foundation and other funding agencies made human rights a focus, channeling millions of dollars toward the cause. The US Congress held hearings, eventually tying foreign aid to a country's human rights record. And President Carter made it a cornerstone of US foreign policy. Human rights had arrived. It had become respectable (Cmiel, 1999, pp. 1234–1238).

AI's success was due to more than good timing, however. It did not simply benefit from the human rights boom. It propelled it. In 1970, AIUSA committed resources to organizing local branches around the country, a tactic that worked remarkably well in expanding its base, and helped bring human rights out of the hallways and offices of the United Nations and into the public arena. This emphasis on building at the grass roots, especially on college campuses, was a by-product of the political milieu; "nearly all of the 1970s AIUSA staff had done antiwar and civil rights work," and assumed mass mobilization was a fundamental feature of progressive politics and social change (p. 1240).

With AI, however, the tactic was not about mass mobilization in the sense of taking to the streets, but mass membership to support well-orchestrated letter-writing campaigns. This was AI's central tactic during the early years. Each AI affiliate, or adoption group, was assigned a political prisoner.

Members then wrote letters to offending governments, journalists, politicians, and international organizations. Done with increasing sophistication, and in large enough numbers, this tactic proved relatively effective in securing the release of prisoners (pp. 1240–1241). What this also meant, however, was that AI had to devote more and more resources to identifying worthy prisoners in order to satisfy the demand of growing numbers of local affiliates.

As a result, AI leaders discovered fairly quickly that not only did the organization not need the masses for street mobilizations, but they did not need a membership to adopt prisoners and write letters. Professional human rights organizations could do the work themselves, saving prisoners in Latin America by lobbying politicians in Washington. Gathering information ceased to be a means to an end, a way of building a mass base. It became the end in itself. AI became a professional organization that gathered facts and then directly lobbied journalists and politicians in an effort to put pressure on human rights violators (pp. 1240–1241). In short, it became a modern human rights organization. Whatever its virtues, this was a different type of politics, one that relied on insider access to political elites and a mass membership whose central purpose was not taking to the streets or writing letters, but writing a cheque to support AI's efforts.

As Kenneth Cmiel outlines, the question as to what path of political engagement to pursue, of whether to be a grassroots-type organization or a professional lobby (or a bit of both), was one that AI leadership debated quite intensely during the 1970s (pp. 1240–1245). The leaders had, after all, come from a tradition of grassroots organizing. However, for other human rights organizations (which were emerging almost on a daily basis during the 1970s, and in many ways became the path within US–Latin American solidarity), the question itself was increasingly off the radar. A new political formula, supported in part by the innovation of direct-mail fundraising and the largesse of philanthropic foundations, had emerged. If a network of professional activists, lawyers, and academics could influence elites, get results, and be financially sustainable through grant writing and fundraising, why bother building a mass base? Key to this, of course, was the capacity of human rights actors to push their cause within the media, in effect shining an international spotlight on human rights victims and violators – which, in turn, would hopefully force governments to take notice.

This was a form of politics that increasingly required being divorced from (traditional) politics altogether. As the central task of human rights organizations became the professional gathering and public dissemination of accurate information about human rights violations, the legitimacy of human rights organizations within the eyes of governments, the United Nations, and the broader public became crucial. Human rights organizations came to deal in information, and that information had to be reliable. This legitimacy rested, at least partially, on ensuring that human rights organizations were themselves not only professionally run, but were neutral and non-partisan, that their activities were independent of politics, particularly the (transformative) political projects of human rights victims, violators, and their supporters. Like most human rights organizations of the period, AI not only "traded on its claim to be above and beyond politics," but "defined itself against the left" (Moyn, 2010, p. 132). This was especially true when it targeted the victims of right-wing dictatorships, as in Chile where AI sought to separate itself from actors advocating political projects. As it developed, the heart of human rights activism did not simply forget or postpone a larger political vision. It actively separated itself from broader political agendas.

The meteoric rise of this brand of human rights did not, then, simply serve to further marginalize a range of left internationalisms, to replace one internationalism with another. Its rise altered the very nature of internationalism itself, of solidarity, by displacing a range of internationalisms that assumed a collective politics of liberation with a form of internationalism that was openly antithetical to political projects or visions rooted in notions of collective emancipation. This was solidarity without politics as the left had traditionally understood it, whereby politics assumes collectively struggling for an alternative way of ordering the world. The emerging human rights movement, by contrast, treated "political problems as moral ones, thereby eliding the deeper political changes that social justice often required," a tendency that would gather steam during the peace movement of the 1980s (Keys, 2014, p. 201).

Many activists recognized this tension, with some reasoning that in order for the human rights movement to be effective its organizations had to be seen as legitimate, and this required a strict separation from partisan politics. This was a strategic decision. The torture had to be stopped, and required a pragmatic, whatever-works, act-now-think-later approach. Some adopted the non-partisan practice and language of human rights quite consciously as a way to attract larger numbers of people into political activism, and as a tool for gaining access to policy makers and the mainstream media. For many, then, human rights remained contested terrain, particularly with respect to whether it should or should not be openly connected to a larger politics. Regardless, however, when the left in both Latin America and the US began to frame opposition to repression through human rights, they not only helped elevate human rights – a remarkably vague and elastic concept – to new heights. They also embraced a concept and set of practices whose broad contours and uses the left would ultimately not control.

What is perhaps even more important than the open tensions within solidarity circles is the fact that this distinction itself, between human rights and various forms of left internationalism, became increasingly invisible to a generation that came of age during the 1980s and 1990s. For many activists who had limited connection with left internationalism and took it for granted that socialism was dead, or who simply "became political" when human rights overshadowed other forms of solidarity, human rights was simply a "progressive" way of engaging the world in a meaningful way. Human rights became the beginning and end of political work. The goal was to end human rights abuses, a supremely worthy cause, and other projects were deemed too complicated, impractical, or (more often) simply not part of a narrowed political imagination.

To be sure, there was always a portion of activists for whom human rights served as a gateway towards a more radical politics. Currents of left internationalism persisted, pushing the human rights movement and attracting activists who were inspired by the urgency of human rights, but ultimately frustrated by its limited political project. Yet, over time, especially as the 1970s slipped into the 1980s and 1990s, the political avenues of left internationalism faded from public view and became increasingly hard to find for new generations of progressives. More importantly, this broader shift towards a solidarity divorced from politics was stimulated by, and brought with it, a very different method of political engagement, one that relied much more heavily on professional staff, lobbying, insider access to political and media elites, etc. This non-governmentalization of solidarity work, which emerged very unevenly during the coming decades, would never become completely hegemonic, but nevertheless became a defining form for much of international solidarity in the coming decades.

* * *

The process by which human rights emerged took place in large part through Latin America, and particularly in Chile, during the 1970s. Almost immediately after the 1973 military coup in Chile, it became apparent – as the Chilean left was murdered, disappeared, or forced into exile – that a human rights politics located in churches would be the only form of opposition possible under US-supported dictatorships in South America. Initially, however, the human rights infrastructure in the US was not in a position to respond. It had been effectively captured by conservatives in order to reinvigorate anti-communism through a focus on human rights abuses in the Soviet Union. Most of what Americans would come to associate with international human rights, including its affiliation with liberals, its principle institutions, and its tight focus on torture and political prisoners, either did not exist or was barely off the ground in 1973. The US section of AI had a total of 3,000 members in 1974, and struggled to find meeting space in Washington, DC. Human Rights Watch did not exist, nor did the Lawyers Committee for Human Rights, the Human Rights Law Group, nor the hundreds of other rights groups that would emerge in the second half of the 1970s (Keys, 2014; Moyn, 2010).

And yet, between religious groups, secular non-governmental organizations, and sympathetic policy makers (the three core constituencies of what would eventually become the human rights movement) there was a sufficient liberal presence to respond to calls for solidarity from Chile. The liberal turn to human rights had happened unevenly during the late 1960s and early 1970s, shaped by events in Greece and Brazil, as well as growing awareness about the Holocaust and political prisoners in South Vietnam. International human rights attracted liberals in part because its limited aspirations fit so well into a moment when there was little appetite for a more ambitious US foreign policy; in part because dictatorships were a very real problem; in part because human rights allowed the US to reclaim the moral high ground without investing much at all; and in part because human rights proved effective at garnering public attention (Hawkins, 2002; Keys, 2014, ch. 7). The increasingly sharp focus on torture and prisoners propelled this process by defining human rights and foreign policy aspirations in narrow terms while framing the issue in a way that captured the public's attention and confirmed the US's moral superiority.

This liberal embrace of human rights could not gain full momentum until after the Vietnam War finally ended in January 1973, in part because it was difficult to lecture the rest of the world about human rights abuses when the US government was committing massive atrocities in Asia. In this respect, the September coup in Chile was timely, and was "the watershed event that would grab headlines and bring liberal human rights concerns – political imprisonment and torture above all – into mainstream public consciousness" (Keys, 2014, p. 148). The human rights movement allowed for a diverse range of people to oppose US intervention in Latin America, in part because the vagueness of the human rights concept allowed people to work together. The net result was that as human rights experienced a meteoric rise in the second half of the 1970s, what passed as anti-interventionism was increasingly disconnected from a left politics. Human rights did not simply marginalize other internationalisms; it also co-opted them while defining the outer limits of opposition to US foreign policy in politically neutral terms.

By the late 1970s, then, the broad contours of Latin American solidarity were set on a shifting ground defined by two differentiated and intertwined currents, left internationalism and liberal human rights, with the latter coming to occupy a dominant place within the movement as a whole. Both strands would blossom and expand in the 1980s on a scale that was unimaginable during the South American solidarity efforts of the 1970s. Left internationalism, which occupied a key place within Chilean solidarity even as human rights became ascendant, would experience a revival during the Central American peace movement. This resurgence was, somewhat ironically, tied to the broader rise of the right and decline of the left.

When Carter embraced human rights in the late 1970s, it seemed quite plausible that human rights would thoroughly capture, and in effect become, progressive internationalism in the US. With Reagan in office, however, conservatives would try with renewed vigor to claim human rights in the fight against communism. And yet, Reagan's obsession with communism, combined with the fact that his foreign policy had horrific consequences in Central America and lacked support in the US, ensured that not only would an important current of human rights remain under the jurisdiction of liberals, but that the left was handed a cause at a time when domestic issues failed to inspire. Activists turned their attention to Reagan's foreign policy with such energy that the progressive wing of the peace movement (in many ways) became the left in the US. They were, however, increasingly isolated.

The Central American peace movement did not, in this sense, represent the reinvigoration of the US left as much as it marked one in a long series of last gasps. The rapid decline of the broader left placed real limits on what a politically isolated peace movement could accomplish in an increasingly conservative climate. Nevertheless, the left internationalism around Central America in the 1980s was quite real, significant, genuinely radical, and had both secular and religious elements. US-based solidarity with Nicaragua was defined not only by an anti-interventionism deeply soaked in anti-imperialism, but more often than not sought to support socialist revolution. Solidarity with El Salvador, which would ultimately be the primary focus of the broader peace movement, was also shaped by a left (primarily through the Committee in Solidarity with the People of El Salvador) that was fighting imperialism to advance socialism in Central America. In the hands of the left, human rights often served as an effective tool (alongside anti-interventionism, self-determination, anti-imperialism, and socialism) that could be disconnected or connected to a larger politics depending on the strategic needs of the moment.

And yet, the broad parameters of US–Latin American solidarity that had been established in the 1970s would hold through the 1980s. That is, as dynamic as left internationalism was during this period, the dominant current of international solidarity was a human rights/peace movement based in church groups, liberal human rights organizations, and Washington, DC-based policy makers. It was also a movement that inherited and deepened a contradiction from 1970s solidarity efforts in South America.

On the one hand, the movement as a whole cohered around a fairly narrow, but important, political project, namely opposition to human rights abuses and US support for military regimes in Central America. To be sure, a significant and important minority saw solidarity in terms of radical transformation, and worked directly with revolutionary movements to advance socialism in Central America. Yet, the core of a heavily faith-based movement, supported by liberal human rights organizations and sympathetic policy makers, saw solidarity not in terms of a long-term struggle to build a new world, but as an urgent call for help to end human rights atrocities and military repression (or to protect its victims). The gravitation towards this limited political project came from a now familiar set of sources. Many church people shied away from taking sides in the civil wars, either because they did not support the revolutionary movements themselves, did not see it as their place to intervene, or simply felt that being "political" would empower anti-communist rhetoric and otherwise undermine a fragile movement that was struggling against a popular president in an increasingly conservative climate. The tendency to cohere around a soft anti-interventionism that avoided connections with broader political projects was also embraced because it was a useful way for communicating with political-media elites and attracting larger numbers to the movement. More than this, the struggle to stop military aid (pushed by Central Americans themselves) had potentially radical implications in that it could undermine dictatorships and allow revolutionary movements to succeed.

On the other hand, although the fact that the movement coalesced around a fairly limited project may explain why it was able to bring thousands of people under its broad umbrella, this narrowed political vision did little to facilitate the movement's own coherence. It never possessed anything resembling an organizational center. As Gosse aptly noted about the movement, "everyone knew it was there, but few, even among its supporters, knew where it came from or how it operated" (Gosse 1995, p. 23). Activism came in a variety of forms, from candlelight vigils, street marches, and traveling to Central American war zones to illegally housing refugees, committing civil disobedience, and pressuring political representatives. National-level entities such as Sanctuary, Witness for Peace, Pledge of Resistance, Neighbor to Neighbor, and Committee in Solidarity with the People of El Salvador gave the movement a certain coherence, but in many ways "the movement" was characterized by the proliferation of local solidarity organizations, most of which were sharply focused in one way or another, working on a particular country/city, organized by or around a particular group (i.e., nuns, students, etc.), or limited to a particular type of solidarity (e.g., lobbying). This was no doubt a strength, lessening sectarianism, inviting broad participation, and making a relatively small and isolated movement appear as though it was everywhere at all times (Gosse, 1995, p. 23).

Yet, it also produced a movement that was, despite some significant national-level organizing efforts, rooted in hundreds of relatively small, autonomous, and semi-isolated organizations that had few resources. They were increasingly sophisticated at political lobbying, fundraising, accessing media attention, and aiding individual victims from Latin America; but they were largely incapable of, or simply unconcerned about, building a political base with the level of coherence required to achieve even short-term goals, let alone to advance a larger political project. That such a description captures today's solidarity landscape is not entirely a coincidence.

In this sense, it was not simply that the broader shift to the right in the US, and the corresponding decline of the left, put serious limits on international solidarity. As Latin Americans pointed out over and over again, the type of international solidarity they needed most was one that would "change things in the US," something that in the long term required precisely what the peace movement could not deliver: a meaningful left that would not only stop military aid but transform the fundamentals of US engagement with the region. More than this, the peace movement, due both to the urgency of its cause, directives from Central Americans, and its increasing political isolation within Reagan's US, was not simply unconcerned with domestic politics, but settled on a mode of politics that resisted cohesion and undermined the possibility of forging a viable left.

The movement's limited political project, combined with its embrace of organizational fragmentation, signaled a form of internationalism that was never designed to outlive its short-term goal of stopping human rights atrocities and the US policies that supported them. It was not simply that a portion of the movement lacked a larger political vision, that activists failed to make connections between human rights abuses and the regressive economic policies being implemented by Central American regimes; or between repression and the political projects being pursued by "human rights victims." It was that much of the peace movement pursued a form of internationalism that actively dissociated itself from politics altogether, offering up instead a form of solidarity whose noble aspiration worked to obscure a limited goal that was to be pursued through an organizational infrastructure that was not built for sustained international solidarity.

Nor was this without long-term consequences for US-based internationalism. At a time when domestic issues were failing to inspire a rapidly disintegrating US left, human rights and the peace movement appeared as a progressive bright spot. It was how increasing numbers of would-be activists came to "progressive" politics in the first place. The urgency of the human rights cause, the limited nature of its political project, and its active separation from left internationalism brought large numbers of people into internationalism relatively quickly. People who shared little in common ideologically, or found the Cold War politically paralyzing, could agree that state violence against its own citizens had to be stopped immediately. The fact that such violence appeared to be on the upswing was being meted out by both right- and left-wing regimes, and engendered deep resistance from Central Americans themselves, making the human rights movement both compelling and attractive to those who wanted to engage in "progressive" politics. People were drawn to a movement that had avenues for political participation and that was addressing an urgent social issue. And they made an important difference.

Yet, ultimately, in part because human rights was not a long-term project rooted in a collective politics of liberation, many international activists considered their work to be "done" once state-led violence was reduced and political prisoners freed. What this meant in practical terms was that once the Cold War was over, and democracies slowly replaced military regimes throughout Latin America, the number of US-based actors engaged "in solidarity" declined dramatically. Perhaps more importantly, those who remained or became active in the 1990s inherited a solidarity infrastructure, complete with established practices, tactics, strategies, and institutions, that had been built through human rights/peace and was often poorly equipped to analyze, let alone effectively challenge, neoliberal capitalism, the central concern of US-based solidarity since the 1980s.

What remained, to oversimplify more than a bit, was a solidarity left that possessed a narrowed political vision, agenda, and imagination, in part because so many activists came of age at a time when left internationalism was all but disappearing from public space and "progressive" international solidarity came to be defined by the very limited politics of human rights. This narrowed vision was accompanied by an understanding of solidarity that is defined more in terms of responding to calls for help than linking struggles, is often disconnected from US political currents, and inhabits an organizational infrastructure that is rooted in the proliferation of non-governmental organizations that have few resources, are not designed to advance political mobilization, and are overly focused on witnessing, exposing, and establishing (largely disconnected) "campaigns" against the most extreme and high profile of abuses.

Discussion questions

1 Is the human rights project political, apolitical, or both?
2 What is the relationship between human rights activism and social movements?
3 How does Latin America fit within the broader history of human rights?

References

Cmiel, K. (1999). The emergence of human rights politics in the United States. *Journal of American History*, 86(3), pp. 1231–1250.

Foner, P. (1988). *US labor movement and Latin America: A history of workers' response to intervention. Vol. I, 1846–1919*. New York: Praeger.

Gosse, V. (1995). Active engagement: The legacy of Central American solidarity. *NACLA*, 28(5), pp. 22–29.

Gosse, V. (2005). *Rethinking the new left: An interpretive history*. New York: Palgrave.

Green, J. (2003). Clerics, exiles, and academics: Opposition to the Brazilian military dictatorship in the United States, 1969–1974. *Latin American Politics and Society*, 45(1), pp. 87–116.

Green, J. (2010). *We cannot remain silent: Opposition to the Brazilian military dictatorship in the United States*. Durham, NC: Duke University Press.

Hawkins, D. (2002). *International human rights and authoritarian rule in Chile*. Lincoln, NE: University of Nebraska Press.

Keys, B. (2014). *Reclaiming American virtue: The human rights revolution of the 1970s*. Cambridge, MA: Harvard University Press.

MacLachlan, C. (1991). *Anarchism and the Mexican Revolution: The political trials of Ricardo Flores Magón in the United States*. Berkeley, CA: University of California Press.

Markarian, V. (2005). *Left in transformation: Uruguayan exiles in Latin American human rights networks, 1967–1984*. New York: Routledge.

Moyn, S. (2010). *The last utopia: Human rights in history*. Cambridge, MA: Harvard University Press.

Further reading

Kelly, P.W. (2018). *Sovereign emergencies: Latin America and the making of global human rights politics*. Cambridge: Cambridge University Press.

Moyn, S. (2014). A powerless companion: Human rights in the age of neoliberalism. *Law and Contemporary Problems*, 77(4), pp. 147–169.

Stites Mor, J., ed. (2013). *Human rights and transnational solidarity in cold war Latin America*. Madison, WI: University of Wisconsin Press.

5   Women, gender, and human rights

Nada Mustafa Ali

Introduction

In the introduction to her book, *Women across cultures*, Shawn Meghan Burn (2010) argues that human rights enshrined in international human rights conventions and declarations constitute an important framework that feminists and women's rights activists looking to understand and to address gender-based discrimination may rely upon to advance gender equality. Feminists and women's rights activists in both Global North and South settings often draw upon the Universal Declaration on Human Rights, the International Covenant on Civil and Political Rights, and the International Covenant on Social, Economic and Cultural Rights to challenge gender-based discrimination and violence. Many feminist and women's rights activists also draw upon tenets of the Convention on the Elimination of All Forms of Discrimination against Women (CEDAW), regional frameworks such as the Protocol to the African Charter on Human and People's Rights on the Rights of Women in Africa (African Women's Rights Protocol) to advocate for law reform, and for women's social, economic, and political rights. Feminists and activists in women's movements working on conflict and peace building often draw on United Nations (UN) Security Council Resolutions on Women, Peace and Security to ensure women's participation in peace building, to call for action to address violence against women, and to ensure that reconstruction of settings affected by conflict take into account the specific experiences, needs, and interests of women, men, girls, and boys.

Yet feminist scholars, and others, have warned against an uncritical reliance on rights discourse. Such criticism questioned this discourse's focus on women as individuals. Critics have argued that the meaning and value of rights depend on the social and political context, and on the social groups and communities to which people belong. As Yuval-Davis puts it: "women are not just 'individuals', but are also members of national, ethnic, and racial collectivities as well as of specific class, sexuality, and life cycle positionings" (1997, p. 38). Yuval-Davis further argues, however, that women should not be mere agents of the collectivities they belong to. Campaigns focused on reproductive rights, for example, "should take account of the multiplexity and multi-dimensionality of identities within contemporary society, without losing sight of the differential power dimension of different collectivities and groupings within it" (Yuval-Davis, 1997, p. 38).

Further questions one must ask include: To what extent is it possible to rely on the universal claims in the various conventions, declarations, and resolutions to seek gender equality, while also ensuring respect for local cultures and avoiding the pitfalls of ethnocentrism? How do we avoid ossifying and homogenizing cultures? How do we avoid losing sight of the embeddedness of cultures in power? Such questions resonate with debates within the field of anthropology, for example. Historically, anthropologists such as Franz Boas, Margaret Mead, and Ruth Benedict challenged racist practices in anthropology by arguing that each culture had its patterns of customs, beliefs, and values that arose from the concerned community's history. Consequently, these anthropologists called on their peers to evaluate cultures and cultural practices on their own terms; see, for example, Benedict (2006 [1934]). Based on these ideas, the American Anthropological Association endorsed the principles of cultural relativism in 1947 and refrained from participating in the process that resulted in the Universal Declaration on Human Rights. It was not until the 1970s that feminist anthropologists started contesting the tendency to tolerate cultural norms that undermined women's rights and bodily integrity by their peers (Donnelly, 2013).

It is worth noting that cultures are dynamic (Yuval-Davis, 1997, p. 39) and are never static or fixed. Abdullahi An-na'im, for example, who defines culture as "the totality of experiences of a given society" (2011, p. 90), draws on a range of studies to explain that cultures are not instinctive, innate, or transmitted biologically. An-Na'im argues that cultures are historically specific and that they often change and adapt according to the surrounding physical, geographical, and social environment (An-Na'im, 2011, pp. 91–2).

I want to add that cultures are gendered. The intersection between gender, race, social class, physical ability, migration, and other aspects of identity and experience also impacts communities' experiences of culture.[1] In addition, as Yuval-Davis argues, in culturalized discourse, gendered bodies and sexuality play pivotal roles as markers and reproducers of the narratives of nations and other collectivities (1997, p. 39). Women often represent the collectivity's common identities. They often also reproduce these collectivities biologically, through giving birth to children, and culturally, through their close association with children (Yuval-Davis, 1997). As such, women, especially among migrant communities and marginalized collectivities, often serve important symbolic functions. In some communities, this can expose women to violence and restrictions on their dress and movement. Leaders in such communities may use arguments of cultural relativism to escape criticism or consequences for undermining the rights of women, for example, as a way to maintain power, and as a way to conceal and suppress internal difference (1997). I discuss this further with reference to a campaign in which Sudanese women's organizations in exile sought to convince opposition parties to commit to ratifying CEDAW if they assumed power in the future.

As I ask above, when thinking about cultural specificity versus the universality of rights: to what extent is it possible to conduct research, write, and advocate on women's human rights and gender equality without reproducing "single stories" (Adichie, 2009) about certain women and communities, constructing African communities as barbarian; or conflating "Arab, Muslim, and terrorist" (Srikanth, 2012, p. 171)? How do we challenge abuses of women's human rights in Global South settings without constructing states and individuals as "Savage," women in the Global South as "Victim (s)," and the human rights corpus as "Savior" (Mutua, 2001)? And without "Othering" women in the Global South (Mohanty, 1984) and women who are part of marginalized communities in Western Europe and North America? These are questions I have been grappling with for over 20 years, in my research, activism, and in my teaching. They are questions that have preoccupied other scholars of Africa, too. In the 1990s, Grinker and Steiner affirmed that "those who teach and study Africa... must learn to problematize the issue of representation in order to locate and unpack the economic, political, personal, and other motivations that might underlie any particular image of Africa" (1997, p. xxvi). Also see Soyinka-Airewele and Edozie (2010). The practice of female genital cutting/mutilation (FGC/M), which has historically been sensationalized in global media and scholarly discourse, can help illustrate this dilemma further.

I argue that it is crucial to draw a distinction between debates on the universality versus cultural specificity of human rights on one hand, and critiques of scholarly and human rights discourses that "Other" women and communities in the Global South on the other. It is important to avoid conflating these two debates.

I also argue that international treaties like CEDAW may constitute important starting points, or "meta-narratives" that women's organizations and activists in countries like Sudan may draw upon to support advocacy around women's social, economic, and political rights. However, it is important to recognize the limitations inherent in such frameworks. It is also important to avoid reinforcing negative stereotypes about women and communities.

The rest of this chapter outlines CEDAW and its tenets. I then discuss some of the arguments that discourage the use of CEDAW for advocacy, with reference to two case studies from Sudan. The first case study focuses on a campaign that Sudanese women organizations in exile in the 1990s and 2000s organized to ensure that a coalition of opposition parties commits to women's human rights enshrined in CEDAW without reservations. This case study reveals the importance of avoiding the homogenizing of political forces when examining approaches to women's human rights in countries like Sudan. It underlines the need to pay attention to the workings of power at the local level (and not only between Global North and South settings) when thinking about the relevance of international human rights conventions like CEDAW to Global South settings. In Sudan, victim-savage-savior narratives, and the sensationalization of issues manifest in the discourses on Female Genital Cutting/Mutilation (FGC/M). I discuss this practice briefly. The chapter concludes with an outline of ways to address challenges of cultural specificity, and to conduct research, write, and advocate on women's human rights without "Othering" women and communities.

The Convention on the Elimination of All Forms of Discrimination against Women

CEDAW, which the UN General Assembly adopted in 1979, and which entered into force in 1981, is the international bill of rights for women. A government that signs and ratifies this agreement commits to safeguarding women's human rights. It also commits to ending all forms of discrimination against women and girls. The Convention is the outcome of advocacy by women's organizations from around the world in the late 1960s and 1970s. While many governments have signed and ratified the treaty – as of March 2018, 189 states have ratified CEDAW – there are countries that have signed but not ratified CEDAW (e.g., the United States (US)). There are also a few countries that did not sign or ratify the treaty. These include the Holy See, Iran, Somalia, Sudan, and Tonga.

Some of the countries that signed the convention have made reservations on some of the articles of the convention, claiming that these articles contradict the country's official religion or undermine its sovereignty. In addition, implementation has been a problem, even for countries that have ratified CEDAW. The treaty thus has so far had a mixed impact on the lives of women and girls worldwide.

CEDAW consists of 30 articles, organized into six parts. The first part prohibits discrimination, negative sex stereotypes, and sex trafficking. Part II covers women's rights in the public sphere, with a focus on politics, representation, and nationality. The third part focuses on women's social and economic rights, including the rights to education, employment, and health. While CEDAW protects women in rural areas and pays attention to their needs and rights, it does not refer to women affected by urban poverty. Part IV safeguards women's equality in marriage, within the family, and before the law. The fifth part supports the establishment of a committee on the elimination of discrimination against women. Established in 1981, the committee, which holds biannual meetings, is a UN treaty body that oversees the development and implementation of CEDAW, including through issuing general comments that elaborate on certain rights. As of March 2018, the committee has issued 32 General Comments. The sixth and final part of CEDAW discusses the effect of the treaty on other international human rights conventions.

To illustrate the complexity of attitudes and practices toward committing to CEDAW and to women's human rights in general, I will discuss a campaign I was involved in in the 1990s and early 2000s. The aim of the campaign was to convince Sudanese political parties operating in exile, particularly in Egypt, Eritrea, and Kenya, under the umbrella of the National Democratic Alliance (NDA),[2] to commit to signing, ratifying, and implementing CEDAW, as a minimum standard to achieve women's rights in Sudan, if they assumed power after overthrowing the regime in power.

A case study: the Sudanese opposition in exile in the 1990s and early 2000s

Sudan is a country in Northeast Africa, with an area of 728,215 square miles, and a population of over 40 million. Sudan is a former British colony that obtained political independence in 1956.[3] Successive postcolonial governments in Sudan followed a pattern of unequal development that created economic, political, and cultural disparities and inequalities between Sudan's different regions. This, among other factors, has contributed to a series of conflicts that started one year before the country obtained political independence.

In the first war, an armed group demanded the secession of South Sudan. The second war erupted in 1983 and ended in 2005 after the government of Sudan, and the Sudan People's Liberation Movement/Army (SPLM/A), signed a Comprehensive Peace Agreement (CPA). The initial goals of the SPLM/A included the establishment of a united Sudan, equal access to the country's political and economic resources by all Sudanese, and a recognition of the country's cultural diversity. In the 1990s, the SPLM/A included the goal of securing the right to self-determination for the people of South Sudan.

In 2003, another war erupted in Darfur, western Sudan. Numerous publications detailed the impact of this war on women, given that government-supported forces used rape as a weapon of war. War also re-erupted in South Kordofan and the Blue Nile areas, in the new south of Sudan, following Sudan's independence in the year 2011. Sudan's conflicts are rooted not only in the country's colonial past, but also in the social, economic, and political marginalization of the people of southern, western, and eastern Sudan by successive governments in Khartoum. They are also rooted in the insistence of successive governments on imposing a single definition of Sudanese identity on a diverse population. Sudan's wars have affected women in distinct ways that I examine in detail elsewhere.

The Bill of Rights in the *Interim National Constitution of the Republic of Sudan* (2005) contains provisions which, if fully respected, could significantly improve the situation of women and advance gender equality and women's rights in Sudan. The Government of Sudan has signed or ratified several human rights conventions including the International Covenant on Civil and Political Rights and the Convention on the Rights of the Child. The government also signed the African Women's Rights Protocol in 2008. In addition, the government signed and ratified the International Conference on the Great Lakes Region's (ICGLR) protocol on the Prevention and Suppression of Sexual Violence against Women and Children in 2008.

Nonetheless, several of Sudan's laws are in conflict with the interim constitution, the African Women's Rights protocol, and the ICGLR protocol. Sudan's Criminal Act and Public Order laws impose a certain dress code on women, violations of which can result in fines, and flogging of up to 40 lashes under article 152 which applies to a variety of vaguely defined "immoral acts," including "indecent or immoral dress." Other problematic provisions include article 149 of the criminal act, which conflates rape with the offence of *zina* (intercourse between a man and a woman who are not married to one another). *Zina* can carry a sentence of up to 100 lashes for unmarried women and men, or death by stoning if married. These laws specifically affect women and girls from marginalized areas of Sudan, who are often arrested for brewing local alcohol.

Article 149 particularly affects women victims and survivors of rape, including in war-affected areas such as Darfur and the Blue Nile. In Blue Nile, interviewees said rape was prevalent before the eruption of conflict in September 2011, but that the majority of offenders were from the armed forces, which complicates access to justice for women. Interviewees said women who failed to prove they were raped were often convicted of *zina*. In April 2012, for example, 28 women were in prison in Roseires locality in the Blue Nile state, awaiting court decisions. Interviewees said although the majority of these women were rape victims or survivors, they were facing charges of prostitution or *zina*.

Similarly, several reports have outlined how these same laws have subjected women and girls who survived rape in Darfur to persecution and hampered their access to justice. In March 2007, two Darfuri women were sentenced to stoning in Al Gezira in Central Sudan after having been convicted of adultery.[4] In addition, in May 2012, a woman was sentenced to death by stoning because of *zina* charges under article 149 of the Criminal Act.

Several Sudanese and regional civil society organizations have campaigned for law reform in recent years. The "No to Women's Oppression" initiative was formed after journalist Lubna Ahmed Hussein was arrested and put on trial for wearing trousers in 2010. The initiative organized several press conferences, sit-ins, and protests in response to specific high-profile cases of discrimination under Sudan's Criminal Act. The Strategic Initiative for Women in the Horn of Africa has also used the African human rights system and legal framework to challenge criminal and public order laws that discriminate against women. The Alkhatim Adlan Centre for Enlightenment and Human Development has carried out research on article 152 and has organized various activities about this law. Numerous organizations and movements are currently advocating for the reform of the Criminal Act and of the Public Order regime. Salmma Women's Centre has produced several booklets, one of which documented state-sanctioned violence against women under article 149. Sima provides psychosocial support to women survivors of violence and supports women convicted under article 149. Al-Manar and Mutawinat provide paralegal services to women in need, and Al-Manar also provides awareness-raising and other support services to women imprisoned for selling alcohol and other women prisoners. International organizations such as Redress, Amnesty International, and Refugees International have also carried out research on laws that discriminate against women.

Customary law is a neglected area that affects women in different parts of Sudan and that warrants additional attention. The Nuba Mountains Women's Education and Development Association (NUWEDA), an organization that has been working with displaced women and communities in remote areas of Khartoum, has identified customary law as an important area for intervention. In addition to education, reproductive health awareness, and legal aid for women, NUWEDA targets male community leaders (*sheikhs, umdas, mukuk,* and *sultans*).

NUWEDA has recently started organizing discussions on customary law, which traditional leaders administer. Women from South Kordofan in Khartoum who report rape or who approach the statutory justice system in cases of rape, domestic conflict, divorce, or child custody are often referred to the customary courts (rather than the relatively friendlier Child and Family Support Unit). Although diverse, customary law often discriminates against women and treats them as the guilty party in domestic disputes. Customary law also often restricts women's property rights. This not only affects women economically, it can undermine their ability to participate meaningfully in training or in political processes given a lack of resources.

Exile politics evolved within the above context. Following the overthrow of a democratically elected government (that reflected the narrow interests of two sectarian parties, the Umma Party and the Democratic Unionist Party (DUP)) in 1989, major political parties and activists went into exile. In exile, the opposition, united under the umbrella of the NDA, organized several meetings that culminated in a major conference that took place in Asmara, Eritrea, in 1995. The opposition agreed on resolutions that united the opposition on an agenda that affirmed the secular nature of the state, and made a commitment to ending the political, economic, and cultural marginalization of populations from historically marginalized areas of Sudan. Moreover, the opposition committed to redefining Sudan's national identity so it reflects the diversity of the country, and to putting an end to the hegemony of a single culture. The Asmara resolutions favored a united Sudan but affirmed the right of the people of South Sudan to self-determination. The resolutions also affirmed the opposition's commitment to safeguarding human rights enshrined in international human rights conventions. However, the opposition limited its commitments to women's human rights based on religion. Article 5 of the Asmara declaration read as follows: "The NDA undertakes to preserve and promote the dignity of the Sudanese woman, and affirms her role in the Sudanese national movement and her rights and duties as enshrined in international instruments and covenants without prejudice to the tenets of prevailing religious and noble spiritual beliefs" (National Democratic Alliance, 1995, p. 1.B.5).

In the years that followed the Asmara conference, much of the activism of women's organizations, women politicians, and activists in exile centered on the need to reword article 5, as it contradicted some of the clauses in CEDAW. Activists and women's organizations argued that a commitment to women's human rights, enshrined in CEDAW, was particularly important given that the ruling party had consistently used religion to oppress women.

In the 1990s and early 2000s, various Sudanese women's organizations were active in exile, especially in Egypt and Kenya. In addition to their activism, many women played important roles in holding communities together. All parties organized under the NDA-made rhetoric that expressed commitment to women's participation. Yet the NDA excluded women from the process that concluded in the drafting and adoption of the Asmara 1995 resolutions. Women were also virtually absent in the NDA leadership structure, which included a woman member of a political party in the NDA's executive office and a veteran woman activist in the institution's leadership council. While predominantly northern women's groups active in Egypt campaigned to ensure that women participate in the NDA, southern Sudanese women based in Nairobi campaigned for women's participation in the structures of the SPLM/A and in peace negotiations. Several women's organizations, especially those based in Cairo, opposed the NDA's restriction of women's rights on a religious basis. Groups said this article contradicted with CEDAW.[5]

At the time, I was active within the Sudanese opposition in exile, and was part of the women's movement that worked to convince opposition parties to commit to CEDAW, and to integrate a concern with gender into their literature and vision for the future, while also working on a multisite ethnography on these same issues. My interviews with the leaders and members of opposition parties in exile showed that although collectively these parties agreed to place restrictions on their commitment to women's human rights, their positions on this issue were not uniform. For example, the representatives of the two sectarian parties, the Umma party and the DUP, argued that CEDAW promoted "promiscuity, prostitution, abortion, and homosexuality [sic]," and that it was thus against Sudanese cultures and social norms.

Left-leaning parties argued they supported the demands of the women's organizations that were active in exile, but they did not want to "offend" their allies at the time: leaders of parties that emerged from Sufi sects. Leaders of southern Sudanese political parties, such as the Union of Sudan African Parties, argued that since most of the members of the party were not Muslims, it was "rude" for the party to challenge a lack of commitment to CEDAW, so as not to "offend" their Muslim colleagues in other parties.

In the interviews, and in advocacy meetings, I asked political leaders who objected to a commitment to CEDAW to name specific clauses they thought contradicted with religion (in this case Islam). Most of the interviewees who objected to a commitment to CEDAW said they had never read the actual convention. Yet, they overwhelmingly cited similar reasons as to why they did not want to commit to women's rights enshrined in this convention. When I probed my interviewees further, most of them said they had read the reporting of (primarily right-wing) Egyptian newspapers on the UN's Fourth Conference on Women (the Beijing Conference)! Reports on the Beijing Conference in much of the Egyptian media constructed this conference as a Western conspiracy against Muslims, and against the cultures of people in countries like Egypt.

The discourse of the two sectarian parties overlapped with the discourses of members of the ruling National Congress Party (NCP). Sumaia Abu Kashawa, who was chair of the quasi-governmental Sudan Women's General Union, wrote in 1995:

> The same issues that rose in the International Conference for Population and Development in Cairo are raised again, especially with regard to reproductive health and promiscuity. Western countries will not spare any effort, through their delegates and non-governmental organisations, in inserting their concepts in the [Beijing] document, in order to uniformly impose these [concepts] on every country. In that way, Western culture, and Western perceptions would form the basis of the New World Order. Third world countries, however, are conscious of this matter and are protesting the articles, which do not reflect their culture.
>
> (Cited in Ali, 2015)

The passage above homogenizes Global South communities as well as "the West." The author strategically places "reproductive health" next to "promiscuity."

The overlap of the government's discourse on one hand, and that of opposition parties of sectarian origins on the other is not accidental. Scholars have argued that claims of authenticity and cultural specificity are often linked to broader processes of neoliberal globalization. Such processes often give rise to anxieties and fears of Western domination. While forces within the ruling party in Sudan and within the two sectarian parties are accepting of the free market ideology, they rely on religion to sustain their power. They thus utilize the fear of communities of Western cultural hegemony to consolidate their power over these communities.

Some of the parties that sought transformation in Sudan committed to women's human rights enshrined in CEDAW. Others argued they would support the demands of women's organizations. These parties, however, were more concerned about maintaining the unity of the exiled opposition against the ruling NCP. The stakes were high at the time: Sectarian parties committed to separation between religion and politics although they depended on religion to reach out to their bases. One of these two parties, the DUP, had historically called for unity between Sudan and Egypt, yet it acknowledged the rights of south Sudanese to self-determination. To ensure that these commitments persisted, other parties made concessions through accepting the limitations the two sectarian parties placed on their commitments to women's rights. This is not to argue that religion or Islam restrict women's human rights. At present, various feminist groups and scholars are exploring ways to achieve gender equality and equity through challenging androcentric interpretations of Islam. The problem is that androcentric interpretations of religion often inform the development of legislations and law. Ruling parties and social groups also often rely on religion to strengthen their power.

Another set of opposition groups consisted of movements with constituencies from historically marginalized areas of Sudan. Representatives of these movements mainly argued that conversations about CEDAW were not a priority for women in their areas. The reason was these areas lacked infrastructure, clean water, food, education, and healthcare. Above all, the population in these areas lacked security. Reflecting on the plight of women in war-affected areas of the Sudan in the 1990s, one interviewee told me:

> In the Nuba Mountains, the government army kidnaps women, men, and children. Women and children are kept in the so called "peace villages." Young women are then used for the nights. Each soldier takes the girl that he fancies and "goes away with her." Kidnappers force elderly women to fetch water and fire wood... These are the kinds of problems that women in the Nuba Mountains emphasize. If you asked them to list their priorities from one to ten, equality between women and men would be priority number ten.
>
> (Hamid, 1999, cited in Ali, 2015)

Another interviewee told me:

> For us as Beja, the issue of women is thorny, that is why we address it with sensitivity. Not that this big talking about women's rights and feminism is not a concern for us, but in our areas, there are real problems facing us right now: there are women who are married off at an early age, and they die at an early age. These are real problems, and not theoretical talk on the rights of women in the NDA or in a state that we might and might not achieve. We are concerned with the existence of women in the area: their life and death. Not their culture or identity but their existence. [So], I will bring copybooks, pencils and a blackboard, and create a conducive atmosphere for women so they can understand, and then [the woman] can decide for herself whether to "contradict with religions."
>
> (Shingirai, 1998)

These concerns are legitimate. They point not to concerns about "cultural specificity," but to the specificity of the *issues, challenges, and abuses* that affect women in marginalized areas of Sudan, and that are present in CEDAW and in the African Women's Rights Protocol. These concerns are also central, at the discursive level, to the 2030 agenda, a set of 17 Sustainable Development Goals that includes commitments to eradicate poverty, hunger, gender inequality, and other inequalities, in order to achieve the highest attainable standard of health and halt climate change by the year 2030.

The above narratives also echo and confirm Gayatri Spivak's argument that "the usually silent victims of pervasive rather than singular and spectacular human rights violations are generally the rural poor" (Spivak, 2004, p. 529). Such concerns, and intersectional analysis, should be part of the agenda(s) of women's organizations that may at times suffer what Spivak refers to as "epistemic discontinuity" (p. 527) with the concerns of marginalized communities. This is specifically important for organizations that aim to transform gender relations in Sudan. However, actors who may want to maintain the status quo in Sudan (e.g., the ruling NCP), or who want to achieve reform – that is, overthrowing the ruling NCP, restoring multiparty democracy, and ensuring women's political participation, without transforming the social, economic, and political structures, institutions, and social relations that prevailed in Sudan since independence – may appropriate such critiques of women's rights and gender equality. Such critiques may serve as tools to challenge the legitimacy of the agendas of women's organizations seeking transformation and gender equality.

Women's activism was not totally in vain. In response to this resistance, the NDA formed a committee that examined article 5, and that was supposed to come up with an alternative text. The committee reached a deadlock, however, because the women representatives of the different parties presented their party lines. The Umma Party suggested the convening of a national women's convention that would draw a charter that reflects the aspirations of the women of Sudan. Short of a conference, women's organizations active in Egypt worked on a charter that was based on CEDAW. Activists put articles of CEDAW to which representatives of the two sectarian parties objected between brackets. The NDA decided to postpone taking a stand on women's human rights, until its second conference, which took place in Massawa, Eritrea in 2000. The DUP halted advocacy on article 5 or CEDAW by threatening to revisit the right to self-determination.

The case of the Sudanese opposition in exile shows that often not all political actors and parties have the same position on women's human rights. While the positions of different political parties were different on whether to commit to women's human rights enshrined in CEDAW without reservations, collectively those parties compromised women's human rights as part of the historic bargain between the "sectarian", "progressive" and "new Sudan" parties to ensure unity. A lack of a strong women's movement with a loosely unified agenda in exile was a key reason for this failure.

The African Union has since adopted another instrument, the *Protocol to the African Charter on Human and People's Rights on the Rights of Women in*

Africa, also known as the Maputo Protocol (hereinafter the African Women's Rights Protocol), following a campaign by women's organizations and activists from across the continent. Most African countries have since signed or ratified this protocol. The Government of Sudan signed the protocol in 2008, but has not ratified it. It would have been difficult for NDA actors to argue that the African Women's Rights Protocol reflected a "Western conspiracy" against countries in Africa and the Middle East.

The African Women's Rights Protocol is a good entry point into the other theme I want to focus on in this article: female genital cutting/mutilation (FGC/M) given that the protocol has prohibited the use of culture to justify violence against women.

Female genital cutting/mutilation and the politics of representation

As I discuss above, questions on the universality versus cultural specificity of human rights, and on the politics of representation, have preoccupied me for the last two decades. While at the Cairo Institute for Human Rights Studies, and in preparation for the United Nations Fourth World Conference on Women, which took place in Beijing in 1995, I carried out research that looked at Arab cultures and human rights from a gender perspective. I also explored questions around culture and women's socio-economic rights in the Middle East and North Africa, as well as FGC/M. I was based in Egypt at the time, and Egyptian academics, activists, and advocates trying to influence policy were running a campaign to overturn a decree by the Minister of Health that legalized FGC/M, provided that the operation took place at a doctor's office. The minister's decision was a reaction to a video "that embarrassed Egypt," that CNN showed about a girl undergoing FGC/M in Egypt at the hands of a male barber. CNN showed the video during the International Conference on Population and Development, which was held in Egypt in 1994.

In the early 2000s, I worked closely with an Eritrean community association in south London on ways to prevent the practice of FGC/M, and to address the needs of women who had undergone FGC/M navigating a health system unequipped to address the reproductive needs and rights of women who had undergone the practice.

In my teaching, however, until recent years, I used to avoid including the topic of FGC/M in my syllabi, unless specifically asked by students to cover this topic at the beginning of the semester. The reason was that the practice has historically been sensationalized by the media or used to label African communities that practice it as barbaric.

The World Health Organization defines FGC/M as "all procedures that involve partial or total removal of the external female genitalia, or other injury to the female genital organs for non-medical reasons" (World Health Organization, 2013).

Individuals in the medical profession, feminists, lawyers, human rights activists, and artists often use the tools at their disposal to effect change.

These strategies sometimes backfire, however. One example of a problematic approach to FGC/M was an installation that Makude Linde, a black artist who is based in Sweden, constructed in 2012. The artist was invited to participate in an exhibit at the Swedish Museum of Modern Art. Linde decided to display a cake that depicted a caricature of an African woman undergoing FGC/M. A letter from a group of African scholars and activists to the Swedish minister of culture, who participated in the event and cut a piece of the cake, provides a good summary of the event:

> On Sunday, April 15, at the Moderna Museet the Swedish Artists Organisation celebrated World Art Day, as well as its own 75th birthday. Lena Adelsohn-Liljeroth, the culture minister, was invited to speak and a number of artists were invited to create birthday cakes for the celebration. The minister was informed that the cake would be about the limits of provocative art, and about female genital mutilation. The event was launched with Lena Adelsohn-Liljeroth cutting the first piece of cake from a dark, ruby red velvet filling with black icing, which we understand was created by the Afro-Swedish artist Makode Aj Linde, whose head forms that of the black woman, and is seen with a blackened face screaming with pain each time a guest cuts a slice from the cake.
>
> (Carre et al., 2012)

The installation, and the attitude of the minister generated criticism from African as well as Swedish organizations. The signatories of the above letter argued that "the racial overtones of this project re-inscribe the exploitation and dehumanization of black African women." They stated,

> Rather disturbingly for many African women, the minister is pictured laughing as she cuts off the genital area (clitoris) from the metaphorical cake, as the artist Makode screams distastefully. The gaze of the predominantly white Swedish crowd is on Lijeroth who is positioned at the crotch end, as they look on at their visibly ebullient culture minister with seemingly nervous laughter as she becomes a part of the performance – a reenactment of FGM on a cake made in the image of a disembodied African woman.
>
> (Carre et al., 2012)

The authors of the letter further compared the installation to Sarah Baartman, an African woman who was exhibited in freak shows in Europe – and who was the subject of public amusement because of her "huge buttocks and peculiar genitalia" (Carre, 2012).

The case of FGC/M is a good example that shows the importance of distinguishing important critiques of sensationalist discourses about FGC/M that construct countries and cultures in the Global South as "barbaric" on one hand and, on the other, debates on the universality of human rights that challenge practices that harm women and girls, even if those were defined as "cultural." Indeed, the African Women's Rights Protocol, which the African Union adopted in 2003, has rejected the tendency to resort to claims of cultural specificity to avoid commitments to women's human rights and to gender equality. For example, the protocol includes an article on harmful cultural practices that requires that state parties take "all necessary legislative and other measures" to eliminate practices such as FGC/M, including through the "prohibition, through legislative measures backed by sanctions, of all forms of female genital mutilation, scarification, medicalization and para-medicalization of female genital mutilation and all other practices in order to eradicate them."

I elaborate on this below, with a focus on Sudan, where recently a debate between US-based Sudan scholars centered on whether it was ethical or legitimate for someone who is not from a culture that does not practice FGC/M to conduct research or uninvitedly challenge the practice (Hale, 1994), or whether the tendency to reduce all the challenges women face in communities that practice FGC/M to this practice warrants a positive engagement with the practice (Gruenbaum, 2014).

FGC/M is prevalent in 28 countries in Africa, in some of the countries in the Middle East, and increasingly among refugee and immigrant populations in Europe and North America. Factors behind the wide prevalence of FGC/M vary from one community to another, but the practice is rooted in patriarchal cultures and in unequal power relations between women and men. The intention is often to protect what some of these communities see as a girl's chastity, respectability, and marriageability. I have argued elsewhere (Ali, 1995) that efforts to eradicate FGC/M should be part of broader struggles to change prevalent social, economic, and political structures and unequal power relationships, including gender relations, as well as value systems that define masculinity and femininity in ways that lead to the subordination of women *and* men (Ali, 1995).

The consequences of FGC/M, especially infibulation, on women's health are often severe. In the short run, it can cause pain, severe bleeding, and infection. In the long run it may cause difficulty in passing urine or menstrual blood. Infibulation also causes severe problems for women during childbirth, as it can cause long, obstructed labor which at times causes maternal injury or mortality (discussed in the narratives in the previous section of this chapter).

A situation analysis of maternal and neonatal healthcare services published by the Population Council in 2010 identified pregnancy and childbirth as serious life-threatening events for many women, especially in historically marginalized parts of Sudan such as eastern Sudan, Darfur, South Kordofan, and including the far north. Deficient healthcare structures often contribute to high levels of maternal mortality and injury in these areas. Living in a marginalized area that lacks healthcare facilities and personnel, compounds the impact of FGC/M.

While a full discussion of the health infrastructure in Sudan is beyond this chapter, it is important to highlight that Sudan's colonial history, as well as postcolonial processes including militarism, authoritarianism, racism, and government neoliberal policies and the imposition of austerity measures, have contributed to the deteriorating health system and to inequalities in access to healthcare. As scholars have argued (e.g., Tsikata, 2007, p. 221), "rights" discourses and international human rights conventions may not be the best analytical frameworks for understanding these challenges. Nor are these frameworks always sufficient for challenging global and local agendas for economic liberalization (Mutua, 2010) that may compound the impact of FGC/M on women and communities.

In Sudan, numerous civil society organizations and other actors have worked to address FGC/M with limited success. One of the creative initiatives that has proved successful in addressing FGC/M in Sudan is "Salima" (whole/intact), which is a partnership between UNICEF, Babiker Badri Scientific Association for Women, the Norwegian Church AID and local government institutions at state level. An important strategy that Salima uses to address FGC/M is tackling derogative descriptions of non-circumcised girls in Sudanese societies. The campaign replaced the derogatory term *ghalfa* (uncut) with *Salima*. Campaign stickers and posters contain the message *"Toulad Salima – Dauha Tanmu Salima"* (she is born whole and uncut – let her grow as whole). The campaign uses cloth with recognizable prints to communicate its message. A cartoon on one of the campaign's posters that shows a man holding the hand of a girl child reads "Salima, because I do not fear change." This message links the decision to abandon FGC/M with community notions of male courage. The campaign has mobilized singers and artists and listed them as Salima's ambassadors.

The campaign has had a significant impact as of this writing. For example, in recent years, several communities have signed declarations to abandon FGC/M as a result of the campaign, which draws upon human rights notions of gender equality. The campaign messages, however, are based on *listening* to communities and unpacking community understandings of the value of FGC/M and problems that arise from the practice of FGC/M.

The case of the Salima campaign shows that a legalistic approach to FGC/M, or a definition of this form of violence against women in merely cultural terms, is not sufficient. However, the sustainability of this campaign will depend on whether it will be able to establish strong connections with activism that seeks to change unequal power relations between women and men in Sudan, given the complexity of culture and its embeddedness in power. A culture often contains aspects that may undermine women's human rights and gender equality. The same culture often also contains features that may promote gender equality and women's human rights. However, power dynamics within communities may result in the dominant groups (often predominantly male) drawing upon the former and using culture as a tool to control women and communities.

Human rights frameworks such as CEDAW, and even regional frameworks like the African Women's Rights Protocol, constitute important normative frameworks that may support claims around specific rights. These are tools that women's organizations could rely on to press for reform. It is important to acknowledge the limitations inherent in these frameworks, however. They should not be considered as a replacement for the hard work that women's organizations and other local actors would need to carry out to achieve change and transformation. Such conventions are not always helpful in enabling activists to analyze the causes of certain gender-based abuses, and the structures, institutions, and unequal power relations within which these abuses are rooted.

Conclusion

What does the case of Sudan teach us? We learn that ensuring a commitment to women's human rights and bodily integrity in Global South settings and beyond is important in its own right. CEDAW and other treaties, conventions, and declarations offer minimum standards and starting points that women's organizations and other actors may draw upon to ensure commitment to women's human rights and gender equality. However, these are not necessarily the *only* tools that organizations and activists can use for advocacy purposes. As I argue above, women's organizations need to develop broader agendas that seek to achieve gender equality, but that also pay attention to the need to transform gendered social, economic, and political structures, institutions, and social relations that sanction sexism, racism, and other forms of oppression and social exclusion. Movements can seek, restore, and draw upon local histories of struggle for women's participation, human rights, and social justice, to legitimize arguments and strategies for social change and gender equality.

Activists and movements who draw upon international human rights conventions, and scholars who use these conventions to frame their research, will need to acknowledge the limits inherent in working within these frameworks: they may facilitate legal and other reform, but they will not inform transformation. Transforming unequal gender relations requires paying attention to, and working to address, local and global socioeconomic and political structures, institutions, and power relations that sanction these inequalities and subordinations.

Importantly, research and activism to achieve women's human rights, especially in Global South settings, should pay specific attention to and avoid ethnocentricity, and the sensationalization of "harmful traditional practices." They should also avoid passing value judgment against cultures of concerned communities when challenging practices that undermine women's bodily integrity and human rights. It is important to historicize and contextualize any rights abuses women may face. This will allow a better understanding of the root causes of such practices, and the power dynamics within which they are rooted. This will also help researchers, activists, and other actors to avoid reinforcing "rescue narratives" and "single stories" about communities. A question that may arise with reference to the Salima campaign, for example, is to what extent have the local and international actors involved in the campaign been able to avoid the pitfalls of collective transnational activism that have plagued campaigns to address gender-based violence (such as acid attacks) in other settings (cf. Chowdhury, 2011)?

Interdisciplinary approaches to human rights that take a critical perspective, that communicate to communities the tenets of international human rights treaties, that explain to communities how the tenets of these treaties relate to their daily lives, and that draw upon local knowledge are thus most helpful when researching, reporting on, and challenging violations to women's human rights in Global South settings, including in Africa. This applies to critical human rights research and activism in other Global South settings, and among marginalized communities in the Global North.

Discussion questions

1   The US signed CEDAW on July 17, 1980, but the country has not ratified the convention yet. Do you think it would be worth your while to be part of the campaigns and advocacy at both state and federal levels to ensure the US ratifies the convention, so it becomes legally binding? Why? Why not?

2   You volunteered to teach English language to new arrivals in Boston, Massachusetts, from a war-affected country. Some of the young women students in your class shared stories about the impact of war on their communities in their country of origin. They also shared experiences and information of intimate partner violence that women in their community in the US face. The students asked you to work with them on a campaign to raise awareness in the US about the impact of the war on women in their country of origin. They also agreed that you write a term paper about their experiences of intimate partner violence. What strategies will you use to make sure the campaign reflects the challenges the women face but does not reinforce negative stereotypes about this community?

Notes

1   For a case study on the change in cultural practices and attitudes, including toward Female Genital Cutting/ Mutilation among Sudanese in the US, see Abdel Halim (2003).
2   The NDA, an alliance of Sudan's opposition parties, was founded in 1989 in Kober Prison. Member parties included the Umma and Democratic Unionist Party, both connected to Sufi sects, the Sudan Communist Party, the Beja Congress, Sudan National Alliance, Sudan National Party, the Free Lions, the Sudan Federal Democratic Alliance, the Sudan People's Liberation Movement, and the Baath party of Sudan. The NDA held meetings in the early 1990s in Egypt, the United Kingdom, Germany, and Kenya that culminated in what came to be known as

the *Asmara Resolutions*, the outcome of the NDA's first conference. The organization was almost exclusively male. All parties agreed on the importance of women's representation in the leadership structures of the NDA. However, there was no consensus on the need to commit to women's human rights enshrined in international human rights agreements such as CEDAW without reservations. The NDA disbanded in 2005, after the signing of the Comprehensive Peace Agreement between the Sudan People's Liberation Movement and the Government of Sudan. Other parties, excluding those representing the people of eastern Sudan (the Beja Party, the Free Lions, and the Democratic Party of the East (the latter was established in 2006)) (Ali, 2015).

3 For an elaborate discussion of the gender politics of Sudan's opposition in exile in the 1990s and early 2000s, see Ali (2015).

4 The women did not have access to lawyers. They also did not have access to interpreters although the court proceedings were in Arabic, which they did not understand well.

5 I discuss the activism of Sudanese women's organizations in Egypt and Kenya around women's human rights elsewhere.

References

Adichie, C. (2009). *The danger of a single story*. Ted talk. Available at: www.ted.com/talks/chimamanda_adichie_the_danger_of_a_single_story/transcript?language=en

Ali, N.M. (1995). *Gender, power, and female genital cutting/mutilation: Case of the Sudan*. Paper presented in the workshop organized by Research, Action and Information Network on Bodily Integrity for Women, NGOs Forum, United Nations Fourth Conference on Women. Huairou, Beijing, China. 30 August–8 September.

Ali, N.M. (2015). *Gender, race and Sudan's exile politics: Do we all belong to this country?* Lanham, MD: Lexington Books.

An-Na'im, A. (2011). *Muslims and global justice*. Philadelphia, PA: University of Pennsylvania Press.

Benedict, R. (1934). *Patterns of culture*. New York: Mariner Books, 2006.

Burn, S.M. (2010). *Women across cultures: A global perspective*. 3rd ed. New York: McGraw-Hill Education.

Carre, C. et al. (2012). *An Open Letter from African women to the Minister of Culture: The Venus Hottentot Cake*. Reproduced in Pambazuka News. https://www.pambazuka.org/governance/venus-hottentot-cake

Chowdhury, E. (2011). *Transnationalism reversed: Women organizing against gendered violence in Bangladesh*. New York: CUNY Press.

Decker, A. C. (2010). Pedagogies of Pain: Teaching 'Women, Militarism and War in Africa'. In T. Falola & H. Haar, eds, *Narrating War and Peace in Africa*. Suffolk: Boydell and Brewer.

Donnelly, J. (2013). *Universal human rights in theory and practice*. Princeton, NJ: Princeton University Press.

Grinker, R.R. and Steiner, C.B. (1997). *Perspectives on Africa: A reader in culture, history and representation*. Oxford: Blackwell.

Gruenbaum, E. (2014). Sondra Hale's 'Ethnographic Residuals': Silence and non-Silence on Female Genital Cutting. *Journal of Middle Eastern Women's Studies*, 10(1).

Hale, S. (1994). A Question of Subjects: The "Female Circumcision" Controversy and the Politics of Knowledge. *Ufahamu*, 22(3), pp. 26–35.

Hamid, W. (1999). Director of the office of the SPLM/A commissioner of South Kordofan. Interview.

Jama, F.M. (2015). Eleven years of the Maputo Protocol: Women's progress and challenges. Society for International Development. Available at: www.sidint.net/content/eleven-years-maputo-protocol-womens-progress-and-challenges [Accessed May 16, 2018].

Mohanty, C.T. (1984). Under Western eyes: Feminist scholarship and colonial discourses. *Boundary 2*, 12(3), pp. 333–358.

Mutua, M. (2001). Savages, victims, and saviors: The metaphor of human rights. *Harvard International Law Journal*, 42, pp. 201–245.

Mutua, M. (2010). Human rights in Africa: The limited promise of liberalism. In: P. Soyinka-Airewele and R.K. Edozie, eds, *Reframing contemporary Africa: Politics, culture, and society in the global era*. Washington, DC: CQ Press.

National Democratic Alliance (1995). *Final communiqué of the conference of fundamental issues*. Asmara, Eritrea: NDA.

Shingirai, A.A. (1998). Former secretary-general of the Beja Congress. Interview. June 6.

Soyinka-Airewele, P. and Edozie, R.K. (2010). Reframing contemporary Africa: Beyond global imaginaries. In: P. Soyinka-Airewele and R.K. Edozie, eds, *Reframing contemporary Africa: Politics, culture and society in the global era*. Washington, DC: CQ Press.

Spivak, G.C. (2004). Righting wrongs. *South Atlantic Quarterly*, 103(2/3), pp. 523–581.

Srikanth, R. (2012). *Constructing the enemy: Empathy/antipathy in US literature and law*. Philadelphia, PA: Temple University Press.

Tohidi, N. (2010). The women's movement and feminism in Iran: A glocal perspective. In: A. Basu, ed., *Women's movements in the global era: The power of local feminisms*. Boulder, CO: Westview Press.

Tsikata, D. (2007). Announcing a new dawn prematurely? Human rights feminists and the rights-based approaches to development. In: A. Cornwall, E. Harrison and A. Whitehead, eds, *Feminisms in development: Contradictions, contestations, and challenges*. London: Zed.

Yuval-Davis, N. (1997). *Gender and nation*. London: Routledge.

Further reading

African Union (2003). *Protocol to the African Charter on Human and Peoples' Rights on the Rights of Women in Africa*. Adopted by the Meeting of Ministers, Addis Ababa, Ethiopia on March 28, and the Assembly of the African Union at the second summit of the African Union in Maputo, Mozambique on July 23. Available at: www.achpr.org/files/instruments/women-protocol/achpr_instr_proto_women_eng.pdf

Basarudin, A. (2016). *Humanizing the sacred: Sisters in Islam and the struggle for gender justice in Malaysia*. Seattle, WA: University of Washington Press.

Basu, A., ed. (2010). *Women's movements in the global era*. Boulder, CO: Westview Press.

Gruenbaum, E. (2005). Feminist activism for the abolition of FGC in Sudan. *Journal of Middle East Women's Studies*, 1(2), pp. 89–111.

Soyinka-Airewele, P. and Edozie, R. N., eds., (2010). *Reframing Contemporary Africa: Politics, Economics and Culture in the Global Era*, Washington, D.C.: CQ press (SAGE)

United Nations General Assembly (1979). *Convention on the Elimination of All Forms of Discrimination against Women (CEDAW)*. Adopted and opened for signature, ratification and accession by General Assembly resolution 34/180 on December 18. Available at: www.ohchr.org/Documents/ProfessionalInterest/cedaw.pdf

United Nations Office of the High Commissioner for Human Rights. Status of ratification interactive dashboard. Available at: http://indicators.ohchr.org/

6 The United States–Mexico border and human rights

Luis F. Jiménez

Introduction

Controversies as to the precise essence of rights, what justifies them, whether we should locate them at the individual or collective level, and what entity should be in charge of protecting them persist. Whatever one might conclude about the nature of rights or their justification, no agreed upon universal entity exists that has either the capacity or the disposition to protect human rights, and thus we are left with states as the main arbiter. Indeed, as Arendt so eloquently argued, the most important right of all is that of citizenship, as this implies the right to have rights, which can only exist within a given political community. As she put it "we are not born equal, we become equal as members of a group on the strength of our decision to guarantee ourselves mutually equal rights" (Arendt, 2003, p. 43).

Consequently, given the unevenness in the capabilities, focus, and priorities of states, the defense of human rights as a practice is riddled with contradictions, inconsistencies, and much lower regard than the universal discourse on the subject might suggest. This is especially true in countries such as the United States (US) which have long wielded the rhetoric of human rights as a foreign policy tool; who consider themselves to be human rights champions, but nonetheless often violate them within their own frontiers. Employing the US–Mexico border as a frame, this chapter aims to explore the gap between these stated principles and practice.

The borderlands are a good place to locate how and why this divergence occurs. First, a physical boundary separating two different authorities ostensibly responsible for the safeguarding of individuals' rights on the two sides of the line puts in sharp relief who can credibly claim their right to have rights, and under what circumstances. Second, the border in question is one of enormous power differential. One side is a global military superpower with vast reservoirs of soft power and at least five times the wealth of its neighbor. The other is a state with a weak monopoly of power over its own frontiers. This dramatically unequal distribution of capabilities shapes not just whose rights can be violated with impunity, but also, the extent to which these rights can be ignored or justified away. Finally, using this frame helps to illuminate how theoretical political constructions translate to the everyday, and how quotidian interactions are suffused with meaning about who belongs and who does not. Indeed, much of the history of the borderlands is one where the experienced reality and the expectations of its denizens clash with the institutions on both sides of the border, but especially Washington – an authority at once distant and ever present.

To accomplish this examination, the chapter focuses on three particular periods: 1) the creation of the border and the subsequent conquest and subjugation of its inhabitants; 2) the establishment of the border patrol and the ways it developed additional forms of control; and 3) the transformation of regulation at the actual boundary between the two countries to one that has enlarged the border to encompass the US as a whole with the installation of internal checks and detention centers across the country. Throughout, the chapter emphasizes how state goals and imperatives of control do far more than their stated purpose. Historically they have dispossessed people, made particular groups vulnerable to violence by individuals later sanctioned by the state, discriminated against those who do not fit within the larger imagined community, and violated the constitutional norms that are supposed to protect all Americans. Moreover, it is not only non-citizens who are subject to human rights violations, but in fact the work shows that throughout history citizenship has offered little protection from local or national authorities when this privilege is at odds with the narrative of who belongs in the polity and who does not.

The first section of the chapter chronicles the dispossession of the native peoples and Mexicans living in the former Mexican territory – individuals who were supposed to have received the protection and privileges of American citizenship as part of the cession treaty. The second section explores the securitization of the boundary between Mexico and the US beginning with the creation of the border patrol in the 1920s and culminating with its militarization in the 1990s where vast swaths of the line became an actual physical barrier and large parts of the border were literally cordoned off. It recounts the unintended consequence of hundreds of undocumented migrants dying from thirst, exposure to the elements, or asphyxiation, but also countless incidents of harassment of American citizens living in the borderlands. The third section examines the dramatic shift that occurred as a result of the 9/11 attacks. It delves into the ways internal controls have proliferated far from the border as detention centers, raids, and local police harassment have multiplied across the country. Moreover, it details how the criminalization of these individuals has given room to pitiful holding conditions and abuse of all types including sexual assault.

The conclusion summarizes the above and underlines the three main points of the narrative. First, human rights abuses in the borderlands are as longstanding as the border itself. Second, although the particulars of who and why have shifted somewhat, the intersection of race and class and the narrative of who belongs and who does not in the imagined community of the nation has always played a role. Finally, whatever the stated purposes of the state in controlling the border, these have always had unintended consequences, much of which has resulted in serious repercussions for the everyday lives of citizens in the area. As a whole, the chapter offers a way to put the current rhetoric and anxiety about the border in context, and problematizes the idea of the US as a champion of human rights.

The establishment of the US–Mexico border and its aftermath

The border itself is, of course, a product of war. The armed conflict that created it, in turn, stemmed in large part over slavery and dubious territorial claims. In the case of the former, slavery became a major issue because the Mexican government, fearing potential encroachment from their northern neighbor on a sparsely populated frontier, thought that an effective way to prevent it was to encourage settlement in Texas – at the time, the Mexican territory most in danger of annexation by the US. Thus, Americans were encouraged to move to Mexico under the provisions of the 1824 General Colonization Law. This promptly led to tensions, however. There were clashes over land titles and allocation, but especially over the 1829 abolition of slavery in Mexico. A threatened revolt by people in Texas was temporarily subdued with a provisional exemption for the region, but as the Mexican government tightened its regulation of enslaved labor, the American immigrants simply ignored the law and eventually decided to declare themselves independent.

The rebellion succeeded and Texas became an independent republic in 1836 – one that Mexico considered an errant colony and one that the US saw as ripe for annexation not least to maintain the political balance between slave and non-slave states. Given the circumstances, war was probably inevitable, but the immediate cause stemmed from Texas alleging its territory to be two and a half times larger than it actually was. By implication this meant that in 1845, when Texas joined the US, the disputed region became American land in the eyes of Washington. So, when there was a military skirmish that ended with the death of 11 American soldiers in the contested area, President Polk saw it as an opportunity to declare war. This was clearly an excuse, however. As President Grant, who served in the army stationed in Texas at the time, explained in his memoirs: "We were sent to provoke a fight, but it was essential that Mexico should commence it… Once initiated there were but few public men who would have the courage to oppose it" (Grant, 1885, p. 67).

Once the fighting began in 1846, US forces promptly overran a weaker and faction-riddled Mexico. In little over a year, they took over the country's capital city and forced the signature of a peace treaty that ceded half of Mexican territory. At the time of the negotiations, there was an estimated 75,000 to 100,000 Mexican citizens and 150,000 to 200,000 Native Americans living in the newly acquired lands. Considering the conditions of power disparity under which it was signed, the agreement hammered out very favorable conditions for the *Mexicanos*, Mexican citizens who suddenly found themselves part of the American polity. The document specifically protected their property and civil rights. Unfortunately for them, however, these were systematically ignored and in practice rescinded (see Griswold del Castillo, 1992). In other words, contra Arendt, in this case, even when these individuals were explicitly granted the right to have rights, the American state opted to disregard them. To be sure, these developments did not always occur specifically because of the federal government. Rather, it was a combination of national, state, and local authorities determining who belonged and who did not regardless of citizenship status with predictable consequences.

Broadly speaking, the abuses can be divided into four general areas: violations of property rights, inadequacy of due process, murder, and lack of judicial recourse. The extent to which these occurred in any given place depended on a number of variables including class unity among *Mexicanos*, demographics, political links, and in the case of property its perceived underlying value. California, for instance, saw a particularly pronounced loss of land ownership as the 1848 Gold Rush transformed the state and created incentives for local authorities to enact laws that dispossessed *Californios* of their estates and mining claims and transferred them to newly arrived Anglo-Americans (Gonzales, 1999, ch. 4). A similar situation ensued in Texas, although more gradually and more as a result of ranching interests than mining. This combined with a state-wide policing force – the Texas Rangers – paved the way for a new status quo (p. 87). Beyond specific state processes, however, the Land Act of 1851, the federal law aimed at processing the land claims of the previous settlers, accelerated the dispossession of *Mexicanos* because it placed the onus on them to demonstrate their ownership. Given their unfamiliarity with American legal processes and the fact that the titles of Spanish land grants were much less precise than the US demanded, *Mexicanos* ended up losing most of their claims either to lawyers or the state (p. 87).

Losing property was one thing, much worse was how often they were targeted for lynching – a disproportionate tactic in the Texas and California borderlands (Gonzales-Day, 2006). Between 1848 and 1928, for example, there were at least 597 Mexicans who were killed in this way (Carrigan and Webb, 2003, p. 413). Many of these were individuals accused of crimes who had little means to defend themselves; their culpability already beyond doubt in the eyes of the mob (Gonzales, 1999, ch. 4). To give a case among many, in June 1874, Jesús Romo was arrested near Puente Creek in California. Before authorities could formally accuse him in a court of law, he was taken and hanged. A local newspaper, the *Los Angeles Star*, praised the decision; it argued that Romo was a criminal who deserved what he got (Carrigan and Webb, 2003, p. 413). A prejudiced legal system only exacerbated conflict as *Mexicanos* had few tools other than violence to defend their rights.

Mexicanos were at least acknowledged as having rights in the treaty; Native Americans were not just explicitly excluded, but the US specifically agreed to use force to prevent Indian raids into Mexico. This meant not just dispatching a military force to do so, but accelerating a process whereby indigenous peoples would be put into reservations and dispossessed of their lands. Indeed, indigenous peoples were not granted US citizenship until 1924, over 75 years after the treaty of Guadalupe Hidalgo. Meanwhile, in the first ten years after it was signed there were over 20 massacres of Native Americans carried out by settlers, local authorities, and the US army. And just as in the case of *Mexicanos*, few if any people were held accountable. This gradual process ended up with a dramatic dwindling of the Native American population. Those who survived saw a near complete destruction of their way of life, first by being forced into reservations and later on into government boarding schools which attempted to erase native culture and language completely through "assimilation" and "Christianization" (see Reyhner and Eder, 2004, chs 5 and 6).

The construction of the modern border

If the immediate period after the creation of the US–Mexico border was a protracted process coupled with human rights abuses that aimed to establish authority over the territory and peoples of the conquered lands, the subsequent era extending roughly from the mid-1920s to the 1990s highlighted whose rights mattered in the borderlands even more and began the process of militarizing the region. This occurred largely because Washington became concerned first with controlling the human flows that crisscrossed the international line, and later with the illegal narcotics that began to flood the country starting in the 1970s. Given that legitimate crossings were not always easy to distinguish from illicit ones, in addition to the biases and perspectives of the (mostly) men in charge, an othering pattern began to develop where phenotype largely shaped the rights a person might expect to possess. Ironically, this weakening of rights transpired even as the US lifted human rights to the top of the international agenda and was central in the enactment of the 1948 Universal Declaration of Human Rights as well as other core components of international law.

Contrary to what one might suppose, at the turn of the century, border authorities did not target Mexicans in particular. In the early 1900s, there were no immigration restrictions on people from Mexico or Latin America at all, and thus, most individuals living in the borderlands experienced the international boundary not as a highly restricted space, but as a neighborhood that happened to encompass two countries (see Hernández, 2010). The exceptions were the Chinese and other Asian peoples that might be perceived that way by immigration authorities. This was because the Chinese were the victims of the nativist politics that assailed the US in the late 19th century. Indeed, although not subjects to the treaty of Guadalupe Hidalgo, their arrival coincided with that particular time period. The influx was especially pronounced in California, where the lure of the Gold Rush attracted thousands, and thus, given the context, they endured similar abuses to those faced by *Mexicanos* and Native Americans. Not only did they experience property loss, discrimination, and confinement to particular areas (Chinatowns), but tragically, even occasional massacres such as the one that took place in Los Angeles in 1871 – the largest mass lynching in American history (see Zesch, 2012). The anti-Chinese campaign culminated with the Exclusion Act of 1882 which banned further migration from Asia and explicitly prohibited those already in the US from becoming citizens. This led to laws in California that targeted individuals unable to become citizens with higher property taxes and fines, and also to the unconstitutional denial of citizenship even to those Chinese who had been born in the US. One of them, Wong Kim Ark, ended up challenging the government and achieving a constitutional precedent for *jus soli*, the principle that established that birth in the US automatically granted citizenship.

The immigration ban slowed but did not eliminate Asian migration. As a result of California agribusiness' broad demand for their labor, Chinese, as well as Japanese and other excluded peoples, continued to come to the US illegally. Given its vastness and relatively unguarded terrain, they did so through the US–Mexico border corridor. This, coupled with the fact that large colonies of Asian peoples, especially Chinese, had begun to flourish on the Mexican side of the border, which in turn was mostly populated by those who had been expelled from American territory, meant that a person aiming to enforce immigration law often relied on phenotypes as a shortcut. Add to that scarcity of labor, where potential unsanctioned entrants could greatly outnumber immigration agents, and it is easy to see how crude stereotypes might arise as an enforcement tool.

If necessity made it inevitable, prejudice ensured the systemic adoption of phenotype stereotyping. By the time the border patrol was created in 1924, this type of practice had already been widely used in the borderlands for decades. Over time, as the Mexican Revolution imbued the southern side of the line with a sense of danger and its northern side with one of peace and prosperity in the minds of Americans, and as immigration restrictions and Prohibition began to criminalize Mexicans, this procedure shifted to target an imaginary wrongdoer that border patrol officials described as "a Mexican male, about 5'5" to 5'8"; dark brown hair, brown eyes, wearing huaraches… and so on" (Hernández, 2010, p. 24). The scholar who uncovered some of this evidence in the correspondence of border agents argued that this profiling could be best thought of as *Mexican Brown*, a useful theoretical distinction because "regardless of immigration or citizenship status, it was Mexican Browns rather than Mexicans in the abstract [who were] within the Border Patrol's sphere of suspicion" (p. 24). By implication, this meant that anyone who was not *Mexican Brown*, but who happened to be with someone who was, would also fall under that shadow.

As the border patrol's focus ebbed and flowed between immigration control and smuggling prevention, internal check points and raids began to occur farther and farther from the international boundary placing more and more Americans under potential scrutiny. In 1953, the government established regulations that allowed the border patrol to have extra-constitutional powers within 100 mile radius of the US borders, in effect nulling the scope of the fourth amendment within that section of the country. Neither local criticism nor court challenges did much to forestall these methods. In 1975, the US Supreme Court ruled in *United States v Brignoni-Ponce* that in order for agents to have enough flexibility to enforce immigration law, Mexican appearance could be *one* of the reasons the border patrol could stop a car, as long as it was not the sole reason. Importantly, the facts of the case showed that "Mexican" had little validity on the ground. Out of three detained men, only one was of that nationality. In 1976, this reasoning was expanded in *United States v Martinez Fuerte*, which held that permanent fixed checkpoints in the southern borderlands were not only legal, but again they could be used to target individuals even when these were brought about "largely on the basis of apparent Mexican ancestry" (1976, p. 428). In 1984, they further determined in *Immigration and Naturalization Service v Delgado* that factory sweeps did not violate the fourth or fifth amendments. As a whole, these rulings stemmed from anxiety over what the court perceived to be out-of-control immigration in the mistaken belief that it imposed enormous social and economic costs (Johnson, 2010).

The common harassment of people that fit the *Mexican Brown* category sometimes escalated into more serious consequences. In 1954, immigration authorities carried out a massive deportation effort. Dubbed Operation Wetback, it clustered around California and Texas in particular, and resulted in hundreds of thousands of individuals being expulsed from the US. The tactics used meant that most people were not allowed to retrieve their property in the US nor permitted to communicate with their families. Even worse, there were cases of immigrants that were beaten before being deported and the removal of hundreds of Americans who were not given a chance to prove their citizenship (Hernández, 2006). The actual conditions under which they were relocated to Mexico were not any better. There was massive boat overcrowding and at least 88 deaths due to sunstroke "because of a round-up that had taken place in 112° heat" (Ngai, 2004, p. 156). At best, deportees would find themselves deep in Mexico – as far from the border as possible, so as to prevent potential attempts to return – without food or money.

In the following decades, these abuses – racial profiling and mistreatment of deportees – continued unabated but were made worse by the militarization of the border and the dramatic expansion of the immigration authorities' manpower. In the 1970s and 1980s there were around 4,000 agents that patrolled the entirety of the US–Mexico border. By September 2001, these numbers had more than doubled to around 10,000. In addition, the international boundary itself became the fulcrum of policy as Washington opted to create concrete barriers to deter unsanctioned crossings. To be sure, the region had long had physical obstructions. In fact, in a rather symbolic measure, the first barricade used along the California line was recycled fencing from the recently closed Japanese internment camps. In the 1990s, however, new construction easily surpassed any previous building efforts. Ramparts, fences, and walls appeared all along the major points of entry. This had predictable effects. Unsanctioned crossings through urban areas dwindled significantly. Illegal immigration, however, did not cease, it merely shifted to more unforgiving terrain such as the Arizona desert. As a result, deaths along the border exploded as immigrants died of thirst and exposure to the elements – since 1994 it is estimated that there have been nearly 10,000 people that have perished trying to cross into the US. In turn, the militarization of the border increased not just the conflict within the surrounding communities, but its social construction as a "war zone" made it more likely that potential abuses could be justified as necessary (see Torres, 2016).

The US–Mexico border in the post-9/11 era

The attacks on New York City accelerated further the previous trends. Public anxiety over terrorism, stoked in part by the Bush administration, brought renewed attention to the international boundary. This time, however, the threat shifted from Mexicans per se to an inchoate fear that radical Muslims would cross through the southern border. Why potential terrorists would opt to do that as opposed to coming into the country the same way the 9/11 attackers had entered the US was never explained. Rather, it became axiomatic within conservative circles that the international boundary was "undefended" and "wide open," and thus the Republican Party-controlled Congress decided to allocate massive funds to the militarization of the borderlands. Both the budget and the border patrol's manpower jumped dramatically once again – as of September 2017, there were around 17,000 agents stationed along the US–Mexico border, roughly the number of FBI officers nationwide. Meanwhile, for the latest year, the border patrol received $3.8 billion from the government – more than double the amount that it was appropriated in 2001 and nearly 15 times what it had been allocated in 1990. Beyond the specific human rights violations these brought about, the construction that resulted had very real consequences for those who owned property along the international boundary. In some cases, individuals lost their land, in other instances, the government divided it so that parts of it became inaccessible, and yet in others, their plots or farms lost some of their value because of the sudden physical barriers built next to them. Most commonly, however, is that those living close to the border suddenly had to deal with border agents on their property as a nearly everyday occurrence. Their presence might usually be no more than a nuisance, but it could also be costly if, for instance, they left cattle gates open.

In addition to these developments, the Bush administration initiated two new trends. The first was a massive reconfiguration of the immigration bureaucracy. It combined disparate functions that had operated under several departments and placed them all within the Department of Homeland Security. The enlargement made the agency at once more powerful – it now ranks as the third largest cabinet department – and less accountable as the already complicated bureaucratic maze became even more so. The second was to increase the level of cooperation with local law enforcement under the 287g section of the Immigration and Nationality Act, and with the creation of special partnerships under the *Secure Communities* program.[1] In both cases, the intent was to maximize the ability to identify and deport unauthorized immigrants.

The shift had two distinct outcomes. First, given that responsibility for immigration policy had now been expanded to police departments nationwide, abuses that had been concentrated on the US–Mexico border suddenly became possible in the rest of the country. This was particularly true because law enforcement is even less familiar with immigration statutes than the border patrol who even with a supposed understanding of the rules still engaged in racial profiling. Second, the resulting expanded capacity to deport people meant that detainees would have to be housed somewhere while waiting for their case to be processed. This shift produced Kafkaesque circumstances because it was coupled with the fact that the judicial system treats violations of immigration law as a civil matter, rather than a criminal one. In other words, a detained person does not have the rights outlined in the constitution, such as a public defender, because the severity of their offense does not merit it, but the punishment they endure does not differ in kind from serious crimes. In fact, given the lack of jail space, those arrested for lacking proper immigration status often end up housed in correctional facilities along with the general population – their status entirely indistinguishable from common criminals (see García Hernández, 2010). In this way, these two Bush-era initiatives spread the conditions already present in the borderlands to include the whole country.

These developments permitted human rights abuses that had existed before to become more prevalent. For instance, deportation of US citizens increased. It is estimated that between 2003 and 2011, about 20,000 Americans were unlawfully evicted (Stevens, 2011). The reasons for this are numerous, but as Stevens puts it: "the most significant cause of US citizens being deported is the absence of accountability and transparency in immigration policy. Widespread, unlawful, racial and ethnic profiling... as well as the resulting unwarranted arrests by the supervisors...are tolerated and then hidden" (p. 654). So, for example, immigration agents might target the wrong person with the same name, might raid locales and prevent people from obtaining ways to identify themselves as citizens, or might assume the individual was lying. This occurs disproportionately with individuals that suffer mental illness. Despite such egregious abuses of power, those responsible suffer little to no consequences. Immigration and Customs Enforcement usually does not even open an investigation into the cases.

In a system where impunity prevails, massive numbers of agents are deemed necessary, detainees hold little to no rights because of administrative neglect, and they lack the necessary knowledge to navigate the bureaucratic maze, other human rights abuses are inevitable. Sexual assault is endemic, for instance. The latest complaint documented 1,016 cases of alleged attacks – an alarming number since this type of act is very likely to go unreported because of fear of retaliation (Community Initiatives for Visiting Immigrants in Confinement, 2017). Mistreatment is also common. In December 2017, the inspector general issued a document that outlined some of the abuse and highlighted in particular unsafe and unhealthy conditions, the delay of prompt medical care, and the incorrect use of punitive measures (Inspector General, 2017). Deaths are less frequent, but also take place. Between 2012 and 2015, 18 detainees perished while in custody, mostly as a result of substandard medical care. According to the Southern Border Communities Coalition, there were also an additional 50 fatalities at the hands of the border patrol between 2014 and 2017.[2] These numbers do not include any indirect fatalities – individuals that might perish as a result of specific border patrol procedures. That would yield a number of unknown victims because immigration agents routinely destroy water supplies left by human rights groups for migrants crossing the desert (Carroll, 2018).

Despite the pervasiveness of human rights violations and the cost this imposes on the freedoms American citizens enjoy, there has been little shift in public opinion or in policy debates within the American polity. To be sure, activists continue to bring attention to the contemporary issues outlined here, but the discussion about the cost of immigration enforcement is simply not very prevalent. The cause for this is the same as the reason for why particular victims suffer abuses in the first place. Those who endure it are seen as deserving of it because of the construction of criminality around them; and in the exceptional cases where a person might be perceived as beyond reproach, the case is assumed to be an error, not part of a systemic problem, regrettable, but necessary to the success of the operation. The Trump administration has, if anything, exacerbated the rhetoric of criminality and deserved consequences. The conversation is now reduced to whether or not there will be a wall erected along the US–Mexico border and, if so, the kind of construction it will be. Occasional circumstances in which public ire materializes on related issues, such as was the case with the Muslim ban, do not lead to sustained challenge, and the public anger quickly exhausts itself. Sustained attention to any particular policy, after all, is difficult generally, but has been especially so with the current presidency. In Mexico and Central America, the public is more likely to be generally aware of mistreatment of their compatriots – whether they share citizenship or not. A large component of their diplomats' jobs is dealing with these types of issues. Unfortunately, they lack the power to do much more than protest.

Conclusion

This chapter has traced how human rights violations have been part and parcel along the borderlands since the creation of the international boundary. Over time, the US has disproportionately persecuted, dispossessed, and at times killed civilians along the border who were perceived as other. Who was most vulnerable has shifted over time, ebbing and flowing as a result of immigration legislation, public anxiety, and the physical capacity of the various enforcement agencies. The American government's rhetoric and push for international laws protecting human rights did little to curtail this trend. If anything, this tendency has accelerated in the last two decades despite court challenges and local criticism. At present, it is hard to see how this might be reverted in the near future.

The account has explicitly focused on chronicling the maltreatment of those holding American citizenship, although, of course, the universe of victims is much larger, and this narrative should not be read as diminishing their ordeal. Rather, it concentrated on these particular cases as a way to contrast how even when a person is recognized as a member of a polity, it does not necessarily mean that their human rights will be protected. This happens largely because having *de jure* citizenship does not always translate to *de facto* membership. Societies that construct measures of belonging atop physical features will invariably discriminate on those characteristics because unlike legal documents, phenotypes are always visible and cannot be easily faked. This is especially evident in areas where states with the power differential of US and Mexico butt against each other.

This creates a conundrum in the human rights debate. On the one hand, if one grants that because of the conditions in the international system only states have the capacity to look after a person's freedoms and dignity, one would also have to recognize that as long as polities retain some type of ethnonational component, individuals who do not possess those physical aspects will remain vulnerable to abuse. In that sense, an internalized moral imperative that treated human rights as global would diminish this possibility. The separation of humanity into independent countries, however, is precisely what makes it difficult to internalize any sense of universality, let alone translate this principle into one consistent with the vagaries that arise from the powers of a nation-state. This would be the case even if we assumed that there would not be a large gap between the rights afforded to citizens of a particular polity and those granted on the basis of a person's humanity – an unlikely proposition. Power inequality and state priorities only serve to exacerbate this problem.

It is also fruitful to be able to distinguish rhetoric from praxis. The problematizing of the US as a human rights champion demonstrates that as difficult as it is to create norms within the international system, it is much harder to follow those internally when the priorities lie elsewhere. Rhetoric is cheap, true commitment that practices those principles is not. This is particularly true when those carrying out orders are far removed from the enacting of the regulations they are supposed to enforce. The US has yet a long way to go.

Discussion questions

1   Why is focusing on the US–Mexico border a good place to explore the topic of human rights?
2   What specific factors have led to a disproportionate level of human rights violations in the territories within the US–Mexico borderlands?
3   How has the shift since 9/11 exacerbated human rights abuses along the border and across the US?

Notes

1   Section 287g was originally codified under the 1996 Illegal Immigration and Immigrant Responsibility Act, but its use was limited. After 9/11 it was enthusiastically employed to screen people for immigration law violations.
2   These included US citizens, but not all occurred while the agents were enforcing immigration law. For details see: www.southernborder.org/deaths_by_border_patrol

References

Arendt, H. (2003). *The portable Hanna Arendt*. New York: Penguin Classics.
Carrigan, W.D. and Webb, C. (2003). The lynching of persons of Mexican origin or descent in the United States, 1848 to 1928. *Journal of Social History*, 37(2), pp. 411–438.
Carroll, R. (2018). US border patrol routinely sabotages water left for migrants, report says. *Guardian*. Available at: www.theguardian.com/us-news/2018/jan/17/us-border-patrol-sabotage-aid-migrants-mexico-arizona?CMP=share_btn_tw [Accessed May 29, 2018].
Community Initiatives for Visiting Immigrants in Confinement (2017). Sexual assault in immigration detention. Press release. April 11. Available at: www.endisolation.org/sexual-assault-in-immigrant-detention/ [Accessed May 29, 2018].
García Hernández, C.C. (2010). Immigration detention as punishment. *UCLA Law Review*, 61, pp. 1346–1414.
Gonzales, M. (1999). *Mexicanos: A history of Mexicans in the United States*. Bloomington, IN: Indiana University Press.
Gonzales-Day, K. (2006). *Lynching in the west 1850–1935*. Durham, NC: North Carolina Press.
Grant, U. (1885). *Personal memoirs of US Grant*. Vol. 1. New York: Charles L. Webster & Co.
Griswold del Castillo, R. (1992). *The Treaty of Guadalupe Hidalgo: A history of conflict*. Norman, OK: University of Oklahoma Press.
Hernández, K.L. (2006). The crimes and consequences of illegal immigration: A cross-border examination of Operation Wetback 1953–1954. *Western Historical Quarterly*, 37(4), pp. 421–444.
Hernández, K.L. (2010). *Migra! A history of the US border patrol*. Berkeley, CA: University of California Press.

110   *Luis F. Jiménez*

Immigration and Naturalization Service v Delgado (1984). 466 U.S. 210 (Supreme Court of the United States).

Inspector General (2017). Concerns about Detainee Treatment and Care at Detention Facilities. Department of Homeland Security. Available at: www.oig.dhs.gov/sites/default/files/assets/2017-12/OIG-18-32-Dec17.pdf

Jonhson, K.R. (2010). How racial profiling became the law of the land: *United States v Brignoni-Ponce* and *Whren v United States* and the need for truly rebellious lawyering. *Georgetown Law Journal*, 98, pp. 1005–1030.

Ngai, M.M. (2004). *Impossible subjects: Illegal aliens and the making of modern America.* Princeton, NJ: Princeton University Press.

Reyhner, J. and Eder, J. (2004). *American Indian education: A history.* Norman, OK: University of Oklahoma Press.

Stevens, J. (2011). US government unlawfully detaining and deporting US citizens as aliens. *Virginia Journal of Social Policy and the Law*, 18(3): 607–720.

Torres, N.I. (2016). *Walls of indifference: Immigration and the militarization of the US–Mexico border.* Oxford: Routledge.

United States v Brignoni-Ponce (1975). 422 U.S. 873 (Supreme Court of the United States).

United States v Martinez-Fuerte (1976). 428 U.S. 543 (Supreme Court of the United States).

Zesch, S. (2012). *The Chinatown war: Chinese Los Angeles and the massacre of 1871.* Oxford: Oxford University Press.

Further reading

Dunn, T. (2010). *Blockading the border and human rights: The El Paso operation that remade immigration enforcement.* Austin, TX: University of Texas Press.

Slack, J., Martínez, D.E., and Whiteford, S., eds (2018). *The shadow of the wall: Violence and migration along the US–Mexico Border.* Tucson, AZ: University of Arizona Press.

St John, R. (2012). *Line in the sand: A history of the western US–Mexico Border.* Princeton, NJ: Princeton University Press.

Staudt, K., Payan, T., and Kruszewski, A.Z., eds (2009). *Human rights along the US–Mexico Border: Gendered violence and insecurity.* Tucson, AZ: University of Arizona Press.

7 Unintended consequences in the postcolonies

When struggling South Africans experience rights discourse as disempowering

Sindiso Mnisi Weeks

Introduction

Almost a quarter of a century since South Africa became a constitutional democracy, the pervasiveness of the concept of "rights" as protected by the Constitution has not led to all citizens and residents feeling empowered and secure. Certainly, many South Africans use the discourse of "rights" – indeed, it is common enough to hear ordinary people announce in various languages, "it's my right!" However, that often does not stop them from then turning around and lambasting "government," "rights," and "the Constitution" – often all in one breath. While poor South Africans may attribute the ineffectiveness of these legal entitlements and protections commonly described using the shorthand of "rights" to systemic factors such as slow transformation and corruption, some (perhaps even many) assign the ultimate blame to "rights" themselves, and the Constitution.

One possible explanation for this "dis/empowerment paradox" (Sigauqwe, 2018) is that the rights discourse that has taken root in the public imagination in South Africa has overpromised and underdelivered. The promised "transformative constitutionalism" has not delivered nearly as much transformation as was hoped or expected, and very slowly at that. One striking fault in the pledges publicly perceived to have been made by the drafters and politicians has been the purported promise that, rather than the document simply being a pivot (a reference point playing a central part in a change of course),[1] the Constitution can bear the weight of South Africans' aspirations for an equal society in which all people have dignity.

This is not to say that the Constitution has delivered nothing. Indeed, popular resistance movements like the Treatment Action Campaign have leveraged it to achieve victories such as the delivery of life-sustaining anti-retrovirals for people living with HIV/AIDS (*Minister of Health and Others v Treatment Action Campaign and Others* 2002 (5) SA 721 (CC)). However, there is a big chasm between what change the Constitution has been able to facilitate and how that is experienced and interpreted by the public. There is also a notable chasm between publics: those who have means contrasted with those who do not; those who are located closer to the urban center who are in many ways distinct from those who are located at the rural periphery; and those who are well supported by vibrant, highly organized, and effective social movements as opposed to those who are not.

For instance, in the groundbreaking decision delivered in the case of *Government of the Republic of South Africa v Grootboom* (2001 (1) SA 46 (CC)), the Constitutional Court declared that the right of access to adequate housing at the very least includes the requirement that government take "reasonable measures... to provide relief for people who have no access to land, no roof over their heads, and who are living in intolerable conditions or crisis situations" (para 99). Yet, famously, Mrs Grootboom, in whose name the case was brought for an order of "adequate basic temporary shelter or housing... pending their obtaining permanent accommodation" applied for through the government's subsidized low-cost housing program, died eight years later without a house; in fact, penniless (De Vos, 2018). As compared to the mobilization behind the Treatment Action Campaign case, Mrs Grootboom stood virtually alone (Budlender et al., 2014).

Such abounding disconnects between the decisions made by the Court in the name of rights and the practical reality in which South Africans live are what contributes to the view from below that "rights" are (often) useless. Yet that is not the primary argument of this chapter. Rather, the chapter seeks to make the case that "rights" are experienced as simultaneously empowering *in rhetorical terms* and disempowering *in practical effect*. This paradox is partly based on what is seen as the "false promise" of socioeconomic transformation made by the Constitution.

This false promise has contributed to what John Carlson and Neville Yeomans (1975) were first to refer to as "lawfare." In the authors' conception, the word blended "law" and "warfare" to refer to the phenomenon they identified as Western legal systems having forsaken alternative dispute-resolution methods and become too adversarial. Hence, Carlson and Yeomans wrote, "[l]awfare replaces warfare and the duel is with words rather than swords" (1975, p. 2). In this sense, then, "lawfare" has arguably become a reality in South Africa as political problems are no longer fervently kept to the political spheres in which negotiation and compromise are inherent; instead, it appears that the adversarial realm of law, which is meant to be the last resort, is now commonly turned to first for solutions. While it is true that the judicial sphere is seen by some as a space for the voice of vulnerable populations to be heard with equal volume as the voices of those in power, the reality remains that access to the judicial sphere is extremely limited and effective access to or use of the formal courts is beyond reach for most South Africans.

As some public intellectuals have aptly argued (e.g., Friedman, 2017), this growing culture of "lawfare" (Comaroff and Comaroff, 2009)[2] has led to the "judicialisation of politics" (Tate and Vallinder, 1995; Hirschl, 2002). As Ran Hirschl defines it, "judicialisation of politics" refers to "the ever-accelerating reliance on courts and judicial means for addressing core moral predicaments, public policy questions, and political controversies" (2006). There have been indications that this "judicialisation of politics" in South Africa threatens the ruling party's regard for the legitimacy of court rulings (Quintal, 2017).

For instance, in July 2008 then general secretary of the African National Congress (ANC), Gwede Mantashe, suggested that the judges on the Constitutional Court were showing signs of being "counter-revolutionaries" (Perry and Lindow, 2015). Later, in August 2011, this same spokesman of the ANC observed that the judiciary were reversing "the gains of transformation through precedents" and said that "the judiciary must depoliticise itself" (Mkhabela, 2011). As recently as May 2017, Mantashe was reported as accusing the judiciary of "playing in the political space and therefore setting a bad precedent" and "tampering with the powers of the executive" in a manner he deemed "embarrassing" (Quintal, 2017). He is not a lone voice in expressing these sentiments on behalf of the ruling party (*Economist*, 2018).

Of course, as these remarks also signify, the "judicialisation of politics" is accompanied by the "politicisation of the judiciary" (Mail & Guardian Political Reporters, 2014). The delicate dance between the popularly elected executive and legislative arms of government and a "counter-majoritarian" (that is, unelected) judiciary, summarized in the Constitutional Court jurisprudence as the "separation of powers,"[3] is consequently undermined. Furthermore, contrary to the democratic ideal, the strength and efficacy of the "checks and balances" between these arms of government are regularly put to the ultimate test of judicial review.

A second potential explanation is that the rejection of "rights" – and, more broadly, the Constitution – based on arguments of "cultural relativism"[4] is a response to the failure of the drafters of the South African Constitution to adequately "vernacularize" rights (Merry, 1996, p. 68). It might therefore be argued that such (rhetorical) rejection of "rights" is to be deemed an expression of resistance to the broader failure of the transition team to adequately reimagine the South African legal system and design a replacement that is truly South African. Hence, the legal system crafted was not representative of the diversity of cultures and values held by South Africans, but largely retained the model of law that came with colonialism (Davis and Klare, 2010). According to this argument, the manner in which customary law is accommodated and traditional leadership and communities provided for in the Constitution is a clear reflection and demonstration of this founding document's failure to effectively respond to the problems created by colonialism and apartheid and transform the whole legal system in view of the need therefore.

A final explanation posited in this chapter is that "rights" under the South African Constitution have become so hegemonic that ordinary people have been given the impression (whether intentionally or unintentionally) that, unless their struggles can be articulated in the precise terms of a legal "case" made on the basis of a "rights" violation, they are not visible, valid, or legitimate. As Pierre Bourdieu (1977) has observed of the juridical field, it separates those who can make "judgments based upon the law" from those who hold only "naive intuitions of fairness" (p. 817). The important word here is "naive" (p. 828). The difficulty presented by the system is that "cases" can only be brought by those with money. At the estimated cost of ZAR 1 million to carry a case through from court of first instance to the highest court, the Constitutional Court is beyond reach for most. In essence, therefore, if only complaints that are explicitly recognized and concretized in law (Oomen, 2005) as "rights" – most surely achieved by means of legislation or litigation – are deemed legitimate and serious, then those who cannot obtain that endorsement must find other ways to legitimate their claims. In such instances, a repudiation of "rights" as necessary for such legitimation is part and parcel of the endeavor.

Furthermore, linked to the previous hypothesis of how largely confined the South African legal system is to the legal model and imagination of pre-democratic legal infrastructure and process, the decisions the Constitutional Court makes often seem distant and/or disconnected from the day-to-day realities, needs, and views of most struggling members of the public. In this way, the "counter-majoritarian" principle on which an ultimate court such as the Constitutional Court of South Africa is based is a genuine challenge for its legitimacy and that of the "rights" it is tasked with protecting and spreading.

This third hypothesis might be likened to the argument made by Ugo Mattei and Laura Nader when they argue that there are times "when the Rule of Law is illegal" because it is in fact used as a form of "plunder" (2008). The argument may similarly be made about "rights" in the South African Constitution as having been experienced as a form of "plunder": a continuation of the colonial pattern of stealing occupied land (then justified using the Roman-Dutch law principle of *terra nullius*), and ignoring, distorting, changing, and replacing indigenous laws at will (because indigenous peoples were regarded as *lex nullius* or "without law"). Now, previously oppressed people experience their "naive intuitions of fairness" as being treated in that same way: only recognized as legitimate if they fit within this purportedly foreign construct of "rights" (for that is how rights are perceived: as principally foreign).

What these hypotheses together suggest is that, while rights are not inherently disempowering (and actually hold tremendous potential for helping people feel empowered), litigation should not be the primary tool accompanying their mobilization. More importantly still, quite arguably, for rights to reach their maximal effect, ordinary people must feel that rights are not fixed and final, or imposed from the top down, but derive much of their content, parameters, and power from the voices and needs of those who struggle from below.

Rights in the Constitution

In terms of the South African Constitution, all law must be consistent with the Constitution and the Bill of Rights (Constitution, 1996: Preamble, and sections 1(c), 7(2), 8(1), and 211(3)). Flowing therefrom is that all "legal" solutions must be consistent with the Constitution's principles. The Constitution recognizes customary law as distinct from common law. However, difficulties invariably arise in identifying and describing customary law; at times, this challenge has resulted in the character of state law being attributed to customary law.[5] Additional difficulty is presented by the fact that "customary law" (like "culture") is not defined in the Constitution.

Nonetheless, the Constitution places the courts (and legislature) under the obligation to respect and accommodate customary law in the South African legal system. Section 211(3) provides that "[t]he courts must apply customary law when that law is applicable, subject to the Constitution and any legislation that specifically deals with customary law." Sections 30 and 31 of the Bill of Rights entrench the individual and group rights to culture, respectively. In subsections 39(2) and (3) customary law is subjected, along with common law, to development by the courts in accordance with "the spirit, purport and objects of the Bill of Rights."

This, however, does not place customary law beyond contention. Subsection 7(2) provides that "[t]he state must respect, protect, promote and fulfil the rights in the Bill of Rights." And, then, subsection 8(1) states that "[t]he Bill of Rights applies to all law, and binds the legislature, the executive, the judiciary and all organs of state." In sections 30 and 31, the right to culture is subject to the qualification that it may not be exercised "in a manner inconsistent with any provision of the Bill of Rights." Since this condition does not accompany other rights in the Bill of Rights, the words obviously cannot be ignored; hence, these qualifications may be read as claw-back provisions. Thus, while no rights in the Constitution are absolute but subject to being balanced against other rights when infringement is alleged, the impression is created that the right to culture is not to be treated like them but is always subordinate to them.

Rights, context, and custom

The argument made in this chapter has been a long time in formation. Below I share excerpts from interviews conducted during fieldwork conducted in 2007–2008 via months of participant observation in a deep rural community in Mpumalanga (the northeastern province) of South Africa known as Mbuzini. The accompanying analysis and discussion of these revelations by members of the community have subsequently been confirmed by numerous studies conducted in different parts of the country, including my own further research in the province of KwaZulu-Natal on the east coast of the country.

Rights, children, wives, and lack of respect

As one middle-aged woman told me, "a person's right is respect." From ongoing discussion with this individual and others, it would appear that "right" here actually means "duty." Thus the person was not referring so much to what the person is her/himself entitled to but to what s/he is con-strained to do. This is exemplified in the statement of another same-aged woman who, when I discussed children's rights with her, said that "a right is only that of a child to have respect: to take the respect taught by their parent at home and practice it at school so that the teachers never have to call the parents in to resolve their disputes."

Women's and children's rights are viewed with similar disapproval. I begin here with women's rights. In an official interview, the chief headman informed me that,

> in this law that exists concerning women's rights, we, as the kingship, as the indigenous, have observed that it is the same as concerning chil-dren's rights. From the start, women had rights, anyway, of course; a woman is respected, she has her station. But not this law that is said to be the constitutional law, that which says that a woman must have the right to do whatever in the home.

A female councilor later echoed this objection in a separate interview where she stated that:

> If I'm living with a man, living in this home, I must know him that he's my husband, and even when he's at work, he's working for me and doing everything for me here at home. I mustn't say that I have the right that my husband must now get up and wash the child's nappies and cook and do everything. No, this is not a right – that's oppressing a person. A right is that my husband must know that I eat here at home and what I want from him he does for me, as the mother of the home. This is the right that I must want... Our rights, we women, are that our husbands maintain us and do for us whatever we want.

One elderly man concluded that "a male person's head is a female person's head; a female person has no other head but the male person." Using his hand to illustrate, he made the point that people take the one side of the hand and not the other side with it; that is, they take modern rights and then forget what they were raised with. This, he said, "makes us say that these rights should stay and work in the cities and towns because when they come here the women misuse them to disrespect the menfolk."

Evidently, modernization comes with many challenges for the community; not least of which are the changing and/or changed views it precipitates. Thus, as demonstrated by these quotations about rights, conceptions of gender, youth, relations, and rights themselves are not changing very rapidly, and people (women and men alike) are quite resistant to changes in this area, rather advocating their own conceptions of these social dynamics. First, the headscarf and apron are still viewed as symbols of femininity and thus as signifiers of (self-)respect and stature and the kitchen remains entrenched as the woman's domain and stronghold. Second, when it comes to children, the community gets even more upset about the promotion of con-stitutionally ordained rights than with regard to women. Cries on behalf of the children are heard in different tones from both sides of the state law line.

Some illustrations of this (roughly summarized for me by one male member of the ward council and presented here in order of the regularity with which they were raised) are instructive. First, the maintenance of family bonds and preservation of ritual and culture by insisting that adoption be observed only within the family is seen, by the state, as resulting in the abandonment and abuse of children.[6] Second, what is customarily seen as a normal romantic relationship – albeit between a significantly older man and a younger girl – providing emotional and economic stability is seen as child abuse and, sometimes, even statutory rape by the state. As highlighted to me by many, what customary law views as discipline the state declares to be degrading treatment that fails to recognize the dignity of children as human beings.[7] Finally, and most inflammatorily, in the abortion debate, what is said to be murder and an abomination or vulgarity by customary law adherents is freedom over one's own body in human rights discourse. By allowing young children[8] to abort without their parents' permission the state law is seen to be teaching young children to disregard their parents' rules and defy authority and discipline; yet the state would retort that it is rather giving effect to children's rights to autonomy, dignity, and bodily integrity (and reducing the number of unwanted babies who will become a burden on the state). In succession, the state is seen as being guilty of the deprivation of multigenerational devolution and provision, while it, in fact, sees the cus-tomary devolutionary principle of male primogeniture as violating gender rights as well as those of equality in terms of age in inheritance.

When I mentioned to one elderly community member that the Constitu-tion and human rights demanded different practices from us than our tradi-tions, he lambasted it saying that they (rural people) hear about the Constitution and its demands but it is imposition.

> For example, if the Constitution tells us that our disciplining our chil-
> dren corporally is *nhlukubeto* (abuse) it is ridiculous because you see
> that its fruits are not good. The government is wrong to allow this
> because they [politicians] were well raised and disciplined under the
> regime of corporal punishment and are, as a result, well-rounded and
> decent, thinking people but now they tell us that we shouldn't do the
> same for our kids but you see that our kids are all the worse for it.
> Thus, the apartheid government (though it abused and oppressed us in
> many ways) was better in that it allowed this. The Bible tells us, "spare
> the rod and spoil the child" and that it is good to beat your children so
> as to discipline them. It is wrong for the government to impose by
> telling us that it is our children's rights not to be disciplined and,
> hence, if we beat our children and they report us to the police we can

be arrested. Where is the right? It is with me, the parent, that I discipline and guide my child.

He added, in frustration, that if he beat his child and they went to report
him to the police he'd be arrested. Then if the child came home and he
kicked them out, the same government would not have room or a place to
put the child. Thus, this makes no sense. Yes, he said, he recognizes and
respects the government but it should not interfere in the way he orders his
house and disciplines his children.

Ultimately, a common view is captured in the words of the chief
headman that:

> if the government is going to say, a child has rights... even back then [in
> the olden days] a child, as every person, had rights. But, how is a child
> raised? By showing them [the correct way]; if you correct them and yet
> they continue not to listen, you use a stick, and when you discipline
> them with a stick, you are not abusing them, you are building them up.
> But, now hear what the government says? No, when you punish a child
> corporally, s/he has the right to go and have you arrested. Today, chil-
> dren here, we no longer control their behavior. A child goes out at night
> and returns the next morning, what will you do to correct him/her? So
> what do you find the child doing then? You find him/her drinking alco-
> hol, at a tavern. What is it? It is this right of the government's. Then
> what does it do to us? It really does us great harm here in the commu-
> nity – especially with regard to the children. It really troubles us. There
> is no longer respect.

Rights, due process, freedom, and power

A relatively elite male member of the community endorsed the traditional
council operating under customary law in the area, as compared to the
magistrate's court where he had had a very bad experience that he claimed
was a show of injustice, saying:

> [the council] are alright because a person can be free there – I mean, a
> person doesn't need an interpreter, they're free because everyone there
> is someone they live with; unlike [at the magistrate's court] where they
> arrive to find that other people are unknown to them because they don't
> live with them and the person becomes intimidated just by entering
> there because they are not used to those people.

He continued to say that another benefit of the community council was that
you went with your entire family whose role was to listen attentively to all of
the proceedings and support you. There, he claimed, you could speak freely
in the language of your choice, without an interpreter, knowing that

the person you're speaking to understands the norms and the values you share. Unlike there [at the magistrate's court] where I'm to speak to "Swanepoel" [who]... when I speak... doesn't hear the impact when I stress things, and when it reaches him it's not the way that I expressed it and it is as though [he] can't understand it properly. That's not right, you see?

And, thus, this interviewee argued that, by contrast, the individual convicted and punished in the council setting could (ostensibly, with the guidance of his family) better see where they had gone wrong and recognize clearly how they might have improved the argumentation of their case. Most importantly, however, they are assured of the fairness of their conviction and do not ever suffer the fate of leaving court pained. He concluded that, in state courts "[t]hey'll say to you, at first you said [such and such], but that person was answering because they are scared, they are not free." He was sure that it was this unfairness that brought about revenge killings after magistrate's court convictions: people would go to prison and return to kill.

Finally, also, some people believe that, as hinted at by the previously quoted gentleman, state law does not comport with their values, and/or that it is impracticable in their circumstances. As pertains to the latter, in a conversation I sat in on with some local women, they discussed the fact that a local woman had told her husband that *ulibele* (he is dull-witted). The women were shocked that she could say that to her husband and still live in "his" house.

Discussion among the group of women then turned to some woman – and it was not clear if it was/was not the same woman who had insulted her husband – who had sued her husband for maintenance. Having done so, she now had to live with him, which was no easy task. The women lamented the fact that the very same people who would have advised her to do such would then be the ones laughing at her when she had thereby ruined her marriage. The lady who had been first to welcome me to their circle said that she would not sue a person she lived with in the same house for that must be very difficult. Her foreign-looking friend agreed that if her husband bought her bread, soap, and built her a house then she would be fine; what more should she want? The first woman offered that people said that this was their right: to sue.

A third (more elderly) woman said that they could keep their rights for "these rights ruin things for us." She repeated this rejection, adding that now that she is as old as she is they come and tell her about rights; they should rather leave her alone. "Rights are fine," she concluded, "for young people like yourself" (pointing at me). But the lady who had befriended me interjected to correct that even for young women folk like myself, rights are a problem because they make us think we can disrespect our husbands, saying it is our right. But then, "will your rights take care of you?" she asked, looking me in the eye. "Take your rights then and sleep outside, on the street."

While people's relationship with their community law is evidently far from perfect, it takes precedence, if only for its familiarity and its being adapted to their life circumstances. They are more open to change than first meets the eye; yet, ultimately, what I heard people say most is well summarized in the chief headman's reflections that people like themselves are not included in the law-making processes and hence do not feel like citizens but rather subjects in the constitutional order. As the chief headman mused,

> what grieves us most is this that when these laws are fashioned, they don't call and sit down with our kings to ask how we operate in these situations, how can we co-operate... They sit on their own and create them, build them, then call our kings to say "now we have this." Then what do you find? Some of it causes us problems.

Part of the objection is to standardization – that is, the disregard and thus suppression of difference. A migrant male community member captured this same sentiment thus:

> it would be better if parliament considered *emalimi* (different tongues) and the fact that each of them have different customs and traditions. There are the Sotho, they have their customs; there are the Pedi, with theirs... But now parliament treats us all the same. When we fought against the Boers we aimed to be united; we didn't think [we would] but now it looks like we might turn on one another. Actually, you see, the Constitution was made by a certain *qembu* (group) – I might say, the [African National] Congress – and they enacted what they wanted.

In light of this, the community members seek to voice their opinions and appeal to the government to reconsider certain rules. But, in the meantime, their solution is just to continue with their practices to the extent that they can without being subject to backlash or arrest. A male member of the council who alleged that the Constitution sabotages traditional people and disadvantages those who do not have money because they cannot sue and challenge people in the Constitutional Court put it in the following terms: "We shall do what we think is best for us... we'll carry on doing that." The chief headman, similarly, put it that "[w]e just carry on with our laws, we don't stop."

Conclusion

In the rich body of remarks collated from the participants in the study described above, one can see the "dis/empowerment paradox" made plain through the comments of rural people who recognize that the Constitution has sought to empower them but also feel that it has had disempowering effects on their lives and communities. Parents reflect on feeling that they can no longer garner respect for themselves or their traditional values because of the threat of being arrested for supposedly abusing their children when they attempt to discipline them. At the same time, those parents feel compelled to indulge their children, thus no longer having their disciplinary trump cards of corporal punishment or even lockouts, even as their children are corrupted by the ever increasing disciplinary threats that present themselves in society.

Husbands express feeling that the Constitution would permit their wives to emasculate and displace them, even requiring them to be subordinate. In the face of such a system of rights, even the husband's fulfilment of his traditional duty to provide for his wives and children would be looked down upon and regarded as inadequate. Even some wives themselves argue that a Constitution that provides for rights that require more of men than that they provide their wives with material security is oppressive toward the men.

One very striking theme that emerges in the author's discussions with participants is the ways in which rights are sometimes conflated (if not totally inverted) with duties. If the right of a child is to show their parents respect, then it is a different kind of right from that which is defined by Western-evolved human rights discourse. Such fundamentally different conceptual understandings could hardly be resolved by a top-down document such as the Bill of Rights embodied in the South African Constitution which draws inspiration from constitutions such as that of Canada.

To be clear, the point here is not to conclude that the beliefs held by the respondents are correct – always or even sometimes. Rather, it is to recognize how the power asymmetries experienced by study participants resound through their reflections on their feelings of having little choice than to (i) negotiate for understanding of their perspectives within the law, (ii) resist (perhaps by acting extra-legally or even illegally), or (iii) comply when forced to do so (also see Ewick and Silbey 1998, p. 224).

There is a long line of studies on legal consciousness that reflect these strategies (Merry, 1990; Sarat, 1990; Silbey, 2005; Nielsen, 2000; Cowan, 2004; Abrego, 2011) and the meanings thereof in different locales. What this chapter argues for is an understanding of the appeal to these strategies within the South African context as one of transitional justice in which people are navigating their attempts to recover from severe national and personal trauma (Gobodo-Madikizela, 2016). When we understand this context for what it is and what it does to how people interact with the law, we can better appreciate the restorative justice role that the Constitution itself (and rights within it) was supposed to play and the potential consequences of its shortfall.

It seems clear that nearly a quarter of a century after South Africa became a constitutional democracy, the concept of "rights" as protected by the Constitution, while pervasive, has not led to all citizens and residents feeling empowered and secure. Poor South Africans such as those in deep rural areas have different explanations for the ineffectiveness of these protections, including political explanations like the dominance of the ANC in the con-stitution-drafting process, but a whole lot of the blame is attributed (at least by some) to "rights" themselves, and the Constitution.

I have argued that one possible explanation for this is that the rights dis-course that has taken root in the public imagination in South Africa has overpromised and underdelivered. The promised "transformative con-stitutionalism" (Klare, 1998; Roux, 2009) has not delivered nearly as much transformation as was hoped or expected, and very slowly at that. Indeed, the people of Mbuzini bemoan the fact that the government's failure to meet basic human needs that they were denied under apartheid, as well as corrup-tion in the access and distribution of existing resources, interferes with the community's ability to receive what was promised when apartheid ended.

Another potential explanation that I have proposed is that the rejection of "rights" – and, more broadly, the Constitution – based on arguments of cultural relativism is a reflection of the failure of the drafters of the South African Constitution to adequately "vernacularize" rights (Merry, 1996). This explanation finds very deep expression in the reflections of the people of Mbuzini on the ways in which they feel excluded by the current political dispensation and, more importantly, feel that their traditions, values, and ways of life are not take into account when imposing rights.

The final explanation posited in this chapter is that "rights" under the South African Constitution have become so hegemonic that ordinary people have been given the impression (whether intentionally or unin-tentionally) that, unless their struggles can be articulated in the precise terms of a "case" made on the basis of a "rights" violation, they are not visible (Fick, 1998, pp. 22–23, 71–72), valid or legitimate. Indeed, the references made by Mbuzini residents to the threat of arrest and their remarks on how exclusive they regard the magistrate's court process as being, when compared to the traditional council process, all gesture to this set of concerns.

These various explanations of how the predominant "rights" discourse in South Africa excludes a significant proportion of South Africans certainly do not suggest that rights are inherently disempowering. In fact, even the people of Mbuzini seem to recognize their potential to be empowering for people when properly conceived and utilized. However, they also make a strong case for the fact that they are not properly conceived or utilized in the South African context of today.

But what does it mean to talk about rights being properly conceived or utilized? It seems obvious that this is not something that the Constitutional Court and ordinary rural South Africans like those in Mbuzini would agree upon off the bat. However, there may be some common ground to be found. For a start, while litigation has become the default space in which to debate important political issues in South Africa, it is fair to say that the democratic system was not crafted with the objective of political issues being settled by courts as a matter of course (Ewick and Silbey, 1998). It is therefore true that litigation through the courts should not be the primary tool accompanying the mobilization of "rights."

More importantly still, I would argue that the evidence points toward the fact that, for rights to reach their maximal effect, ordinary people must feel that rights are not fixed and final, or imposed from the top down. Instead, they must derive much of their content, parameters, and power from the voices and needs of those who struggle from below (Mamdani, 1990; Nyamu Musembi, 2005). Hence, the views of the people of Mbuzini have to be reflected as part of the discussion and formation of rights. To merely ignore them is to allow (and even encourage) them to ignore "rights" as irrelevant. After all, as Gordon Woodman has written, "those who are said to weaken the rule of state law are contributing to the rule of customary law" (Woodman, 1996, p. 160).

In my view, incorporating these divergent public views does not necessitate wholesale adoption. Empowerment is ultimately more about process participation than about content outcomes. However South Africa elects to proceed, it seems self-evident that the task of vernacularizing rights and radically transforming the legal order to make the South African legal system a true reflection of the country's diverse people(s) is urgent.

Discussion questions

1   Describe what you understand by Sally Engle Merry's concept of "vernacularizing" rights.
2   In what ways is "rights" discourse experienced by subsets of the South African population as disempowering, and what "legal consciousness" strategies do they use in attempts to respond to their perceived disempowerment?
3   One of the study participants remarks, "Will your rights take care of you?... Take your rights then and sleep outside, on the street." What is the meaning and significance of this female participant's statement, and how does it contribute to/support the scholarly argument that is presented in this chapter?
4   Discuss your ideas for how rights might be effectively used to advance "transitional justice" and "restorative justice" in South Africa.

Notes

1   The Oxford English Dictionary Online (2014) defines "pivot" as "the central point, pin, or shaft on which a mechanism turns or oscillates; a person or thing that plays a central part in a situation or enterprise; the person or position from which a body of troops takes its reference point when moving or changing course."
2   In their discussion of "lawfare," Comaroff, and Comaroff (2009) refer back to Walter Benjamin's essay (1978 [1921]). Writing in December 1920 and January 1921, Benjamin critiques the law as being founded in and operating by means of

violence (the use of force). In Benjamin's precise words: "all violence as a means is either lawmaking or law-preserving" (p. 243) He further warned that, "[w]hen the consciousness of the latent presence of violence in a legal institution disappears, the institution falls into decay" (p. 244).

3 Even though the "rule of law" is named as a founding value in section 1 of the Constitution of South Africa, the "separation of powers" is not explicitly mentioned. Nonetheless, the doctrine is arguably implied by the provisions of the Constitution and the Constitutional Court has expressed this in a number of cases such as *Glenister v President of the Republic of South Africa and Others* 2009 (1) SA 287 (CC) at para 28. In the certification judgment, *In re: Certification of the Constitution of South Africa, 1996* 1996 (4) SA 744 (CC) at paras 108–109, the Constitutional Court described the "separation of powers" doctrine within the context of its intimate relationship with the principle of "checks and balances" between arms of government: "There is, however, no universal model of separation of powers, and in democratic systems of government in which checks and balances result in the imposition of restraints by one branch of government upon another, there is no separation that is absolute... because of the different systems of checks and balances that exist... the relationship between the different branches of government and the power or influence that one branch of government has over the other, differs from one country to another."

The principle of separation of powers, on the one hand, recognizes the functional independence of branches of government. On the other hand, the principle of checks and balances focuses on the desirability of ensuring that the constitutional order, as a totality, prevents the branches of government from usurping power from one another. In this sense it anticipates the necessary or unavoidable intrusion of one branch on the terrain of another. No constitutional scheme can reflect a complete separation of powers: the scheme is always one of partial separation. In Justice Frankfurter's words, "[t]he areas are partly interacting, not wholly disjointed."

Also see *De Lange v Smuts* 1998 (3) SA 785 (CC) at para 60.

4 See for example Holomisa, 2011; Koyana and Bekker, 1998; and Mqeke, 1996. Also see Nhlapo, 2000; Nyamu Musembi, 2005; Cowan et al., 2001; and Mamdani, 1990.

5 *Bhe and Others v Magistrate, Khayelitsha and Others; Shibi v Sithole and Others* 2005 (1) SA 580 (CC). See discussion in Comaroff and Comaroff, 2009 and in Mnisi Weeks, 2015.

6 No crimes of neglect and ill-treatment of children are recorded (the same is true of three of the previous five years), and only one incident was recorded in 2003/2004 and once again in 2005/2006. Refer to *Crime in the R.S.A. April to March 2001/2002 to 2006/2007* (2007). South African Police Service, Mbuzini.

7 Abolition of Corporal Punishment Act 33 of 1997.

8 Of 14 years of age.

References

Abrego, L.J. (2011). Legal consciousness of undocumented Latinos: Fear and stigma as barriers to claims-making for first- and 1.5-generation immigrants. *Law and Society Review*, 45(2), pp. 337–370.

Benjamin, W. (1978 [1921]). Critique of violence. In: P. Demetz, ed., *Reflections: Essays, aphorisms, autobiographical writings*. Translated by E. Jephcott. New York: Schocken Books, pp. 237–252.

Bourdieu, P. (1977). The force of law: Toward a sociology of the juridical field. *Hastings Journal of Law*, 38, pp. 814–853.

Budlender, S., Marcus, G., and Ferreira, N.M. (2014). *Public interest litigation and social change in South Africa: Strategies, tactics and lessons.* Atlantic Philanthropies. Available at: www.atlanticphilanthropies.org/wp-content/uploads/2015/12/Public-interest-litigation-and-social-change-in-South-Africa.pdf [Accessed May 18, 2018].

Carlson, J. and Yeomans, N. (1975). Whither goeth the law-humanity or barbarity. In: M. Smith and D. Crossley, eds, *The way out: Radical alternatives in Australia.* Melbourne: Landsdowne Press.

Comaroff, J.L. and Comaroff, J. (2009). Reflections on the anthropology of law, governance and sovereignty. In: F. Von Benda-Beckmann and J. Eckert, eds, *Rules of law and laws of ruling: On the governance of law.* Farnham: Ashgate.

Cowan, D. (2004). Legal consciousness: Some observations. *Modern Law Review,* 67 (6), pp. 928–958.

Cowan, J.K., Dembour, M.-B., and Wilson, R. (2001). *Culture and rights: Anthropological perspectives.* Cambridge: Cambridge University Press.

Davis, D.M. and Klare, K. (2010). Transformative constitutionalism and the common and customary law. *South African Journal on Human Rights,* 26(3), pp. 403–509.

De Vos, P. (2018). Irene Grootboom died, homeless, forgotten, no C-class Mercedes in sight. *Constitutionally speaking.* Available at: https://constitutionallyspeaking.co.za/irene-grootboom-died-homeless-forgotten-no-c-class-mercedes-in-sight/ [Accessed March 14, 2018].

Economist (2018). South Africa and its courts: Judges uncowed. Available at: www.economist.com/news/middle-east-and-africa/21660540-judiciary-has-refused-so-far-toe-governments-line-judges- uncowed [Accessed March 14, 2018].

Ewick, P. and Silbey, S. (1998). *The common place of law: Stories from everyday life.* Chicago, IL: University of Chicago Press.

Fick, A.C. (1998). Limited possibilities: Agency and subaltern subjectivity in four South African allegories. Master's thesis, University of Cape Town.

Friedman, S. (2017). The judicialisation of politics. *Seventh Annual Public Interest Law Gathering.*

Gobodo-Madikizela, P. (2016). Interrupting cycles of repetition: Creating spaces for dialogue, facing and mourning the past. In: P. Gobodo-Madikizela, ed., *Breaking intergenerational cycles of repetition: A global dialogue on historical trauma and memory.* Toronto: Barbara Budrich Publishers, pp. 113–134.

Holomisa, P. (2011). Balancing law and tradition: The TCB and its relation to African systems of justice administration. *South African Crime Quarterly,* 35, pp. 17–22.

Hirschl, R. (2002). Resituating the judicialization of politics: Bush v. Gore as a global trend. *Canadian Journal of Law and Jurisprudence,* 15(2), pp. 191–218.

Hirschl, R. (2006). The new constitution and the judicialization of pure politics worldwide. *Fordham Law Review,* 721. Available at: http://ir.lawnet.fordham.edu/flr/vol75/iss2/14 [Accessed March 14, 2018].

Klare, K.E. (1998). Legal culture and transformative constitutionalism. *South African Journal on Human Rights,* 14(1), pp. 146–188.

Koyana, D.S. and Bekker, J.C. (1998). *The judicial process in the customary courts of Southern Africa.* Umtata: University of Transkei.

Mail & Guardian political reporters (2014). Judiciary, legislature, executive: What is Zuma planning? *Mail & Guardian.* Available at: https://mg.co.za/article/2014-05-08-zuma-judges-to-dominate-constitutional-court [Accessed March 14, 2018].

Mamdani, M. (1990). The social basis of constitutionalism in Africa. *Journal of Modern African Studies*, 28(3), p. 359.

Mattei, U. and Nader, L. (2008). *Plunder: When the rule of law is illegal.* Hoboken: Blackwell.

Merry, S.E. (1990). *Getting justice and getting even: Legal consciousness among working-class Americans.* Chicago, IL: University of Chicago Press.

Merry, S.E. (1996). Legal vernacularization and Ka Ho'okolokolonui Kanaka Maoli, the People's International Tribunal, Hawai'i 1993. *Political and Legal Anthropology Review*, 19, p. 67.

Mkhabela, M. (2011). Full interview: ANC's Mantashe lambasts judges. *Sowetan Live.* Available at: www.sowetanlive.co.za/news/2011-08-18-full-interview-ancs-mantashe-lambasts-judges/ [Accessed March 14, 2018].

Mnisi Weeks, S. (2015). Customary succession and the development of customary law: The Bhe legacy. In: M. Bishop and A. Price, eds, *A transformative justice: Essays in honour of Pius Langa.* Johannesburg: Juta, pp. 215–255.

Mqeke, R.B. (1996). Customary law and human rights. *South African Law Journal*, 113, p. 364.

Nhlapo, T.R. (2000). The African customary law of marriage and the rights conundrum. In: M. Mamdani, ed., *Beyond rights-talk and culture-talk: Comparative essays on the politics of rights and culture.* Cape Town: David Philip Publishers, pp. 136–148.

Nielsen, L.B. (2000). Situating legal consciousness: Experiences and attitudes of ordinary citizens about law and street harassment. *Law and Society Review*, 34, pp. 1055–1090.

Nyamu Musembi, C. (2005). Towards an actor-oriented perspective on human rights, inclusive citizenship: Meanings and expressions. In: N. Kabeer, ed., *Inclusive citizenship: Meanings and expressions.* London: Zed Books, pp. 31–49.

Oomen, B. (2005). *Chiefs in South Africa: Law, power and culture in the post-apartheid era.* Woodbridge: James Currey.

Perry, A. and Lindow, M. (2015). South Africa's ruling-party turmoil: A boost for democracy? *Time Magazine.* Available at: http://content.time.com/time/world/article/0,8599,1843631,00.html [Accessed March 14, 2018].

Quintal, G. (2017). Abuse of courts or the last line of defence? *Business Day.* Available at: www.businesslive.co.za/bd/opinion/2017-05-12-abuse-of-courts-or-the-last-line-of-defence/ [Accessed March 14, 2018].

Roux, T. (2009). Transformative constitutionalism and the best interpretation of the South African Constitution: distinction without a difference? *Stellenbosch Law Review*, 20(2), pp. 258–285.

Sarat, A. (1990). Law is all over: Power, resistance and the legal consciousness of the welfare poor. *Yale Journal of Law and the Humanities*, 2, p. 343.

Silbey, S. (2005). After legal consciousness. *Annual Review of Law and Social Science* 1(1): 323–368.

Sigauqwe, G. (2018). *Using of courts as a resistance tool: A case study of Makause Community Development Forum (Macodefo).* Master's thesis. University of the Witwatersrand.

Tate, C.N. and Vallinder, T., eds (1995). *The global expansion of judicial power.* New York: New York University Press.

Woodman, G.R. (1996). Legal pluralism and the search for justice. *Journal of African Law*, 40(2), p. 152.

Further reading

Gobodo-Madikizela, P. (2008). Transforming trauma in the aftermath of gross human rights abuses: Making public spaces intimate through the South African Truth and Reconciliation Commission. *Social Psychology of Intergroup Reconciliation*, pp. 57–75.

Lushaba, L.S. (2015). New South African review 4: A fragile democracy – twenty years on. *South African Historical Journal*, 67(3), pp. 375–378.

Michelman, F.I. (2011). Liberal constitutionalism, property rights, and the assault on poverty. *Stellenbosch Law Review = Stellenbosch Regstydskrif*, 22(3), 706–723.

Modiri, J.M. (2015). Law's poverty. *Potchefstroom Electronic Law Journal/Potchefstroomse Elektroniese Regsblad*, 18(2), pp. 223–273.

Sibanda, S. (2013). Not quite a rejoinder: Some thoughts and reflections on Michelman's "Liberal Constitutionalism, Property Rights and the Assault on Poverty". *Stellenbosch Law Review = Stellenbosch Regstydskrif*, 24(2), 329–341.

Part II
Critical areas in human rights

8 The mysterious disappearance of human rights in the 2030 Development Agenda

Gillian MacNaughton

Introduction

At the United Nations (UN) Summit in September 2015, the UN General Assembly (UNGA) adopted the resolution *Transforming our world: The 2030 agenda for sustainable development*. The 2030 Agenda sets out a global plan of action, including 17 Sustainable Development Goals (SDGs), upon which the UN and its members will focus their funding, expertise and efforts over the 15 years from 2016 to 2030. While the introduction to the resolution states that the 2030 Agenda is grounded in the Universal Declaration of Human Rights and international human rights treaties, there is a striking absence of references to human rights in the goals designed to implement the plan. The SDGs on food, health, education, water and sanitation, and decent work, for example, might all have been framed in terms of human rights as they correlate directly with the economic and social rights recognized in the International Covenant on Economic, Social and Cultural Rights (ICESCR) and other international human rights treaties. The failure to fully integrate human rights into the global development plan for 2016–2030 reinforces the separate but parallel tracks of development and human rights at the UN to the detriment of both agendas.

This chapter examines the disparity between the SDGs and the human rights legal obligations of UN members, and explores the implications of this striking disjuncture in international law, policy, and planning. It begins with a brief history of human rights and development at the UN, explaining the parallel trajectories of these two projects. The chapter then examines the success as well as the critiques of the Millennium Development Goals (MDGs; 2010–2015). With this background, the chapter focuses on the 2030 Agenda, examining the solid commitment to human rights in the resolution, followed by the mysterious disappearance of human rights from the 17 goals elaborated to implement the agenda. Analyzing the content of the 2030 Agenda, the chapter points to many inconsistencies with the international human rights obligations of UN member states. Finally, in view of the absence of human rights in the explicit language of the goals, the chapter calls for integrating human rights into the development agenda through its implementation phase.

Human rights and development at the United Nations

In 1945, at end of World War II, 51 nations came together to establish the UN with three purposes: (1) to maintain peace and security, (2) to promote economic and social development, and (3) to protect human rights (UN Charter, articles 1, 55, 56). While the UN Charter establishes that ensuring respect for human rights is a core function of the organization, it does not spell out specific human rights, except non-discrimination. In 1948, however, the UNGA adopted the Universal Declaration of Human Rights, which sets out the human rights, merely referenced in the UN Charter, that all members of the UN pledge to uphold. Unfortunately, the Cold War then set in and it was decades before significant progress was made at the UN level in promoting and protecting human rights. This is especially true for economic and social rights, the rights to food, housing, water, health, education, decent work, and the benefits of science, which are closely related to poverty elimination and social development. For decades, these rights were marginalized by the wealthy Western countries, which characterized them as socialist rights, although President Franklin D. Roosevelt had advocated for these rights as a Second Bill of Rights in his 1944 State of the Union Address, and the majority of constitutions in the world recognized at least some of these rights.

The UNGA eventually adopted the ICESCR and the International Covenant on Civil and Political Rights (ICCPR) in 1969, but it was not until 1976 that they came into effect. Further, it was not until the end of the Cold War that the UN began to make significant progress toward holding states accountable for their obligations for economic and social rights under the ICESCR. In 2018, however, there were 169 state parties to the covenant. Further, in 1989, the UNGA adopted the Convention on the Rights of the Child (CRC), which also recognizes a broad array of economic and social rights. UN members rapidly ratified the CRC, and today only one country in the world, the USA, is not a party to this treaty.

In addition to the Universal Declaration of Human Rights and the international human rights treaties, in 1986, the UNGA adopted the Declaration on the Right to Development. Article 1 of the declaration states: "The right to development is an inalienable human right by virtue of which every human person and all peoples are entitled to participate in, contribute to, and enjoy economic, social, cultural and political development, in which all human rights and fundamental freedoms can be fully realized."

The Declaration on the Right to Development, however, was little more than a rhetorical victory for developing countries, as the wealthy countries ensured that the right would not be legally binding, that it carried no obligations of resource transfers, and that it would not be of greater priority than the civil and political rights to which they were devoted (Uvin, 2010, p. 164). Although the UN Commission on Human Rights (and then the Human Rights Council) appointed an independent expert on the right to development, Arjun Sengupta (1999–2004), a working group on the right to development (1998–present) and a special rapporteur on the right to development, Saad Alfaragi (2017–present), the right to development remains, according to many human rights experts, "operationally meaningless" (Uvin, 2010, p. 165). Still, the right is invoked frequently in the preambles to the resolutions adopted by the UNGA.

During the 1990s, the UN also held a series of international conferences, which reinvigorated the human rights movement and linked it once again to the UN purposes of maintaining peace and security and promoting economic and social progress (UN Charter article 1, p. 55). These included, among others, the 1990 World Conference on Education for All in Jomtien, Thailand, the 1992 UN Conference on Environment and Development (the Earth Summit) in Rio de Janeiro, the 1994 International Conference on Population and Development in Cairo, the 1995 World Conference on Women in Beijing, the 1995 World Summit for Social Development in Copenhagen, and the 1996 World Food Summit in Rome. At each of these conferences, UN members made specific commitments to achieving economic and social progress and environmental protection.

Importantly, the 1993 World Conference on Human Rights culminated in the Vienna Declaration and Program of Action, which set forth commitments for the global realization of all human rights. Addressing the tendency of many countries to marginalize some rights – notably women's rights or economic and social rights – the Vienna Declaration emphasized the indivisibility and interdependency of all rights, as enshrined in the Universal Declaration of Human Rights and emphasized in the preambles to the ICCPR and the ICESCR, stating:

> All human rights are universal, indivisible and interdependent and interrelated. The international community must treat human rights globally in a fair and equal manner, on the same footing, and with the same emphasis. While the significance of national and regional particularities and various historical, cultural and religious backgrounds must be borne in mind, it is the duty of States, regardless of their political, economic and cultural systems, to promote and protect all human rights and fundamental freedoms.
>
> (para. 5)

Recognizing the need for greater attention to human rights around the world, the Vienna Declaration called for prioritizing the promotion of democracy, development, and human rights at the international and national levels; increasing financial and other resources for human rights; and improving coordination on human rights in the UN system. The 1993 World Conference on Human Rights started a new age – post-Cold War – for economic and social rights in which these rights have become accepted as legitimate rights by human rights organizations and many governments as well. Notably, human rights and development both seek to improve the wellbeing of people, and both agendas were reinvigorated following the Cold War. Nonetheless, at the UN, their paths would rarely cross (Alston, 2005).

The Millennium Development Goals: a missed opportunity

In 2000, the UNGA adopted the Millennium Declaration, which reaffirmed the UN members' commitment to the purposes and principles of the UN Charter, including peace and security, development and poverty eradication, protecting the environment, human rights and democracy, and protecting the vulnerable (UNGA, 2000). The declaration also unified in one instrument selected economic, social, environmental, and human rights commitments made at the international conferences of the 1990s. The following year, the UN secretary-general issued his report "Road Map towards the Implementation of the United Nations Millennium Declaration," outlining strategies and best practices to meet each of the commitments in the declaration (UN Secretary-General, 2001). Significantly, the annex to the report elaborated the MDGs, a nested hierarchy of eight goals, 18 targets, and 48 indicators to measure progress made in reaching the targets and goals. The eight MDGs, shown in Table 8.1, formed the basis of the first global agenda and monitoring system for human development.

The MDGs quickly became the "consensus framework" for the development efforts of the UN, the international financial institutions, bilateral donors, private foundations, national governments, and non-governmental organizations (Fukuda-Parr and Yamin, 2013; Langford, 2010). They also "raised the profile and popular awareness of development issues, changed the terms of international development policy, and helped to bring together a stronger focus on neglected social rights, such as the rights to food, education and health" (Darrow, 2012). UN Secretary-General Ban Ki-Moon declared, "The global mobilization behind the Millennium Development Goals has produced the most successful anti-poverty movement in history" (UN Department of Economic and Social Affairs (UNDESA), 2015, p. 3). MDG 6 on combating HIV/AIDS was a "stunning success," and there were

Table 8.1 The Millennium Development Goals (2001–2015)

Goal 1	Eradicate extreme poverty and hunger
Goal 2	Achieve universal primary education
Goal 3	Promote gender equality and empower women
Goal 4	Reduce child mortality
Goal 5	Improve maternal health
Goal 6	Combat HIV/AIDS, malaria, and other diseases
Goal 7	Ensure environmental sustainability
Goal 8	Develop a global partnership for development

also major achievements on MDG 2 (universal primary education), MDG 4 (child survival), and MDG 7 (water and sanitation) (Fukuda-Parr and Yamin, 2013). On the other hand, there was little progress on the MDG 1 targets on hunger and decent work and MDG 8 on a global partnership for development, including aid, debt, trade, and technology transfer (Fukuda-Parr and Yamin, 2013). Moreover, there were many unintended negative consequences, providing lessons for future efforts to formulate a global development agenda.

Unlike the commitments to poverty eradication and development, the human rights commitments made in the Millennium Declaration were not translated into a framework for implementation, monitoring, and accountability (Office of the High Commissioner for Human Rights (OHCHR), 2008). Moreover, they were not integrated into the MDG framework like the environmental commitments, which were enshrined in MDG 7 (Langford, 2010). Nonetheless, the UN human rights mechanisms on economic and social rights, the OHCHR, and human rights advocates urged all UN agencies and governments to adopt a comprehensive human rights-based approach to realizing the MDGs (Joint Statement, 2002; OHCHR, 2008; Robinson, 2010). While some UN agencies adopted human rights-based approaches to development, most governments, both donors and recipients, failed to integrate their human rights obligations into their development work.

Although the MDG agenda proved to be an unprecedented success at mobilizing global support for reducing poverty, the MDGs have also received considerable criticism, in particular from human rights advocates (Alston, 2005; Saith, 2006; OHCHR, 2008; Langford, 2010; MacNaughton and Frey, 2010; Darrow, 2012). Darrow (2012) summarizes them as follows:

> [C]ritics of the MDGs have pointed to the secretive circumstances of their birth, their technocratic and reductionist nature, their lack of ambition, their failure to address root causes of poverty, their failure to factor in legal obligations pertaining to social rights, their gender-blindness, their failure to address poverty in rich countries, their weak accountability mechanisms, their limited uptake by social movements in the Global South, the potentially distorting character of target-driven policy-making, and the propensity of the MDGs to "crowd out" attention to important issues that didn't make it into the global list, for example, social security or social protection.
>
> (pp. 59–60)

These criticisms implicate five core human rights principles: (1) participation, (2) accountability, (3) universality (4) equality and non-discrimination, and (5) interdependency. First, the process for selecting the MDGs and the targets was not transparent or *participatory*. According to Hulme (2010), the MDGs were selected by a task force of experts from the Organisation for

Economic Co-operation and Development (OECD), Development Assistance Committee (DAC), the World Bank, the International Monetary Fund, and the UN Development Programme, which drew primarily from the International Development Goals published by the DAC in 1996, rather than from the Millennium Declaration (p. 18). Hulme surmises, "[T]hese organizations ensured that the MDGs fully recognized the centrality of income growth to poverty reduction and that the variant of human development the MDGs pursued was based on a basic needs approach and not human rights or reduced inequality" (p. 19).

Contrary to a central tenet of human rights requiring transparency and participation in policy making, the formulation of the MDGs involved no consultation with the people who would be targeted by this agenda or with their government representatives. Indeed, it was a top-down process in which wealthy countries decided on the goals to impose on poor countries in a so-called global development agenda that emphasized primarily the responsibilities of poor countries for their own development (Saith, 2006).

Second, the goals aligned closely with economic and social rights and yet were not framed in terms of the international human rights legal obligations of the UN member countries, which usefully entail systems for monitoring and *accountability*. For example, MDG 1 on eradicating poverty and hunger aligned with the right to an adequate standard of living and the right to food, and MDG 2 on achieving universal primary education aligned with the right to free and compulsory primary education. The failure to explicitly frame the goals in terms of human rights missed the opportunity to bring coherence to the development and human rights agendas. After all, both human rights and the MDGs aim to improve individual and community wellbeing. More importantly, however, by failing to frame the MDGs explicitly in terms of human rights, the UN appeared to downgrade many economic and social rights from international legal obligations to mere development strategies (OHCHR, 2008). Rather than enhancing monitoring and accountability for achieving the closely related economic and social rights, the framing of the MDGs undermined human rights as legal obligations.

Third, the MDGs were not *universal*. MDG 1 through 7, encompassing human development targets – on food, education, health, housing, water, and sanitation – applied only to developing countries, while MDG 8, on the global partnership, applied to developed countries. The MDGs thereby did not apply universally to all countries, and consequently, they did not apply universally to all people living in poverty. Specifically, the MDGs ignored poverty, hunger, homelessness, lack of decent work, and other human development needs in developed countries (Saith, 2006, p. 1184; OHCHR, 2008, p. 4). In this respect, the MDGs conflicted with human rights obligations – which guarantee the rights to food, housing, decent work, an adequate standard of living, and so on for everybody universally – by excluding poor people living in rich countries, and rich countries from their obligation to address poverty within their own borders.

Fourth, the MDGs did not adequately address the human rights principles of *equality and non-discrimination* (Fukuda-Parr and Yamin, 2013). In general, the MDG framework called for aggregation of data to produce averages across a country, masking gross discrepancies and growing inequalities (Darrow, 2012). For example, MDG 1C called for halving the proportion of people who suffer from hunger. To achieve this target, countries are likely to focus on those populations easiest to reach, thus leaving those most marginalized further behind (OHCHR, 2008). The MDGs also ignored discrimination, except in the MDG 3 targets on the elimination of the gender disparity in education and in national parliaments. These targets, however, grossly oversimplified gender discrimination. Moreover, the MDGs failed to consider discrimination on the basis of ethnicity, language, religion, disability, age, or other status (Darrow, 2012). These omissions made it more likely that states would (intentionally or not) discriminate against women and other disadvantaged groups to achieve the MDG targets as it would be more difficult to reach these groups. In contrast, human rights calls for non-discrimination in processes and outcomes, and thus requires disaggregated data to ensure that policies and programs do not further impair the enjoyment of rights by marginalized groups.

Fifth, while the MDGs successfully focused attention and support on a narrow set of targets, they also resulted in marginalizing other important objectives that did not get included in the MDG framework (Fukuda-Parr and Yamin, 2013). For example, the goal of universal primary education sidelined early education, as well as secondary and tertiary education. Fukuda-Parr and Yamin explain further, "Several studies found that the goals/targets encouraged implementation approaches that were conceptually narrow, vertically structured and relied heavily on technological solutions, neglecting the need for social change and the strengthening of national institutions" (2013, p. 61).

Sidelining all but a few targets and adopting vertical interventions to address them directly conflicts with the human rights principle of *interdependency*. As recognized in the Vienna Declaration and Program of Action, as well as in the preambles to the ICCPR and the ICESCR, all human rights are indivisible, interdependent, and interrelated. Therefore, addressing one human right, while ignoring related human rights will not result in the realization of human rights for all. Transformative change in the enjoyment of the rights to food, education, and health requires building sustainable and interrelated national and local systems that abide by the human rights principles of *participation, equality and non-discrimination, accountability, universality,* and *interdependency.*

Finally, some of the goals are simply inconsistent with human rights standards. For example, MDG 1C aimed to reduce by half those people suffering from hunger, leaving the other half still suffering from hunger 15 years later. Human rights demands the immediate fulfillment of a minimum core of each social right. A state party to the ICESCR violates the right to food when it fails "to ensure the satisfaction of, at the very least, the minimum essential level required to be free from hunger" (Committee on Economic, Social and Cultural Rights, 1999, para. 17). Similarly, MDG 7D was extraordinarily unambitious as it aimed to significantly improve the lives of 100 million slum dwellers, which was only 10 percent of those living in slums (Darrow, 2012). Although technically the world achieved target 7D, the situation is worse today than it was in 2000, as the absolute number of people living in slums has risen from 792 million in 2000 to over 1 billion today (UNDESA, 2015; UN Habitat, 2016). These targets, and others, set the benchmarks far too low and thereby undermined the human rights regime, which establishes legal obligations with far higher standards and obliges parties to international human rights treaties to meet them in far less time.

The 2030 Development Agenda: another missed opportunity

The success of the MDGs, as well as the criticism of the framework, led to early discussions on a subsequent development agenda. The deadline for most of the MDG targets was 2015; however, in 2010, in its report *Keeping the promise: United to achieve the Millennium Development Goals*, the UNGA requested that the Secretary-Gneral make recommendations in his annual MDG reports for developing the post-2015 agenda (para. 81). The Secretary-General responded in his 2011 report *Accelerating progress towards the Millennium Development Goals: Options for sustained and inclusive growth and issues for advancing the United Nations development agenda beyond 2015*, stating "The post-2015 development framework is likely to have the best development impact if it emerges from an inclusive, open and transparent process with multi-stakeholder participation" (para. 68). Accordingly, the politics, formulation, purpose, and content of the SDGs differed greatly from that of the MDGs.

Participation

First, in response to criticism about the lack of *participation* in formulating the MDGs and targets, the UN led a broad global consultation on a post-2015 development agenda. In 2011, the secretary-general established a UN system task team, which brought together member states, civil society, academia, and the private sector to provide expertise and undertake research on key areas for the post-2015 framework. The task team issued 18 "Thematic Think Pieces," including one on human rights, *Towards freedom from fear and want: Human rights in the post-2015 agenda*. The think piece on human rights declared, "The central challenge of 2015 is the challenge of equality" (UN System Task Team, 2012, p. 4). It maintained that the narrow focus on economic growth in development circles has meant inadequate attention to equity, widening disparities, and growing social unrest. The human rights think piece, therefore, called for a stand-alone goal on equality, and explicit integration of equality across all other goals through disaggregation of data and equality benchmarking and monitoring (p. 6).

Additionally, in 2012, the Secretary-General appointed the High-Level Panel of Eminent Persons on the Post-2015 Development Agenda composed of 27 members from civil society, government, and the private sector, who were tasked with advising the UNGA on the post-2015 agenda. The High-Level Panel issued its report, *A new global partnership: Eradicate poverty and transform economies through sustainable development,* in May 2013, recommending 12 goals and providing illustrative targets for each goal. The UN also established an online survey, *My world 2015,* in which almost 10 million people participated by indicating the topics they thought were most important to address in the post-2015 agenda. In 2012, the UN Conference on Sustainable Development in Rio de Janeiro resulted in the UNGA resolution, *The future we want,* which committed governments to formulate a set of SDGs to replace the MDGs when they expired in 2015 (UNGA, 2012).

Importantly, in January 2013, the UNGA created the 30-member Open Working Group (OWG), which was tasked with preparing a proposal on the SDGs to be considered by the UNGA. The OWG led an inclusive process on the formulation of the SDGs, establishing 26 thematic clusters. "Human Rights" was one of the thematic clusters, and the UN Technical Support Team (TST) prepared a brief on human rights, which recommended that each SDG "should explicitly refer to the corresponding human rights standards... in a way that imports and reinforces the actual content of those rights as recognized in international law" (TST, 2013, pp. 5–6). Additionally, the TST recommended that targets "be closely and explicitly aligned with their corresponding human rights standards" (p. 6). In July 2014, the OWG issued its final report to the UNGA with its proposal for 17 SDGs and 169 targets. At the September 2015 UN Summit, the UNGA adopted the resolution *Transforming our world: The 2030 agenda for sustainable development,* embracing the OWG's 17 goals and 169 targets in substantially the same form.

The consultation on the 2030 Agenda was no doubt the broadest global consultation in history, involving governments, civil society organizations, academics, business organizations, and UN agencies. The resulting goals are listed in Table 8.2. Reactions to the SDGs were mixed (Fukuda-Parr, 2016). Certainly, there was greater participation in their formulation and the goals and targets were more comprehensive – but perhaps overwhelmingly so. Moreover, despite calls from civil society and within the UN system for the SDGs to be grounded explicitly in human rights, for the most part, they are not (Winkler and Williams, 2017). Rather, like the MDGs, they turn human rights legal obligations into mere aspirational policy goals.

Universality

One positive feature of the SDGs, in comparison to the MDGs, is that they are *universal*. They apply to all countries. While the MDGs were driven by development ministers and heads of development agencies with the purpose

Table 8.2 Sustainable Development Goals (2015)

Goal 1	End poverty in all its forms everywhere
Goal 2	End hunger, achieve food security and improved nutrition and promote sustainable agriculture
Goal 3	Ensure healthy lives and promote wellbeing for all at all ages
Goal 4	Ensure inclusive and equitable quality education and promote life-long learning opportunities for all
Goal 5	Achieve gender equality and empower all women and girls
Goal 6	Ensure availability and sustainable management of water and sanitation for all
Goal 7	Ensure access to affordable, reliable, sustainable, and modern energy for all
Goal 8	Promote sustained, inclusive, and sustainable economic growth, full and productive employment, and decent work for all
Goal 9	Build resilient infrastructure, promote inclusive and sustainable industrialization, and foster innovation
Goal 10	Reduce inequality within and among countries
Goal 11	Make cities and human settlements inclusive, safe, resilient, and sustainable
Goal 12	Ensure sustainable consumption and production patterns
Goal 13	Take urgent action to combat climate change and its impacts
Goal 14	Conserve and sustainably use the oceans, seas, and marine resources for sustainable development
Goal 15	Protect, restore, and promote sustainable use of terrestrial ecosystems, sustainably manage forests, combat desertification, and halt and reverse land degradation and halt biodiversity loss
Goal 16	Promote peaceful and inclusive societies for sustainable development, provide access to justice for all, and build effective, accountable, and inclusive institutions at all levels
Goal 17	Strengthen the means of implementation and revitalize the global partnership for sustainable development

of mobilizing support for international aid to poor countries, the SDGs were driven by environmental ministers from countries in the Global North and Global South with the purpose of creating a global agenda for sustainable development (Fukuda-Parr, 2016). In the resolution *Transforming our world*, the UNGA states,

> This is an Agenda of unprecedented scope and significance. It is accepted by all countries and is applicable to all, taking into account different national realities... These are universal goals and targets which involve the entire world, developed and developing countries alike. They are integrated and indivisible and balance the three dimensions of sustainable development.
>
> (UNGA, 2015, para 5)

As Fukuda-Parr explained, the SDGs "are universal goals that set targets for all – not just poor – countries, and are as relevant for the USA as for Liberia" (Fukuda-Parr, 2016, p. 44). Thus, while the MDGs addressed people living in poverty only in poor countries, the SDGs demand that all countries – including the USA – reduce poverty within their borders (SDG 1), achieve universal health coverage (target 3.8), and adopt fiscal, wage, and social protection policies to progressively achieve greater equality (target 10.4). Although the universality of the SDGs and targets aligns well with universal human rights, the absence of explicit human rights standards in the goals (and the vast majority of targets) is a major drawback, which negatively impacts on both the international human rights and development agendas.

Equality and non-discrimination

The attention to *equality and non-discrimination* in the SDGs is another positive feature of the 2030 Agenda. While the MDG framework called for monitoring averages across countries, thereby ignoring inequalities, the 2030 Agenda commits to leave no one behind. Toward this objective, the SDGs include SDG 10, a stand-alone goal on reducing inequality within and between countries, and SDG 5, a goal on achieving gender equality, as well as a commitment to require monitoring data be "disaggregated by income, sex, age, race, ethnicity, migration status, disability and geographic location and other characteristics relevant in national contexts" (UNGA, 2015, para. 74(g)). Consequently, at first glance, the 2030 Agenda looks promising. Digging deeper, however, the targets do not fully carry out the objectives of those who advocated for these commitments.

SDG 10, for example, calls for reducing inequality within and among countries. Target 10.1 is the sole target to address the extreme income inequality within countries. It states: "By 2030, progressively achieve and sustain income growth of the bottom 40 percent of the population at a rate higher than the national average" (UNGA, 2015, para. 21). This target addresses only the bottom 40 percent; it does not address the extreme inequality between the bottom 40 percent and the top 10 percent or top 1 percent (MacNaughton, 2017). Overall, inequality between the top and the bottom might actually increase while the bottom 40 percent rises faster than the average. Additionally, the target depends on income growth. If there is no income growth, the bottom 40 percent gets no benefit (MacNaughton, 2017). Finally, the target is not a target at all. It is a *means* to reduce *poverty*, not an *end* evidencing a reduction in *inequality*. A meaningful target on income inequality would require, at minimum, that the bottom 40 percent have a greater share of national income by 2030 and that the top 10 percent have a smaller share (Pogge and Sengupta, 2015).

SDG 10 includes two other targets that might be more promising. SDG target 10.2 calls for promoting "social, economic and political inclusion of all, irrespective of age, sex, disability, race, ethnicity, origin, religion or economic or other status" (UNGA, 2015, p. 21). Unfortunately, the target does not define any benchmark for countries to achieve; it merely calls for *promotion* of inclusion. Target 10.3 states, "Ensure equal opportunity and reduce inequalities of outcome, including by eliminating discriminatory laws, policies and practices and promoting appropriate legislation, policies and action in this regard" (p. 21). Again, the "target" does not define any specific outcome, nor does it include a deadline. Both targets 10.2 and 10.3 provide little in concrete terms upon which civil society may demand accountability, although both targets are closely related to international human rights standards on non-discrimination.

Beyond SDG 10, several targets focus on reaching specific marginalized groups (Winkler and Satterthwaite, 2017). For example, target 2.3 on small-scale food producers refers to indigenous peoples and pastoralists, and target 4.5 seeks to ensure equal access to education for persons with disabilities and indigenous peoples. Winkler and Satterthwaite maintain, however, that target 17.18 is perhaps the most important target in terms of addressing inequalities as it calls for capacity building to enable developing countries to produce data "disaggregated by income, gender, age, race, ethnicity, migratory status, disability, geographic location and other characteristics relevant in national contexts" (UNGA, 2015, p. 27). Only with such disaggregated data can inequalities be identified and addressed to ensure that no one is left behind. In their recent study, however, Winkler and Satterthwaite find that "racial and ethnic variables have been largely ignored in the first few years of SDG monitoring, despite the fact that racial and ethnic discrimination are among the most prevalent and persistent forms of discrimination" (2017, p. 1074). In sum, the stand-alone goal on inequality and the commitment to disaggregated data are not likely to fulfill the desired outcomes unless linked to human rights standards.

Accountability

From a human rights perspective, perhaps the most disturbing thing about the SDGs is that, despite strong support from the UN human rights mechanisms and civil society, they are not stated explicitly in terms of human rights. In its preamble, the resolution *Transforming our world* refers to human rights 11 times, including in two references to the Universal Declaration of Human Rights. Indeed, the resolution states,

> The new Agenda is guided by the purposes and principles of the Charter of the United Nations, including full respect for international law. It is grounded in the Universal Declaration of Human Rights, international human rights treaties, the Millennium Declaration and the 2005 World Summit outcome. It is informed by other instruments such as the Declaration on the Right to Development.
>
> (UNGA, 2015, para. 10)

Yet, the 17 goals are not framed in terms of human rights. They do not aim to achieve the rights to food, water, housing, health, education, and decent work for all. And only one target, target 4.7, specifically mentions "human rights" as part of the content of education. Although targets here and there mention specific rights – such as labor rights in targets 8.7 and 8.8 and sexual and reproductive rights in target 5.6 – this is not a human rights-based agenda. This is curious in view of the strong advocacy for grounding the 2030 Agenda in human rights, the explicit commitment in the *Transforming our world* resolution to grounding the 2030 Agenda in human rights, and the commitments that all UN members have made in the Universal Declaration of Human Rights and international human rights treaties to realizing these rights. However, there is no doubt, given this background, the UN members intentionally chose not to frame the SDGs in explicit human rights language.

The failure to do so has several consequences. First, this means that development and human rights continue on parallel tracks, while they could be reinforcing each other (see Alston, 2005). In some circumstances, it will result in conflicts between the development agenda and the human rights agenda, although human rights must take priority as they impose legal obligations. Most importantly, however, by failing to align the two agendas, the 2030 Agenda misses the opportunity to enhance accountability for the SDGs by linking them to human rights legal obligations and human rights mechanisms of accountability. Moreover, the commitment to a review of each country's progress every four years was removed from the 2030 Agenda final language and the "monitoring and accountability" chapter was renamed "follow-up and review." These signs suggest that "the accountability gaps that have plagued development policy and practice for decades" will continue under the SDG framework (Donald, 2016). Indeed, it is likely the desire to avoid a robust system of accountability that motivated UN members to choose not to frame the SDGs explicitly in terms of human rights legal obligations.

Interdependency

Finally, some of the SDG targets are inconsistent with human rights standards. They simply set the bar far too low. For example, SDG target 1.1 states, "By 2030, eradicate extreme poverty for all people everywhere, currently measured as people living on less than $1.25 a day" (UNGA, 2015, p. 15). In contrast, the Universal Declaration of Human Rights states, "Everyone has the right to a standard of living adequate for the health and well-being of himself and of his family, including food, clothing, housing and medical care and necessary social services" (article 25). There is no doubt that the right to an adequate standard of living requires more than pushing people over the target 1.1 threshold for "extreme poverty." Target 1.1 sets the bar too low (Pogge, 2004). Moreover, target 1.2 reiterates the problem in the MDGs, by calling for a reduction by half the proportion of people living in poverty under national definitions. This target, like MDG target 1.A, would leave half the population still living in poverty 15 years later. SDG targets 1.1 and 1.2 are also interdependent with many other targets, making it difficult, if not impossible, to reach them. Given the extreme wealth in the world, there is no reason for anyone to live in poverty today, much less for targets that aim to leave them in poverty beyond 2030.

Conclusion

The SDGs improve upon the MDGs in many ways. The formulation of the goals and targets was carried out through an unprecedented global consultation involving millions of people. The SDG framework is universal in that it applies to all countries, and it gives more attention to equality and non-discrimination through a stand-alone goal (SDG 10) and commitments to disaggregated data for many targets. The framework is also far more comprehensive than the MDG framework, recognizing that development objectives for food, housing, water, education, health, and decent work, among others, are all interrelated and interdependent, and therefore, it is not sustainable to address these issues in silos. Nonetheless, the SDG framework leaves the development and human rights agendas following separate paths, like "ships passing in the night" as Philip Alston once said (2005, p. 755). The failure to unite development and human rights agendas is to the detriment of both. Certainly, in the context of the new SDG framework, the failure to explicitly ground the goals and targets in the human rights legal obligations of the UN members detracts from the ability of civil society, as well as UN and domestic human rights mechanisms, to hold states to account for the commitments they made in the 2030 Agenda. Yet, there are still opportunities to unite the two agendas in the implementation strategies, which would improve policy coherence, as well as monitoring and accountability, helping to achieve the SDG targets and realize human rights and dignity for all.

Discussion questions

1   What are the advantages and disadvantages of using quantitative targets for a global development agenda?
2   In what ways have the MDGs and SDGs conflicted with the human rights obligations of UN members?
3   Why are UN member states reluctant to adopt their international human rights obligations as explicit development policy goals?
4   How could global human rights and development agendas be aligned and integrated to reinforce each other?

Key primary documents on human rights and development

Charter of the United Nations (UN Charter) (1945). Available at: www.un.org/en/cha rter-united-nations/

International Covenant on Civil and Political Rights (ICCPR) (1966). UNGA res. 2200A (XXI), UN Doc. A/6316.
International Covenant on Economic, Social and Cultural Rights (ICESCR) (1966). UNGA res. 2200A (XXI), UN Doc. A/6316.
United Nations General Assembly (UNGA) (1986). *Declaration on the right to development.* UN Doc. A/41/128. December 4.
World Conference on Human Rights, Vienna Declaration and Programme of Action, UN Doc. A/CONF.157/23 (June 25, 1993).
United Nations General Assembly (UNGA) (2000). *United national millennium declaration.* UN Doc. A/RES/55/2. September 18.
United Nations Secretary-General (UN Secretary-General) (2001). *Road map towards the implementation of the United Nations millennium declaration.* UN Doc. A/56/326. September 6.
United Nations General Assembly (UNGA) (2015). *Transforming our world: The 2030 agenda for sustainable development.* UN Doc. A/Res/70/1. October 21.

References

Alston, P. (2005). Ships passing in the night: The current state of the human rights and development debate seen through the lens of the Millennium Development Goals. *Human Rights Quarterly*, 27(3), pp. 755–829.
Committee on Economic, Social and Cultural Rights (1999). General comment 12: The right to adequate food (art. 11). UN Doc E/C.12/1999/5, May 12.
Darrow, M. (2012). The Millennium Development Goals: milestones or millstones? Human rights priorities for the post-2015 development agenda. *Yale Human Rights and Development Law Journal*, 15(1), pp. 55–127.
Donald, K. (2016). Promising the world: Accountability and the SDGs. *Health and Human Rights Journal Blog*. Available at: www.hhrjournal.org/2016/01/promising-the-world-accountability-and-the-sdgs/ [Accessed May 1, 2018].
Fukuda-Parr, S. (2016). From the Millennium Development Goals to the Sustainable Development Goals: Shifts in purpose, concept, and politics of global goal setting. *Gender and Development*, 24(1), pp. 43–52.
Fukuda-Parr, S. and Yamin, A.E. (2013). The power of numbers: A critical review of MDG targets for human development and human rights. *Development*, 56(1), pp. 58–65.
Hulme, D. (2010). Lessons from the making of the MDGs: Human development meets results-based management in an unfair world. *IDS Bulletin*, 41(1), pp. 15–25.
Joint Statement by the UN Committee on Economic, Social and Cultural Rights and the UN Commission on Human Rights' Special Rapporteurs on Economic, Social and Cultural Rights (2002). *The Millennium Development Goals and economic, social and cultural rights*. Available at: www2.ohchr.org/english/bodies/cescr/docs/statements/MDGandESCRs-2002.doc [Accessed May 1, 2018].
Langford, M. (2010). Poverty of rights: Six ways to fix the MDGs. *IDS Bulletin*, 41(1), pp. 83–91.
MacNaughton, G. (2017). Vertical inequalities: Are the SDGs and human rights up to the challenges? *International Journal of Human Rights*, 21(8), pp. 1050–1072.
MacNaughton, G. and Frey, D.F. (2010). Decent work, human rights and the Millennium Development Goals. *Hastings Race and Poverty Law Journal*, 7(2), pp. 303–352.

Office of the High Commissioner for Human Rights (OHCHR) (2008). *Claiming the Millennium Development Goals: A human rights approach.* Available at: www.ohchr.org/Documents/Publications/Claiming_MDGs_en.pdf [Accessed May 12, 2018].

Pogge, T. (2004). The first United Nations Millennium Development Goal: A cause for celebration? *Journal of Human Development* 5(3), pp. 377–397.

Pogge, T. and Sengupta, M. (2015). The Sustainable Development Goals (SDGs) as draft: Nice idea, poor execution. *Washington International Law Journal*, 24(3), pp. 571–587.

Robinson, M. (2010). The MDG-human rights nexus to 2015 and beyond. *IDS Bulletin*, 41(1), pp. 80–82.

Saith, A. (2006). From universal values to Millennium Development Goals: Lost in translation. *Development and Change*, 37(6), pp. 1167–1199.

UN Habitat (2016). *Slum Alamanc 2015 2016: Tracking improvement in the lives of slumdwellers.* Nairobi: UN Habitat.

UN System Task Team on the Post-2015 U.N. Development Agenda (2012). *Towards freedom from fear and want: Human rights in the post-2015 agenda, Thematic think piece.* Geneva: OHCHR. Available at: www.un.org/en/development/desa/policy/untaskteam_undf/thinkpieces/9_human_rights.pdf. [Accessed May 1, 2018].

United Nations Department of Economic and Social Affairs (2015). *The Millennium Development Goals report 2015.* New York: United Nations.

United Nations General Assembly (UNGA) (1948). *Universal Declaration of Human Rights.* UNGA res. 217A (III), UN Doc. A/810 at 71. December 10.

United Nations General Assembly (UNGA) (2010). *Keeping the promise: United to achieve the Millennium Development Goals.* GA Res. 65/1, UN Doc A/RES/65/1.

United Nations General Assembly (UNGA) (2012). *The future we want.* UN Doc A/RES/66/288. September 12.

United Nations Inter-Agency Technical Support Team (TST) (2013). *TST issues brief 18: Human rights including the right to development.* Presented for the UN General Assembly Open Working Group 6th Session. Available at: https://sustainabledevelopment.un.org/content/documents/2391TST%20Human%20Rights%20Issues%20Brief_FINAL.pdf [Accessed May 1, 2018].

Uvin, P. (2010). From the right to development to the right-based approach: How "human rights" entered development. In: A. Cornwall and D. Eade, eds, *Deconstructing development discourse: buzzwords and fuzzwords.* Rugby: Practical Action Publishing and Oxfam.

Winkler, I.T. and Satterthwaite, M.L. (2017). Leaving no one behind? Persistent inequalities in the SDGs. *International Journal of Human Rights*, 21(8), pp. 1073–1097.

Winkler, I.T. and Williams, C. (2017). The Sustainable Development Goals and human rights: A critical early review. *International Journal of Human Rights*, 21(8), pp. 1023–1028.

Further reading

Civil Society Reflection Group on the 2030 Agenda for Sustainable Development (2017). *Spotlight on sustainable development: Reclaiming policies for the public.* Available at: www.2030spotlight.org/sites/default/files/download/spotlight_170626_final_web.pdf

MacNaughton, G. (2015). Human rights education for all: A proposal for the post-2015 international development agenda. *Washington International Law Journal*, 24(3), pp. 537–569.

Nelson, P. and Dorsey, E. (2018). Who practices rights-based development? A progress report on work at the nexus of human rights and development. *World Development*, 104, pp. 97–107.

Reflection Group on the 2030 Agenda for Sustainable Development (2016). *Spotlight on sustainable development*. Available at: www.2030spotlight.org/sites/default/files/contentpix/spotlight/pdfs/Agenda-2030_engl_160713_WEB.pdf

Williams, C. and Blaiklock, A. (2018). Human rights informed the Sustainable Development Goals, but are they lost in New Zealand's neoliberal aid program? In: G. MacNaughton and D. F. Frey, eds, *Economic and social rights in a neoliberal world*. Cambridge: Cambridge University Press, pp. 236–260.

9 Addressing General Recommendation no. 35 from an intersectional perspective on violence, gender, and disability in Mexico

Ana María Sánchez Rodríguez

Introduction

Violence is a human rights violation that affects disproportionally more women than men worldwide (World Health Organization, 2014, p. 8). The Convention on the Elimination of All Forms of Discrimination against Women (CEDAW) defines the term "discrimination against women" as

> any distinction, exclusion or restriction made on the basis of sex which has the effect or purpose of impairing or nullifying the recognition, enjoyment or exercise by women, irrespective of their marital status, on a basis of equality of men and women, of human rights and fundamental freedoms in the political, economic, social, cultural, civil or any other field.
>
> (CEDAW, 1979, article 1)

The CEDAW committee adopted by the United Nations General Assembly in 1979 has articulated 37 general recommendations (GRs). GRs are a tool used by the committees of the United Nations human rights treaties which elaborate these to address a pressing issue that needs further interpretation for state parties to implement the CEDAW.

This chapter focuses on GR no. 35 on gender-based violence against women to analyze intersections amongst gender, violence, and disability. The CEDAW committee updated its GR no. 19: "25 years of CEDAW General Recommendation No. 19 (1992): Accelerating efforts on violence against women," and invited interested parties to submit comments. The CEDAW committee stressed on the first draft of GR no. 19 "that women affected by particular circumstances or who belong, or are perceived as belonging to certain groups, may be subject to specific and intersecting forms of discrimination." At the same time the CEDAW committee is acknowledging "that gender-based violence may affect some women to different degrees, or in different ways than other women because they experience varying and intersecting forms of discrimination" (CEDAW Committee, 2016).

GR no. 35 on gender-based violence against women was adopted by the CEDAW committee in July 2017 and like GR no. 19 addresses the intersecting forms of discrimination between gender and other intersections such as disability. Intersectionality is a cross-cutting issue in human rights conventions that refers to multiple discrimination (Chow, 2016). This chapter argues that a better understanding of intersectionality in GR no. 35 can be used to implement comprehensive policies to end violence against marginalized women such as women and girls with disabilities. The purpose of this chapter is to analyze intersectionality in GR no. 35 focusing on gender and disability. Then, this chapter addresses Mexico as a case study and explores intersectionality policy analysis in Mexican policies and how these are equipped to implement GR no. 35 in relation to women with disabilities. The chapter's objective is to demonstrate the need for a deeper understanding of an intersectionality analysis in human rights instruments to address multiple discrimination and the importance in policy to understand intersectionality.

The first section of the chapter explains intersectionality focusing on the intersectional analysis for policy and further discussing it as a tool to design and implement policies. Intersectionality is a critical feminist theory that focuses on power and inequalities across diverse groups (Bowleg, 2012; Choo and Ferree, 2010; Dhamoon, 2010). Human rights benefits from an intersectional analysis by taking into account different forms of discrimination and recognizing that different groups of women experience violence otherwise. There are different approaches of intersectionality in policy analysis (Hankivsky et al., 2012) that can be used to implement the CEDAW and the committee's GRs. This chapter explores how to address intersectionality as a conceptual model to put human rights into practice.

The second section explores GR no. 35 by looking at the main additions and focusing on the state's role to end violence against women. The purpose of the second section is to understand how intersections interplay with violence and use this to clarify the role of the state in addressing intersectionality in gender and disability as well as other intersections. This section explores how intersectionality addresses intersections amongst gender and disability that can be useful for state parties to address violence against women.

The third section explores Mexico as a case study and a signatory country of the CEDAW (1981) and the Convention on the Rights of Persons with Disabilities (CRPD; 2007). This section analyzes Mexican policies by applying intersectional policy analysis to tackle violence against women and looks in particular at women and girls with disabilities and GR no. 35. This last section reviews policies in place to end violence against women and raises the question of how to use intersectionality in state policies to end violence against women with disabilities and support state human rights compliance of the CEDAW and other related human rights international treaties.

The chapter concludes with the challenges ahead to implement policies with an intersectional approach by having discussed the following research questions: What is intersectionality and how can it be used in policy analysis (first section)? How is intersectionality addressed in GR no. 35 in relation to violence against women, in particular women with disabilities (second section)? What does intersectionality applied in policy analysis to end violence against women look like in the case of Mexico (third section)?

Intersectionality as an approach for policy analysis

Intersectionality is a major contribution of feminist scholarship and is considered a theory and a research method (Hancock, 2007). The intersectionality approach is rooted in critical race theory traced in Crenshaw (1989, 1991) and Collins (1986). The intersectionality theory recognizes and analyses different systems of oppression impacting the lives and experiences of different groups of women. Crenshaw was the first to coin the term of intersectionality (1989) to analyze violence against black women in the United States and to explain legal discrimination against them. Crenshaw's iconic "traffic in an intersection" metaphor is used to explain the intersections between race and gender:

> Discrimination, like traffic through an intersection, may flow in one direction, and it may flow in another. If an accident happens in an intersection, it can be caused by cars traveling from any number of directions and, sometimes, from all of them. Similarly, if a Black woman is harmed because she is in the intersection, her injury could result from sex discrimination or race discrimination.
>
> (Crenshaw, 1989, p. 149)

Intersectionality as a research paradigm recognizes the hegemonic (ideas, cultures, and ideologies), structural (social institutions), disciplinary (bureaucratic hierarchies and administrative practices), and interpersonal (routinized interactions among individuals) (Hancock, 2007, p. 74). Hancock incorporates other dimensions to the intersectional complexity: (1) diversity within; (2) categorical multiplicity to explain the categories and their dimensions; (3) categorical intersections between categories; (4) time dynamics or context analysis; and (5) individual institutional interactions (Hancock, 2013, pp. 282–283). Categorical multiplicity requires an understanding to acknowledge intersections that are most troubling and significant for particular groups such as women with disabilities.

Aiming to have a more coherent understanding of what intersectionality is, and considering a growing consensus, Collins defines it as a feminist theory of identity with the purpose of "fostering critical examination of how social structures and related identity categories such as gender, race, and class interact on multiple levels, resulting in social inequality" (Collins, 2015, slide 10). Intersectionality is also defined as a system of interactions "between inequality-creating social structures (i.e. of power relations), symbolic representations (social practices, norms and values that operate within a society, Winker and Degele, 2011, p. 59) and identity constructions that are context-specific, topic-orientated and inextricably linked to social praxis" (2011, p. 54). Choo and Ferree (2010, p. 131) reviewed three dimensions that have become important for theorizing intersectionality: "(1) the perspectives of multiply-marginalized people; (2) a model that analyzes main effects into interactions; (3) and a model that focuses on systems where multiple institutions overlap to reproduce inequalities."

Intersectionality is a complex concept, attempting to capture the multi-dimensional categories that contribute to a person's vulnerability, at the same time taking into account the socioeconomic and political contexts that reproduce inequalities.

There are different ways in which intersectionality analysis is conducted and that alone is not sufficient for understanding all the complex interactions (Lombardo and Agustín, 2012; Walby, 2007; Verloo, 2006). Walby (2007, pp. 451–452) describes at least five approaches to doing intersectionality analysis, which could be divided into two sets of analysis: the first set addresses the concept of system and the second set rejects the notion of system. The approaches analyze social inequalities and the system in which they are located such as class and the economic system. The second set of approaches rejects the notion of a single system and analyzes the complexity of social relations in different systems, taking into account different domains of institutions in the polity, economy, and civil society areas. The intersections in the second set of approaches are analyzed considering overlapping systems that produce inequalities respectively to race, gender, class, and disability. Other intersectionality policy analysis methods include McCall's approach of intracategorical analysis, which observes the relationships of inequality in social groups by understanding categories as dynamic, not static, and explores whether these inequalities existed before (2005, p. 1785).

Intersectionality remains an ongoing theoretical and methodological problem to scholars; intersections are multidimensional and multilayered and that makes it hard to address all at the same time (McCall, 2005, p. 1772). Intersectionality analyses focus on power relations and the crossing nodes where intersections meet and reproduce discrimination and exclusion. Intersectionality also challenges how power is conceived and given by depriving some groups and providing privileges to other groups. In the end, the purpose of an intersectional analysis is to contribute to disabling the structures of oppression by considering power relations and the geographical and historical context (Weber, 1998, 2001). The structures of oppression of disability or any other category are systems that are simultaneously expressed and embedded in all social institutions (1998, p. 18).

In sum, intersectionality is a theory concerned with structures that produce and reproduce exclusion and inequalities tackling intertwined identities of discriminated groups. The intersectionality is also a method for research, providing the researcher the multidimensional lenses to analyze complex interactions at the individual and collective levels to explain inequality.

Intersectionality applied to policy analysis seeks to understand why and how inequalities are produced against different groups (Hankivsky and Cormier, 2011). Lombardo and Verloo (2009, p. 470) left Crenshaw's "political intersectionality" to revise the dynamics of privilege and exclusion that overlook intersections. Hankivsky and Cormier (2011, p. 220) identified three approaches to incorporate intersectionality in policies: (1) space as an analytical dimension in intersectionality policy analysis (Rönnblom, 2008); (2) an intersectional policy process analysis (Bishwakarma et al., 2007 in Hankivsky and Cormier, 2011); and (3) the multistrand project (Parken and Young, 2008).

The first approach, developed by Rönnblom, addresses the importance of "space" in policy analysis (Hankivsky and Cormier, 2011). Rönnblom defines "space" as relational, interactive, and in constant change to contextualize power dynamics. The "space" is a key component in policy analysis that situates the researcher at the intersections of categories that are excluded for examining how the space, as defined above, is produced. The space(s) contextualizes and provides the researcher an understanding of her/ his position in relation to the categories and their intersections explored (Rönnblom, 2008, pp. 52–53). The second approach addresses intersectionality in all the policy-making process stages (agenda setting, policy formulation, policy implementation, and policy assessment). These authors considered intersectionality as a theory and a method that captures the complexity of the policy problems of marginalized populations. In addressing the policy process, Rönnblom argues that the intersectional case study of problem definition and policy formulation is the first step in multidimensional thinking. Parken and Young (2008) developed the third approach. This approach, known as the multistrand project, considers a "six-strand" equal treatment legislation covering gender, disability, race, sexual orientation, age, and religion to promote equality and human rights (Hankivsky and Cormier, 2011).

Parken and Young's intersectional model incorporates gender equality and human rights in policy work, an exercise that was undertaken in Wales in 2007 with the multistrand project. They identified five steps in their method: (1) using equality expertise to identify areas of inequality ripe for investigation; (2) mapping the equality dimensions of the policy field, data collection of the different strands; (3) visioning and implementing the redesigned policies; (4) road testing, including uncovering unintended results; and (5) monitoring and evaluating the results (2008). The intersectional approach facilitates a cross-strand examination avoiding any hierarchy across the six strands.

The intersectionality-based policy analysis (IBPA) developed by Hankivsky et al. (2012), is another approach to analyzing policy. The IBPA provides core guiding principles and 12 overarching questions with which to analyze intersectionality in policies, in particular health policies. The principles are: intersecting categories, multilevel analysis, power, reflexivity, time and space, diverse knowledge, social justice, and equity. These constructs are incorporated in the analysis of policies and can be used to explore policies of state and policy proposals of non-state actors that address gender-based violence against women with disabilities. IBPA questions focus on the current policies, e.g., how are groups differentially affected by this representation of the "problem"? Additional questions target policy implementation and tackle inequalities among groups, such as where and how interventions can be made to address the problem (by reducing inequities among groups). Other IBPA questions target social change and power structure analysis, e.g., how the process of engaging in an IBPA has transformed the ways in which researchers, policy makers, and civil society organizations engage in the work of policy development, implementation, and evaluation. The IBPA remains a tool for policy analysis attempting to address policy implementation and the stages of policy formation and policy evaluation. Hankivsky et al. remind us that policy implementation should take into consideration accountability and policy monitoring, and should include questions related to policy implementation, should address who is responsible to implement the policy and encourage solidarity and coalition across different interested groups (Hankivsky et al., 2012, p. 41).

The intersectional policy analysis approaches presented here show different angles to address how policies consider intersectionality and put it into practice. Nonetheless, an intersectional analysis of policy will focus first on the representations of the intersections and if these are taken into account in policy, and how. The Mexican case study will address the question of how women with disabilities are being brought into policies to end violence and how GR no. 35 offers better guidance to comply with state human rights obligations.

Intersectionality is not a novel concept in human rights, but it remains undefined in the international human rights conventions (Chow, 2016). The concept of intersectionality in the CEDAW is used to recognize differences amongst women experiencing violence and as criteria to understand the scope of state obligations addressing appropriate measures (CEDAW Committee, 2017, p. 12). The CEDAW was adopted in 1979 by the United Nations General Assembly and does not address intersectionality. The CEDAW recognizes discrimination on the basis of sex and not on other categories such as disability, ethnicity, and nationality (1979, article 1).

The CEDAW highlights discrimination between men and women based on their sex, and differences amongst women are not addressed (article 1). The CEDAW Committee GR no. 28 on core obligations of state parties defines intersectionality as

> a basic concept for understanding the scope of the general obligations of States parties contained in article 2. The discrimination of women based on sex and gender is inextricably linked with other factors that affect women, such as race, ethnicity, religion or belief, health, status, age,

class, caste and sexual orientation and gender identity. Discrimination on the basis of sex or gender may affect women belonging to such groups to a different degree or in different ways to men.

(2010, para. 18)

GR no. 28, para. 26 goes further and endorses policies to: "identify women within the jurisdiction of the State party (including non-citizen, migrant, refugee, asylum-seeking and stateless women) as the rights-bearers, with particular emphasis on the groups of women who are most marginalized and who may suffer from various forms of intersectional discrimination."

GR no. 28 makes progress in conceiving the importance of intersectionality but remains imprecise on how the states can interpret intersectionality to legislate and design policies. Getting intersectionality right in human rights remains a struggle in law and practice (Bond, 2001). Many laws addressing discrimination account for one or two forms of intersecting forms of discrimination but fail to capture the complexities of women's lives and the intersection with their identities.

The next section analyzes intersectionality in GR no. 35, how intersectionality is defined, and how the intersections are framed in relation to violence against women. This section pays special attention to gender, disability, and violence to explore policies to end violence against women with disabilities.

General Recommendation no. 35 on gender-based violence and intersectionality: a focus on gender and disability

CEDAW does not include a definition on violence against women and gender-based violence, and the CEDAW committee attempted to clarify it. GR no. 19 issued by the CEDAW committee is on violence against women, the term employed in this GR is violence against women and gender violence interchangeably. GR no. 19 defines gender-based violence as "a form of discrimination that seriously inhibits women's ability to enjoy rights and freedoms on a basis of equality with men" (CEDAW Committee, 1992, para. 1). Gender-based violence is included in the definition of discrimination in article 1 of the CEDAW (CEDAW Committee, 1992, para. 6). GR no. 35 distinguishes between violence against women and gender-based violence, clarifying that the definition in article 1 of GR no. 19 refers to violence against women. GR no. 35's preference is the term "gender-based violence against women," indicating that this term stresses violence against women not as an individual problem but as a social problem (CEDAW Committee, 2017, para. 9). However, the use of one or the other term is problematic. Even though GR no. 35 attempts to clarify the scope of gender-based violence and differentiate it from violence against women, the term is elusive in human rights instruments (Mason, 2013).

GR no. 35 refers to intersectionality as intersecting forms of discrimination in relation to gender-based violence. It highlights the negative impact on women that different intersecting forms of discrimination have and refers to some of these intersections, including:

> women's ethnicity/race, indigenous or minority status, colour, socioeconomic status and/or caste, language, religion or belief, political opinion, national origin, marital status, maternity, parental status, age, urban or rural location, health status, disability, property ownership, being lesbian, bisexual, transgender or intersex, illiteracy, seeking asylum, being a refugee, internally displaced or stateless, widowhood, migration status, heading households, living with HIV/AIDS, being deprived of liberty, and being in prostitution, as well as trafficking in women, situations of armed conflict, geographical remoteness and the stigmatization of women who fight for their rights, including human rights defenders.
>
> (CEDAW Committee, 2017, para. 12, pp. 4–5)

Disability has been excluded as a category that interrelates with gender, ignoring that women with disabilities are at more risk of suffering violence compared to other women (International Network of Women with Disabilities, 2010 in Ballan and Freyer, 2012, pp. 1083–1084). Policies to end violence rarely address specific measures for women with disabilities. Disability becomes an issue of the CRPD and gender an issue addressed by the CEDAW.

The CRPD recognizes the multiple discrimination against women and girls and emphasizes gender- and age-sensitive support for persons with disabilities to end violence against women (CRPD, 2006, articles 6 and 16). Moreover, the CRPD committee published General Comment no. 3 on article 6: Women with disabilities (CRPD Committee, 2016), and highlighted three main areas of concern: (1) violence; (2) sexual and reproductive health and rights; and (3) discrimination and concern for "the prevalence of multiple discrimination and intersectional discrimination against women with disabilities, on account of their gender, disability and other factors" (para. 10). GR no. 3 describes the acts of violence against women with disabilities, e.g., abandonment; the absence of free and informed consent and legal compulsion; neglect, including the withholding or denial of access to medication; the removal or control of communication aids; and the refusal to assist in communicating (2016, para. 31).

Recognition of intersectionality amongst violence and disability is necessary to move forward to defining policies that address women with disabilities' specific needs. GR no. 35 ensures that all prevention and protection services are accessible including information and facilitating the inclusion of discriminated groups (CEDAW Committee, 2017). In this sense, in GR no. 35, intersectional analysis for making policies would include questions for policy such as: (1) What are the lived circumstances (risks) of women with disabilities suffering violence (compared to women without disabilities)? (2) How are women with disabilities represented and included in policy to end violence (compared to men with disabilities and to women without disabilities)? (3) What are the institutions, their practices, and interactions with women with disabilities? The next section analyzes the Mexican case by looking at these questions.

Implementing General Recommendation no. 35: intersections between violence, gender, and disability in Mexico

Mexico has a population of 120 million: 61.5 million women and 58.5 million men. 7.1 million people have disabilities: 3.8 million women and 3.3 million men (INEGI, 2014). The disadvantages of the disability population in Mexico are numerous: there are barriers to accessibility, health, work, and education, but violence against women with disabilities has not been a priority in policy. Furthermore, there are few organizations led by persons with disabilities, and other organizations have been founded by family members of persons with disabilities to rectify the problem of lack of state services, but not necessarily to address violence against women with disabilities (Brogna, 2009). In relation to violence against persons with disabilities there are not consolidated data and there are no disaggregated data for the number of women with disabilities that have suffered violence compared to women without disabilities. The survey that gathers data on intimate partner violence and gendered violence is the National Survey on Households (ENDIREH). The 2016 ENDIREH survey indicated that in Mexico 43.9 percent of women older than 15 have suffered intimate partner violence. This survey provides data on the prevalence of different types of violence against women; for example, 49 percent of women have suffered psychological violence, referring to receiving threats, being humiliated, and underappreciated. Economic violence is another form of violence against women impacting 29 percent of women and occurs when women are forbidden from working and studying or restricted from access to property and money. Physical violence represents a life-threatening form of violence against women and has affected 34 percent of women. Sexual violence is a form of violence against women in which a woman is forced by her partner to have sexual relations and has impacted 41.3 percent of women.

Historically, persons with disabilities were under the mandate of the National System for Integral Family Development (in Spanish: *Sistema Nacional para el Desarrollo Integral de la Familia-SNDIF*). The SNDIF is a social affairs entity and its mission is to promote welfare in particular for children, women, indigenous migrants, displaced populations, the elderly, persons with disabilities, persons with addictions, etc. (Social Affairs Act, 2014, article 4). The SNDIF provides care and describes the services for persons with disabilities to fulfill their basic needs that include legal and social counseling, rehabilitation, and work inclusion. Social affairs policy bodies do not address gendered violence against women with disabilities and defines persons with disabilities as persons with impairments or special needs, while other policy bodies such as the National Commission to prevent and eradicate violence against women (Conavim) and the Women's National Institute (Inmujeres) address violence against women, but do not define women with disabilities' specific needs. Welfare institutions support persons with disabilities, but do not recognize persons with disabilities as having rights (Soto Martínez, 2011). Social affairs institutions support persons with disabilities because of their disability without addressing their rights (p. 35). The differentiated focus of programs to support persons with disabilities and those to end violence result in making women with disabilities invisible. There is a lack of policy and there are no resources allocated for specific actions, prevention campaigns, or professionalized staff to support the specific needs of women with disabilities (Sánchez Rodríguez, 2017).

Mexico has advanced in legislation to end violence against women. The General Act on Women's Access to a Life Free of Violence enacted in 2007 highlights the policies to end violence against women and incorporates the principle of non-discrimination, but does not address intersectionality. The act establishes a national structure, which includes federal and local government, and it is chaired at the highest political level; this system discusses the strategies to end violence. Violence against women is defined as a harmful act based on their gender (GAWALFV, 2007, article 5, IV), and gender perspective is defined as an approach to uncover gender oppression as inequality and injustice (IX).

Mexican legislation, policies, and programs for persons with disabilities are separated from those targeting violence against women. National policies include the National Comprehensive Program to Prevent, Assist, Punish and Eradicate Violence against Women 2014–2018 (PIPASEVM, 2014) and the National Program for the Development and Inclusion of Persons with Disabilities 2014–2018. These programs are conducted by different policy bodies, the PIPASEVM by the National Commission to prevent and eradicate violence against women (Conavim) and the second by the National Council for the development and inclusion of persons with disabilities (Conadis). Both Conadis and Conavim do not coordinate actions to end violence against women with disabilities when both of them mention specific actions. The PIPASEVM under Conavim adopts a so-called differentiated and specialized approach for the implementation of policies that recognize that there are groups such as persons with disabilities that are worse off and that the state needs to assist them accordingly (2014, p. 48). The second program addresses specific actions to end violence against women with disabilities such as: (1) to promote that all emergency shelters for women victims of violence adapt their spaces for women with disabilities; (2) to develop programs or actions to prevent, protect, and assist persons with disabilities against exploitation, violence, abuse, torture, and other cruel, inhuman, or degrading treatment; (3) to support civil society organization projects that promote the rights of persons with disabilities; (4) to create mechanisms to highlight gender-based violence and discrimination against women, girls, and older women with disabilities; and (5) to promote legal counseling services on disability, discrimination, and violence given by institutions and civil society organizations.

The CRPD committee in their concluding observations (2014) on the initial report submitted by Mexico in February 2011 made specific recommendations regarding women and girls with disabilities emphasizing intersectional discrimination and clarifying some of the measures that the Mexican state should adopt, such as compiling disaggregated data and having indicators to account for intersectional discrimination. The CRPD committee also expressed its concern regarding the limited access to justice for persons with disabilities and, in particular, women and girls with disabilities who are victims of violence. It recommended implementation of article 13: access to justice (CRPD Committee, 2014). In relation to article 16, the committee urged the state:

> To implement existing legislative and policy measures to prevent violence against women and girls with disabilities and to provide protection and reparation to those who fall victim to it. The Committee requests the State party to periodically compile data and statistics on the situation of women and girls with disabilities in respect of violence, exploitation and abuse, including feminicide.
>
> (article 16, para. 34)

In the end, it is important to understand how the policy bodies that serve women and persons with disabilities are directly incorporating these strategies. The Mexican government has initiated and concluded numerous programs to address their human rights obligations, but these programs are fragmented and do not contribute strategies or goals to end violence against women with disabilities (Sánchez Rodríguez, 2017). The General Act on Women's Access to a Life Free of Violence refers to the CEDAW and the human rights recognized in other international treaties; however, in terms of content, this law needs to be revised under the new GR no. 35 and an explicit intersectionality approach added.

An intersectional analysis of policies in Mexico indicates that disability and violence against women are addressed by different policy bodies with a multiplicity of programs. Until recently, disabilities policies were not addressing violence or vice versa. An example is the National System for Integral Family Development (in Spanish: Sistema Nacional para el Desarrollo Integral de la Familia), which addresses persons with disabilities but does not consider violence, and Conavim, which does not take into account women with disabilities. Clara Jusidman, president and founder of the organization Citizen Initiative and Social Development, INCIDE Social AC (In Spanish: Iniciativa Ciudadana y Desarrollo Social, Asociación Civil) remarks: "There are two frameworks, [disability and gender]. I believe that the agenda is pushing forward the rights of persons with disabilities in general but there is little from a gender perspective... this happened with the indigenous women... They fought for their indigenous rights and then for their rights as women" (personal communication with Clara Jusidman, December 2013, in Sánchez Rodríguez, 2017).

Another issue to discuss is that violence against women is typically a one-dimensional policy issue, meaning that conditions such as race, ethnicity, class, and disability are absent from gender concerns. Gender equality is used to refer to equality between men and women, but not equality amongst women. The absence of an intersectional analysis results in policy cracks and institutional monopolies addressing violence against women as one dimensional. The statistical information focuses on the types of violence rather than on the lived circumstances of women. A definition of violence has in mind a woman that is different to a man, but does not consider factors such as "disabled," "indigenous," or "from another nationality." Yet, the National Program for Equal Opportunities and Non-Discrimination Against Women 2013–2018 (Pro Igualdad, 2013) carried out by Inmujeres addresses equal opportunities for women and men and seeks equity for women in vulnerable situations such as women with disabilities, indigenous women, single mothers, girls, and young women. The specific actions to end violence against women with disabilities include incorporating prevention programs into their (migrant and women with disability) special programs, but there is no reference to what those special programs are (p. 44). Again, the inclusion of marginalized groups remains as a "paragraph or a subsection" in policy documents (focus group, Marite Fernández, December 2013, in Sánchez Rodríguez, 2017). Furthermore, the Pro igualdad strategy falls short of addressing the systemic discrimination and violence suffered by these groups. There are few policies that aim to tackle different intersections across women victims of violence. The state of Querétaro has applied a specific model to support indigenous women with specialized units. Units called "MAI," for indigenous support units, work to familiarize women into the indigenous culture in Querétaro and together with the craft center promote services. In spite of this, services such as MAI are targeted to a certain group of women, indigenous women, and other social categories. Intersecting these categories are unobserved dimensions; for example, poverty is commonly addressed but disability is not. Even more, disability is perceived differently in each specific indigenous community; MAI could be an important strategy in Querétaro but not so in other regions.

Feminists in Mexico have worked hard to establish violence as a priority in the national policy agenda, and yet accounting for other women that belong to vulnerable groups is missing. Women with disabilities are a forgotten agenda in Mexican feminism. The former director of Indesol explained, "they are not in their agenda. Even if you search for them, you will not find women with disabilities, because it was like the revindication of us strong women, using the word of empowered and that does not get along with the inclusion of other groups [referring to other vulnerable groups]" (personal communication with Maria Angelica Luna Parra, Director of Indesol, September 2015, in Sánchez Rodríguez, 2017).

The absence of intersectionality that tackles inequalities in violence raises questions of the kind of women who are ideologically constructed and used to design and apply policies. Gender and disability constructions in the Mexican case trace back to a distinct set of institutions, one set addressing violence and the other disability. Both gender and disability have not met in policies addressing violence, resulting in general policies that emphasize gendered violation but no other traits such as disability.

GR no. 35 offers an opportunity for advocates and policy makers to address the policy gap amongst violence, gender, and disability. GR no. 35 highlights intersectionality and can propel a discussion between the different Mexican policy bodies to harmonize the law and programs and to seek collaboration to tackle violence against women with disabilities. GR no. 35 is specific on actions to prevent and protect women from violence that are pointed by advocates from disability and feminist organizations to push forward inclusive policies. The role of the state as duty bearers is addressing all women by making and implementing the appropriate policies.

Conclusion

This chapter described what intersectionality is and highlighted it in the recently adopted GR no. 35. Intersectionality is a loaded notion and conceptually hard to address in full, but the approach helps to close the policy gap in laws and programs whose purpose is to end violence by disclosing which women are most affected. Human rights standards, such as GRs, have developed complex conceptual terms and may fall short in describing policy actions. GRs establish a road map to support states to fulfill their human rights obligations. The purpose of this chapter was not to evaluate how well intersectionality is addressed in human rights but to support the idea that intersectionality is important for human rights, in particular in the issue of violence against women. The recent adoption of GR no. 35 is an opportunity for signatory countries such as Mexico to evaluate and amend their policies to end violence against women. Intersectionality has to be at the heart of policy discussions and at all stages of policy making, from policy design to policy evaluation. The case study showed that there are entrenched approaches that exclude women with disabilities from policies to end violence and that intersectionality is not yet addressed. Furthermore, GR no. 35 can be used by civil society organizations, in particular those representing the most discriminated women to advocate for their rights. In the end the challenge for policies to end violence against women with disabilities is to address both gender and disability in violence, accounting for gender relations and disability-based discrimination.

Discussion questions

1   What is internationality and how can it be used in policy analysis?

2   How is intersectionality addressed in GR no. 35 in relation to violence against women and in particular against women and girls with disabilities?
3   How does intersectionality applied in policy analysis to end violence against women look in the case of Mexico?

References

Ballan, M. and Freyer, M. (2012). Self-defense among women with disabilities: An unexplored domain in domestic violence cases. *Violence against Women*, 18(9), pp. 1083–1107.

Bond, Johanna E. (2001). International Intersectionality: A Theoretical and Pragmatic Exploration of Women's International Human Rights Violations. *Emory Law Journal*, 52(1), pp. 71–186.

Bowleg, L. (2012). The problem with the phrase women and minorities: intersectionality: An important theoretical framework for public health. *American Journal of Public Health*, 102(7), pp. 1267–1273.

Brogna, P. (2009). *Las representaciones de la discapacidad: la vigencia del pasado en las estructuras sociales presentes. Brogna, Patricia [comp.], Visiones y revisiones de la discapacida*. México: Fondo de Cultura Económica.

Campbell, M. (2016). CEDAW and women's intersecting identities: A pioneering approach to intersectional discrimination. Oxford University. Working paper vol. 2, no. 3. Available at: https://ohrh.law.ox.ac.uk/wordpress/wp-content/uploads/2015/07/Working-Paper-Series-Vol-2-No-3.pdf [Accessed March 10, 2018].

CEDAW Committee (UN Committee on the Elimination of Discrimination against Women) (1992). General Recommendation no. 19 Violence against Women. 11th session. Available at: www.ohchr.org/EN/HRBodies/CEDAW/Pages/Recommendations.aspx [Accessed March 11, 2018].

CEDAW Committee (UN Committee on the Elimination of Discrimination against Women) (2010). General Recommendation no. 28 on the Core Obligations of States Parties under Article 2 of the Convention on the Elimination of All Forms of Discrimination against Women. Available at: www.ohchr.org/EN/HRBodies/CEDAW/Pages/Recommendations.aspx [Accessed March 11, 2018].

CEDAW Committee (UN Committee on the Elimination of Discrimination against Women) (2016). Draft update of General Recommendation no. 19: 25 years of CEDAW General Recommendation no. 19(1992): Accelerating efforts on gender-based violence against women. Available at: www.ohchr.org/EN/HRBodies/CEDAW/Pages/DraftUpdateGR19.aspx [Accessed March 11, 2018].

CEDAW Committee (UN Committee on the Elimination of Discrimination against Women) (2017). General Recommendation no. 35: On Gender-Based Violence against Women, Updating General Recommendation no. 19. Available at: www.ohchr.org/EN/HRBodies/CEDAW/Pages/Recommendations.aspx [Accessed March 11, 2018].

CEDAW, Convention on the Elimination of All Forms of Discrimination against Women (1979). United Nations General Assembly, Available at: www.ohchr.org/EN/ProfessionalInterest/Pages/CEDAW.aspx [Accessed March 10, 2018].

Choo, H. and Ferree, M. (2010). Practicing intersectionality in sociological research: A critical analysis of inclusions, interactions, and institutions in the study of inequalities. *Sociological Theory*, 28(2), pp. 129–149.

Chow, P. (2016). Has intersectionality reached its limits? Intersectionality in the UN Human Rights Treaty body practice and the issue of ambivalence. *Human Rights Law Review*, 16(3), pp. 453–481.

Collins, P. (1986). Learning from the outsider within: The sociological significance of black feminist thought. *Social Problems*, 33(6), pp. s14–s32.

Collins, P. (2015). Sharpening intersectionality's critical edge. 11th Social Theory Forum, University of Massachusetts Boston.

Crenshaw, K. (1989). Demarginalizing the intersection of race and sex: A black feminist critique of antidiscrimination doctrine, feminist theory and antiracist politics. *University of Chicago Legal Forum*, 1, p. 139.

Crenshaw, K. (1991). Mapping the margins: Intersectionality, identity politics, and violence against women of color. *Stanford Law Review*, 43(6), pp. 1241–1299.

CRPD (Convention on the Rights of Persons with Disabilities) (2006). United Nations General Assembly A/61/61, Sixty-first session Item 67 (b). Available at: www.un.org/esa/socdev/enable/rights/convtexte.htm [Accessed March 11, 2018].

CRPD Committee (UN Committee on the Rights of Persons with Disabilities) (2014). Concluding observations on the initial report of Mexico (CRPD/C/MEX/CO/1). United Nations, Convention on the Rights of Persons with Disabilities. Available at: http://repository.un.org/bitstream/handle/11176/310323/CRPD_C_MEX_CO_1-EN.pdf?sequence=1&isAllowed=y [Accessed March 11, 2018].

CRPD Committee (UN Committee on the Rights of Persons with Disabilities) (2016). General comment no. 3 on article 6: Women with disabilities (CRPD/C/GC/3). United Nations, Convention on the Rights of Persons with Disabilities. Available at: www.ohchr.org/EN/HRBodies/CRPD/Pages/CRPDIndex.aspx [Accessed March 11, 2018].

Dhamoon, R. (2010). Considerations on mainstreaming intersectionality. *Political Research Quarterly*. doi: 1065912910379227

ENDIREH (2016). Principales resultados. Instituto Nacional de Estadística y Geografía, México. Available at: http://internet.contenidos.inegi.org.mx/contenidos/productos/prod_serv/contenidos/espanol/bvinegi/productos/nueva_estruc/promo/endireh2016_presentacion_ejecutiva.pdf [Accessed March 11, 2018].

General Act on Women's Access to a Life Free of Violence (2007). Available at: www.dof.gob.mx/nota_detalle.php?codigo=4961209&fecha=01/02/2007 [Accessed March 11, 2018].

Hancock, A. (2007). When multiplication doesn't equal quick addition: Examining intersectionality as a research paradigm. *Perspectives on Politics*, 5(1), pp. 63–79.

Hancock, A.M. (2013). Empirical intersectionality: A tale of two approaches. *UC Irvine L. Rev.*, 3, 259.

Hankivsky, O., ed. (2012). *An intersectionality-based policy analysis framework*. Vancouver, BC: Institute for Intersectionality Research and Policy, Simon Fraser University.

Hankivsky, O. and Cormier, R. (2011). Intersectionality and public policy: Some lessons from existing models. *Political Research Quarterly*, 64(1), pp. 217–229.

Hankivsky, O., Reid, C., Cormier, R., Varcoe, C., Clark, N., Benoit, C., and Brotman, S. (2010). Exploring the promises of intersectionality for advancing women's health research. *International Journal for Equity in Health*, 9(5), pp. 1–15.

INEGI (Instituto Nacional de Estadística y Geografía) (2014). La discapacidad en México, datos al 2014. Available at: http://internet.contenidos.inegi.org.mx/contenidos/productos/prod_serv/contenidos/espanol/bvinegi/productos/nueva_estruc/702825090203.pdf [Accessed March 11, 2018].

Lombardo, E. and Agustín, L. (2012). Framing gender intersections in the European Union: What implications for the quality of intersectionality in policies? *Social Politics: International Studies in Gender, State and Society*, 19(4), pp. 482–512.

Lombardo, E. and Verloo, M. (2009). Institutionalizing intersectionality in the European Union? *International Feminist Journal of Politics*, 11(4), pp. 478–495.

Mason, C. (2013). *Manufacturing urgency: Development perspectives on violence against women*. Ottawa: University of Ottawa.

McCall, L. (2005). The complexity of intersectionality. *Signs: Journal of Women in Culture and Society*, 30(3), pp. 1771–1800.

National Program for the Development and Inclusion of Persons with Disabilities (2014–2018) (2014). Available at: www.gob.mx/conadis/acciones-y-programas/p rograma-nacional-para-el-desarrollo-y-la-inclusion-de-las-personas-con-discapacidad-2014-2018-5882 [Accessed March 11, 2018].

Parken, A. and Young, H. (2008). *Facilitating cross-strand project*. Cardiff: WAG.

PIPASEVM (National Comprehensive Program to Prevent, Assist, Punish and Eradicate Violence against Women 2014–2018) (2014). Available at: www.gob.mx/ segob/acciones-y-programas/programa-integral-para-prevenir-atender-sanciona r-y-erradicar-la-violencia-contra-las-mujeres-2014-2018 [Accessed March 11, 2018].

Pro igualdad (National Program for Equal Opportunities and Non-Discrimination against Women 2013–2018) (2016). Available at: www.gob.mx/sre/documentos/ programa-para-la-igualdad-entre-mujeres-y-hombres-2015-2018 [Accessed March 11, 2018].

Rönnblom, M. (2008). "How is it done?" On the road to an intersectional methodology in feminist policy analysis. In: L. Gunnarsson and A. G. Jónasdóttir, eds, *Proceedings from GEXcel Theme 1: Gender, sexuality and global change conference of workshops 22–25 May, 2008 J GEXcel Work in Progress Report*, volume IV, 51, pp. 51–54. Available at: www.diva-portal.org/smash/get/diva2:901162/FULLTEXT01. pdf#page=51 [Accessed March 11, 2018].

Sánchez Rodríguez, A. (2017). Civil society organization practices to end violence against women and girls with disabilities in Mexico. Graduate Doctoral Dissertations, p. 342. Available at: https://scholarworks.umb.edu/doctoral_dissertations/ 342 [Accessed May 18, 2018].

Social Affairs Act (2004, last reform 2014) Available at: www.diputados.gob.mx/ LeyesBiblio/pdf/270_191214.pdf [Accessed March 11, 2018].

Soto Martínez, A. (2011). La discapacidad y sus significados: notas sobre la (in) justicia. *Política y cultura*, 35, pp. 209–239.

Verloo, M. (2006). Multiple inequalities, intersectionality and the European Union. *European Journal of Women's Studies*, 13(3), pp. 211–228.

Walby, S. (2007). Complexity theory, systems theory, and multiple intersecting social inequalities. *Philosophy of the Social Sciences*, 37(4), pp. 449–470.

Weber, L. (1998). A conceptual framework for understanding race, class, gender, and sexuality. *Psychology of Women Quarterly*, 22(1), pp. 13–32.

Weber, L. (2001). *Understanding race, class, gender, and sexuality: A conceptual framework*. New York: McGraw-Hill Humanities/Social Sciences/Languages.

Winker, G. and Degele, N. (2011). Intersectionality as multi-level analysis: Dealing with social inequality. *European Journal of Women's Studies*, 18(1), pp. 51–66.

World Health Organization (2014). Global status report on violence prevention. Available at: www.who.int/violence_injury_prevention/violence/status_report/2014/ report/report/en/ [Accessed March 11, 2018].

164   *Ana María Sánchez Rodríguez*

Further reading

Álvarez de Lara, R. and Pérez Duarte y Noroña, A., eds (2014). *Aplicación práctica de los modelos de prevención, atención y sanción de la violencia de género contra las mujeres: protocolos de actuación.* 4th edn. México, DF: UNAM, Instituto de Investigaciones Jurídicas. Available at: https://archivos.juridicas.unam.mx/www/bjv/libros/8/3936/17.pdf [Accessed March 11, 2018].

Anthias, F. (2013). Intersectional what? Social divisions, intersectionality and levels of analysis. *Ethnicities*, 13(1), pp. 3–19.

Björnsdóttir, K. and Traustadóttir, R. (2010). Stuck in the land of disability? The intersection of learning difficulties, class, gender and religion. *Disability and Society*, 25(1), pp. 49–62.

Bond, J. (2001). International intersectionality: A theoretical and pragmatic exploration of women's international human rights violations. *Emory Law Journal*, 52(1), pp. 71–186.

DEVAW (1993). The Declaration on the Elimination of Violence against Women. United Nations General Assembly A/RES/48/104, 85th plenary meeting. Available at: www.un.org/documents/ga/res/48/a48r104.htm

Frohmader, C., Dowse, L., and Didi, A. (2015). Preventing violence against women and girls with disabilities: Integrating a human rights perspective. Think piece document for the development of the National Framework to Prevent Violence against Women. Available at: http://wwda.org.au/wp-content/uploads/2015/04/Think-Piece_WWD.pdf

Ortoleva, S. and Lewis, H. (2012). Forgotten sisters: A report on violence against women with disabilities: An overview of its nature, scope, causes and consequences. Northeastern University School of Law research paper no. 104–2012. Available at: https://ssrn.com/abstract=2133332

Parken, A. (2010). A multi-strand approach to promoting equalities and human rights in policy making. *Policy and Politics*, 38(1), pp. 79–99.

10 Global LGBTQ politics and human rights

Jamie J. Hagen

Introduction

While not everyone identifies with the experiences of those who are members of LGBTQ communities, everyone has a sexual orientation and a gender identity. The landscape for global LGBTQ[1] politics is unfolding before our eyes as citizens of a global society began to include attention to sexual orientation and gender identity within discussions of human rights. The last quarter century (1990–2015) in particular presents a time of rapid change for those advocating for human rights using sexual rights-based claims. But this advancement of LGBTQ rights as human rights at the United Nations (UN) is just one indicator of progress and not everyone in the world is equally impacted, with 75 countries still criminalizing consensual same-sex behavior.

Though activists have been pushing for LGBTQ rights on the local, regional, and international levels for decades, little progress was made in the international human rights arena until recently. It is only in the past decade that states have begun to step up to the international stage at the UN and voice support for issues important to LGBTQ communities, like the need to decriminalize any laws banning certain sexual orientations or gender identities.

This chapter includes four sections. The first section defines key terms that may be new to those reading about LGBTQ rights for the first time. The next section reviews the landscape of global LGBTQ organizing with attention to feminist organizing, organizing for sexual rights, and organizing at the UN over the past 50 years. The third section focuses on LGBTQ human rights in three country-specific situations. The fourth section provides a conclusion.

Key words for understanding global LGBTQ politics

People who are marginalized because of their sexual orientation or gender identity may be discriminated against as a result of their sex, gender, or both. Some people identify as a member of the LGBTQ community because of who they are attracted to sexually while others do so because of their gender expression. For example, a lesbian living in a state that bans same-sex relationships may be criminalized for having sex with another woman, but she may also be policed for her hairstyle or clothing, in other words her gender presentation. This policing of LGBTQ individuals' behavior, dress, and desire is due to strict social norms that generally define two distinct categories, one for men and one for women.

There are a number of definitions pertinent to global LGBTQ politics and human rights. Sexual orientation and gender identity are related but distinct terms. *Sexual orientation* refers to a person's physical, romantic, and/or emotional attraction towards other people. On the other hand, *gender identity*

> reflects a deeply felt and experienced sense of one's own gender. A person's gender identity is typically consistent with the sex assigned to them at birth, although that is not always the case and may change over the course of a lifetime. For transgender people, there is an inconsistency between their sense of their own gender and the sex they were assigned at birth. In some cases, their appearance and mannerisms and other outwards characteristics may conflict with society's expectations of gender-normative behavior.
>
> (Free & Equal, 2017)

People may also experience discrimination and violence because of their perceived sexual orientation and gender identity or for advocating on behalf of those with LGBTQ identities.

While the shorthand of describing sex as relating to the body and gender as relating to the mind is commonly used, this explanation is incomplete. Sex as a biological descriptor usually refers to male and female categories; however, queer and trans theorists reject the exclusive use of these binary categories, arguing that just as gay, lesbian, bisexual, and transgender identity labels are socially constructed, so are male and female biological categories. Intersex awareness advocates also point out that biological sex characteristics such as chromosomes and genitalia are not always sex-specific and may not fit neatly into binary categories.

Though many people are familiar with the labels lesbian, gay, and bisexual to describe sexual orientation, trans and queer may require more explanation. In this chapter the T is used as a category that is inclusive of gender non-conforming people or a gender-diverse community as a whole whose members may include those who identify as transgender, transsexual, genderqueer, androgynous, agender, bigender, two spirit, and gender nonconforming. Importantly, the *Free & Equal* fact sheet explains in their definition of LGBT, "While these terms have increasing global resonance, in different cultures other terms may be used to describe people who form same-sex relationships and those who exhibit non-binary gender identities (such as hijra, meti, lala, skesana, motsoalle, mithli, kuchu, kawein, travesty, muxé, fa'afafine, fakaleiti, hamjensgara and Two-Spirit)."

Queer is an umbrella term that includes lesbian, gay, bisexual, transgender, intersex, and radical sexual communities. Other identities that may also fall under "Q" or queer include genderqueer and questioning. Queer is used to mean both a politics and identity category. Other acronyms that may be used include LGBTQIA or LGBTI with the A standing for asexual and the I for intersex. Some members of the intersex community see their advocacy as part of the work of global LGBT advocacy while some do not identity with this community.

Two terms are critical to understanding the forms of discrimination faced by the community: homophobia and transphobia. As defined by David A. B. Murray, *Homophobia* is "a socially produced form of sexual discrimination" (2009, p. 3). Murray also notes that "antigay prejudice" and "gay-hatred" are related terms used as a way to recognize that this type of discrimination is not actually a fear that can be understood in only psychological terms (2009, p. 4). *Transphobia* is "a set of negative attitudes toward, fear and hatred of transgender and gender non-conforming people" (Grollman, 2012). Using labels and categories that are inclusive and representative presents a challenge to the human rights community. For example, the movement in the United States that is now called the LGBTQ movement was once largely referred to as the gay rights movement or the lesbian and gay rights movement with a narrow focus on gay men. Transnational advocacy has largely moved towards using the LGBT identification as a way to include lesbian, gay, bisexual, and transgender individuals. The words people use to define populations are political in and of themselves. As an example of one act of resistance to this homophobia and transphobia, the words queer and dyke were once used as slurs against lesbians and gays but many people in LGBTQ communities now self-identify with those terms as a way to positively reclaim them.

The abbreviation SOGI is sometimes used as a way to refer to sexual orientation and gender identity together. For example, an intersex individual being denied healthcare may not necessarily be personally impacted with the same political concerns of a gay man living in a country where same-sex marriage is banned. However, these political concerns are grouped together because they are both a result of similar discriminations resulting from a heteronormative political system. Heteronormativity is the assumption by individuals or institutional practices that everyone is heterosexual, and that heterosexuality is superior.

Transnational LGBTQ organizing

Mobilizing for "gay rights as human rights" on the international stage has largely taken shape through transnational networks. This organizing has involved complicated and sometimes contentious exchanges between communities in the Global North and the Global South. The role of large global civil society organizations like OutRight International often represent the public-facing side of this organizing, though there are many more involved behind the scenes. How these organizations integrate and represent local actors presents opportunities as well as challenges for transnational organizations.

United States activist Julie Dorf launched the International Gay and
Lesbian Human Rights Commission (IGLHRC) in 1990 as an organization
focused on gaining asylum status in the United States for lesbian- and gay-
identified refugees. IGLHRC, which changed its name to OutRight Action
International, defines itself as "a leading international organization dedicated to human rights advocacy on behalf of people who experience discrimination or abuse on the basis of their actual or perceived sexual
orientation, gender identity or expression" and the organization is a pio-
neer in combating homophobia and transphobia globally (OutRight Action
International, 2018).

Amnesty International was the first of the larger "gatekeeper model of
human rights" organizations to publish a widely circulated monograph of
gay and lesbian rights in 1993. Julie Mertus uses the term "gatekeeper" to
problematize the role of organizations setting the global agenda for what
issues are taken up as human rights concerns and how this may be exclusionary to other agendas. Human Rights Watch (HRW) began reporting and
monitoring the persecution of gay men and lesbians in 1996. The HRW
approach to human rights advocacy is "to name the abuse being observed as
a human rights violation, to blame the violator for its actions, and then
shame the responsible states and other culpable entities into taking correc-
tive actions" (Mertus, 2007).

OutRight began working with HRW in 1998 and two years later
HRW launched its own LGBT rights program. Other large transnational
organizations advocating for issues of sexual orientation and gender
identity include Arc International and ILGA (International Lesbian,
Gay, Bisexual, Trans, and Intersex Association). These transnational
organizations centralized in the North have largely targeted their
resources on gathering information, reporting it, and then mobilizing
members to particular action. Often these actions include making phone
calls, signing petitions, or donating money to continue to support this
work. The thought behind this reporting and mobilizing is that it will
lead to increased protection for those who are experiencing violence
because in-state actors will be publicly shamed by being openly called
out for either failing to protect citizens or in some cases causing the
harm at the hand of the state.

However, the naming and shaming model used by the larger "gatekeeper"
organizations raises many challenges for an organization such as OutRight,
dedicated to working with and amplifying the voices at the grassroots level.
Mertus addresses this paradox in her work, stating,

> Throughout the world, many sexual minorities[2] simply do not view
> their identities in terms of the hetero/homo dichotomy, and rather pre-
> sent a wide variety of sexual identities unrecognizable in the west. For
> them, the globally transplanted "ideas" of "gay liberation" serve "not as
> emancipatory slogans" but impose external categories onto widely

divergent peoples, thus obscuring the inherent value of fluidity and deliberation in sexual identity.

(Mertus, 2007)

Negotiating the right time to amplify these stories and finding ways to partner with grassroots organizations is part of the process transnational organizations navigate in this human rights work. This can be especially sensitive when working with populations of people who may not have disclosed their SOGI for fear of retaliation from family, work, or even the police.

Still, some argue the presence of attitudes of neocolonialism persist through models of advocacy for LGBTQ human rights modeled on an agenda of the Global North. Although the resource advantage remains with Northern non-governmental organizations (NGOs), feminist and queer organizations are increasingly looking to partnerships in the Global South as a way to address these racial and economic divides between different organizations. This takes shape in a number of different ways including hosting workshops for networking, training, capacity-building projects for smaller organizations, and financial support to bring advocates to the UN during annual meetings. But the way sexual freedom and human rights are presented for those who participate in queer or same-sex relations are a contentious topic. Suparna Bhaskaran, who writes about decolonization, queer sexualities, and transnational projects, highlights how this occurs in India. Bhaskaran complicates the notion of a fixed Western identity for gay men as a path to sexual freedom and group identification (2004, pp. 97–101). She writes, "Group affiliations such as sexual categories and their political economies in India are not always the same as in the 'west' but are always marked by it in uneven ways" (p. 97). Because of this, the predominantly Western narrative that "coming out" as a gay man is a path to sexual freedom and liberation may not prove true to some men who participate in same-sex sexuality in other contexts such as India and whose experiences may not be represented by this narrow understanding of sexual practice.

Additionally, the terms of global and local are also loaded in the context of transnational advocacy. Sally Merry writes about the paradox between the global and local in global human rights advocacy, highlighting the challenge that comes with transnational organizations being an untrustworthy intermediary due to this positioning:

In the context of discussions of transnationalism, local tends to stand for a lack of mobility, wealth, education, and cosmopolitanism, as well as recalcitrant particularity, whereas global encompasses the ability to move across borders, to adopt universal moral frameworks and to share in the affluence, education and cosmopolitan awareness of elites from other parts of the world.

(Merry, 2006)

This can manifest in a number of different ways, including homonationalism and pinkwashing.

Pinkwashing is a technique used in marketing or political campaigning to appear progressive by promoting LGBT human rights, despite the reality of harm and violence perpetrated against the community. A notable example is how this occurs during Pride season in marches around the world. Queer activists have protested the inclusion of police and the military in Pride marches, arguing that their presence neglects the violence queer people of color still face at their hands. Corporations such as alcohol distributors and banks have also been charged with using participation in Pride events to pinkwash. One of the most prominent charges of pinkwashing is against the state of Israel, a country that promotes being a great place to travel for LGBT individuals while being charged with continued violence against Palestinian people, LGBT and otherwise.

Homonationalism is a term coined by queer theorist Jasbir Puar to describe the post-9/11 nationalist rhetoric that promotes a progressive LGBT human rights narrative in the West as civilized and in contrast to homophobic barbaric and backwards Islamism in the Middle East. The language is used to promote the continued dominance of hierarchical ideals intended to maintain an ideology of class, race, gender, and nation-state based in a politics privileging heteronormative masculinity (Puar, 2007). At times this homonationalist rhetoric is used to justify military intervention to protect the human rights of LGBT individuals from their failed or failing state. This simplistic binary argument is made despite the persistence of homophobia, lesbophobia, biphobia, and transphobia in those states that make claims to progressive human rights for LGBT individuals including the United States and the United Kingdom.[3] The binary framing also erases the identities of queer Muslims around the globe.

In recent years, the rise of authoritarian movements has also presented a stark challenge to the perception of LGBTQ human rights as always moving in a positive direction with continued support and protection around the globe. This backlash against the spread of LGBTQ rights has taken many forms. For example, Bermuda voted to repeal the right for same-sex marriage in February 2018. Under the Trump presidency, a number of threats to protections for LGBTQ individuals have been raised, including a possible ban on transgender members from serving in the military.

Feminist organizing and LGBTQ organizing

Feminist organizers have long argued that lesbian concerns were too marginal to be taken up by women's rights organizing, the politics of sexual orientation and gender identity too radical. This is in part because lesbian feminists reject the assumed normalcy of heterosexuality and patriarchy. Direct action by members of the Lesbian Avengers is one form of rejection of this insistence that lesbians wait their turn to be a part of feminist organizing. Direct action can take many forms including protests and sit-ins. The Dyke March is one event that was started by the Lesbian Avengers that continues in United States cities today including in New York, Boston, and Chicago.

Lesbian feminists did much of the work to highlight ways in which gay liberation politics in the 1980s continued to exclude women and promote patriarchal power structures privileging white males. Lesbian activists like Charlotte Bunch, the former head of the Center for Women's Global Leadership, played a big role in getting lesbian and gay issues on the human rights agenda in the early 1990s. Lesbian activists also worked to get lesbian issues on the agenda at the 1993 World Conference on Human Rights and 1995 World Conference on Women.

Transnational feminist work and the women's rights movement offer insights into transnational work for global LGBT rights. Lesbian feminist theorists also contribute to the field of queer theory in important ways. The Astraea Lesbian Foundation for Justice, founded in 1977, continues this vision of lesbian feminist work and is the only philanthropic organization that works exclusively to fund human rights projects focused on LGBTQI human rights. The group "came out" as a national lesbian foundation in 1990 and has funded the work of many lesbian writers including Audre Lorde, Adrienne Rich, and Sarah Schulman (a co-founder of the Lesbian Avengers), as well as activism in 27 countries.

LGBTQ rights as sexual rights

Another frame that is sometimes used for discussing issues important to LGBTQ communities is that of sexual rights. Issues that fall within this paradigm of advocacy might include sex workers' rights, reproductive healthcare, or healthcare for people living with HIV/AIDs. The public health community often uses the identifications MSM (men who have sex with men) and WSW (women who have sex with women) to provide services to these communities. However, some human rights advocates resist this framing, arguing that while it does recognize that all men who have sex with men may not identify with the LGBT community, the MSM framing is also problematic. As described earlier, not everyone identifies with a binary category of man or woman. Additionally, some argue that these categories perpetuate a stigma about embracing LGBT identities that human rights advocates are working to address. Nevertheless, it is important for transnational advocates to model advocacy on local and regional advocates that in some cases may make more sense in a sexual rights framework:

> a sexual rights framework, which speaks to the rights of bodily integrity and sexual and gender autonomy and expression, provides for advocacy strategies which embrace a larger community. Working transnationally and/or in international arenas necessitates an organizing strategy that

takes into account geographically and historically specific concepts of sexuality and gender and gives deference to local activists' preferred ways of thinking of and expressing any gender which falls outside of social and cultural norms; it requires modes of organizing that do not reify gender binaries.

(Budhiraja et al., 2010, p. 141)

Human rights related to sex, sexuality, and the right to healthcare for women are particularly contentious in the international area. This means that lesbian, bisexual, and transgender women face hurdles that filter through patriarchy and misogyny in ways that other issues on the LGBTQ human rights agenda may not. Other advocacy that may fall within this category includes the right of lesbian partners to parent without interference from the state as well as same-sex adoptions. In many states same-sex partners are not granted the same security when it comes to adoption and parenting as heterosexual partners. In most cases lesbians are also denied the same kinds of access to medical care for fertility treatments granted to heterosexual women.

Intersex individuals may also advocate within the public health and sexual rights framework. Intersex individuals and advocates who reject medical intervention have appealed to the international human rights framework arguing that these interventions inhibit bodily integrity.

Bringing LGBT human rights to the UN

Following the first reports on discrimination against lesbians and gays in the 1990s a small number of NGOs continued to publish reports about these communities. As a way to provide guidelines for the application of international human rights law in relation to sexual orientation and gender identity, human rights experts met in Yogyakarta, Indonesia in 2006. The culmination of this meeting was the Yogyakarta Principles. In the introduction to the principles, co-chairs Sonia Onufer Correa and Vitit Muntarbhorn explain,

The Yogyakarta Principles address a broad range of human rights standards and their application to issues of sexual orientation and gender identity. The Principles affirm the primary obligation of States to implement human rights. Each Principle is accompanied by detailed recommendations to States. The experts also emphasize, though, that all actors have responsibilities to promote and protect human rights. Additional recommendations are addressed to other actors, including the UN human rights system, national human rights institutions, the media, nongovernmental organizations and funders.

Five years later, in 2011, the UN Human Rights Council released the first report to address homophobia and transphobia, *Human rights, sexual orientation and gender identity from the Human Rights Council*. The report identified discriminatory laws criminalizing homosexuality and imposing arbitrary arrest and detention, or in some cases the death penalty, for LGBT people as violations of international standards and obligations under international human rights law. The report outlines disturbing realities for LGBT people: in 76 countries, for example, it remains illegal to engage in same-sex sexual behavior; in five of those, the penalty is death. In 2013 the UN unveiled the *Free and Equal* campaign to highlight the LGBT community globally. The issues raised by the UN in this campaign, along with emerging data about targeted violence against the LGBTQ population is/has been documented by NGOs.

Without documentation and data, it remains a challenge to promote and protect the human rights of the global LGBTQ population. Because of this, the UN established the first independent expert on issues of SOGI (IESOGI) in 2016. The special representative is charged with investigating discrimination based on sexual orientation and gender identity around the world. This appointment was met with significant resistance at the UN, but nevertheless was successful and is a groundbreaking accomplishment. The following year the first person to serve in this role, Vitat Muntarbhorn, began a three-year term. Unfortunately he was unable to complete the term because of illness and the health of a family member, but before his resignation the first statement of the IESOGI was presented to the Human Rights Council in June and the General Assembly at the UN in October.

Following the appointment of the first IESOGI, experts once again gathered to develop a supplement to the Yogyakarta Principles after ten years, the Yogyakarta Principles plus 10. The update to the document includes nine principles as well as 111 additional state obligations. One notable update to the principles is Principle 36, "The right to enjoyment of human rights in relation to information and communication technologies." As the principle states:

> Everyone is entitled to the same protection of rights online as they are offline. Everyone has the right to access and use information and communication technologies, including the internet, without violence, discrimination or other harm based on sexual orientation, gender identity, gender expression or sex characteristics. Secure digital communications, including the use of encryption, anonymity and pseudonymity tools are essential for the full realization of human rights, in particular the rights to life, bodily and mental integrity, health, privacy, due process, freedom of opinion and expression, peaceful assembly and association.

While this right to protection online is important for everyone, it can be especially important to those who do not see visibility of their sexual orientation or gender identity in their own community. Lack of visibility for marginalized identities occurs for a number of reasons, including stigma. As a way to avoid this stigma within one's own family and community, some people have found ways to find community and solidarity through online communities for information about everything from trans health, intersex advocacy, lesbian dating, and living with HIV/AIDS. Members of the LGBTQ community have also looked to online media to create a representation of their own identity to educate people who may not be familiar with experiences like asexuality, same-sex adoption, or being pregnant as a transgender man. By using social media platforms, these individuals have bypassed more traditional and mainstream mechanisms of information sharing, communicating everything from art and music to information about medical and mental healthcare.

Resistance to LGBTQ human rights

Though progress for LGBTQ human rights has been remarkable over the past quarter century, there has also been immense resistance. As outlined above, many continue to face violence and oppression from states who simply do not recognize freedom of sexual orientation and gender identity as a matter of human rights. But some resistance to LGBTQ human rights framing comes from those who argue against the dangers of a narrow universal human rights paradigm and liberal identity categories.

In his ethnographic study of brokers at OutRight, Ryan Thoreson addresses this challenge directly, writing, "Brokers frequently worked on cases where the persons involved did not necessarily identity as LGBT or queer, but were persecuted for behaving or organizing in ways others deemed unacceptable. It proved difficult, if not impossible, to do transnational LGBT work using a single lens for understanding sexuality" (2014, p. 99). Here Thoreson is referring to those actors who worked at OutRight to liaise between activists and the UN or state governments as brokers. Thoreson notes that during his fieldwork at OutRight the most common acronym used was LGBT; however, many other combinations of letters and terms were used depending on any given context or actor in the specific context. Advocates also note that often people are discriminated against because they are perceived to be LGBTQ whether or not it is actually true and it is important to advocate on their behalf as well.

Advocating for LGBTQ human rights in the local and national contexts

Listening to local community members speak about their experiences as members of LGBTQ communities organizing outside the UN offers another perspective on LGBTQ rights. Issues of concern for LGBTQ human rights include but are not limited to decriminalizing sex work, legalizing same-sex marriage, the right to bodily autonomy for intersex people, adoption rights for lesbians, and access to healthcare for transgender people. These concerns cross into many other areas of political concern, including international law, global health, reproductive rights, and criminal justice.

Below are a number of different country-specific examples of the ways that transforming local media coverage of sexual and gender diversity, rejection of anti-sodomy laws, and resistance to racism and economic injustice offer different emphases and approaches to LGBTQ advocacy.

Palestine: transforming local media

The way the media portrays LGBTQ individuals is of great importance in making changes on both a social and political level. By providing training, toolkits, and current media practices, activist organizations are able to hold the media accountable through research of current practices as well as provide educational resources for best practice. In this way activists can work with the media to help shift the public's perception and understanding of LGBTQ communities.

Over the past ten years the Palestinian organization alQaws has worked to transform local media as well as cultural and media production as it relates to addressing sexual and gender diversity issues. In describing their efforts to transform local media they explain, "Moving forward, we will advocate among professional Palestinian journalists and media agencies to fundamentally shift their approach to gender and sexual diversity issues, encouraging positive coverage and thoughtful debate of otherwise taboo or maligned topics, such as homosexuality, violence targeting gender and sexual minorities, women's sexuality, and more" (alQaws, 2014).

India: colonial anti-sodomy laws

Activists in some countries have also worked at the local and national levels to resist sodomy laws. In India, as well as in some other countries including Uganda, the sodomy laws are a legacy of being under colonial rule during the British Empire. Anti-sodomy laws were intended to impose a form of European morality making certain sexual acts "perverse" while others were viewed as "natural." The colonial legacy of anti-sodomy laws persisted in India until very recently, where same-sex relationships were still criminalized until September 2018.

With this historical awareness it becomes clear that rather than homosexuality and same-sex relationships being an import of the Global North, anti-sodomy laws and the homophobic rhetoric used to enforce them are the foreign import. Local activists have worked to bring this historical awareness to campaigns that argue that LGBTQ identities are not part of their communities. Reflecting on this the lesbian poet, Kaushalya Bannerji, writes, "To be a lesbian is not, as I used to think, a Westernized rejection of our Indian identities. We can look to our own societies and cultures for examples of strong female friendships and the heroic rebellion of all women dealing with aspects of patriarchy, including sexual and economic degradation" (1993, p. 63).

United States: racism and economic injustice

In the United States, a number of organizations choose to focus their agendas in ways that differ from the larger international organizations, such as the national LGBTQ task force organizations Black and Pink and Queers for Economic Justice. These organizations prioritize queer people of color in their organizing and focus primarily on issues such as youth homelessness, police brutality, and incarceration that impact members of queer communities of color at a disproportionate rate.

Black and Pink advocates on behalf of queer and trans people living in prison. Their campaign work is primarily centered on providing resources to LGBTQ people living behind bars, including a pen pal program. The radical queer non-profit organization Queers for Economic Justice, defunct as of 2014, worked to draw attention to class inequality. Their anti-capitalist organizing was also critical of the focus on justice and liberation at the heart of the original Pride parades in many locations. As one of the founding members of the organization, Amber Hollibaugh explains while reflecting on the role of the organization in the larger NGO landscape, "We're not trying to be one more included constituency that gets named in this fight... it doesn't solve the deeper question of gender conformity and inequality because of capitalism" (Taterka, 2014).

Conclusion

The scope of human rights concerns addressed by organizations promoting rights for LGBTQ individuals has grown over the last quarter century. The role of feminist and trans communities in transnational intersectional organizing is critical to advancements today. Framing human rights work with a queer feminist lens moves the conversation beyond the narrow approach of single-issue identity advocacy to a larger vision that also recognizes how issues like race, class, and colonialism also impact LGBTQ individuals. The struggle for LGBTQ human rights is one that involves many actors: citizens, politicians, lawyers, protesters, and allies. The LGBTQ human rights community includes those who advocate through political protest as well as those who fight for legal protections through the courts. The role of allies is also important when it comes to recognizing the need to include gender-neutral restrooms and supporting diverse family structures in their communities.

In measuring progress for advocacy for LGBTQ human rights of the last 25 years it is also important to consider the ways local stakeholders view this progress. Some questions to consider are: Who defines the issues for conversations about LGBTQ rights? How do patriarchy and misogyny continue to operate even in organizing for LGBTQ human rights? This is a question that transnational feminists have been asking about women's rights. How do we understand the many varied communities who exist under the same umbrella of LGBTQ? An intersectional approach to these questions requires considering multiple aspects of a person's identity including but not limited to race, class, gender, and how privilege operates for different members of the same community.

Just as feminists have argued that the personal is political, this is also true when it comes to advocating for sexual orientation and gender identity-specific human rights. LGBTQ politics is present in the everyday experience of those who have access to healthcare for transgender women and housing for homeless youth. Having the right to serve in the military matters little to a gay couple who is unsafe holding hands while walking home at night. The shape LGBTQ politics takes varies over time and place and challenges the simplifying narrative of universal human rights. Grassroots activists working in partnership with transnational activist organizations are increasingly challenging global norms about LGBTQ communities.

Discussion questions

1 How can international human rights groups work intersectionally to include attention to the sexual orientation and gender identity of individuals in all of their campaigns?
2 How can advocates best represent the rights of those who do not necessarily identify with LGBT identity labels but still engage in same-sex sexual practices?
3 How would you respond to someone who said that some parts of the world oppose same-sex relationships because of "cultural beliefs"?
4 In 2015 Hillary Clinton stated: "gay rights are human rights." In what ways does the Universal Declaration for Human Rights include ways to promote and protect LGBTQ human rights?
5 Have you seen any institutions (school, church, family, business) change in how they address the needs of LGBTQ individuals? Give some examples.

Notes

1 In this chapter I use LGBTQ to refer to lesbian, gay, bisexual, trans, and queer as the most common identifiers used in writing about sexual orientation and gender identity categories within the human rights space. The section on key words as well as the section on sexual rights expands on other terms often used when discussing non-normative sexual orientations and gender identities.
2 At times people also use the phrase "sexual minorities" to identify those who practice non-normative sexual practices such as same-sex partnership, however, some advocates reject this framing arguing that it suggests that heterosexual partnership and heterosexual practice are normal while practices outside of that are not.
3 Transgender women of color in the United States continue to face incredibly high rates of violence with at least 28 transgender individuals murdered in 2017 alone, serving as a startling example of the ways in which the protection for SOGI-based human rights has yet to reach all citizens of the country.

References

alQaws (2014). *Our projects: Social and cultural change.* Available at: www.alqaws.org/our-projects/Social-Cultural-Change [Accessed March 15, 2018].

Bannerji, K. (1993). No apologies. In: R. Ratti, ed., *A lotus of another color: An unfolding of the South Asian gay and lesbian experience.* New York: Alyson, pp. 59–64.

Bhaskaran, S. (2004). *Made in India: Decolonizations, queer sexualities trans/national projects.* New York: Palgrave Macmillan.

Budhiraja, S., Fried, S.T., and Teixeira, A. (2010). Spelling it out: From alphabet soup to sexual rights and gender justice. In: A. Lind, ed., *Development, sexual rights and global governance.* London: Routledge, pp. 131–144.

Free & Equal (2017). *Fact sheet LGBT rights: Frequently asked questions.* Available at: www.unfe.org/wp-content/uploads/2017/05/LGBT-Rights-FAQs.pdf [Accessed March 15, 2018].

Grollman, E.A. (2012). What is transphobia? And, what is cissexism? *Kinsey Confidential.* Available at: http://kinseyconfidential.org/transphobia/ [Accessed March 3, 2016].

Human Rights Council (2011). Resolution 17/19, Human rights, sexual orientation and gender identity. A/HRC/RES/17/19, adopted June 17.

Merry, S.E. (2006). Transnational human rights and local activism: Mapping the middle. *American Anthropologist*, 108(1), pp. 38–51.

Mertus, J. (2007). The rejection of human rights framings: The case of LGBT advocacy in the US. *Human Rights Quarterly*, 29(4), pp. 1036–1064.

Murray, D. A. B. (2009). *Homophobias: Lust and Loathing Across Time And Space.* Durham, NC: Duke University Press.

OutRight Action International (2018). *Where we work.* Available at: www.outright international.org/where-we-work [Accessed March 15, 2018].

Principle 36 (YP+10) (2016). *The right to the enjoyment of human rights in relation to information and communication technologies.* Available at: http://yogyakartaprinciples.org/principle-36-yp10/ [Accessed March 15, 2018].

Puar, J.K. (2007). *Terrorist assemblages: Homonationalism in queer times.* Durham, NC: Duke University Press.

Taterka, M. (2014). Queers for Economic Justice closes its doors thanks to lack of economic justice. *Autostraddle.* Available at: www.autostraddle.com/queers-for-economic-justice-closes-its-doors-thanks-to-lack-of-economic-justice-224520/ [Accessed March 15, 2018].

Thoreson, R.R. (2014). *Transnational LGBT activism: Working for sexual rights worldwide.* Minneapolis, MN: University Of Minnesota Press.

Further reading

Brettscheneider, M., Burgess, S., and Keating, C., eds (2017). *LGBTQ politics: A critical reader.* New York: New York University Press.

Butler, J. (1993). Critically queer. *GLQ: A Journal of Lesbian and Gay Studies*, 1(1), pp. 17–32.

Butler, J. (1999). *Gender trouble.* New York: Routledge.

Human Rights Watch (2009). "They want us exterminated": Murder, torture, sexual orientation and gender in Iraq. *Human Rights Watch Online.* Available at: www.

hrw.org/report/2009/08/17/they-want-us-exterminated/murder-torture-sexual-orientation-and-gender-iraq [Accessed March 3, 2016].

Quinn, Sarah. (2010). An Activist's Guide to the Yogyakarta Pinrciples. Available at: http://ypinaction.org/wp-content/uploads/2016/10/Activists_Guide_English_nov_14_2010.pdf. [Accessed on September 19, 2018].

Picq, M. and Thiel, M. (2015). *Sexualities in world politics: How LGBTQ claims shape international relations*. Abingdon: Routledge.

Stryker, S., Currah, P., and Moore, L.J. (2008). Introduction: trans-, trans, or transgender? *WSQ: Women's Studies Quarterly*, 36(3/4), pp. 3–4.

Weiss, M.L. and Bosia, M.J. (2013). *Global homophobia*. Urbana, IL: University of Illinois Press.

11 Refugee camps and the (educational) rights of the child

Rajini Srikanth

This essay takes as its starting point the child's "right to education" and focuses in particular on children in refugee camps to understand how this right is implemented and what opportunities the child's right to education provides for the future in shaping a global citizen. I argue that the circumstances of refugee children present the international community with an opportunity to cultivate future adults with agile and empathetic minds who could serve as constructive facilitators for a complex and uncertain global future. State interests and state sovereignty have long held sway as organizing principles of global society; though the last 20+ years have seen a gradual shift to a focus on human rights and the "sovereignty of peoples" (Barnett, 2011, p. 166), with human security rather than state security taking precedence among officials at United Nations' agencies (pp. 162–163), there is nonetheless an insufficiently robust global governance imagination to address the ravages of the destructive wars of the latter half of the 20th century and the nearly two decades of the 21st century – the US-led "global war on terror," the Saudi offensive in Yemen, the Syrian president's bombings of Syrian citizens, Israel's assaults on Gaza and in the occupied territories of the West Bank, the civil war in Sudan and the raids by the Janjaweed militia, and the ethnic cleansing of Rohingya Muslims in Myanmar, to name a few.

Among the many groups displaced by these forces of violence are children, who, if they are "fortunate" are able to flee with their families, and, if they are not, are sundered from family and left to navigate the future alone. Humanitarian agencies and the governments of the countries of first asylum have had to house hundreds of thousands and even millions of displaced people, including children, while Western nations largely abdicate their global responsibility to these fellow humans. Education of displaced children is one of the many tasks that fall to governments of first asylum and humanitarian agencies, once the medical, housing, and food security needs of displaced populations have been addressed.

In focusing on the education of displaced children, I draw in part on the frameworks of speculative fiction to offer ways of imagining the future that "depart from consensus reality [and] embrace a different version of reality than the empirical-materialist one... as a quest for the recovery of the sense of awe and wonder" (Osiewicz, 2017, p. 2). I don't at all mean to suggest that the conditions in refugee camps and the immense challenge of educating displaced children can be treated as the raw material for fictional landscapes; rather, what I argue is that the value of using fictional tools and fictional sensibilities lies in their ability to bring us close to that which is not immediately observable, reportable, and measurable. The conditions of refugee experience often border on the surreal, beyond our expectations of reality (Mohsin Hamid's 2017 novel *Exit West*, about refugees and displacement, "mixes the real and the surreal," as Michiko Kakutani observes in her review, 2018). It is in recognition of the many inexplicabilities of refugee life that I turn to speculative fiction, not so much as a methodology of inquiry but as a mental orientation to heighten awareness of what is not immediately provable about refugee education but which could gesture to future transformations of global society.

Speculative fiction, as Osiewicz explains, has been deemed an "imaginative necessity" (2017, p. 22), a mode of thinking that looks beyond the devastating disruptions and upheavals of the current moment to a future that "could be"; it "represents a global reaction of human creative imagination struggling to envision a possible future at the time of a major transition from local to global humanity" (p. 2). It is not surprising that populations that have embraced with gusto the fluid category of speculative fiction have been traditionally marginalized – e.g., indigenous peoples, Latin, Black, and Asian American writers, and postcolonial peoples (p. 21). Osiewicz observes that speculative fiction is "politically scrappy, cognitively empowering, and affectively stimulating" (p. 22). His use of the descriptor "scrappy" is telling, with its dual connotations of something disorganized and fragmented as well as someone argumentative and aggressive.

The many challenges that those who deliver education to children in refugee camps encounter can be overwhelming – everything from lack of space, availability of teachers, resource commitments from governments of first asylum in which the refugee camps are located, decisions about the language of instruction when the refugees speak a language that is not that of the first-asylum country, assuring the safety of children as they go every day from their camp dwellings to the school; within this complicated and daunting landscape, the idea of education emerges as the one avenue of promise and hope. It is this resilient belief in a future that is "better," whatever the obstacles, that characterizes both the teachers and children as operating in the speculative mode.

While there is no doubt about the severe mental health challenges that refugee children experience (Sirin and Rogers-Sirin, 2015), research has shown that even small investments in educating refugee children yield enormous results in terms of reducing the deleterious impact of the violence of war or the upheavals of natural disasters. The everyday routine of attending "school" (however rudimentary the physical space may be), the opportunity to interact with a caring adult and other children, the invitation to focus on something other than the hardships of survival are all factors that contribute to the salutary effects of an educational setting and activities. Education holds the promise of an improved future and introduces a semblance of normalcy into the chaos and tumult of displacement. This essay considers refugee education as holding the possibilities of transformative ways of living even as it acknowledges the many obstacles in realizing these optimistic speculations.

Education and envisioning the landscape of the future

The Convention on the Rights of the Child (CRC) was opened for ratification in November 1989 and put "into force" in September 1990. One of the clauses of the preamble of this covenant reminds us that the focus on children in international law began in 1924 in the Geneva Declaration on the Rights of the Child, and children were underscored as a special group in several legal instruments that followed: the Declaration of the Rights of the Child adopted by the General Assembly on November 20, 1959, in the International Covenant on Civil and Political Rights (in particular in articles 23 and 24) adopted in 1966, in the International Covenant on Economic, Social and Cultural Rights (in particular in article 10) also adopted in 1966, and "in the statutes and relevant instruments of specialized agencies and international organizations concerned with the welfare of children" (OHCHR, Convention on the Rights of the Child). Within the legal framework of the United Nations, a child is any person under the age of 18, unless laws in specific countries specify that "majority" is attained earlier (article 1 of the CRC).

Article 13 of the CRC states: "The child shall have the right to freedom of expression; this right shall include freedom to seek, receive and impart information and ideas of all kinds, regardless of frontiers, either orally, in writing or in print, in the form of art, or through any other media of the child's choice." Article 17c "encourages the production and dissemination of children's books" and article 28 spells out the right of the child to education, especially primary education, with every effort made to provide secondary and higher education as well. The United Nations as well as other international humanitarian organizations that respond to emergency situations, for example, the International Rescue Committee (IRC) and Save the Children, are invested in ensuring that children are provided nurturing and supportive educational environments so that their recovery from the traumas of war and forced migration is hastened.

The right to education leads to other rights: General Comment no. 13 of the Committee on Economic, Social, and Cultural Rights at the 21st Session, in December 1999, notes, "as an empowerment right," education allows both adults and children to overcome poverty, and avoid "hazardous labour and sexual exploitation." However, as the comment further clarifies, education confers more than just practical benefits: "*a well-educated, enlightened and active mind, able to wander freely and widely, is one of the joys and rewards of human existence"* (OHCHR, General Comment no. 13, emphasis added). The diction used is decidedly not "practical" and verges on the affective. That policy makers and career bureaucrats would consider a mind "able to wander freely and widely" as desirable and would resort to emphasizing "joys and rewards" is not typical. I would argue that it is the terrain of education that enables this expansive speculative vision and leads to relatively "poetic" declarations.

The IRC, which was founded in 1933 to provide humanitarian aid and relief, has an elaborately developed "healing classrooms" program that pays close attention to the holistic needs of children. The curriculum and activities of the healing classroom stress such pedagogical practices as writing in a journal every day, creating poetry and short stories, drawing pictures, making puppets and masks, singing, dancing, acting, working in groups, taking field trips to learn about science, discussing and implementing conflict-resolution practices, and doing projects important to the community. Teachers are also encouraged to design "multidisciplinary units focused on crises" (IRC, 2006, p. 13), in which students acquire math, science, and language skills by engaging the crisis at hand. The copyright page of the IRC's healing classroom curriculum guide lists the places in which it has been piloted: Iraq, Liberia, northern Ethiopia, and Aceh. It has also been used in the United States for children affected by Hurricane Katrina (IRC, copyright page).

The healing classroom can become a site for the cultivation of future adults who imagine the world as an interdependent ecosystem of living beings (animals, humans, and plants) and natural resources. IRC research shows that of those children who have gone through traumatic displacement, "70% are resilient, 20–25% are vulnerable, and 3–5% require specialized intervention" (IRC, 2006, p. 4). These statistics indicate that excessively biomedicalizing the condition of refugee children undermines their ability and capacity to recognize themselves as change agents of their own world and diminishes, in the minds of planners and policy makers, the possibilities that could be made available to the children. It is crucial not to reduce the children to the condition of "victimhood" in which the milieu of their present suffering is seen to extend indefinitely into the future.

The interplay between past, present, and future is an important domain of refugee studies. Education, in this interplay, provides promise of a destination that is currently beyond one's reach but that is surely reachable. It beckons to a desirable future and a different future with greater possibilities than the one currently at hand. But the paradox of education is that it is also an activity that structures one's thinking and therefore has the possibility of disciplining. Education can create compliant subjects or creative individuals, future global citizens who either patiently await the promises of a dignified and fulfilling life or boldly and perhaps even aggressively seize hints of opportunity to restructure their situations. Henry Giroux exhorts us to embrace "a politics and a pedagogy of hope... [a]gainst the tyranny of market fundamentalism, religious dogmatism, unchecked militarism, and ideological claims to certainty" (2006, pp. 189–190). For children in refugee camps, hope is not a luxury; it is a necessity. A prominent vector through which hope is delivered is almost invariably education.

Matiop Wal, who was forced to flee Sudan in 1987, when he was 7 years old, and was one of the thousands of unaccompanied children who trekked to Ethiopia and from there to Kenya, after having lived for four years in a refugee camp in Ethiopia, speaks about his own efforts to educate himself. At the Kakuma refugee camp in Kenya, Matiop learned to love learning and to value education. He remembers,

> When we started school in Kakuma in 1993, there were no classrooms and there were no books. Our classes were held in the shades of acacia trees. And our writing boards were made out of pieces of discarded cardboard boxes. We used to buy charcoals from the local people (Turkana people) with portions of our meager rations, and we used the charcoals as chalks.[1]

Despite the bare-bones material conditions of their lives, the yearning for education led Matiop and other Sudanese youth to barter what little they had in exchange for writing implements and to use the leveled dust of the ground under the acacia trees as the notebooks, desks, and chairs of their pedagogical encounter. He speaks with great fondness of his teachers, adult Sudanese refugees:

> The teachers were the books, since they taught us from their memories... In the beginning of the schooling in the Camp in Kenya, those teachers just volunteered themselves to teach us, but the UN acknowledged their effort later on when the camp was well established. So they were employed and they continued teaching us. Seeing those teachers working with the UN was one of the inspiring reasons that encouraged so many children who did not know the value of education. But when we saw that they were refugees just like us children, and that what they had in their heads differentiated them from us, that was so convincing that every child wanted to learn so that they can work and be able to support themselves someday, through what they would learn in school. I was one of the children who were inspired by those south Sudanese teachers in the refugees camp.[2]

Matiop's recollection highlights a number of important points about the significance of education in "emergency settings": it provides structure, establishes routine, generates a sense of purpose for both adults and children, and enables the projection of a vastly improved future. Matiop left the camp in Kenya in 2001, when he was 21 years old. I met Matiop when he was a student at the University of Massachusetts Boston in the mid-2000s. The extensive length (nearly ten years) of Matiop's stay in the Kakuma refugee camp is not at all unusual. Many refugees are "warehoused" in refugee camps for decades; in fact, Kenya is home to two of the largest refugee camps in the world, Dadaab and Kakuma, which have been in existence since 1991 and 1992, respectively.[3]

Matiop's enthusiasm for the schooling he received at Kakuma is implicitly echoed in this description by Dryden-Peterson of two children who developed "vacant eyes" and "resigned attitudes" (2006, p. 391) when the informal refugee-run school that they were attending in Kampala, Uganda was forced to shut down because of resistance from the local population. The sense of "awe and wonder" that speculative narrative provides of a future replete with possibilities is powered in refugee camps by the activity of learning. The violence that brings children to refugee camps, that tears them from their homes and their families is, through the educational encounter, pushed back from the forefront of their consciousness to make room for an alternate reality.

Education that emphasizes a common humanity

For refugee children, the connection to the world outside their refugee camps is a crucial aspect of their hope of belonging to a global community (this is especially true for children who are 14 and above). In this context, the Global Citizenship Education (GCE) program developed by the United Nations Educational, Scientific, and Cultural Organization (UNESCO) in 2013 is significant. Countries in sub-Saharan Africa have received UNESCO encouragement to implement the curriculum in their primary schools and, in the case of Uganda, in refugee settlement camps within its borders. GCE is also used in the United Nations Reliefs and Works Agency (UNRWA) camps in Palestine, and its impact there is discussed later in this essay. GCE was conceived as a means to foster a new kind of thinking among children and youth of the world, an education that foregrounds the importance of connection among the peoples of the globe: UNESCO conceives of GCE as cultivating "a sense of belonging to a global community and a common humanity, a feeling of global solidarity, identity and responsibility that generates actions based on and respect of universal values" (UNESCO, n.d.).

The director of the Division of Education for Peace and Development at UNESCO describes GCE as aiming to "empower learners to engage and assume active roles both locally and globally, and to face and resolve global challenges such as peace building or environmental issues." She notes as well that GCE "contributes to increasing individual competitiveness of learners in a globalizing world" (UNESCO, n.d.). There is something schizophrenic in an initiative that seeks to foster global understanding while simultaneously increasing individual competitiveness. It is not clear how teachers are trained to negotiate this curious contradiction. There is nothing inherently detrimental about self-enrichment and the pursuit of individual passions in cultivating global citizenship, but if competitiveness is prioritized as a mode of being, then it is more than likely that competitiveness will foster precisely those attitudes that militate against global citizenship. "Learning to live with others" (UNESCO, n.d.) – one of the goals of GCE – is difficult when collaboration and cooperation are subordinated to individual competitiveness. In Uganda, GCE is embedded within one of the goals of the country's education frameworks: "*to promote understanding of the value of national identity, patriotism and cultural heritage, with due consideration of international relations and beneficial inter-dependence*" (Uganda National Commission for UNESCO). It is not impossible to develop an attitude toward life that both takes pride in local and national imperatives and also recognizes the value of peoples and nations other than one's own – "rooted cosmopolitanism" as Appiah has termed it. But such an attitude requires skilled pedagogy and the ability to cultivate in children and youth the capacity to reconcile seemingly contradictory feelings.

The rhetoric of GCE privileges such attitudes as "empathy" and "solidarity"; one of the key learner attributes that is sought is "motivation and willingness to care for the common good" (UNESCO, 2015, p. 29). The learning objectives articulated in detail for different age groups, in UNESCO's GCE guide, are impressive, especially with the attention paid by the framework designers to power dynamics and the impact of asymmetrical power on such matters as whose voice gets heard and how structures of educational governance are established. The age categories differentiated by UNESCO's GCE guide are: 5–9 (pre-primary and lower primary), 9–12 (upper primary), 12–15 (lower secondary), and 15–18+ (upper secondary) (UNESCO, 2015, p. 31).

The ambition of the GCE curriculum can only be realized, however, with appropriate teacher training and the resources of space, time, and materials to deliver it. Refugee education suffers from acute shortages of all necessary facets of infrastructure. GCE at best is an aspirational idea and, at worst it is a feel-good rhetorical and pedagogical planning exercise that serves the self-congratulatory interests of bureaucrats, non-governmental organizations, and donor organizations. Sarah Dryden-Peterson observes that it is crucial for teachers to prepare refugee children for "unknowable futures" (2017). I would go one step further and note that the refugee children's situation of uncertainty is *not* debilitating, *not* handicapping. Rather, its very uncertainty and the children's ability to dream in these circumstances hold within them the potential for cultivating innovative, creative, and responsible future thinkers and leaders.

In making this suggestion, I am not trying to depoliticize the condition of displacement and warehousing by projecting a sanitized and hopeful ground for reconstruction; on the contrary, I wish to underscore that precisely because the conditions of displacement create flux and disruption they are ripe for reshaping imagination and re-envisioning the future. Dryden-Peterson's observation that "Teachers of refugees are not a private, national good but a public, global one" (2017) further confirms my view that refugee camps provide teachers with a unique opportunity to understand that they are educating citizens for the future of the world and not for narrowly conceived national futures. However, in the case of Palestinian refugee camps run by UNRWA, the question of nationalism takes on complex weight and power, as I discuss later in this essay. Nonetheless, it is possible, some would argue, that Palestinian identity and its deep historical attachments to land that is currently under Israeli control can coexist with the vision of a future in which Palestinian and Jewish identities can flourish in a single binational state (Farsakh, 2011; Karmi, 2011).

The future is always uncertain, but for refugee children, in particular, it is characterized by "radical uncertainty" (Dryden-Peterson, 2017). Kim LeBlanc and Tony Waters underscore that education anywhere is a political project and especially so in refugee camps. They explain that "education packages for refugee camps, like food reserves, are borrowed from a stockpile in the host country or elsewhere, and little attention is paid to broader questions to do with the kind of future children will have" (2005). They articulate the problem of socializing refugee children, through education, into the national project of citizenship:

> the world's refugees as a stateless "them" provide an unusual challenge for understanding the relationships imagined between school curriculum and modern citizenship... [I]ssues taken for granted in "normal" societies, such as language choice, history, gender, and religion become a focus for contention within the community itself, host country education ministries, and the humanitarian relief community.
> (Waters and Le Blanc, 2005, p. 130)

I agree that the stateless condition of refugees does present a problem for the nationalizing project of nation-state-designed curricula; but I also see the situation as an opportunity for instilling new pedagogies and underscoring new urgencies that don't polarize place-based and community-specific cultural attachments, on the one hand, and global visions on the other.

Palestinians living in refugee camps run by UNRWA and living in the West Bank and Gaza, who experience the everyday effects of living under Israeli control, present a special case within the context of refugee education. Nadera Shalhoub-Kevorkian, among others, has described their condition as a "perpetual 'refugee status'" (2010, p. 336). She observes that education's power lies in its being one of the "few optimistic avenues left to the colonized to struggle toward emancipation... [S]tudents... consequently value education as a means to an end towards freedom" (p. 337). Attending school, despite the multiple hardships, becomes an act of resistance. Shalhoub-Kevorkian observes that her conversations with Palestinian children show that "schools have become a site of opposition for many: by attending school, they refuse to give in to the horrors of life around them and to lose the source of support, love, and belonging, and perhaps most importantly, stability" (p. 345). She detects a "counter-hegemonic language... in the children's thoughts and voices" (p. 346), and she offers us the words of one young girl:

> I believe that I, Hidaya, the very simple person, is much stronger than all of them. Otherwise, why would they send a tank, big computerized planes and machines to kill me. They fear the Palestinian child, and therefore we must stay strong, love each other, help and support the needy, and be educated.
>
> (p. 346)

Ozlem Eskiocak is the human rights education program coordinator for UNRWA. She writes about UNRWA's delivery of its "Human Rights, Conflict Resolution and Tolerance Education Programme" and the integration of its values into all subject areas including mathematics. The 19,000 teachers in the UNRWA camps are all trained to deliver this curriculum to the approximately 500,000 refugee children in the various camps for Palestinians in Gaza, the West Bank, Jordan, and Lebanon (2018). The video "If the world were 100 people" shows how human rights education is put into practice in a lesson on statistics, percentages, and ratios. The video, which is approximately 8.25 minutes long, offers a fascinating and upbeat view of a vibrant classroom in which students and the teacher (depicted as computer animated figures) engage in a lesson that seamlessly integrates mathematical concepts with issues of diversity and human rights. The children discuss such subjects as access to clean water, toilets, and safe homes alongside the multiplicity of religions and cultures and the varying levels of comfort they feel about interacting with those who are "different" (UNRWA, n.d.). The students are aware of the fact that they themselves do not have "safe homes," and they are shown in this video as developing a consciousness of the wider world in which large numbers of people suffer deprivations of basic needs such as clean water, food, and toilets. The Palestinian refugee children also learn that there is 100 percent literacy in their communities. This last bit of information, delivered by the teacher, provides a source of pride, I would argue, and underscores the primacy placed on education as a tool of freedom and possibility.

Aspirational futures meet present realities

Eskiocak reminds us that though human rights education in the UNRWA camps is a strong vehicle for empowering both Palestinian children and teachers, the ambitious curriculum does not erase from their consciousness the harsh realities of their lives. She writes,

> The students were going through one of our human rights activities in which they were asked to draw their ideal world. Some of these 8 year-old

children drew rockets directed at their homes because that was their reality. In other words, even the blue skies in their drawings were littered with rockets.

Similarly, teachers asked, "how can I teach human rights when my own rights as refugees are not respected?" Community members were equally skeptical (Eskiocak, 2018). These sentiments find parallels in Jennifer Hyndman's (2011) observations that education within the camps (her focus is on camps in Kenya) may introduce and underscore the values of global citizenship, but the actualities of life within the camps and the opportunities for the future for young people in the camps meet the hard facts of host country policies surrounding refugees as well as the developed countries' policy of "externalizing asylum" and erecting barriers to mobility and opportunity for refugee youth.

The irony of the 21st century is that as the United Nations has made global citizenship a priority, the international community, particularly the developed nations, have instituted policies that stymie the realization of one of the principal tenets of global citizenship: i.e., the common humanity we all share. The global education curriculum may create confidence in the refugee students, may make them feel that they are connected to a wider humanity and not alone. However, does it prepare children for the long fight? Refugee camps are sites of containment. They are necessary places of crisis management, essential places of shelter, but they also enable the perpetuation of a state of hope perennially deferred, or elusive hope that holds the promise of a realization that will never come. If the confidence that the children in the GCE video "MyVoiceMySchool" (Eskiocak, 2018) display is the quality that is instilled in them through global human rights education, then can this confidence be sustained through the long-term disappointment of unrealized hope? Does repeated frustration of hope turn the children's and youth's confidence into resignation or does it harden into defiant insistence that they will not be deterred? Can solidarity be forged across children and youth in different countries and sustained into adulthood, so that, at a future date, as adults they can work together to realize a full life? Is GCE a kind of salve that makes it possible to endure the unconscionable realities of the present, or is it an infusion of necessary aggressive hope that demands the construction of a meaningful reality?

Though Agamben's "bare life" formulation is often applied to refugee existence, critics of well-meaning Western interventions into refugees' lives resist it as a characterization. Refugees and refugee children do not lack the inner resources to find meaning in their lives, they observe. In fact, in the case of refugee children living in circumstances of prolonged conflict and dispossession, a political stance of resistance can provide a strong bulwark against despair and allow for the positing of a meaningful future. Veronese et al. note that "While on the one hand signs of the ongoing violence are clearly identifiable, for example in schools that have been bombed, or in the daily challenge of trying to study when the electricity is cut off every 6/8 hours, on the other hand, Gazan children at school are constantly engaged in constructing *meaning* in relation to their own lives and that of their community" (2017, p. 371). Rather than psychologizing the children and reading them through the lens of a Western psychological model of post-traumatic stress disorder, the authors of this study insist on recognizing the children's resourcefulness in constructing their own forms of resistance and reimagining in order to infuse their lives with purpose and possibility. For example, when children play in the rubble of bombed buildings in Gaza, their activity is a form of resistance to the dangers that pervade their environment. Studies show that "Running the risk of playing in a dangerous environment is an active way for these children to claim the right to exist" (p. 371).

I have discussed the optimistic and hopeful vision of UNESCO's GCE. Whether such education politicizes or depoliticizes children and youth is complicated to assess, because the process of politicization can be gradual, incremental, and cumulative over time such that there is no easy way to trace the causal link between a type of curriculum and pedagogical process, on the one hand, and the awakening into political consciousness and self-determination on the other. GCE does not, unlike explicitly decolonizing pedagogies and curricula, identify oppressors and systems of power that must be challenged and resisted. One could see it as a defanged and depoliticized curriculum because of its emphasis on hope rather than anger, and collaboration rather than defiance. I would argue, however, that the oppositions are not so simple, and to see the children and youth as malleable into compliant and patient global citizenship is to underestimate their capacity for complex understanding.

Ann-Christin Wagner (2017) critiques the depoliticized education provided to the youth in refugee camps in Jordan. One of the thought-provoking examples she provides is of the German political foundation that came to Mafraq to conduct a one-day workshop for refugee youth on "democratic institutions." The 12 youth participants, she writes, engaged in heated debate about citizenship and participatory democracy, but "there was a striking mismatch between participants' goodwill and opportunities for political participation in Jordan, let alone Syria." As a result, she "question[ed] the value of *citizenship* as a concept of development work: reclaiming refugee integration makes little sense when even Jordanian *citizens* lack civil and political rights" (p. 115). Wagner asserts that this type of misguided programming, because of its lack of attention to pragmatic realities, shows how "political education can become depoliticized." But my challenge to Wagner's argument lies in her understanding of the descriptor "depoliticized." I would argue that though the refugee youth are outside any (nation-state) political spaces in the present, one cannot therefore dismiss the possibility of their participating in or reshaping such spaces in the future. Agamben is right that the refugee is "the only thinkable figure" (2008, p. 90) for imagining a future political community. There is the possibility of crafting a new kind of political consciousness – one that imagines a new type of belonging in a reconfigured world. However speculative such a vision might be, it might provide the only avenue for refugee youth and children to project an alternate future to the one that they are experiencing.

We Love Reading

In this regard of hope for the future, Rana Dajani's "We Love Reading" (WLR) initiative, which started off as what could have been seen as an outrageously impractical idea, is now an influential reading program for young children in all types of communities – refugee, immigrant, impoverished, urban – in many parts of the world. Dajani was deeply troubled by the statistic, included in the 2011 Report on Cultural Development issued by the Arab Thought Foundation (Amin-Ali, 2017, p. 223), that in the Arab world people spend a bare six minutes a year reading for pleasure (i.e., reading material unrelated to work, religious education, or secular education). Whether or not this statistic is accurate or an exaggeration (Caldwell, 2012) is less important than that it provoked Dajani into action. She was determined to change the situation, because she carried within her treasured memories of having read for pleasure as a child.

Dajani is a scientist, a professor of biology and biotechnology at Hashemite University in Jordan, and yet she was driven by a desire to tap the community-building potential of reading to children (aged 4–10). There was nothing intentionally political in the genesis of "We Love Reading," but the types of books that were selected to be read aloud – that "included themes of empathy, responsibility, and respect" (Dajani and Abdullah-Awad, 2017, p. 17) – indicate clearly that there was a latent social objective in mind: call it one of cultivating in young readers the capacity to care for and connect with others so as to shape a world that is less riven with hostile divisions. Dajani and Abdullah-Awad aver that "[L]iterature, as opposed to textbooks used for school, is primarily a humanistic product, encouraging empathy, ambivalence, tolerance, and self-reflection… Developing a relationship with literature at a young age encourages a generation to deploy such qualities in their everyday life afterwards" (p. 18). The training provided to the adult volunteers who read further underscores the thematic agenda of the WLR project:

> Empathy, respect and acceptance are core values, transmitted in the training. They shall enable the women to teach approaches such as if a person disagrees with somebody, he or she can at least appreciate the background of the counterpart and respect different opinions. This attitude fosters inclusion and respect among the trainees who in turn become role models for others.
>
> (p. 19)

The act of reading has ripple effects for the women volunteers. It builds confidence in them, brings the community together, and can lead to initiatives that tackle problems faced by the neighborhood, such as trash on the streets. Dajani observes that because the WLR readers come from local communities, it is perceived as being a homegrown initiative, not something imposed by the West, and it is tailored to local contexts and delivered in the local language.[4] What started out as a project that she piloted in her mosque in Jordan has grown into a global movement that is in 41 countries as of this writing, and its impact is felt not only by children aged 4–10 in refugee camps and in non-refugee spaces but also by the adults who read and in the communities where the adults and children reside.

Initially, the books that WLR uses were drawn from available titles in Arabic: the two conditions that the books had to fulfill were, "they had to be fun, and the illustrations had to be bright and cheerful." The success of the WLR program drew interested donors and UNICEF who saw it as a useful vehicle to communicate themes of positive coexistence, sustainability, and empathy. Dajani insists that even with donors who come with large amounts of money and a desire to promote particular kinds of themes, she foregrounds the "fun" aspect of the experience for the children. "If the children don't enjoy the book and don't share it with family members, then it's no use," she says. WLR has a growing catalogue of titles of books that it has commissioned and published, working with Jordanian writers, illustrators, and designers. "We work with the writers and illustrators sometimes for a year, until we have the kind of book we want." The illustrations are lively, vibrant, and compelling. The themes of the WLR-created and published books include "environmental protection, acceptance of mental and physical disabilities, refugees, anti-violence, social unity, and gender equality" (from the electronic catalogue).[5] The titles are categorized into three age groups: 4–6, 5–8, and 7–10. There are separate symbols for each of the environmental themes – water, energy, and anti-littering – and separate symbols for each of the social issues – non-violence, social inclusion, disabilities, empathy, gender, and refugees.

WLR and the donors hope that the reading and discussion of books can lead to heightened awareness of the themes that animate them and so create a "world" that is more inclusive and concerned with care for others and for the environment. Dajani has been working with several university researchers to run studies that measure the impact of the books and the program on children's attitudes to particular issues. Neurobiologist Jean Decety has been studying the impact of WLR on the development of empathy in children. Recently, Dajani received $3 million from UNICEF and other donors to conduct research on the effectiveness of the WLR program in Jordan, including in the refugee camps.[6]

Conclusion

There are a number of players involved in the education of children and youth in refugee camps. In addition to the relevant agencies of the United

Nations (UNESCO, UNICEF, and UNRWA), several non-governmental humanitarian organizations and donor organizations, along with the governments of countries of first asylum, take on the overwhelming responsibility of ensuring that millions of displaced children acquire the cognitive and social skills to forge a meaningful life in the future, wherever that future might be. These children are not victims and they are not potential recruits for nefarious purposes. They are resilient and hopeful human beings who, infused with a bit of confidence and provided with a vision of an enriched future, could prove to be among the most thoughtful, empathetic, and complex participants of a global community.

Discussion questions

1 How does fulfilling the right to education for children enable the realization of other rights?
2 If the future that awaits children in refugee camps is an uncertain one, what skills and attributes would most enable them to navigate this uncertainty?
3 What is GCE, and what is its value as a curriculum for educating children in refugee camps?
4 Refugees are often seen as vulnerable and helpless populations. How would you describe refugee children? How do the humanitarian agencies perceive them? Based on your understanding of their realities, what essential components should their education include?

Notes

1 Matiop Wal, in an email communication to the author dated January 22, 2018.
2 Matiop Wal, in an email communication to the author dated January 21, 2018.
3 "Warehousing" describes the "practice of keeping refugees in protracted situations of restricted mobility, enforced idle-ness, and dependency – their lives on indefinite hold – in violation of their basic rights under the 1951 UN Refugee Convention." See Merrill Smith, n.d.
4 I met Rana Dajani in Cambridge, Massachusetts in February and March 2018. Dajani was at the Radcliffe Institute at Harvard University, as a Rita E. Hauser fellow for the academic year 2017–18.
5 Dajani sent me the electronic catalogue at my request.
6 See Yazji (2014) for a study of the impact of the WLR program at the Zaatari refugee camp in Jordan that provides compelling though not conclusive evidence of its positive effects on the psychsocial wellbeing of children.

References

Agamben, G. (2008). Beyond human rights. *Social Engineering*, 15, pp. 90–95.
Amin-Ali, K. (2017). United Arab Emirates: An overview. In: S. Kirdar, ed., *Education in the Arab world*. New York: Bloomsbury Academic, pp. 217–243.
Barnett, M. (2011). *Empire of humanity: A history of humanitarianism*. Ithaca, NY: Cornell University Press.

Caldwell, L. (2012). The Arab reader and the myth of six minutes. *Al-Akhbar English*. Available at: https://english.al-akhbar.com/node/3168 [Accessed April 28, 2018].

Dajani, R. and Awad, Abdullah Z.J. (2017). We Love Reading: A women's literacy program in the Arab world. *Ohio ASCD Journal*, Winter/Spring, pp. 15–24.

Dryden-Peterson, S. (2006). I find myself as someone who is in the forest: Urban refugees as agents of social change in Kampala, Uganda. *Journal of Refugee Studies*, 19(3), pp. 381–395.

Dryden-Peterson, S. (2017). How teachers can prepare children for unknowable futures. *Refugees Deeply*. Available at: www.newsdeeply.com/refugees/community/2017/03/16/how-teachers-can-prepare-refugee-children-for-unknowable-futures [Accessed April 7, 2018].

Eskiocak, O. (2018). Making global education possible for refugees. Available at: www.opendemocracy.net/wfd/ozlem-eskiocak/making-global-citizenship-education-possible-for-refugees (Accessed April 11, 2018).

Farsakh, L. (2011). The one-state solution and the Israeli-Palestinian conflict: Palestinian challenges and prospects. *Middle East Journal*, 65(1), pp. 55–71.

Giroux, H. (2006). Reading Hurricane Katrina: Race, class, and the biopolitics of disposability. *College Literature*, 33(3), pp. 171–196.

Hyndman, J. (2011). A refugee camp conundrum: Geopolitics, liberal democracy, and protracted refugee situations. *Refuge: Canada's Journal on Refugees*, 28(2), pp. 7–15.

International Rescue Committee (IRC) (2006). Creating healing classrooms: Guide for teachers and teacher educators. Available at: http://healingclassrooms.org/downloads/CHC_Guide_for_Teachers_TEs.pdf [Accessed April 6, 2018].

Kakutani, M. (2018). In *Exit west*, Mohsin Hamid mixes global trouble with a bit of magic. *New York Times*. Available at: www.nytimes.com/2017/02/27/books/review-exit-west-mohsin-hamid.html [Accessed April 29, 2018].

Karmi, G. (2011). The one-state solution: An alternative vision for Israeli-Palestinian peace. *Journal of Palestine Studies*, 40(2), pp. 62–76.

LeBlanc, T. and Waters, T. (2005). Schooling in refugee camps. *Humanitarian Practice Network* Available at: https://odihpn.org/magazine/schooling-in-refugee-camps/ [Accessed April 14, 2018].

OHCHR (n.d.). Convention on the Rights of the Child. Available at: www.ohchr.org/EN/ProfessionalInterest/Pages/CRC.aspx [Accessed April 6, 2018].

OHCHR (n.d.). General Comment no. 13: The Right to Education. Available at: www.ohchr.org/EN/Issues/Education/Training/Compilation/Pages/dGeneralCommentNo13Therighttoeducation(article13)(1999).aspx [Accessed April 6, 2018].

Osiewicz, M. (2017). Speculative fiction. In: P. Rabinowitz, ed., *Oxford research encyclopedia of literature*. Available at: http://literature.oxfordre.com/view/10.1093/acrefore/9780190201098.001.0001/acrefore-9780190201098-e-78?rskey=d2vZm0&result=1

Shalhoub-Keverkian, N. (2010). Palestinians, education, and the Israeli "industry of fear." In: A.E. Mazawi and R.G. Sultana, eds, *The world yearbook of education 2010: Education and the Arab World: Political projects, struggles, and geometries of power (Part IV: Knowledge imaginaries)*. New York: Routledge, pp. 335–349.

Sirin, S.R. and Rogers-Sirin, L. (2015). The educational and mental health needs of Syrian refugee children. In: R. Capps and K. Hopper, eds, *Young children in refugee families*. Washington, DC: Migration Policy Institute, pp. 1–27.

Smith, M. (n.d.). Warehousing refugees: A denial of rights, a waste of humanity. Available at: http://refugees.org/wp-content/uploads/2015/12/Warehousing-Refugees-Campaign-Materials.pdf [Accessed May 18, 2018].

Uganda National Commission for UNESCO. Pilot testing global citizenship education (GCED) curricula and training materials in refugee settlement camps primary
schools, Kiryandongo District, Uganda. Available at: www.unesco-uganda.ug/ug/
dnews/41/Pilot-Testing-Global-Citizenship-Education-(GCED)-Curricula-and-Tra
ining-Materials-in-Refugee-Settlement-Camps-Primary-Schools,-Kiryandongo-Dis
trict,-Uganda-.html [Accessed April 14, 2018].

United Nations Educational, Scientific, and Cultural Organization (UNESCO) (2015).
Global citizenship education: Topics and learning objectives. Available at: http://unes
doc.unesco.org/images/0023/002329/232993e.pdf (Accessed April 14, 2018).

United Nations Educational Scientific and Cultural Organization (UNESCO) (n.d.)
Teachers for 21st century global citizenship. Available at: https://en.unesco.org/news/
teachers-21st-century-global-citizenship [Accessed April 6, 2018].

United Nations Relief and Works Agency for Palestine (UNRWA) (n.d.). *If the world
were 100 people.* Available at: www.youtube.com/watch?v=JNOJdbLmfE4&feature=
youtu.be [Accessed April 11, 2018].

Veronese, G., Pepe, A., Jaradah, A., Murannak, F., and Hamdouna, H. (2017). We
must cooperate with one another against the enemy: Agency and activism in
school-aged children as protective factors against ongoing war trauma and political
violence in the Gaza Strip. *Child Abuse and Neglect*, 70, pp. 364–376.

Wagner, A. (2017). Frantic waiting: NGO anti-politics and "timepass" for young
Syrian refugees in Jordan. *Middle East: Topics and Arguments*, 9, pp. 107–121.

Waters, T. and Le Blanc, K. (2005). Refugees and education: Mass public-schooling
without a nation-state. *Comparative Education Review*, 49(2), pp. 129–147.

Yazji, S. (2014). Final report: the impact of the We Love Reading pilot program on
the psychosocial health of participating children in Zaatari Refugee Camp. Available at: https://d3gxp3iknbs7bs.cloudfront.net/attachments/c4abdf61-4f5d-4cde-a4ab-
6717c57ee643.pdf [Accessed April 14, 2018].

Further reading

Dill, J.S. (2013). *The longings and limits of global citizenship education: The moral pedagogy of schooling in a cosmopolitan age.* New York: Routledge.

Dryden-Peterson, S. (2015). *The educational experiences of refugee children in countries of
first asylum.* Washington, DC: Migration Policy Institute.

Mahasneh, R.A., Romanowski, M.H., and Dajani, R.B. (2017). Reading social stories in the
community: A promising intervention for promoting children's environmental knowledge and behavior in Jordan. *Journal of Environmental Education*, 48(5), pp. 334–346.

Mundy, K., Dryden-Peterson, S., and Steiner-Khamsi, G., eds (2011). *Educating children in conflict zones: Research, policy and practice for systemic change.* New York:
Teachers College Press.

UNHCR (2016). Missing out: Refugee education in crisis. Available at: http://uis.
unesco.org/sites/default/files/documents/missing-out-refugee-education-in-crisis_
unhcr_2016-en.pdf [Accessed April 14, 2018].

Wright, L. and Plasterer, R. (2010). Beyond basic education: Exploring opportunities
for higher learning in Kenyan refugee camps. *Refuge: Canada's Journal on Refugees*,
27(2), pp. 42–56.

12 Persistent voices

A history of indigenous people and human rights in Australia, 1950s–2000s

Maria John[1]

Introduction

While those at the Paris Peace Conference in 1919, or in Dumbarton Oaks and San Francisco in 1944–1945, gave little thought to the concerns of indigenous Australians in their deliberations about human rights, the growth of the new legal paradigm and the new institutions to which it became attached were closely observed by those working for Aboriginal rights within Australia, and quickly became the context and language of their activism. As evinced in the poetry of acclaimed Aboriginal activist and artist Oodgeroo Noonuccal, by the start of the 1960s the language of human rights was firmly ingrained in Australian indigenous political discourse. In 1962, Noonuccal penned what would become one of her most cited works; a poem titled "Aboriginal Charter of Rights." In it, she juxtaposed the secure enjoyment of basic social, political, and civil rights by Australians, with their glaring absence in Aboriginal peoples' lives. Her memorable lines calling for "Status, not discrimination; Human rights, not segregation" (1962, p. 14) also indicated how at this historical and political juncture, Aboriginal people in Australia were not unlike many disempowered and marginalized peoples around the world who, under the mantle of this new human rights discourse, were fighting both inside and outside of empire for just and equal treatment.

At this time, Aboriginal people in Australia faced some of the worst mistreatment enacted on a people by its own government. In the 1950s and 1960s they were still excluded from many basic social, economic, and political rights. Indeed, Aboriginal people were not even counted in Australia's national census until 1967, indicating just how peripheral they were to the nation. Given the nature of their mistreatment, it is easy to understand why Aboriginal activists centered on human rights in this period. The 1948 Universal Declaration of Human Rights was brimming with protections for basic civic and social equality, and the genocidal horrors of World War II had engendered a more receptive world stage for those who criticized the injustice of state policies employing invidious racial distinctions. Consequently, Aboriginal people, like many others, seized on human rights in the immediate heyday of the 1948 declaration as a tool that could be wielded to help keep the excesses of the (in their case colonial) state in check.

In this vein, throughout the 1960s Aboriginal campaigners like Charles Perkins drew directly on international events in this new human rights era to argue that Australia's domestic policy towards Aboriginal people was being rendered ethically and politically untenable by the new norms of international morality (Read, 1990). In 1961, upon being elected vice president of a newly formed national pressure group, the Federal Council for Aboriginal Advancement (FCAA), Perkins joined the campaign to abolish the oppressive South Australian Aborigines Act,[2] telling one journalist, he was "trying to kick Little Rock clear out of South Australia" and that Australian state governments were behaving "like the Belgians in the Congo" (Perkins, cited in Read, 1990, p. 5). In fact, some Australian campaigners in the 1960s, like prominent white suffragette Jessie Street, had long felt, "the best hope for the advancement of Aboriginal rights lay with international exposure of Australian practices" (Sekuless, 1978, p. 8).[3] In order to appeal directly to global forums for protections, claims to equal rights for Aborigines thus steadily became expressed by activists in the international language of human rights.

Yet, the precise meaning of this borrowed language to its new users, and the extent to which international human rights norms would *continue* to serve Aboriginal people in Australia beyond their immediate struggles for equality and basic citizenship rights, are important and difficult questions to confront and grapple with. In order to understand the unique position in which Aboriginal people found (and continue to find) themselves, in relation to the logic and function of human rights, we have to remember that in their political struggles during the 1950s–1960s, unlike other (non-indigenous) peoples under conditions of colonialism, Aboriginal people in Australia were not yet appealing to human rights frameworks in order to be granted political independence. Rather, more like African Americans or other minority populations, Aboriginal people appealed to the United Nations (UN) during this time because they were being oppressed and treated unequally by the Australian state. In this respect, human rights discourse was tailor-made to respond to their most pressing needs. Their early appeals to human rights were thus an attempt to use this legal framework to make the Australian state's use of its sovereign powers more just and equitable. Importantly, however, these appeals to human rights norms did not settle, let alone address, questions about the legitimacy of the Australian nation's sovereign claims over Aboriginal peoples more fundamentally. It is this latter, more far-reaching question on which greater indigenous political aspirations ultimately turn.

Many of the more far-reaching political aspirations of indigenous politics have always sat somewhat uncomfortably within a human rights framework. Historically speaking, indigenous peoples' political concerns have been stretched between the stronger aspirations of decolonization (akin to former colonies seeking independence from colonizing states), and the less radical, but more pressing need to reckon with the ongoing *effects* of colonialism (more akin to claims of mistreated minorities, seeking equal rights and treatment). The turn to human rights discourse to advance the latter (less strident) demand has thus been accompanied by critiques that the human rights model is ultimately ill-suited and even assimilationist in relation to indigenous peoples' politics. As these arguments go, at least politically speaking, the human rights framework is ultimately only responsive to questions of whether the authority of the colonial state is being justly wielded (that is, in accordance with human rights and equality standards). When it comes to questioning the historical legitimacy of that colonial authority over indigenous people in the first place, the UN human rights framework has ranged over time from a conspicuous silence to a strategic ambiguity. According to this line of criticism, the human rights model therefore involves a buried assumption, or at least the practical entailment, that indigenous peoples need only be treated just like any other citizen. But indigenous political aspirations went (and continue to go) beyond this assumption by challenging the very authority of the colonial state itself. This challenge, as I have indicated already, is not well (or at least easily) addressed by the human rights framework.

We can discern these sorts of misgivings in much of the latest scholarship on indigenous peoples' engagements with the UN. Indeed, in this literature something of a critical consensus has been reached that however progressive the 2007 UN Declaration on the Rights of Indigenous Peoples (UNDRIP)— and indeed, the entire international legal system built around human rights—these instruments also contain significant oversights and compromises (Engle, 2010, 2011; Churchill, 2011; Wiessner, 2011). In particular, contemporary critics argue that embedded in the 2007 declaration are serious limitations to the very rights it is praised for containing. These scholars have argued that while the UN and the 2007 declaration may have made significant strides in protecting indigenous cultural heritage, land rights, and development, they have done so in ways that are potentially undermined by their ultimate commitment to the existing boundaries and prerogatives of state sovereignty and to an especially individualistic and liberal form of human rights. In short, by re-enshrining a commitment to liberal individualism and to the unbridled sovereignty of nation-states that continue to oppress indigenous peoples, the UN system has become an extension of colonization in the present.

Chapter outline

In this chapter I use the example of Australia to chart a history of activism that prefigures the critical views of human rights to which I refer above. I show that while the 1948 Human Rights Declaration served Aboriginal activists well for a while, the limitations of a human rights framework for the protection of *specific* indigenous rights and interests eventually led to a movement in the closing decades of the 20th century to develop a legal regime specifically tailored to the needs, demands, and rights of indigenous peoples – as distinct from other minority groups. The political demands and aspirations of the world's indigenous peoples are of course diverse, but the primacy within their politics of relationships to specific ancestral lands and historical and continuing aspirations for independent political community commonly distinguishes them from other minorities dispossessed in terms of power or wealth. For these reasons, once the initial battles for citizenship rights and equality had been waged, it became necessary for Aboriginal people to reach beyond what an individualist human rights framework could offer, and strive for new protections that could accommodate their collective rights and aspirations – most of all, the protection of their threatened heritages, languages, rituals, and lands.

In some respects, the 2007 UNDRIP was a major milestone in this regard, but as I will discuss, while the document has been lauded by many for its recognition of collective rights, the right to culture, and self-determination for indigenous peoples, it is also heavily critiqued for not doing enough – if only because at the end of the day, legally speaking, UN declarations, like most resolutions by the General Assembly, are of a mere aspirational nature: "recommendations" without legally binding character. More problematically than this, though, was the way in which, throughout negotiations leading to the 2007 declaration, it was clear the UN system actively sought to adopt a stance of ambiguity towards the meaning of self-determination as specifically applied to indigenous peoples. Finally, as many critics point out, a close reading of the rights protected by UNDRIP shows that they are both less powerful than they appear on the surface, and that they are limited and superseded by the human rights framework in which they are embedded.[4] Legal scholar Karen Engle expresses this last problem succinctly when noting that the indigenous right to self-determination recognized by UNDRIP takes the form of "a collective human rights demand rather than a claim for statehood" (2011, p. 148).

I will elaborate on these critiques of UNDRIP within the final section of this chapter. For now, however, I want to tell the historical story behind the critical turn in indigenous engagements with human rights. And for this we need to examine the shift within indigenous political activism on the international stage that occurred during the mid- to late 20th century. In this time indigenous peoples pivoted from an expression and advocacy of their grievances to an international forum in the language and framework of human rights, to a more transformative effort seeking to ensure that uniquely indigenous political concerns and rights were accommodated within the legal and political instruments of the international forum to which they appealed. In an effort to account for how and why indigenous peoples (broadly speaking) historically moved toward and then away from a human rights framework, I examine the intertwined histories of Aboriginal rights advocacy and human rights advocacy in Australia during two distinct periods: the post-war era of the 1950s–1960s, and the closing decades of the 20th century. In many ways, the historical case study I offer here might be regarded as a representative story. Through it, we can draw some general lessons and pose some pointed questions about how useful or detrimental a human rights framework has ultimately been for indigenous peoples.[5]

Within interdisciplinary conversations about human rights, historians offer an important contribution, which is to provide a longer view. Whether one agrees or disagrees with recent criticisms of the 2007 declaration or of the UN more generally as a forum for pursuing indigenous rights, there is something to be gained from remembering and attempting to understand the strategic purposes with which indigenous peoples initially chose, and continue, to engage with the UN system, and to put it to work for them. Moreover, this history reminds us that post-war and subsequent campaigns within the UN for indigenous rights have been part of a global story of disempowered peoples making use of an international theater to attain a political transformation of their local circumstances. It is often said that indigenous people in Australia and elsewhere are positioned on the margins of international politics. However, when we are aware of the long history of indigenous attempts to strategically engage with the instruments and institutions of international politics, we cannot ignore that indigenous peoples have been persistent voices in the arena of international affairs. In the specific context of the UN, few people, for instance, realize the political seeds of UNDRIP were in fact sown in 1923 and 1925, respectively, when Haudenosaunee Chief Deskaheh and Maori TW Ratana, sought access to the League of Nations to expose Canada and New Zealand's violations of treaties with their peoples (Moreton-Robinson, 2011). While the League denied Chief Deskaheh and TW Ratana access to the Assembly (Britain, Canada, and New Zealand successfully petitioned that their complaints were domestic rather than international matters), their efforts nonetheless paved a pathway for contemporary global indigenous rights activists. This chapter can thus also be read as an attempt to bring indigenous political actors firmly into the story of international politics in the 20th and 21st centuries.

Aboriginal rights in Australia: a local and global story

If, as I propose here, the history of post-war Aboriginal activism in Australia can be told as both a local and global story, the local story must surely begin with 40 Aboriginal nomads who were found sick and malnourished in the Central Desert in 1956. Their plight, due to Cold War nuclear weapons testing over their territories, started a "shame campaign" by local Australian media, and became the impetus for the report of a select committee tabled in the Western Australian parliament, which inquired into the state of Aborigines. According to this report, malnutrition, blindness and disease, abortion, infanticide, burns, and other injuries were all commonplace among the

Wongi people of the Warburton Ranges. On January 9, 1957 the Sydney Communist Party newspaper, *Tribune*, described this report as ripping aside "the screen that has veiled the cruel plight to which our Governments condemn Australian Aborigines" (Attwood, 2003, pp. 149–50).

The global story I propose to tell begins with the activism this incident in the Central Desert sparked. At this time, one might have said Australia consisted of two largely separate worlds. One was characterized by all the trappings of middle-class comfort; running water and power, laws that ensured social order, employment, access to food, and even government support in times of economic hardship. Largely city-living folks, most non-indigenous Australians believed they lived in a uniquely fair and just democracy, unhindered by the rigid class stratification of Britain, or the acute racial tensions that dominated the US or South Africa. The other world in this nation's borders was inhabited by people whose ancestors had lived on the land since the beginning, but who by the 1950s had lost almost all their territories and lived in poverty on the fringes of non-indigenous society. Many Aboriginal people at this time were ineligible for government allowances, state, or other federal benefits that Australians received. State laws also controlled where Aboriginal people lived, where they could or couldn't move, and whom they could marry. Indeed, many Aboriginals were not legal guardians of their own children and were not permitted to manage their own earnings (Attwood, 2003).

Against this backdrop, and specifically, the revelations of the gross mistreatment of Aboriginal people in the Warburton Ranges, the Victorian Aborigines Advancement League (VAAL) formed in 1957 with the goal of achieving full citizens' rights for Aboriginal people. In 1958 VAAL joined forces with eight other similar bodies to form the FCAA (Taffe, 2005). One of their strategies for attaining citizens' rights was the amendment of the Australian Constitution through a referendum, to give the Commonwealth government power to legislate for Aboriginal people. Australia's 1901 Constitution had included several racist provisions that prevented oversight by the national government of states' management of indigenous affairs: section 51(26) withheld for the states all legislative power concerning the "aboriginal races"; and section 127 prevented the counting of Aboriginal people in the national census (Attwood and Markus, 2007). The FCAA therefore campaigned to repeal section 127 and the clause of section 51(26) limiting national reform of indigenous affairs. If achieved, this would not have conferred on Aboriginal peoples either citizenship or the right to vote in Australia, but it was seen to be significant for establishing Aboriginal peoples' presence in the nation in positive and equal terms (Attwood and Markus, 2007).

The history of the FCAA, as I will discuss further below, is one of a globally savvy body of campaigners (Taffe, 2005). It is clear that activists within Australia not only found inspiration and strength from looking to other disempowered peoples engaged in civil rights struggles and movements to decolonize within the former European empires, but were also starting to imagine themselves as fighting parallel causes. What this history illustrates is how during the 1950s and 1960s, an emergent human rights discourse was seized upon by activists of all kinds, as a means to hold national governments accountable before the world stage.

First steps: citizenship rights as human rights, 1950s–1960s

In Australia, as elsewhere, the post-war environment was fertile for the formation of new organizations seeking to implement social and political change. For campaigners in Australia, unlike in the decolonizing states to which they had looked for inspiration, the concern was mostly for the welfare and citizenship rights of Aboriginal people, rather than claims for sovereignty and statehood.[6] Though white reformers often dominated these post-war organizations, as time went on, Aboriginal people played an increasingly significant role.[7] The prominence of white advocates in the early period, when demands aligned more closely with calls for inclusion and equality, should be contrasted against the later period, when the rise of Aboriginal voices within activist circles precipitated a distinctive shift to advocating for harder forms of self-determination and decidedly anti-assimilationist forms of inclusion.

The first active group was the Democratic Rights Council, established in Melbourne in 1950. This led to an Australian People's Assembly for Human Rights that formed commissions on various aspects of human rights, including an Aboriginal Commission (Chesterman, 2005). Other coalitions of white and black activists quickly followed suit. In 1951, the Council for Aboriginal Rights (CAR) organized a rally where Charles Duguid (president of the South Australian Aborigines Advancement League) detailed Australian infringements of the Universal Declaration of Human Rights (Chesterman, 2005). At this rally, people learned that the principle of *habeas corpus*, which protected citizens against arrest unless they were charged with an offence, did not apply to Aboriginal people. They also learned that Aboriginal people could not drink alcohol unless they were exempted from the Aboriginals Ordinance, that their movement in towns was controlled, and that they could be displaced from their homes whenever the authorities dictated (Chesterman, 2005). In light of these abuses, CAR quickly determined it would be guided by the UN's 1948 Human Rights Declaration (Taffe, 2005).

The Australian Aboriginal Fellowship (AAF) was another significant organization established in the mid-1950s by prominent campaigners Faith Bandler and Pearl Gibbs. One historian argued it was "led by Aborigines who felt that black leadership was essential to ensure the active support of other Aborigines" (Taffe, 2005, p. 50). Yet, it also intended to be a "fellowship" of black and white co-operation (Bandler and Fox, 1983). At a meeting in 1957 at Sydney Town Hall, the AAF helped initiate the move to change the Australian Constitution. Their early petitions for a constitutional referendum had reflected campaigner Jessie Street's appreciation of "the values encoded in the Universal Declaration of Human Rights" (Lake, 2002, p. 66). Street was among the most vocal figures in this era connecting domestic movements with international discourse. In 1945, she was a member of the Australian delegation to the inaugural UN conference in San Francisco, going on to become active in the Status of Women Commission, a subcommittee of the new UN Economic and Social Council. In 1955, she joined the Aborigines Protection Society (APS) (Lake, 2002). The APS identified the need for a national indigenous organization to participate in the international human rights dialogue, so they prepared a questionnaire on the social, political, and legal circumstances of Aborigines, hoping to submit a report for the UN Commission of Human Rights' Sub-Committee on the Prevention of Discrimination and the Treatment of Minorities. Their letter of appeal read: "this Society, having consultative status with the United Nations, is in a position to suggest a subject for its enquiry. It proposes to act only at the request of Australians... until some coordinating body of Australian opinion has gained consultative status and can act for itself" (APS, cited in Lake, 2002, p. 172). In traveling extensively across Australia for the purposes of this report, Street met Shirley Andrews of the Victorian CAR, who connected her with activists Charles Duguid, Mary Bennett, Don McLeod, and John Clements, as well as many other (mostly white) activists from all states. These relationships yielded significant outcomes. For example, Bennett drew Street's attention to the International Labor Organization (ILO) Convention 107 concerning "the protection of indigenous and other tribal and semi-tribal populations in independent countries" (ILO Convention, 1957). Whereas the 1948 Human Rights Declaration had emphasized the universal rights of all people, the ILO Convention looked specifically at the rights of indigenous peoples who were colonized. The focus of Convention 107 was on equal rights and integration but it also went further, stating: "The right of ownership, collective or individual, of the members of the populations concerned over the lands which these populations traditionally occupy shall be recognized" (ILO Convention, 1957). Australia, however, did not sign the convention.

With all these influences at play, the agenda of the second annual conference of the FCAA, held in Melbourne in 1959, was now shaped according to the articles of Convention 107 (Rowse, 2000). The FCAA's first resolution called on Australian state and federal governments "to implement the provisions of the ILO Convention 107... ideally suited as standards for future plans for raising the status of the Australian Aborigines" (*Smoke Signals*, 1959, p. 14). By 1960, the FCAA was explicitly seeking the expertise of the ILO: "Due to the inability of the Northern Territory (NT) Administration to provide adequate employment for Aborigines in the Territory, this Conference calls on the Federal Government to invite an ILO expert... to advise the NT Administration" (*Smoke Signals*, 1960, p. 8). Meanwhile, in parliament,

Gough Whitlam and other Australian Labor Party members regularly raised the issue of ratification of ILO 107 (Whitlam, 1985).

Regardless of whether these international instruments and language firmly implanted the liberal ideology of equal individual rights as an end goal for the project of Aboriginal rights, the point is, at this historical juncture, they certainly helped local activists to frame their own use of that ideology for their own ends. These activists did more than just hint at Australian short-comings that international law could address; they ushered in a period when the "politics of embarrassment" became standard practice, connecting Australia to wider forums as Aboriginal people and their advocates became adept at using the media. While in Australia it became very hard for the national government to ignore activists as they increasingly sought to bring their struggles to an international audience, it must be emphasized that the agenda for change among the government and their critics alike was still firmly on the great nation-building theme of inclusion, never more confidently expounded than in the quest for constitutional reform that accompanied the 1967 Referendum.

Away from human rights and towards self-determination in the 1970s

The postscript to this early history of human rights discourse in Aboriginal rights campaigning in Australia, and the second historical moment I wish to highlight, comes soon after the 1967 Referendum, when Aboriginal voices within activist circles started to become more prominent. Many Aboriginal campaigners saw that the promises of both the 1948 Human Rights Declaration and the 1967 Australian Constitutional Referendum might not extend far enough. Activists soon realized that Aboriginal peoples' desires for equality could not be met if that equality came hinged to an assimilationist ideal of national inclusion, that a) didn't question the legitimacy of Australian sovereignty over Aboriginal people in the first place; and b) aimed, ultimately, at the erasure of their unique cultural and political identities. As such, by the 1970s, after initial struggles for citizenship rights and equality had been waged, the inherent limitations of a human rights model for indigenous peoples started to become more of a sticking point for those within the Aboriginal rights movement, whose aim was to reject assimilation. The work of Aboriginal activist and artist Oodgeroo Noonuccal is once again a marker of this political shift. Whereas Noonuccal's earlier poetry (cited at the start of this chapter) had lauded the goals of equality and inclusion, by 1969 she wrote disapprovingly of the referendum's naive optimism in these goals and her work instead expressed a new commitment to Aboriginal independence, black culture, and political solidarity: "Only fools and Dreamers," proclaimed her poem, "Black Commandments," "convince themselves that races in Australia can become one people" (1969, p. 25). As many Aboriginal activists increasingly sought to articulate, the reinforcement of liberal individualism at the very heart of the human rights project sat at odds with many of the core political projects driving indigenous politics; collective rights to land and resources being the main one (Attwood, 2003).

In the 1970s, clear divergences therefore started to develop in the political opinions of Aboriginal Australians, and between them and their non-indigenous supporters. It is clear much of this stemmed from the growing awareness among Aboriginal activists in Australia of decolonization and radical struggles for liberation. It is well known, for example, that many young Aboriginal activists in the 1970s were inspired by, and felt an affinity with black nationalist politics in the US, as demonstrated by the emergence of an Aboriginal Black Power Movement in the 1970s (Goodall, 1996). Another pivotal moment in Aboriginal political organizing in Australia during the 1970s was the establishment of the Aboriginal Tent Embassy. On January 26, 1972, four Aboriginal activists arrived in the nation's capital to establish what they were calling an "Aboriginal Embassy" by planting a beach umbrella on the lawn in front of Parliament House (now Old Parliament House). The embassy was a response to the government's refusal to recognize Aboriginal land rights and its insistence on a new general purpose lease for Aborigines that would be conditional upon their "intention and ability to make reasonable economic and social use of land" and which would exclude all rights they had to minerals and forestry (Goodall, 1996, p. 98). Several tents soon replaced the beach umbrella, and supporters quickly came from all over to join the protest. To this day, the Aboriginal Tent Embassy remains outside Old Parliament House as a symbol of the ongoing Aboriginal struggle to have their land rights and sovereignty recognized.

One way to understand this prominent and highly symbolic protest is that it was, of course, a powerful example of a new indigenous transnationalism that demonstrated how Aboriginal activists were adapting the radical and global discourse of decolonized nationalism to their own struggles (Goodall, 1996). What emerged from this new injection of energy into Aboriginal campaigning in Australia was a dramatic shift from the deployment of the human rights discourse to argue for citizenship and equality (as advanced by the FCAA and others), to the pressing of claims for special Aboriginal rights as Australia's "first peoples," including land rights, strong forms of self-determination and sovereignty, and Aboriginal "nationhood." This shift in the Aboriginal movement brought with it an entirely new set of claims upon the Australian nation, and meant that to continue using the international forums and instruments to which they had become accustomed, Aboriginal people in Australia (along with indigenous peoples globally) also had to start modifying these to their needs as well. The UN Permanent Forum on Indigenous Issues, UNDRIP, and the emergence of the global indigenous movement mark the history of these changes. As I will explain next, the compromises embedded in UNDRIP, its non-legally binding character, and the way in which it ultimately pivoted back towards a human rights framework, also mark the inherent limitations and challenges indigenous peoples will continue to face within an international system that is structured, at the end of the day, to shore up the existing nation-state system. By striving to simply make this system better, as opposed to recognizing the ways in which colonialism continues through the system itself, critics stress that the UN can only go so far in supporting indigenous peoples' rights.

Toward the UN Declaration on the Rights of Indigenous Peoples, 1980s–2000s

In many ways, the efforts of indigenous peoples to codify their political aspirations of self-determination and indigenous rights within the UN framework is largely a story of frustration. Indeed, the various political compromises that were necessary to get a charter of indigenous rights recognized in the UN resulted in a document that although seemingly aligned with the more strident political demands of indigenous activism of the 1970s, was, in reality, perhaps closer in practice (if not in spirit) to the goals of the earlier moment in Australian Aboriginal rights advocacy. That is, much as the engagement with human rights discourse was (for many) strategic in the 1950s and 1960s, I think we can also regard the final 2007 declaration as a similarly strategic compromise on the part of indigenous peoples. Strident disagreements have since ensued over whether efforts to work for indigenous rights within the UN framework have proven powerless, perhaps even counterproductive.

By and large, critiques of the 2007 declaration typically fall along three main lines: a) UNDRIP is not legally binding; b) UNDRIP hems in the demands of indigenous peoples for self-determination to internal forms of self-governance only (such as in the realm of culture); and c) to the extent that UNDRIP recognizes indigenous peoples' collective rights, it does so within a framework that still defers to both existing nation states and the primacy of human rights. In this final section of the chapter, I wish to return to the last of these criticisms since it gets us back to the concept of human rights.

Much of the controversy throughout negotiations in the 1990s and early 2000s concerned article 3 of the 1993 draft, which was retained in the adopted 2007 declaration. It read, "Indigenous peoples have the right of self-determination. By virtue of that right they freely determine their political status and freely pursue their economic, social and cultural development."[8] Disagreements over the potential meaning of the terms "self-determination" and "peoples" were central to the inability of states and indigenous groups to agree upon a text for the declaration.[9] Concerns over these concepts also led the United States, Canada, Australia, and New Zealand to vote against the declaration's final adoption. These four states and many others had expressed concern that the indigenous right to self-determination might be read to include the right to statehood. This was even in spite of the fact that article 46(1) of the declaration specifies that it does not support such "strong" forms of self-determination. Rather, it states that the declaration should not be "construed as authorizing or encouraging any action which would dismember or impair totally or in part, the territorial integrity or political unity of sovereign and independent States" (UNDRIP, 2007, article 46(1)). Moreover, the declaration is clear in limiting its recognition of indigenous self-determination to "internal" matters only, stating: the right to self-determination guarantees only "the right to autonomy or self-government in matters relating to their internal and local affairs, as well as ways and means for financing their autonomous functions" (UNDRIP, 2007, *supra* note 1, at article 4). This language makes it clear that strong forms of indigenous self-determination, which might threaten the sovereignty and territorial integrity of nation states, would not be recognized or protected by the UN. Moreover, as legal scholar Karen Engle points out, in the final version of the declaration, article 46 (quoted earlier) not only restricts the meaning of self-determination in these ways, but also potentially affects the meaning and application of *all* the rights contained in the declaration (2011). Paragraph 2 of article 46 reads in part, "The exercise of the rights set forth in this Declaration shall be subject only to such limitations as are determined by law and in accordance with international human rights obligations" (UNDRIP, 2007, article 46). Paragraph 3 calls for the interpretation of rights in the declaration "in accordance with the principles of justice, democracy, respect for human rights, equality, non-discrimination, good governance and good faith" (UNDRIP, 2007, article 46). What this does is to effectively subordinate any collective rights indigenous peoples may have secured through the declaration, to the individual rights framework of the human rights legal regime. On numerous scores, then, critics have argued that the political compromises that were required to get even these minimal protections recognized, has resulted in a document that is studiously non-committal, and while nominally recognizes indigenous rights, does so in a way that ultimately aims to blunt, or thwart the stronger political aspirations of indigenous peoples.

While even at the time, this compromise language concerned many indigenous peoples involved with the declaration, most who were party to the negotiations ultimately decided to support it with the assurance that other key provisions would remain intact, including those on land and resource rights and free and informed consent, which would in some sense protect indigenous peoples' territorial integrity. The United States, Canada, New Zealand, and Australia were the only states to vote against the declaration in 2007, which was endorsed by 144 member states constituting the majority of the UN General Assembly. The significance of their votes against the declaration is perhaps put into sharp relief when we recognize that almost half the indigenous population of the world lives within the borders of these four nations (Moreton-Robinson, 2011). Moreover, coming to terms with why these particular nations were so reluctant to fully endorse a document of this kind gets us to the very heart of the reason why indigenous peoples' strong claims for political sovereignty will remain hampered within an international system that continues to defer to the political and territorial prerogatives of colonial states. While as of 2010 all four nations reversed their position and endorsed the declaration, as numerous scholars and critics of the document point out, much remains to be done. Their capitulation, after all, was to a document that basically made concessions to their ultimate sovereign authority.

If we look at the many frustrated attempts of indigenous peoples over the 1990s and early 2000s to get their stronger forms of self-determination recognized within the UN system, we see that rather than being thwarted completely, the final version of the 2007 declaration is the acquiescence (some might say detrimental compromise) of indigenous campaigners, to accept a more limited understanding of self-determination as something restricted to internal forms of self-governance only, and which seeks to contain any recognition and protection of their collective rights to relatively non-threatening areas only, such as culture. By softening their stance on self-determination, indigenous rights advocates arguably succeeded in broadening the general liberal model of human rights so as to incorporate a collective right to culture, and to allow for difference within an equality model. The reason I suggest we might look upon this turn as a political move akin to the earlier moment in Aboriginal rights advocacy, is that by shifting to articulate their claims primarily in terms of the human right to culture (sometimes understood as an individual right and sometimes as a collective one), indigenous activists arguably went for an easy "win" in order to secure protections for at least *some* indigenous rights within the international system. However, as many critics point out, the limitations imposed on indigenous rights and the shoring up of protections afforded to colonial state sovereignty by the declaration raise additional questions. Does the reinstantiation of nation-state sovereignty achieved by this softening of indigenous calls for self-determination ultimately work to entrench the authority of nation states over indigenous peoples? And finally, if, as Canada, New Zealand, the United States, and Australia also assert, the declaration is a moral and political document that is not legally binding, then what use is it?

Conclusion

It is possible to return to our historical discussion now by pointing out that at the moment when Aboriginal Australians were radicalizing, similar events were taking place globally. Indigenous peoples across the world in the 1970s were realizing more deeply the circumstances and nature of their particular oppression and were celebrating and rediscovering culture as the ground of unique political expression (Pritchard, 1998). Recognition of the simultaneity of the indigenous experience led to stronger networks of information and solidarity. These interacted with new movements of non-indigenous peoples and drew on deeper realizations of the implications of human rights, as well as its limits in protecting specifically indigenous interests (Pritchard, 1998). Indigenous people in Australia and elsewhere played a significant role on the international stage during this period. Organizations such as the World Council of Indigenous Peoples emerged and began to exert pressure on a UN system hitherto concerned with the civil and political rights of individuals and minorities. This pressure created space within the UN system where an agenda of indigenous rights to land, culture, and heritage could systematically be pursued, most notably with the passage of the UNDRIP and the UN Permanent Forum on Indigenous Issues. However, as noted here and in much recent scholarship on indigenous rights within the international legal system, as long as the declaration defers to the dominance of state sovereignty and to human rights as the primary limit on that sovereignty, its potential to truly support indigenous peoples in their ongoing struggles to combat continuing colonialism will continue to be hampered. Meanwhile, indigenous peoples persist in finding other ways to uphold and protect their sovereign rights.

Discussion questions

1   Why did the human rights framework initially appeal to indigenous peoples (in the post-war era)?
2   When and why did indigenous peoples end up pushing for more than the human rights framework could offer them? Do you agree that they needed to push beyond a human rights framework?
3   What is different about the protections offered to indigenous peoples by the UNDRIP (as compared to the protections offered by a human rights framework)?
4   On balance, has indigenous peoples' engagement with the UN and the human rights framework been more beneficial or counterproductive for the goals of indigenous politics?

Notes

1   The author wishes to thank Emilio Mora and Christopher Norton for their assistance with this article.
2   The South Australia Aborigines Act 1934–1939 consolidated certain acts relating to the protection and control of the Aboriginal and so-called "half-caste" population of South Australia. Parts of the act controlled the free movement of Aboriginal people through the requirement of exemptions, or permits for example. The amendment to the act in 1939 made the Aborigines Protection Board the legal guardian of all Aboriginal children and it also introduced the Exemption Certificate which allowed certain Aborigines to become "non-Aborigines" if they fulfilled the government requirements for assimilation. If not exempted, Aboriginal people could not open a bank account, buy land, or legally drink alcohol. Exempted people, on the other hand, were not permitted to live on reserves or mix with non-Aborigines. A full copy of the act can be accessed at: www.indigenousrights.net.au/document.asp?iID=598

3   Indeed, many issues dominating domestic Australian politics in the 1950s and 1960s already situated Aboriginal concerns in a global context. Britain's rocket ranges and nuclear testing in the Woomera, Warburton, and Maralinga regions of central Australia had exposed Aboriginal people to the perils of the atomic age. Meanwhile, the steady incursion of international mining conglomerates onto the lands of remote Aboriginal communities placed them at the mercy of transnational capitalism.

4   As I explain later, what this means is that to the extent that indigenous peoples' right to self-determination has been protected by UNDRIP, this has been limited to the realm of self-determination in their cultures only. That is, UNDRIP allows for the recognition that indigenous peoples have a human right to (the self-determination of) their cultures.

5   While I have chosen to highlight the representative nature of this case study, it must also be acknowledged that this is perhaps only especially true in the case of indigenous peoples whose communities fall within the territorial and national boundaries of settler nation states like the US, Canada, Australia, and New Zealand. As the extensive literature on indigenous peoples and the UN clearly shows, the particular situations of indigenous peoples globally has made for a diverse and wide-ranging set of experiences and struggles within and against the international system.

6   Although calls for self-determination would follow, as I later discuss.

7   The historian Peter Read has argued that this first phase of post-war activism attracted Aboriginal people who had access to the education and esteem available in relatively tolerant spaces such as churches, sporting clubs, and unions, hence we encounter individuals like Doug Nicholls (a pastor) and Joe McGinness (a union worker) (1990, p. 62).

8   This provision specifically applies to common article 1 of the two major covenants on human rights to indigenous peoples.

9   The history of these thwarted attempts is more than I have room to discuss here, but is the focus of many books and articles on UNDRIP – some of which are referred to in the "Further reading" section at the end of this chapter.

References

Attwood, B. (2003). *Rights for Aborigines*. Sydney: Allen and Unwin.

Attwood, B. and Markus, A. (2007). *The 1967 referendum: Race, power and the Australian constitution.* Melbourne: Aboriginal Studies Press.

Bandler, F. and Fox, L. (1983). *The time was ripe: A history of the Aboriginal-Australian fellowship (1956–69).* Sydney: Alternative Publishing Cooperative.

Chesterman, J. (2005). *Civil rights: How indigenous Australians won formal equality.* St Lucia, Qld: University of Queensland Press.

Churchill, W. (2011). A travesty of a mockery of a sham: Colonialism as "self-determination" in the UN Declaration on the Rights of Indigenous Peoples. *Griffith Law Review,* 20(3), pp. 526–556.

Engle, K. (2010). *The elusive promise of indigenous development.* Durham, NC: Duke University Press.

Engle, K. (2011). On fragile architecture: The UN Declaration on the Rights of Indigenous Peoples in the context of human rights. *European Journal of International Law,* 22(1), pp. 141–163.

Goodall, H. (1996). *Invasion to embassy: Land in Aboriginal politics in New South Wales, 1770–1972.* Sydney: Allen and Unwin.

ILO Convention 107 (1957). Available at: www.indigenousrights.net.au/files/f77.pdf

Lake, M. (2002). *Faith: Faith Bandler, gentle activist*. Sydney: Allen and Unwin.

Moreton-Robinson, A. (2011). Virtuous racial states: The possessive logic of patriarchal white sovereignty and the United Nations Declaration on the Rights of Indigenous Peoples. *Griffith Law Review*, 20(3), pp. 641–58.

Noonuccal, O. (1962). Aboriginal Charter of Rights. *Smoke Signals*, 2(1), p. 14.

Noonuccal, O. (1969). Black commandments. *Koorier*, 1(10), p. 25.

Pritchard, S. (1998). *Indigenous peoples, the United Nations and human rights*. Sydney: Federation Press.

Read, P. (1990). *Charles Perkins: A biography*. Melbourne: Viking.

Rowse, T. (2000). *Obliged to be difficult: Nugget Coombs' legacy in indigenous affairs*. Cambridge: Cambridge University Press.

Sekuless, P. (1978). *Jessie Street: A rewarding but unrewarded life*. St Lucia, Qld: University of Queensland Press.

Taffe, S. (2005). *Black and white together FCAATSI: The Federal Council for the Advancement of Aborigines and Torres Strait Islanders, 1958–1973*. St Lucia, Qld: University of Queensland Press.

UNDRIP (2007). Available at: www.un.org/esa/socdev/unpfii/documents/DRIPS_en.pdf

Whitlam, E.G. (1985). *The Whitlam government, 1972–1975*. Melbourne: Viking.

Wiessner, S. (2011). The cultural rights of indigenous peoples: Achievements and continuing challenges. *European Journal of International Law*, 22(1), pp. 121–140.

Further reading

Anaya, J. (2004). *Indigenous peoples in international law*. Oxford: Oxford University Press.

De Costa, R. (2006). *A higher authority: Indigenous transnationalism and Australia*. Sydney: University of New South Wales Press.

Hartley, J., Joffe, P., and Preston, J., eds (2010). *Realizing the UN Declaration on the Rights of Indigenous Peoples: Triumph, hope, and action*. Saskatoon: Purich Publishing.

Watson, I., ed. (2018). *Indigenous peoples as subjects of international law*. New York: Routledge.

Part III
Praxis and human rights

13 So, you want to work in human rights?

Jean-Philippe Belleau

Many, maybe most undergraduate students I have had in my courses seem incredibly interested in working in human rights. I do everything to lower their expectations: you will be poor; there is almost no job in human rights; it's not all black and white; it is not intellectually rewarding; many of your colleagues will have a "missionary" mentality that will put you off. And then, there is the rest.

My first experience in human rights happened incidentally and did not incite me to continue. In mid-1994, as I was starting my PhD, a friend (the above-mentioned "missionary" type) called and matter of factly asked me to replace him: I would need to go to a non-governmental organization (NGO) headquarter and take the testimony of "an old political exile from Burma" traveling through Europe at the time. These were actually two nuns and they were from Tibet. I must have been uninterested for I do not remember other circumstances. I sat down to take their testimonies through a voluntary interpreter. I may not have even looked at the two nuns when I entered the room. Yet, conscientiously, I started to take notes and within minutes I remember vividly feeling I was unprepared for the hell I was listening to. I raised my head and finally met their eyes. They probably had been looking straight at me since the beginning. For most of that afternoon they told their story. What I had learned in an anthropology course, that people from "traditional" societies do not talk openly to a stranger, especially women, and especially about intimate matters, was being refuted in front of me. Horrors were being enumerated, humiliations meticulously depicted, the unspeakable was being spoken without much of these inhibitions "traditional cultures" are supposedly made of. Yet, I was feeling that there were gaps in their story of escape and terror. Gaps are problematic when you need to build a case – they undermine it. I remembered what a professor in ethnographic methods had told us: "You need to have the courage to ask tough questions." Today, I would say "the nerve." But suddenly facing the closed, yet talkative faces of the two nuns, I did not feel like being courageous. I must have mumbled at first but I eventually raised my head, looked at them and did ask: the men who raped you, did they wear uniforms? I was more surprised, and still am, by how they answered than by the answer itself. I could hardly finish my question. They were expecting it; they were hoping for it. They answered, and answered at length. I continued. If they inserted a knife into your vagina, how were you able to walk all the way into Nepal afterward? This other nun you had started the journey with, did they kill her in front of you, was there no witness? They were closing the gaps, and I felt embarrassed for having been suspicious in the first place.

The interview lasted for most of the afternoon. At some point, we all realized it was over and we parted ways. There was something deeply unscientific about meeting someone from another cultural universe, not having a clue about it, asking a few questions through an interpreter, and making a conclusion three hours later. Yet, the most unpleasant part of the experience was not being exposed to a horrible story. It was to have been responsible for its extraction. A total stranger asked about the most horrible and intimate suffering in their lives and then disappeared for ever. I had to create intimacy in an instant, extract information, and then leave them. There was something abnormal, unscrupulous about it. Nobody with some basic ethical standard and empathy would want to do this type of job – human rights.

* * *

Located right outside the historical district of Cap Haitian, Haiti's second largest town, Shada is its oldest shantytown. Families migrating from the countryside in the 1970s were the first to settle there. Built on a swamp, it has no street names or recognizable landmarks; it would be easy to hide there. I was driving on Shada's central dirt street in an early afternoon in October 1995, a street rendered even more impractical by earlier rains. I was then working for the International Civilian Mission to Haiti (MICIVIH), a human rights mission sent by the United Nations (UN) to investigate violations committed during a military regime (1991–1994). Victims, especially those from the most disenfranchised sectors of society, often were not bringing their cases to outsiders or to the judicial system. We had to look for them. We were also looking for the perpetrators.

I finally found the house I was looking for. A woman in her mid-30s welcomed me at the doorstep, with two skinny children at her side. I handed her the piece of paper her imprisoned husband had given me. I entered. The woman made me sit down in what was passing for a living room. A little girl, maybe 8 or 9, with a sad face and an enormous bandage covering her right eye, sat beside her. She stared, mute, at the strange man in front of her during my entire stay in the house. I sat in a wooden armchair, memory of wealthier times. I was listening to the mother but kept looking at the bandage. It was too big and covered half of the face. It had been cut with scissors or a knife from a large piece of white fabric: they could not afford a doctor. I was listening and writing what the woman was saying about her husband when my eyes finally ventured around the room. She was struggling. With her husband no longer providing, the family was plunging further into indigence.

If anthropology is in a position to communicate something effective to human rights work, it would not just be about anthropology's track record of methods, or about its own library of ethnographic knowledge. It would be about the thickness of details. Pierre Clastres (1972), who studied a dis-appearing indigenous society, believed that details are not benign and often lie in facial expressions. There lies also an anthropological truth: of what a face says about what happened. A year after Clastres' classical work, anthropologist Clifford Geertz (1973) wrote his own and there also famously focused on the face. What does it mean when an informant is contracting his eyelid: is it a twitch or a wink? Is his eyelash moving because of a piece of dust or is he communicating something? Geertz simply but crucially meant that a critical evidence can lie in an ephemeral detail and in the researcher's ability to detect it. Yes, such interpretation is subjective – but that is all we have.

The evidence I suddenly saw was a face stuck in that living room in the Shada shantytown. It was a framed picture. When I finally saw it, the little girl, her misery, the slum, the mother's despair, all evaporated. I immediately recognized the man I had been visiting at the horrendous prison of Cap Haitian for the past few weeks and understood why he looked so proud. It all came into place. He had been arrested for a misdemeanor at a road check – he had an unregistered handgun in his car. He started to trust me and asked me to go to the place his family had just moved to. Talk to my wife, tell her everything, I will soon be released. You are my only friend. He scribbled a few words for her on a piece of paper I had handed him and then the address to deliver it. I was no longer paying attention to the little girl's bandage or what her mother was saying; my eyes were stuck on the framed picture. A small, color photograph, maybe 5 by 6 inches. More arresting than the white uniform he was wearing on the picture was the self-confidence that radiated from his facial expression and his posture. A true military officer. This man used to command and be obeyed. His wife had opened her door to me and now she would be poor forever.

The assault on anthropology carried out by academic currents known as postmodernism and postcolonialism in the 1980s questioned anthro-pologists' pretense to *know* other cultures simply because they have been "there." Yet, they did not really propose an alternative – except, probably, to hand over the job. Having been and spent some time *there* is certainly no guarantee of getting things right; it is still better than staying on a campus or a café terrace in Paris. Yet, postcolonialism knew where to hit: ethnography is anthropology's great contribution to the study of humanity. Post-colonialist scholars, essentially people who stay in their office and reproach anthropologists to get out of theirs, would predictably assert that the differ-ence between a twitch and a wink lies in the eye of the beholder. The proud inmate at the Cap Haitian prison was not twitching or winking: he had looked straight at me every time we engaged in a conversation and, with a perfect posture and in a prison filled with petty thieves, he looked unusual.

He was too neat to be honest. Were his posture and facial expression the only details that got me to continue investigating? Nothing else.

When I myself became a father, the memories of the little girl somehow came back. Was she only wounded or just sick? Or had she lost her eyesight? What has she become now that her father could no longer provide for her health and education? I also think about the two peasants who had been executed by this man, in a remote village in the center of the country during the military regime. They were supporters of Aristide, the democratically elected president deposed by the military in 1991. I had traveled to their village too, months earlier; I had met and stayed with their families, now economically devastated. I had done all that before the prisoner scribbled words for the wife he loved. Before he told me that I was his only friend and before I put my hand on his shoulder, looked convincingly in his eyes and quietly told him "You can trust me."

So, you want to work in human rights?

* * *

Trou-du-Nord is a middle-sized town in northern Haiti with a strange, rather ungraceful name ("Hole of the North"). Leafy, at least when I was last there, it is a pleasant place. In late 1995, a strange incident occurred. A child was killed in a ritualistic fashion in Trou-du-Nord. Killed and eaten. The killer had been duly arrested by the police and was in prison, awaiting trial. However, the judge's report said, *"pratique de sorcellerie"* (witchcraft practice) and not "murder." Yet everybody, the police, the public rumors, and a radio channel were talking about the murder.

I was assigned the case mainly because of its location. As a human rights officer, I was at the bottom of the UN bureaucracy's food chain – that is, everybody above me was a boss and therefore utterly unwilling to travel to the countryside. In October or November of that year, the MICIVIH office in Cap Haitian received a report that a man had been imprisoned in Trou-du-Nord for practicing witchcraft. It should have qualified as a human rights violation because the Haitian Constitution and international conventions ratified by the Haitian state protect freedom of religion – and witchcraft is just another man's religion.

I went to the prison, met the suspect, then met the investigative judge who had written the report. Whose child had been killed? Nobody knew. What was her name? Nothing about that. I went to the morgue, then to the police, and nobody seemed bothered. I went to the suspect's house, now in prison – he had been living by himself, which was unusual. I went to interview the neighbors. They had seen the whole thing: how the child was captured, killed, cooked, and ingested. (Apparently this man did everything outside.) Outraged, the neighbors finally intervened and gave the man to the police. So, whose child was this, I asked? They could not say. Was it a boy or a girl? What did she look like? Like any other, they said. In the weeks that followed, I kept investigating, traveled to neighboring towns and morgues and tried to find out if any child was missing. In vain. This child, it seemed, had dropped from the sky, and now that she was in someone's belly, there was little evidence she had ever existed.

The human rights mission in Cap Haitian had a staff of about 12 people and a coordinator. I gave an oral report on the Trou-du-Nord case, emphasized its legal aspects, anti-witchcraft laws having been explicitly abolished in Haiti by the 1987 Constitution, and asked to continue the investigation. Unwisely, I also argued that, likely, no act of cannibalism had taken place and that we should request the judge to release the imprisoned "witch": do you think anyone anywhere would stand by while a child is being killed, cooked, and eaten? With this piece of universalism, things started to unravel in the UN office. I do not remember much of the conversation that followed, except that it was tense and at the end the coordinator angrily shouted (that, I remember word by word): "You do not understand. This is their culture!" Cannibalism, long ago a marker of barbarism, had become a marker of cultural authenticity – that had to be respected, defended, preserved. No longer an anti-value, cannibalism was becoming "cultural." The UN coordinator was defending Haitian culture and I, well, what did that make me?

The coordinator forbade me from further investigating. A few weeks later, though, after the coordinator was replaced (that is, in UN practice, promoted) following allegations of incompetence (that is, suspected of much worse), I resumed my investigation and returned to the people who were key to the story: the neighbors and especially the woman who lived immediately adjacent to the suspect's house. I kept thinking about her because, when I had first asked pointed questions about the child and the cooking, her eyes were going in all directions and her voice lowered. So, I went to talk to her on several occasions. We became friends. I was allowed to enter her house. We made jokes, laughed together. And then, at some point, she admitted it: the child had turned into a chicken right before being killed. It was a child – that, there was no doubt about it. Except that the witch had the power to turn him into a chicken – another evidence he really was a witch. The other neighbors later admitted to the metamorphosis version, with some variations to the story, maybe a sign that they had not rehearsed it together. The suspect had cooked and eaten a chicken – the banality of culture.

A few neighbors, chief among them that woman, had an old grudge and coveted his land. Petty sentiments, envy, and distrust of witches sealed the man's fate. There had never been a child and probably not even a chicken. The pots of cannibal societies are usually empty. At some point, a heated discussion took place between the two neighbors (the lady and the voodoo priest), then other neighbors intervened, sided with her, then turned into a mob when the police finally intervened and saved the priest by arresting him. Students will ask: did the neighbors lie or did they believe in their cannibal story? Well, my UN colleagues, for sure, believed in cannibalism.

* * *

As I entirely rewrote this chapter, cutting off gruesome experiences for more appropriate ones for undergraduate readers, such as the one above, what I could not expurgate are ubiquitous observations about the UN bureaucracy, ineptitude, and irresponsibility. The disgust one can acquire for this organization while working for them – which is not uncommon – hinder reflections about the how and why of this situation. The most problematic is not just the colonial situation of having highly paid and overly young expatriates working in a destitute country; it is the status and the symbolic power irresponsible and clueless UN officials carry with absolute impunity in political landmines. In 1993, two members of the MICIVIH convinced Antoine Izméry to attend a mass against the military regime. Izméry was a wealthy member of the Haitian elite who openly supported and funded the pro-democracy movement. They told him that his presence at this mass would fire up the resistance to the military. He hesitated. They went to his home where he was protected by bodyguards and insisted that he would be safe if he were to attend mass at the Sacré Coeur church, that they would stand with him publicly as UN officials and would prevent the military from harming him. So, he left the safety of his home, entered the church, and was executed by a death squad in the middle of the mass. These two human rights officials sent him to his death. They never paid a price and did not even engage in self-reflection, putting all the blame on the military regime. They continued to work for the UN and sanctimoniously wrapped themselves up in the self-righteous and heroicized mantle of human rights – who in his right Western mind would dare question the validity of human rights and human rights work in public? I met countless such individuals in international organizations. At the end, you feel this recurring question deep in your stomach: does the UN produce such individuals, or does it merely attract them?

* * *

The strangest thing about small towns in rural Haiti might be the morgue. A village can lack water, electricity, a sewage system, and live in extreme poverty, but it almost always has a top-notch morgue, equipped with a cold chamber and a generator. The rest of the town can live in a continuous blackout year after year, yet the morgue shines. People commonly say that the dead are better treated than the living. Anthropologists repackage it by saying that the dead are more respected in traditional societies than in industrial societies, or something along this line. In any case, the dead are kept intact for a while before being buried.

It was 2000 and I was working for the Organization of American States' (OAS) electoral mission to Haiti – as much as I disliked working for the UN, I loved the OAS, a genuinely caring, if sometimes messy international organization. In April, a group of opposition leaders came storming into my small OAS office in Cap Haitian: "They are killing us!" A member of the opposition had been shot and killed in Grande-Rivière-du-Nord, about 30 miles south of Cap Haitian. Lavalas, the government party, was killing opponents, they shouted. The body of the OPL operative (OPL was the main opposition party then) had been found by a lake in the hills, kilometers away from his hamlet.

I went to read the judge's death report: the victim died of drowning. No mention of shooting, bullets, assassination. No foul play. He had fallen into a lake and died. Did the opposition leaders who stormed into my office make the whole thing up? Then, I read the time of death on the report: 3am, a rather strange time for a farmer to go around, especially to the middle of nowhere. I went to meet the judge in Grande Rivière for more explanation. She was a scared cat. It was 2000 and everybody knew that Aristide would be back in power within a few months – Aristide and his feared followers. Her eyes said: please, do not drag me into this. Had she traveled to the area? No. Had she seen the body? No. What she wrote was what the police had told her.

On her office wall, she showed me the lake on a large map. We were in April. It was already dreadfully hot and humid, and that lake was a day's walk in the hills. There was likely no road leading to that lake and I might have to spend the night somewhere in a farm. The scorching heat was telling me to believe the judge and stay put.

At grad school, an advisor, after having read an ethnographic report I had written, compared me to "a truffle dog." Truffle dogs have a unique talent for putting their nose fearlessly into dirt to find ugly mushrooms worth hundreds of dollars. It is an acquired technique. This advisor meant well, I think, although I am not sure most people would find the metaphor dignified enough to embrace it. Yet, since I was embracing a profession that screams for evidence, I thought the truffle dog could be an appropriate totem, and in key investigative moments I would ask myself: what would a truffle dog do?

I went up the mountain. The hilly landscapes were beautiful and still wooded. I found a farm where I could spend the night, I even found a farmer willing to rent me his mule – for those who do not know, you cannot ride a donkey, but you can ride a mule. I had to bring it back to the farmer on my way down. After a day, I finally found the "lake." It was a pond. And it was three inches deep. To drown there, you had to be incredibly talented. In addition, there was nobody around. No farm, no hamlet, no cultivated field, nothing. Just that strange, lonely pond. What on earth did that farmer do there at night? I went back to the judge to let her know about my findings and the lake's depth. She told me she would investigate. I went to the dead man's farm, talked to his family, friends, and neighbors: nobody knew anything, except that he had left his home in the middle of the night. Was there anyone with him that night? Nobody knew.

I had to see the body. I felt it was my last chance to figure out if there had been foul play or not. The opposition leaders who stormed into my office loudly had asserted the man had been shot; maybe it was true. If the body had bullet holes or even knife wounds, that would be it. I became obsessed with the morgue, I imagined I could sneak in at night and find out how the body looked: with bullet holes or not. Two days after the hills trip, I went to the morgue. I met the undertaker in his office and convinced him to show me the body. He hesitated, then agreed, but insisted he would not do more.

Finally, I was going to know. We went to the chamber. There was a huge wall with about a dozen drawers. The undertaker knew which one I was looking for. He opened and I immediately peered over. The body was there. But the dead man was fully clothed, in his best outfit. Seconds passed. I kept looking, as if my eyes could pierce the cloth. At that moment, a family entered the morgue and the panicked undertaker rushed back to his office, leaving me alone for a few minutes. I was by myself in the chamber, with the dead man in its open drawer. What do I do now? The body was a few inches away, with the absolute proof on it. I just had to take the clothes off. I imagined the headlines: "OAS official strips a dead man naked." I closed the drawer.

Meanwhile, the judge issued a new death report. It got better – she now concluded it was a suicide. The old farmer left his farm in the middle of the night, walked hours to a picturesque location, and ended his life there, pondering on the moon and the landscape. Maybe a 19th-century German poet, but a small-town farmer and political party operative in 2000 in the Caribbean? I had interviewed the whole family, the OPL's supporters, the neighbors, the people who found the body; nothing came out from these. As an observer, I did not have a mandate to carry out an investigation, order anyone within the judiciary or the police to do anything, I could only observe, although in practice, international observers worked hand in hand with both judges and the police. Yet, nobody was willing to ask the family to remove the dead man's clothes, not even me. I gave up. And I think many human rights investigations end up as such, nowhere.

* * *

For elections in developing countries (not sure what the new words are now, maybe "transitioning to democracy"), member countries of international organizations often send short-term electoral observers. They are usually the lowest of the low: politicians' relatives, unemployed spouses of oligarchs, unemployed children of the unemployed spouses, local political operatives needing to be rewarded, and other unsavory characters. The nepotistic machine found a nest there. International organizations have no say on how these observers are selected but have to manage and dispatch them once they are on the ground. They arrive one to two days before the elections and leave right after. I dealt with that several times. For the May 2000 parliamentary elections, Canada's governing party then, the Liberal Party, had sent low-level political operatives. It was a reward, a paid trip in a tropical country. I had never heard about Canada's Liberal Party before, and I still have no idea what it stands for and if it still exists, but to send the kind of observers I saw, you really had to have no respect for Haiti. About a dozen arrived in Cap Haitian, a number that did not augur well. My Jamaican colleague, a woman who always had a good word for everybody, received them. This time, she was speechless (she later fended off two assailants armed with an M16 who attempted to steal an envelope with electoral results; the man they worked for is now a senator).

Meanwhile, the political situation in Cap Haitian was deteriorating rapidly. Tensions, rumors, threats were making everybody nervous. It made me worried about the safety of the electoral observers we were sending in the field. The elections took place, almost six months behind schedule, on May 26, 2000. They proceeded without any real incident, at least in the north of the country. That day, I regularly checked by radio if the dirty dozen were OK. At 6pm, the voting stations closed and the observers were supposed to observe the counting and tabulations, almost always carried in silence and at the light of candles. By 10pm though, I still had not heard from two observers we had dispatched in Dondon, a small town of about 5,000 people, in the highlands about 40 miles south of Cap. I was radioing them every minute, in vain. By 11pm, I still had no news and started to imagine the worst. At midnight, as most of the votes had been counted in Cap Haitian and as the situation was calm, I decided to drive to Dondon. It was a dirt road and I could not go very fast. When crossing hamlets, I could see some homes lit by candles on the roadside: electoral workers counting ballots. I entered in Dondon two hours later. It was pitch dark. The situation seemed calm. In the town's center, I could still see some animation, some candles inside homes, and some polling personnel walking home.

As I was driving toward the town's center, I saw two bodies lying by the right side of the street, in the gutter, face down. I braked and rushed. The worst had happened indeed and the reputation of the OAS would be tainted forever. These were my two observers and they were completely drunk. They did not look well but they were alive. One had lost a shoe. I remember that detail because, well, an electoral observer, drunk and missing a shoe at night in central Haiti was a rather uncommon occurrence. I raised my head and saw a group of young people, likely electoral workers or local party representatives on their way home after a long counting. They were willing to help. We picked up the glory of the Liberal Party and carried them inside a house. An elderly woman brought some food while another cleaned the dirt and vomit from their faces. I remember that other detail because their gentle gestures strikingly looked similar to Candomblé (the Afro-Brazilian religion) priestesses in Brazil ceremonies. One of the two men regained consciousness. They had also lost their radio, their notebook, and whatever material they carried and were blaming locals for it. A local political candidate in the house took me apart and explained that they had been drinking rum all day. I will skip the other details. They had also made a racket inside a polling station. We put the two observers on the back of my truck. As I was about to leave, I remember a group of young people running towards the car. They had found the radios, two wallets, and a shoe.

We drove back on the same country road. Then, one hour later or so, I had one of the most extraordinary encounters I ever had. We were about half-way between Dondon and Cap Haitian. The Haitian night had engulfed everything in pitch dark while a tight and mesmerizing yellow spot was shining to the left of the road, about 200 yards away – it really looked like a

224 Jean-Philippe Belleau

tropical version of a Van Gogh, dark blue with a bright yellow touch. This was more than unusual. No organized event ever happens at night. The voodoo ceremonies that foreigners are obsessed about do not happen in shining houses either, and never that late. This was deeply unusual. I stopped, left the two Liberals snoring in the back and walked through the field towards the light. As I got close, I heard the loud noise of a generator, which explained the improbable light. It was a farm, and I was about to enter from the back. Dozens of people were there. They were dressed up. It looked like a normal social event, except that it was in the middle of the night in the middle of nowhere. And it looked like a wedding – at 3 or 4 in the morning. As I peered from the back, they suddenly noticed me. They got frightened first, but then invited me inside. There was an enormous cake on a table, I remember wondering how they had found the ingredients as Haiti had just exited an economic embargo. The cake was extremely sugary, almost uneatable, I remember that also. I looked around. These impoverished farmers had obviously put a lot of money into this event. An elderly man took my hand and took me to the groom. He was ecstatic. He welcomed me and offered me cake again. But I could not see a bride. Their Kreyol and their accent were difficult for me to understand, but then he said it: I am marrying Erzuli Dantor. I asked him to repeat it and then I understood: it was a *marriage-bague* – a "ring wedding." Haitianist anthropologists wait their whole life in vain to witness this. The groom was marrying Erzuli Dantor, aka St Catherine, the "spirit" (or *lwa*) of love and beauty. I felt a wave of gratitude for Canada's Liberal Party. A priest had advised this marriage to the young man (the groom) as a cure for some ailment or for a situation he wanted to get rid of. It had to take place at night, and there it was, in full view and yet hidden. Immune to the country's political situation or the troubles of a passing truck from an international organization, the peasant world was continuing unscathed, curled up in the night.

* * *

I have to be the only Western civilian who has stayed an entire week on a Pakistani military base. For six days, I woke up to the sound of boots, picked up some pashtun, observed soldiers and officers, ate chapatis, and a few times engaged in philosophical conversations about the meaning of life or the manipulation of automatic weapons. Although I was not there to spy, I also realized Pakistani officers had a covert resource: the best cooks an army could dream of, although I would learn the truth about it only months later. For one week, I ate seekh kebabs, chapatis, aloo gobi, and a dish they called "bong," a curry which seemed to be the soldiers' favorite. Unfortunately, the few who knew how to make it could not communicate much in English.

There was also a tent where soldiers would go in the evening for entertainment. Some officers, I soon noticed, disapproved of it, although I occasionally saw them go there as well. So, the fourth or fifth day, after emerging from the morphine treatment that had kept me in the medical unit, I finally went to that tent, burning with curiosity – as Peter Sloterdijk has said, humans are the species that need an explanation. As soon as I entered the tent, a couple of soldiers silently showed me a place on a bench and invited me to sit. These bulky, mustachioed men were watching films. Indian films. A tree, a dance around the tree, a wedding, and many songs. Love stories.

I ended up on that military base because of Captain Shaheed, whom I had met a few months earlier in the premises of a Catholic convent – these stories cannot be made up. The Pakistani Battalion, known as PakBat, was one of three foreign Blue Helmet units posted by the UN in the north of Haiti. The PakBat had set up an entire base with a full medical unit a few miles from Cap Haitian. When I became suddenly ill with a hemorrhagic fever in early 1996, I had a medical choice worthy of globalization: Guatemalan, Dutch, or Pakistani. I thought of Shaheed and asked my driver to take me to the PakBat base – although he later said I could not tell him anything and he chose the PakBat on his own.

I stayed in the medical unit for the first few days but as I recovered, I wandered around the base and observed military life. A truck left the base every morning around 10 or 11. Every day, the Pakistani battalion was preparing and sending food to the dire Cap Haitian penitentiary. There was no cooking facility there and the inmates were fed only if their families brought them food. The Pakistani military at some point had realized that and taken it upon themselves to remedy that situation. The most humane individuals I observed in the international community wore a uniform. The human rights unit of the UN, myself included, as well as all other human rights NGOs in town, never brought a loaf of bread to that prison. It was not part of their mandate either to take me in when I was ill and they did it.

I had met Shaheed months earlier in a mountain town close to the Dominican border. There were partial elections there and I was to monitor them. The only quiet place offering a bed was a small convent run by three gracious Canadian nuns. The convent also had a large compound where the first day I saw a couple of military vehicles enter and park; they would spend two nights there – I have no recollection where the soldiers and officers slept. For this convent in this remote village, it was the event of the decade. For two nights, each evening, two soldiers went up the staircase to give the three nuns and myself a full hot meal. The first evening, I was talking with one of the nuns on the second-floor veranda when the soldiers unexpectedly brought mutton, vegetables, and chapatis, followed by Captain Shaheed. Overwhelmed with gratitude and cultural cluelessness, the nun thanked him by giving him a chain with a wooden cross, waiting for the appreciation by looking straight in his eyes with a smile. I saw the captain smile gently in return, accept the cross, open his hand, his face betraying nothing else, and put the cross in his shirt's pocket. I remembered that scene months later when the hemorrhagic fever kicked in. If the PakBat doctor had as much medical competence as Shaheed had class, I should be in good hands. My driver later told me that I was covered with blood when we arrived at the base. I had lost consciousness. I regained it two days later with multiple IVs. Someone had washed me. I would soon start my ethnographic observation of Pakistani military life and Bollywood movies. Only months later, through a casual encounter with a lieutenant did I learn the truth about the military cuisine I ate: a major had ordered the camp's cook to make special meals for me every day. This time, I had missed the wink.

* * *

As in a bad, abusive marriage, I have never forsaken working in human rights (obviously, the abuses are reciprocal). I still carry out human rights missions. My unsolvable contradiction is that anthropologists tend to be highly critical individuals and lean (I hope) towards a Voltairian mind. But human rights – as a set of political values and as a professional field have been construed in the past decades as the Good – a moral absolute. And to question the good is universally regarded as obscene. The lack of reflexivity of this field – and possibly of humanitarian organizations in general, as proven by the moral disintegration of the British flagship NGO Oxfam in early 2018, then by scores of other celebrated NGOs, when it was revealed that its employees commonly used donors' money to organize sex parties with prostitutes – is predicated on that self-assigned goodness and led to moral disarray. The professionalization of human rights in the 1990s made it attractive as a career – and for careerists – and created a gap between highly paid – and not always educated or sensitive – expatriates and a local population surviving on meager salaries, if any: the relation can only be neocolonial. The sex parties are just the grotesque tip of the iceberg. The lack of accountability and meritocracy in international organizations with a heavy bureaucracy, their culture of silence and impunity, and the political bias of their personnel magnify the type of behavior I sketched in this chapter, especially in countries where the state is too weak or inept to control foreign expatriates and organizations. Yet, my reflection here should not be a deterrent. Undergraduate students tend to be moral individuals, are (hopefully) hungry for justice, and some are far to the left, as I was at their age. My plea is for the distance, for students to take human rights as an object that is neither good nor bad but deserves a scientific and critical outlook, and for the belief that nothing is sacred, even the sacred. Human rights work is ethically messy. For this reason, it is a good education: in the end, I recommend it.

Discussion questions

1　Do you think a professional should reveal his past experiences, including accounts that may bring bad press to a former employer?
2　How would you reconcile professional ethics with personal ones? How would you deal personally with ethical dilemmas?

3   Do you think that methods are a detail or essential to know?
4   Where would you draw the line for critical inquiry? Or should we draw the line at all?

References

Clastres, P. (1972). *Chronicle of the Guayaki Indians.* New York: Zone Books, 1998.
Geertz, C. (1973). Thick description: Towards an interpretative theory of culture. In: *The interpretation of culture: Selected essays.* New York: Basic Books, pp. 3–30.

Further reading

Holmes, K. (1996). The new world disorder: A critique of the United Nations. *Journal of International Affairs,* 46, pp. 323–340.
Katz, J.M. (2013). *The big truck that went by: How the world came to save Haiti and left a disaster behind.* New York: St Martin's Press.
Schuller, M. (2012). *Killing with kindness: Haiti, international aid and NGOs.* New Brunswick: Rutgers University Press.
Wilde, R. (2007). Colonialism redux? Territorial administration by international organizations, colonial echoes, and the legitimacy of the "international." In: A. Hehir and N. Robinson, eds, *State building: Theory and practice.* London: Routledge.

14 Migrant workers in the Gulf
Theoretical and human rights dilemmas

Amani El Jack

Introduction

This chapter examines the challenges of labor migration in the Persian Gulf region and explores its theoretical and policy dilemmas. I will locate the debate on labor migration in the Gulf within its broader global context, a context that is currently being shaped by anti-migration sentiments and policies and accelerating waves of populism/nativism characterized by the control of national borders.[1] The chapter addresses two main aspects of the problematics informing transnational migration theories and praxes: first, international human rights policy on transnational migration advocates a hierarchy of rights that privileges civil and political rights over the protection of the human rights of migrant workers; and second, international labor laws advocated by the United Nations (UN) and institutions such as the International Labor Organization (ILO) have led to the adoption of the International Convention on the Protection of the Rights of All Migrant Workers and Members of Their Families. In the Gulf region, its contested immigration sponsorship policy that is commonly referred to as the *Kafala* system has undergone various reforms in an attempt to improve the working conditions of the region's migrants by emphasizing wage protection and the provision of employment benefits. However, in reality, these international and regional labor regulation measures tend to be symbolic in nature and lack an enforcement mechanism that would enable them to protect the basic human rights of migrant workers. By drawing on my ongoing field research on migrant workers in the Gulf coupled with secondary data and scholarly surveys, the first section of this chapter examines the theorization on transnational migration, while the second section interrogates labor migration policies in the Gulf region.

Interrogating transnational migration theories and praxes

Existing scholarship on transnational migration has advanced our understanding of the human rights implications of migration, its gendered consequences, and addressed the violations of the human rights of refugees/

migrant workers as well as their restricted access to legal residency status, citizenship, and naturalization processes. However, in the present moment, transnational migration is facing a growing global backlash that renders refugees and labor migrants a threat to national identities and attributes current economic and cultural questions to factors such as globalization, diversity, and the openness of national markets/societies to transnational migrants. Witness to the rise in popularity of such nativist ideology is the Brexit vote in the United Kingdom in 2016 along with the resurgence of anti-immigration politics in the United States and across Europe. Indeed, the discourse surrounding these new developments is infused with elements of xenophobia, Islamophobia, and racism. This negative development has severely impacted the lives of migrant women, men, and children and has posed significant theoretical and methodological challenges to academic and policy-related fields. Thus, in this section, I will highlight three main problems informing transnational migration theories and praxes.

First, one of the main shortcomings of transnational migration scholarship lies in the false distinction between migrant workers and refugees, which has serious consequences not only at the theoretical level but more importantly with regards to its human rights implications (El Jack, 2007). As Ray Jureidini and Latife Reda argue, "distinguishing labor or economic migrants from refugees is important from the perspective of humanitarian agencies distributing donated resources earmarked for refugees, but not necessarily from the general principles of human rights" (2017, p. 227). The conceptualization of the "migration–asylum nexus" is in recognition of this difficulty in distinguishing between forced and economic migration, where similarities between the migratory processes lack differentiation in policy responses to both asylum seekers and (economic) migrants, particularly in Europe. Jureidini and Reda further argue that "the distinction between migrants and refugees is that "refugees," by definition in international law, are deemed to be deserving of special protection and assistance; so-called "economic migrants" are not" (2017, p. 225). Moreover, international human rights policy on transnational migration clearly advocates a hierarchy of rights, which privilege civil and political rights over the protection of gender, economic, social, religious, and cultural rights. Human rights discourses and international conventions/protocols have focused for the most part on assessing protracted refugees' situations instigated by wars and militarized conflict. Indeed, articles 1, 55, and 56 of the UN Charter, as well as the UN 1951 Convention only provide political and legal frameworks for the protection of refugees and forcibly displaced women, men, and children (Choelwinski et al., 2009). Informed by the ideological debates of post-war European geopolitics (e.g., post-World War I and II), these UN instruments were designed to apply to refugees in Europe displaced by historic threats of the Holocaust and Communism. Thus, these instruments remain Eurocentric and limited, even today.

Another problematic feature of transnational migration theories and praxes is that international organizations such as the ILO have also advocated for labor migrants' rights, which led to the adoption of the ILO Declaration on Fundamental Principles and Rights at Work. Moreover, the UN passed the International Convention on the Protection of the Rights of All Migrant Workers and Members of Their Families. The UN convention and ILO declaration both advocate for the rights of migrant workers, which include wage protection and the provision of social security along with employment benefits. As the next section illustrates, the Gulf region's contested immigration sponsorship policy (the *Kafala* system) has been nominally reformed over the past few years in order to address international criticism regarding violations of the human rights of migrant workers. The *Kafala* system reforms focused on wage protection and the provision of employment benefits in an attempt to improve the working conditions of migrant workers in the region. However, these international and regional labor measures tend to be symbolic in nature and lack the enforcement mechanisms that enable them to protect migrant workers' human rights. Both globally and within the Gulf region, the majority of countries that host migrant workers, including the United States and the Arab Gulf states, have not signed or implemented many of these international instruments, thus rendering them ineffective.

The third shortcoming of mainstream migration scholarship on labor migration is that it tends to predominantly focus on the economic impact of migration, specifically the remittance behavior of migrants in the Global North/South, while overlooking the multidimensional complexity of migrant experiences. Such scholarship can be divided into perspectives either belonging to the structural/historical critical approach, which examines the causes of migration (e.g., push and pull factors) and directly links migration to structural inequalities at the global scale (Papademetriou, 1985; Probsting, 2015) or to liberal perspectives that highlight the cost–benefit dimensions of migration and its implications for migrants, their families, host countries, and homelands (Harris and Todaro, 1970; Keely and Tran, 1989; Schiff, 1999; Verloo, 2007). Neoclassical theorists such as Harris and Todaro argue that transnational migration is caused by a geographical imbalance between the demand and supply of labor. They assert that workers tend to migrate to high-wage countries from countries where wages and economic productivity are low. Thus, their theory assumes that migration waves will decline when wage differentials are eliminated (Harris and Todaro, 1970). On the other hand, Piore's dual labor market theory argues that labor migration is induced by the workforce needs of industrial countries (e.g., pull factors) rather than being motivated by the push factors from sending countries (Piore, 1972). In contrast, the new economics of labor migration theory assumes that transnational migration patterns are not merely based on individual decisions, but rather are attributed to complex decisions collectively made by women, men, and other members of their households (Stark and Bloom, 1985).

While some of these mainstream migration theorists attempt to address the causes and consequences of migration, for the most part their focus depicts migrants as a burden on host governments. As a result, they have not accurately captured the fluidity of modern-day migration patterns. For example, in the Gulf region, both "skilled" and "unskilled" migrant workers have been instrumental to the current economic development and modern transformation of the region through their engagement in the high-demand fields of construction, security, and domestic services. They do not only earn an income that contributes to enhancing their own wellbeing, but also provide financial support to their families through regularly sustained remittances that contribute significantly to the development of their home countries. In addition to this economic component, labor migration has contributed to the social and cultural enrichment of both sending and receiving countries.

At the international level, there has also been a long tradition of recognition of the worker-related rights of economic migrants. Almost a century ago, international workers' rights organizations began to understand the important correlation between the protection of rights of workers in societies in general and the inclusion of migrant workers within national labor protections. The preamble to the ILO's 1919 constitution highlights this commitment by explicitly mentioning its interest in protecting workers who are "employed in countries other than their own."[2] Over the decades, a number of host countries have adopted the international labor standards and migrants' rights conventions of the ILO. In addition to the eight fundamental rights provided in the 1998 ILO Declaration on Fundamental Principles and Rights at Work, specific instruments comprise a host of ILO conventions that refer to the needs of labor migrants including wage protections, occupational health and safety, employment policies, labor inspections, social security provisions, and the rights of domestic workers (Babar, 2017). This represents one of the UN's core human rights protocols for migrant workers and widens the discussion of migrant protections beyond merely ensuring labor rights already established through ILO instruments to more holistic norms for the inclusion of migrants within national human rights agendas (International Labor Organization, 2018). However, as the next section will demonstrate, any discussion of migrant protections must address the complexity of forces that lead to the abuse of migrant workers, including the types of protection(s) either afforded to or withheld from them by the Gulf *Kafala* system, as well as international human rights conventions on migrant labor.

Labor migration in the Gulf

The process of recruiting labor migrants to work in the Gulf region is not distinct in comparison to other worker migration systems in other parts of the globe. However, what distinguishes the contested Gulf immigration sponsorship policy, commonly referred to as the *Kafala* system, is the degree of restrictions that government agencies, recruitment companies, and private sponsors impose on migrant workers under their sponsorship. The *Kafala* system regulates the recruitment and oversight of foreign workers, strictly controlling migrant entry, residency, and departure processes. It gives the sponsor the responsibility and authority over a migrant worker's living, accommodation, and working conditions (Diop et al., 2017). Thus, the *Kafala* system enables migrant laborers to enter the Gulf region legally with a work permit as temporary workers in sectors such as construction, security, agriculture, and domestic services while simultaneously undermining their basic human rights.

Since its establishment in the 1950s, the *Kafala* system has stipulated that labor migrants should be sponsored by state agencies, recruitment companies, or private citizens in order to obtain work visas and residence status in the Gulf. Heather Murray argues, "because the system requires that an employee work only for his or her sponsor, many sponsors often take away their migrant workers' passports and identification cards"[3] (2012, p. 467). For instance, the six Gulf Cooperation Council (GCC) states, comprising Bahrain, Kuwait, Oman, Qatar, Saudi Arabia, and the United Arab Emirates, impose severe restrictions on "unskilled" or "low-skilled" migrant workers. International human rights organizations and scholars such as Abdoulaye Diop, Trevor Johnston, and Kien Trung Le have compared the *Kafala* system to systems of "indentured servitude" and argued that it enables sponsors to hire migrant workers and pay them low wages, forcing them to work long hours under exploitative working and living conditions. In addition, due to salary stipulations and entry/exit requirements, many such workers are not allowed to bring spouses and family members to the receiving country or visit relatives in other GCC states. For example, in Qatar, all expatriate workers are required to provide proof of a minimum monthly salary of 10,000 QAR (slightly less than 3,000 USD) in order to sponsor residence permits for their wives or children. For "unskilled" or "low-skilled" migrant workers, whose typical salary is substantially less than this amount, such regulations bar them from bringing their families to Qatar for the duration of their employment abroad. In addition, none of the GCC states offers any pathway to permanent residence or citizenship to migrant workers. Instead, these states link workers' residency status to restricted contractual agreements, which is in itself contradictory to international human rights laws and regulations (Amnesty International, 2018; Babar, 2017; Diop, 2017; Human Rights Watch, 2017; International Labor Organization, 2018).

Despite recent changes introduced to the *Kafala* system in the Gulf region, a significant number of "unskilled" or "low-skilled" migrant workers are still under threat of labor exploitation in the six GCC states. For instance, the state of Qatar has reformed its *Kafala* system and introduced a contract-based system under Law no. 21 of 2015 that came into force in

December 2016. However, even within the new contract-based system, migrant workers still require the permission of their recruiters to leave the country or change their sponsor if they want to leave before the end date of their contract.[4] These new reforms still lag far behind the requirements of international human rights standards and there exists no mechanism or political will for their implementation (Human Rights Watch, 2017).

Despite the limitations of these marginal reforms, the ILO estimates that the GCC states host around 22 million migrant workers, who constitute a majority of the regional labor force. In the state of Qatar alone, migrants constitute about 94 percent of the country's economically active population and 99 percent of the private sector's labor force. Since the state of Qatar won the rights to host the FIFA 2022 World Cup, the number of migrant workers within its labor force continues to significantly increase. Most of the migrant labor force originates from regions such as the Middle East, South-East Asia, South Asia, and Sub-Saharan Africa (Qatar Statistics Authority, 2017). It is, however, important to note that labor migrants are not a homogenous group but are rather diverse. As a result, their experiences vary based on how gender, class, race, education, language, religion, and national identity with other power relations intersect to shape their life stories and migratory journeys.

Despite the application of the *Kafala* system for the recruitment of all foreign labor within the Gulf, there emerges clear distinctions between the experiences of "unskilled" or "low-skilled" migrant workers and those of "high-skilled" expatriates. For instance, expatriates experience a certain level of relative privilege in contrast to migrant workers. This privilege is often based on such factors as class, education, language, nationality, or social status and often translates to flexible employment agreements, freedom of movement, competitive work packages, luxurious accommodation, and generous family benefits for education and healthcare. However, this is in stark contrast to the experiences of many "unskilled" or "low-skilled" migrant workers who comprise most of the regional labor force and are often employed in the fields of construction, security, agriculture, and domestic services (Longva, 1999). In field research conducted with some of the African migrant workers who live in workers' camps near the city of Al-Khor about 50 kilometers outside Doha in 2017, many of the workers indicated that they are completely isolated from society and urban life. Compared to those within the city limits, the roads in the camps are unkempt, dirty, and narrow and the living conditions are extremely harsh. This particular camp houses a total of 113 workers from seven different countries (Nepal, India, Ghana, Nigeria, the Philippines, Kenya, and Sri Lanka). As one of the research participates articulates:

> We are cramped here in small rooms each accommodating up to 10 people. The rooms are not suitable for the harsh weather conditions. Sometimes we are forced to cook inside our rooms because the camp

lacks the basic facilities like a suitable kitchen. The bathrooms are few and people have to wake up so early to get a chance to get ready without getting delayed... Life in this labor camp is worst than the city slum life in Kenya. Being one among the many, I have been trying very hard to cope with life since I first arrived here.

As the above testimony illustrates, labor camps are segregated from the lavish, main estates of the capital city of Doha. This is because its thousands of migrant workers, oftentimes young and male, are perceived as security threats within Gulf societies, where a demographic imbalance between a small ratio of nationals in comparison to foreign workers complicates issues of national identity and exacerbates social tensions between nationals and foreign workers (Forstenlechner and Rutledge, 2011; Kapiszewski, 2015). By and large, these young males are confined to isolated areas where they are housed in residential camps or collective housing communities. Such areas are characterized by poor living standards, where workers are not permitted to organize themselves within civil society organizations or socio-cultural and political networks. These types of living conditions experienced by "unskilled" or "low-skilled" migrant workers in the Gulf are a violation of article 2 of Universal Declaration of Human Rights that states, "Everyone is entitled to all the rights and freedoms set forth in this Declaration, without distinction of any kind, such as race, color, sex, language, religion, political or other opinion, national or social origin, property, birth or other status." While the unique situation of migrant workers in the Gulf differs with those of migrant workers in other regions of the Global North in regards to the specifics of their day-to-day realities, migrant workers across the globe encounter the same types of human rights violations and are isolated from mainstream society.

Although their experiences differ from male migrant workers, my female research participants also reveal how women working in the domestic sector are negatively impacted by the *Kafala* system. My findings show that the experiences of women and men are gendered, complex, and varied. While men dominate the public sector, women are predominantly employed in the private sphere. Moreover, the socially and culturally constructed gender roles for women influence the details of their employment in the domestic sector. Thus, they are bound by stereotypical notions of gender roles and predominantly confined to household service as cleaners, cooks, and nannies, whereas male domestic workers perform tasks outside the home as gardeners, drivers, and security guards. This is in line with the Gulf's male-dominated society within which domestic work is considered a family matter. Also, the patriarchal personal status codes of the region designate the husband as head of the household, which relegates wives, children, any adult female relatives, and domestic workers (both males and females) as subservient members of the family. Sharon Nagy's study of female, Filipina domestic workers within Gulf households illustrates how this patriarchal relationship between domestic workers and their sponsors disproportionately impacts women in a negative fashion (Nagy, 1998). This is demonstrated in the gender-specific vulnerabilities that female domestic workers face including wage discrimination, sexual harassment, sexual exploitation, and gender-based violence in the unregulated domestic sector.[5] In its 2008 report, Human Rights Watch draws attention to such gender-based violence, documenting the physical and sexual abuse of Mina, an Indonesian domestic worker in Riyadh, Saudi Arabia. Recounting her experience, Mina states:

> You have only two choices: either you work without a salary, or you will die here. If you die, I will tell the police that you committed suicide... Even if I worked without a salary, it did not guarantee that I would not be beaten. That is why I escaped. All the doors were locked so there was no way out, the windows had iron bars, but there was a hole for ventilation in the bathroom from which I escaped. Before I escaped, I prayed and asked Allah for help although my body was very dirty since she did not allow me to take a bath for a month. I prayed.

As shown by Mina's experience, the *Kafala* system does not guarantee protection of the basic human rights of domestic workers. Indeed, none of the GCC states offer standard protections against domestic violence. Instead, traditional cultural and prevailing customs and practices within these six countries pose major obstacles to the protection of women inside the home. The ILO country reports on the Gulf indicate that violence against women is rarely addressed. Moreover, it is cloaked in secrecy and oftentimes is either underreported or not reported at all due to social stigma. Hence, female domestic workers face a unique set of dangers inherent to the nature of their work and should not be consigned to the status of mere "servants." Quite the contrary, these workers deserve special protection under local and regional labor laws and international human rights regulations.

It is important to note that all "unskilled" or "low-skilled" migrants within the Gulf share a sense of social isolation, albeit of varying degrees. This is partially due to the persistence of a negative perception of migrant workers within Gulf society as a threat to local culture and identity. As a result of this perception, foreign laborers rarely interact with nationals beyond their work environment. Such isolation was demonstrated by a study conducted in Qatar in 2010 with a sample of 1,114 construction workers. The study differentiated between Qatari neighborhoods and neighborhoods comprised of either foreign expatriates or migrant workers and explored the composition of the residents of each neighborhood, relationships between neighbors, and their sense of community. These studies find that there is a lack of communication among workers and residents who often lack a common language or culture (Al-Emadi et al., 2012; Al-Ghanim et al., 2010). It also reflects a growing sense of social isolation among migrant workers and a widening gap between nationals and foreign residents, a gap that may negatively affect social cohesion in the future. These studies also indicate that the *Kafala* system does not adequately protect migrant workers from further isolation and exploitation by their employers. Due to the vastly different economic, social, and living conditions that it entails for "unskilled" or "low-skilled" migrant workers, "skilled" workers, and citizens, the *Kafala* system creates and reinforces social boundaries among these three groups. Whereas expatriates and their families can intermingle with citizens to some extent based on their economic, educational, and social status, there is no chance for other groups of migrant workers to integrate within urban life in GCC states. In fact, in most cases, these workers are often prevented from entering public spaces such as shopping malls, parks, or museums under the guise of prohibitory practices including "family days" (e.g., days where admission to such public venues is only permitted to families), which constitutes a clear violation of their human rights.

The presence of such social isolation was confirmed by Abdoulaye Diop, Trevor Johnston, and Kien Trung Le in a similar nationally representative survey through the Social and Economic Survey Research Institute at Qatar University with 2,394 Qatari citizens in 2012. It examined the attitudes of Qataris towards migrant workers in addition to providing an assessment of the current socio-economic and political bias against migrant workers (Diop et al., 2017). Their findings reiterate that negative perceptions of foreign labor continue to persist. They argue that Qataris harbor fears about the negative influence of domestic workers on their national culture and traditions. One growing concern among Qatari nationals was the threat posed by nannies and domestic workers due to their direct influence on the upbringing of their children and youth. Therefore, nationals fear that such workers will change the social fabric of Qatar by changing the behavior of its children and youth and their way of life (e.g., manner of dress, appearance, language, etc.). This, in turn, is perceived to endanger Qatar's ability to preserve the unique identity of its small local population. Thus, despite international human rights and labor organizations such as Amnesty International, Human Rights Watch, the International Organization for Migration, and ILO criticism of Gulf states for their discrimination against migrant workers under the *Kafala* system, these studies illustrate continued public support for the *Kafala* system and the opposition of business owners and social groups to its reform (Amnesty International, 2017; Human Rights Watch, 2014).

In response to growing international criticism, many Gulf states have been repositioning themselves on the global stage as beacons for international diplomacy, trade, and cultural exchange. This attempted transformation is reflected in the 2030 national visions of many GCC countries, which emphasize holistic socio-economic, political, and structural changes. Within the proposed changes, governments in Bahrain, the Kingdom of Saudi Arabia, Kuwait, Qatar, and the United Arab Emirates have included a comprehensive review of the *Kafala* system. These states have recently adopted policies to reform their regulatory systems of labor migration not only to address existing shortcomings of their protection of migrant workers, but also to comply with international human rights laws aimed at improving the situation of migrant workers.[6] For instance, Qatar introduced the concept of migrant worker welfare, which is defined by the ILO to broadly include services, facilities, and amenities that enable migrant workers to perform their duties in healthy surroundings. In this regard, welfare measures do not only include monetary and legal terms but also the enhancement of working and housing conditions, the provision of health services, industrial relations, and insurance against diseases, accidents, and unemployment for both workers and their families.

In addition, the ILO *Domestic Workers Convention* was adopted in 2011, which puts in place new standards within the informal employment sector, often the site of substantial exploitation of migrant workers. The convention provides provisions for the protection of fundamental principles and rights at work including the freedom of association and the right to collective bargaining, the elimination of forced or compulsory labor and child labor, and the eradication of employment and occupational discrimination. Under this convention, domestic workers within the Gulf region should have fair employment terms, decent living and working conditions, and should be protected from all forms of abuse, harassment, and violence. Nevertheless, a significant gap continues to exist between the stipulations of international conventions and regional initiatives and the actual application and practice of such stipulations. Implementation of these conventions and initiatives has faced a number of obstacles. First, some public- and private-sector players are hesitant to adopt them due to their explicit acknowledgment of the financial burden associated with the ratification of these conventions in comparison with very limited benefits. Second, some Gulf states argue that some of the provisions are incompatible with their existing laws. Third, several states have not ratified the UN Convention on the Protection of Migrant Workers due to claims of its redundancy (e.g., that rights stipulated are already protected by existing national laws). Amidst such claims, it appears that such regulations are symbolic gestures, which have yet to be implemented by GCC countries. Instead, such reforms are often superficial public relations ploys to mitigate international outrage without addressing the root causes of the issue. As Diop et al. (2017, p. 177) argue, "despite real desire to change their immigration policies, GCC states encounter entrenched economic interests and broad popular resistance, which together have stymied any genuine political will for reform."

Conclusion

In conclusion, there exists a clear conflict between the regulations of international law and the UN-based protections provided to migrant workers by established conventions and the predatory regulations of the *Kafala* system as it currently exists in the GCC states. The recent attempts of GCC states to reform their *Kafala* systems have hitherto only consisted of symbolic modifications that do not adequately address the myriad of factors currently contributing to the abuse and exploitation of migrant workers within the Gulf region borders. Indeed, at its core, the *Kafala* system is intimately linked to the anti-migrant sentiment that is partially attributable to local concerns regarding demographic imbalances and the increasing number of migrants within the labor force. Such sentiments among GCC nationals share key characteristics with the anti-immigrant rhetoric that has spread at the global level, particularly those prevalent among the public in North America and Europe. Currently, these societies share a belief that migrants are a threat to both national culture and security. Whether in the Global North or the Gulf region, these populations attribute negative socio-economic and cultural challenges to factors such as globalization and diversity. However, if GCC governments are to fulfill the social, economic, and cultural goals set forth in their 2030 national strategic visions, then the challenge of creating an atmosphere of positive engagement between its predominantly foreign labor force and its locals must be adequately addressed. Furthermore, a comprehensive reform of the *Kafala* system is urgently required. Yet, such reforms must address the importance of not only acknowledging but also enforcing existing international human rights laws and conventions aimed at guaranteeing the protection of migrant worker rights and welfare. Thus, such reforms would not only demonstrate a recognition of the unique circumstances of migrant workers within Gulf society, but also their invaluable contribution to Gulf society as a whole.

Discussion questions

1 Gulf states have reservations on UN conventions and regulations. What should happen when local culture conflicts with international human rights laws?
2 Why do we need to pay attention to gender, class, race, education, language, religion, and national identity in understanding migrant human situations in the Gulf?
3 What are some factors that influence government policies on migrant labor in the Gulf? Are these static or do they engage with the changing social, political, and economic dynamics of the region? If yes, how so?

Notes

1 In the Global North, this has been demonstrated by the Brexit vote in the United Kingdom, the presidential election of Donald Trump in the United States, the defeat of Chancellor Angela Merkel's immigration agenda in Germany, and the overall rise of "closed door" immigration policies across Europe. The anti-refugee/immigrant

sentiments within the Gulf region and the Middle East share intrinsic characteristics with other parts of the globe and have been heavily influenced by xenophobia, ethnocentrism, and racism. For instance, the Trump administration's anti-immigration policies popular in the current political rhetoric surrounding immigration in the United States center on the control of borders via the construction of walls in addition to the large-scale deportation of illegal migrant workers as well as those asylum seekers whose claims for refugee status have not yet been granted.

2 International Labor Organization Constitution, 1919.

3 Confiscating the passports of migrants would make it difficult for them to leave their sponsors. As a result, such workers would be forced to continue to work under abusive working conditions. If they should manage to leave their employers, migrant workers will encounter stiff monetary penalties and be forced to leave the country immediately at their own expense instead of having their employers cover return travel costs as was stipulated in their original job agreements.

4 The new law uses the word "recruiter" instead of "sponsor."

5 Although the gender gap exists among GCC nationals, expatriates, and migrant workers alike, it disproportionately impacts female migrant workers, particularly those engaged in domestic work. For instance, domestic workers in Qatar are paid less than 30 percent of the country's average wage while domestic workers in Bahrain earn around 20 percent of the earnings of national workers.

6 For instance, the state of Qatar enacted a law in 2014 that emphasized the prompt payment of workers' salaries while the Kingdom of Saudi Arabia created a wage protection system in 2013 that imposed penalties on companies that delayed payments. Similarly, Kuwait has also implemented measures to guarantee the payment of worker salaries.

References

Al-Emadi, D. (2012). *From Fareej to metropolis: A social capital survey of Qatar*. Doha: Qatar University Social and Economic Survey Research Institute.

Al-Ghanim, K., ed. (2010). *Awḍā' al-'umāl ghayr al-mahra fī qiṭā' al-nashā'āt fī Qatar*. Doha: National Human Rights Committee.

Amnesty International (2017). Qatar: Abuse of migrant workers remains widespread as World Cup stadium hosts first match. Available at: www.amnesty.org/en/latest/news/2017/05/qatar-world-cup-stadium-first-match/ [Accessed August 14, 2018].

Amnesty International (2018). Qatar finally joins two human rights treaties – but what does it really mean for migrant workers? Available at: www.amnesty.org/en/latest/news/2018/06/qatar-finally-joins-two-key-human-rights-treaties-but-what-does-it-really-mean-for-migrant-workers/ [Accessed August 14, 2018].

Babar, Z. (2017). The "humane economy": Migrant labor and Islam in Qatar and the UAE. *Sociology of Islam*, 5(2–3), pp. 200–223.

Choelwinski, R., Guchteneire, P., and Pecoud, A. (2009). *Migration and human rights: The United Nations Convention on Migrant Workers' Rights*. Cambridge: UNESCO Publishing/Cambridge University Press.

Diop, A., Le, K., Johnston, T., and Ewers, M. (2017). Citizens' attitudes towards migrant workers in Qatar. *Migration and Development*, 6(1), pp. 144–160.

El Jack, A. (2007). Gendered implications: Development-induced displacement in the Sudan. In: P. Vandergeest, P. Idahosa, and P. Bose, eds, *Development's displacements: Ecologies, economies and cultures at risk*. Vancouver: UBC Press, pp. 61–81.

Forstenlechner, I. and Rutledge, E. (2011). The GCC's "demographic imbalance": Perceptions, realities and policy options. *Middle East Policy*, 18(4), pp. 25–43.

Harris, J. and Todaro, M. (1970). Migration, unemployment and development: A two-sector analysis. *American Economic Review*, 60(1), pp. 126–142.

Human Rights Watch (2008). "As if I am not human": Abuses against Asian domestic workers in Saudi Arabia. Available at: www.hrw.org/reports/2008/saudiarabia 0708/ [Accessed May 6, 2018].

Human Rights Watch (2014). I already bought you: Abuse and exploitation of female migrant domestic workers in the United Arab Emirates. Available at: www.hrw. org/sites/default/files/reports/uae1014_forUpload.pdf [Accessed August 14, 2018].

Human Rights Watch (2017). #MeToo, say domestic workers in the Middle East. Available at: www.hrw.org/news/2017/12/08/metoo-say-domestic-workers-middle-east [Accessed August 14, 2018].

International Labor Organization (2018). Exploratory study of good policies in the protection of construction workers in the Middle East. An ILO white paper by Jill Wells. ILO Publications. Available at: www.ilo.org/beirut/publications/WCMS_ 618158/lang–en/index.htmhttps://www.hrw.org/reports/2008/saudiarabia0708/ [Accessed May 18, 2018].

Jureidini, R. and Reda, L. (2017). The convergence of migrants and refugees. *Sociology of Islam*, 5(2–3), pp. 224–247.

Kapiszewski, A. (2015). Arab versus Asian migrant workers in the GCC countries. In: P. Jain and G. Oommen, eds, *South Asian migration to Gulf countries*. 1st ed. London: Routledge India, pp. 66–90.

Keely, C. and Tran, B. (1989). Remittances from labor migration: Evaluations, performance, and implications. *International Migration Review*, 23(3), pp. 500–525.

Longva, A. (1999). Keeping migrant workers in check. *Middle East Report*, 29(211), pp. 20–22.

Murray, H. (2012). Hope for reform springs eternal: How the sponsorship system, domestic laws, and traditional customs fail to protect migrant domestic workers in GCC countries. *Cornell International Law Journal*, 45(2), pp. 461–485.

Nagy, S. (1998). "This time I think I'll try a Filipina': Global and local influences on relations between foreign household workers and their employers in Doha, Qatar. *City and Society*, 10(1), pp. 83–103.

Papademetriou, D. (1985). Illusions and reality in international migration: Migration and development in post-World War II Greece. *International Migration*, 23(2), pp. 211–224.

PioreM. (1972). Notes for a theory of labor market stratification. In: R. Edwards, D. Gordon, and M. Reich, *Labor market segmentation: A research report to the US Department of Labor*. Cambridge, MA: Harvard University, Centre for Educational Policy Research.

Probsting, M. (2015). Migration and super-exploitation: Marxist theory and the role of migration in the present period of capitalist decay. *Critique*, 43(3–4), pp. 329–346.

Qatar Statistics Authority (2017). Labor force survey: The first quarter (January–March 2017). Doha: Ministry of Development and Planning. Available at: www. mdps.gov.qa/en/statistics/Statistical%20Releases/Social/LaborForce/2017/Q1/Labor Force-Quarter1-2017-webreport.pdf [Accessed May 6, 2018].

Schiff, M. (1999). Trade, migration and welfare: The impact of social capital. Policy Research Working Paper Series 20144. Washington, DC: World Bank.

Stark, O. and Bloom, D.E. (1985). The new economics of labor migration. *American Economic Review*, 75(2), pp. 173–178.

Verloo, M. (2007). *Multiple meanings of gender equality: A critical frame analysis of gender policies in Europe*. Budapest: Central European University Press.

Further reading

Adler, L. and Gielen, U., eds (2003). *Migration: Immigration and emigration in international perspective*. Santa Barbara, CA: Greenwood Publishing Group.

Arrighi, G. and Silver, B. (1984). Labor movements and capital migration: The United States and Western Europe in world-historical perspective. In: C. Berquist, ed., *Labor in the capitalist world-economy*. Beverly Hills, CA: Sage, pp. 183–216.

Auwal, M. (2010). Ending the exploitation of migrant workers in the Gulf. *Fletcher Forum for World Affairs*, 34(2), pp. 87–108.

Azhar, M. (2016). Indian migrant workers in GCC countries. *Diaspora Studies*, 9(2), pp. 100–111.

Baldwin-Edwards, M. (2011). *Labor immigration and labor markets in the GCC countries: National patterns and trends*. London: LSE Kuwait Program on Development.

Gardner, A. (2017). *City of strangers: Gulf migration and the Indian community in Bahrain*. Ithaca, NY: Cornell University Press.

Gardner, A., Pessoa, S., Diop, A., Al-Ghanim, K., Le Trung, K., and Harkness, L. (2013). A portrait of low-income migrants in contemporary Qatar. *Journal of Arabian Studies*, 3(1), pp. 1–17.

Gardner, A., Pessoa, S., and Harkness, L. (2014). *Labor migrants and access to justice in contemporary Qatar*. London: Middle East Centre, LSE.

Hamza, S. (2014). *Migrant labor in the Arabian Gulf*. Knoxville: University of Tennessee, Tennessee Research and Creative Exchange.

Jain, P. and Oommen, G., eds (2015). *South Asian migration to Gulf countries: History, policies, development*. London: Routledge.

Kamrava, M. and Babar, Z. (2012). *Migrant labor in the Persian Gulf*. London: Hurst.

Khory, K. ed. (2012). *Global migration: Challenges in the twenty-first century*. 1st ed. New York: Palgrave Macmillan US.

Martin, S., Weerasinghe, S., and Taylor, A., eds (2014). *Humanitarian crises and migration: Causes, consequences and responses*. London: Routledge.

Moretto, M. and Vergalli, S. (2011). Analysis and European policies of migration flows: The uncertainty effect. *Equilibri*, 15(1), pp. 139–148.

Omoniyi, T. (2007). *The cultures of economic migration: International perspectives*. London: Routledge.

Peer, B. (2013). A maid's execution. *New Yorker*. Available at: www.newyorker.com/news/news-desk/a-maids-execution [Accessed May 6, 2018].

Piore, M. (1974). The dual labor market: Theory and implications. In: D. Gordon, ed., *Problems in political economy: An urban perspective*. Lexington, MA: DC Heath & Co.

Qatar Statistics Authority (2012). *Bulletin labor force statistics 2012*. Doha: Ministry of Development and Planning. Available at: www.mdps.gov.qa/en/statistics/Statistical%20Releases/Social/LaborForce/2012/Labour_Force_Statistics_QSA_Bu_AE_2012.pdf [Accessed May 6, 2018].

Qatar welcomes opening of ILO office in Doha. *Gulf Times*. Available at: www.gulf-times.com/story/590884/Qatar-welcomes-opening-of-ILO-office-in-Doha [Accessed April 29, 2018].

Rajan, S., ed. (2016). *South Asia migration report 2017: Recruitment, remittances and reintegration.* London: Taylor & Francis.

Schrover, M. and Molony, D., eds (2013). *Gender, migration and categorization: Making distinctions between migrants in Western countries, 1945–2010.* Amsterdam: Amsterdam University Press.

Shah, N. (2013). Labor migration from Asian to GCC countries: Trends, patterns and policies. *Middle East Law and Governance,* 5(1–2), pp. 36–70.

Todaro, M. and Maruszko, L. (1987). Illegal migration and US immigration reform: A conceptual framework. *Population and Development Review,* 13(1), pp. 101–114.

Wachter, M., Gordon, R., Piore, M., and Hall, R. (1974). Primary and secondary labor markets: A critique of the dual approach. *Brookings Papers on Economic Activity,* 5(3), pp. 637–694.

Winckler, O. (2010). Labor migration to the GCC states: Patterns, scale, and policies. Migration and the Gulf. Washington, DC: Middle East Institute, pp. 9–12.

15 Ethical reckoning

Theorizing gender, vulnerability, and agency in Bangladeshi *Muktijuddho* film

Elora Halim Chowdhury

Films about the *Muktijuddho* (Bangladesh Liberation War of 1971[1]) are formative of Bangladeshi national cinema. Many of these films represent the struggle for independence through a gendered and sexualized lens of male valor and female shame. This defining event of self-determination has been presented as a glorious nationalist occurrence, highlighted by the heroism of freedom fighters and the sacrifice of women. At the same time, the *Muktijuddho* has not been adequately recognized globally, or even regionally, nor has there been meaningful reckoning with loss and trauma suffered by survivors whether at the state, judicial, or interpersonal levels. State-level negotiations involving India, Pakistan, and Bangladesh have failed to foster dialogue or reconciliation, let alone recognition of the crimes against humanity committed during the war. Instead, national governments have cultivated the notion of "the inspiration of 1971" (*shadhinotar chetona*) to promote their varied political agendas.

In this context, film and literature have been the mediums through which collective memory, interpersonal reckoning, and national solidarity have been shaped and maintained. The relationship between film, literature, and human rights and the contested terrain of representation, articulation, and artistic approximation of unspeakable violence is well documented, particularly in the genre of Holocaust cinema (Goldberg, 2007) as well as Palestinian cinema (Dabashi, 2006). The genre of human rights cinema then is crucial for attending to and generating deeper and effective consciousness, even political action. A small number of noteworthy contemporary Bangladeshi films, such as *Itihash Konna* (Daughters of History, 1999), *Guerilla* (2011), *Ekattor er Shongram* (The Struggle for Love and Survival – Bangladesh 1971, 2014), and *Meherjaan* (2011), grapple with the contested and difficult questions about war and gender justice that have been mostly relegated to the margins of historical memory. These films engage critically with the multifaceted narratives of the birth of a nation, the foundational struggle over identity, the intimate relationship between gender, nation, and sexuality, the legacy of war, and ethical reckoning with trauma. All four films narrate war stories through the lens of gendered vulnerability, agency, and suffering, within the larger frame of national upheaval for self-determination. *Muktijuddho* film in Bangladesh as a genre serves what human rights cinema does in its contribution to the creation of collective consciousness about genocide, gendered violence, and other mass atrocities. In this paper, I want to build on the idea of Bangladeshi national cinema as *human rights cinema* to explore its role in documenting and engendering understanding about women, vulnerability, and agency within a *Muktijuddho* gender ideology. Drawing from feminist sociologist Patricia Hill Collins' (2004) conceptualization of a black gender ideology, I propose that in cinematic traditions, an idealized *Muktijuddho* gender ideology influences and entrenches gendered social norms and reinforces perceptions of war, masculinity, and femininity. Not a benign set of perceptions, these serve to justify patterns of legibility, recognition, and rejection for discursive practices of national inclusion and exclusion. The paper is divided into two sections. The first provides a historical context for *Muktijuddho* films as iconic national cinema that speaks to a human rights consciousness, and the second analyzes a noteworthy recent film from this newer genre of critical national cinema that exposes and illuminates the ambiguities and contestations around gender, national belonging, and citizenship. Finally, I conclude with comments about national cinema as a mode of human rights advocacy engendering a discourse that contributes to/detracts from a broader quest for gender justice.

The Bangladesh *Muktijuddho* has figured prominently in films produced both in the commercial film industry and outside of it. Although these films vary widely in terms of originality and quality, the liberatory inspiration of 1971 is the main identifiable characteristic that sets Bangladesh war cinema apart as a national phenomenon. Film historian Zakir Hossain Raju (2015) argues that national cinema in third-world contexts is a vehicle to engage with the predicaments of nationhood and identity within colonial and postcolonial conditions. In Bangladesh, cinema as an institution has grown during a period of contestation over debates regarding nationhood, modernity, and cultural identity. Categories such as Bengali, Bengali-Muslim, and Bangladeshi have been shaped over the last century in different social, economic, and political circumstances and have interacted "with and upon the roles and functions of the cinema." Raju continues, "So this cinema, by constructing 'Bangladeshi' identity as the one-size-fits-all umbrella for all Bengali Muslims as well as non-Muslims and non-Bengalis living in Bangladesh, worked towards imagining the sense of a Bangladeshi modernity" (p. 3).

Historical events, such as the Partition of the Indian subcontinent[2] and the *Muktijuddho*, have become points of reference in the region as touchstones against which the magnitude of postcolonial suffering and loss of human life and the birth of freedom and self-determination are measured. Literature, memoir, and film in Bangladesh have become a crucial component in the project of nation building and deeply influence how, as witnesses far removed from the time of these events, we memorialize national history with sentimentality. Thus, it is important to question how national cinema, and its iconic depiction of *Muktijuddho* cinema, has evolved in representations of gender and identity and to what extent this genre allows for a complex representation/recognition of multifaceted experiences of the war. A close reading of films pertaining to 1971 will highlight the instability of paternalist post-war nationalism that lies at the heart of nationalist cinema and how in remembering the war and serving as memorials to it, films also retain the ambiguity of the nationalist project as well as the struggle for meaning over gender justice.

In a study mapping a comprehensive log of *Muktijuddho* films, Kaberi Gayen (2013) categorizes 26 full-length and seven key telefilms into three camps: films that are set in the pre-war, war, and post-war contexts. Gayen further categorizes the films by each decade since national independence as well as within industrial and alternative cinema camps. Referring to the *Muktijuddho* films of the early to mid-1970s, Gayen argues that sexual violence against women serves as a trope. Women's roles are inevitably tied to sacrifice or loss of innocence leading to a loss of respectful place in society. Fewer *Muktijuddho* films were released in the post-1975 era during the period of military dictatorships,[3] a period when films were less critical of the Liberation struggle. In the 1980s, the influence of Bombay cinema in the region became more pervasive and there was a noted increase in commercialization, song and dance sequences, and the commodification and sexualization of women. Parallel social and political mobilizations have set the context of more critical cinematic representations of war in the 1990s and beyond, namely the People's Tribunal (1992)[4] and the War Crimes Tribunal[5] set up in 2010 by the Awami League Government[6] to bring perpetrators of the 1971 genocide to justice. Gayen, however, is equally critical of the parallel and industrial cinematic representations of women as they continue to relegate them to the private sphere, where women stand in for the suffering of the nation. In this critical political turn, however, a newer genre of popular cinema has emerged that attempts to unravel the collapsing of public national suffering and women's embodiment of it even as they reconstitute *Muktijuddho* gendered tropes.

A few guiding questions animate my engagement with *Muktijuddho* cinema: (1) What social roles do women occupy in Liberation War films? (2) What do these cinematic representations imply about women's place in society? (3) What modes of participation in the Liberation struggle are available to/imagined for women? (4) What are the terms through which subjects can become legible/visible as victims/survivors of violence and agents of nation? Elsewhere, I have written about influential *Muktijuddho* films in relation to peace, reconciliation, and healing for the nation; therefore, in this essay I will focus on an important and critically acclaimed war film, *Guerilla*.

Guerilla

A freedom fighter[7] himself, director Nasir Uddin Yousuff's *Guerilla* (2011) is the first commercially released *Muktijuddho* film that centers around a female combatant. The film is based on acclaimed writer Syed Shamsul Haque's novel, *Nishiddho Loban* (Forbidden Salt, 1990). *Guerilla* traces the story of Syeda Bilqis Banu, a middle-class Bengali Muslim[8] woman through whose increasing involvement and awakening we see the freedom struggle unfold. Breaking with the cinematic tradition of deeply gendered representation of the war where the combat role is reserved as masculine in contrast to the feminization of vulnerability through the victimization of women, *Guerilla* invokes a double meaning of combat and struggle played out on the frontlines of war as well as social and cultural norms of patriarchy. The heroine Bilqis Banu is both a freedom fighter (*Muktijoddha*) for national liberation and woman's emancipation.

In December 2017, in celebration of the 46th anniversary of Bangladesh's Victory Day, 157 outlets featured historic films about the *Muktijoddho*. Joya Ahsan, the lead actor of *Guerilla*, attended one of the open admission screenings of *Guerilla*. Commending this initiative, Ahsan noted its significance in reviving a popular tradition of community film and theater culture as well as promoting the spirit of 1971 (*shadhinotaar chetona*) among younger generations of audiences. In an interview with *Prothom Alo*, a national daily newspaper, Ahsan invited readers to join her in this exemplary initiative, calling it an artistic blueprint to *Muktijuddho*, and she spoke about her own personal investment in it as the daughter of a freedom fighter. "When I was working on this film, I thought of myself as a fearless guerilla fighter just like my father. It was a feeling like no other" (interview by Masud in Prothom Alo, December 16, 2017).

The film opens to the impending violence of the night of March 25 or Operation Searchlight[9] when the Pakistan army unleashed a military strike on unarmed civilians of its eastern wing massacring thousands. Bilqis and Hasan, Bilqis' husband, are in their home, while Sheikh Mujib's[10] declaration of independence is ringing in the background amidst widespread agitation on the streets. Hasan tries to placate an anxious Bilqis with humor foreshadowing his imminent disappearance. He suggests that if he does not return home from work, she can take pride in his sacrifice (*Korbaan*) for the country in resisting Pakistani occupation. When indeed Hasan does not return home that night, Bilqis embarks on a search for her missing husband and joins the freedom struggle alongside ordinary Bengalis from all walks of life.

Guerilla is a quintessential nationalist, as well as political film, intended to narrate a particular story of the birth of Bangladesh. The government not only partially funded the film's production but it also waived the tax on the sale of tickets. The film went on to win the National Film Awards in a record-breaking ten categories. Its massive popularity and high-level recognition speak to several motifs that have come to be mythologized in the memorialization of the war specifically at a time when the ruling Awami League Party came into power on the platform of justice for martyrs and healing for the nation. The opening scene shows Sheikh Mujib (affectionately called *Bongobondhu*, Friend of Bengal) as the unequivocal leader and

proclaimer of independence (when Awami League's arch rival the Bangladesh Nationalist Party in more recent times has claimed that its deceased
leader President Ziaur Rahman[11] was the first to declare it) and aligns the
film's allegiance to the revolutionary and leftist vision of the Bengali cultural
intelligentsia.

There is a moment in the film where we come to visualize the freedom
struggle through a revolutionary lens, spanning across class, gender, religion,
urban, rural, and global geographical divides to articulate a shared vision of
truth through love, peace, and revolution. In this scene, the adolescent
daughter of the real-life martyr Altaf Mahmud,[12] who is portrayed by
Ahmed Rubel in the film, sings *Joy Shotter Joy* (Victory to Truth). The *Muktijuddho* is depicted through a montage where the Bengali freedom struggle is
personified through an image of its charismatic leader, Mujib, as the culminating figure in an array of other revolutionary leaders in the region and
around the globe including those of Fidel Castro, Che Guevara, Martin
Luther King, and M.K. Gandhi. Altaf is shown sitting in a breezy verandah
clad all in white, nodding to and encouraging his daughter's passionate singing. His wife, wearing a cotton sari, comes in with a cup of tea and joins
father and daughter, completing the picture of the Bengali middle-class cultural
activist home space.

In Hasan's absence, Bilqis carries on with her day job at a bank, all the
while acting as an insurgent collecting donations for the war, transporting
spools of revolutionary poems and songs composed by Altaf Mahmud to
the underground networks of *Shadhin Bangla Betar Kendro*, [13] arranging
medical care and transportation for comrades, and even planting explosives
at high-level Pakistani military events. In one such scene, Bilqis arrives
wearing a red sari, dramatically transformed into an elegant, high-class
woman who speaks English and sips wine (under duress which she then spits
out) accompanying Mrs Khan, who in contrast is dressed in black. She is an
upper-class woman, widow, and mother who consorts with Pakistanis in
order to aid the Bengali freedom struggle. At this party, Mrs Khan makes
the ultimate sacrifice by acquiescing to the request of the Pakistani army
officers and staying back with them at the party even though she knows a
guerilla attack is about to take place. Bilqis had planned it with her cadres
and planted an explosive in the bathroom. Mrs Khan's farewell gesture to
Bilqis is a raised fist signifying both goodbye and the revolutionary symbol
of solidarity and resistance.

Bilqis is thus an insurgent in the war as well as a woman resisting patriarchal social norms. Although the film traces her awakening, she always
stands apart as different, as Other. At a security check post, the Pakistani
guard inspects her identity card and notes that she doesn't look Bengali.
When Bilqis returns home late, her mother-in-law admonishes her as
"manly" in her activities as well as high and mighty in her demeanor and
likens her to "Maharani Queen Victoria." Here the film exposes the patriarchal double standard upheld even by women. Despite Bilqis' unwavering

service to her mother-in-law, the old woman on her deathbed calls her the monster who devoured her son and left her life empty of meaning.

In another scene, Bilqis asks Hasan why he married her since she did not measure up to his Dhaka University women friends who were "smart" and "modern" and totally unlike her (*gaaiya* and "unsmart"). Hasaan in return reflects another patriarchal standard whereby the woman has to be both demure and sexy as well as feisty and compliant. He states that Bilqis may come across as a village belle but inside she is a savage (*aasto jongli*) – a trait that arouses him. He reaches for her with a passionate embrace and Bilqis responds coyly, "I can bite" (*kamrabo kintu*).

The turning point in the film occurs when the narrative and the warfront shift from urban to rural Bangladesh. With the death of Bilqis' mother-in-law and the capture of her comrades, namely Altaf Mahmud, she has no more refuge in the city. Mahmud's wife, another female combatant, hurries over to Bilqis' home and asks her to flee and go undercover. Donning a burkha[14] for protection and as a form of disguise (clothing in the film is shown to have alternative meanings as insurgent practice, or religious allegiance), Bilqis boards a train to return to her ancestral home of Joleswari. On the train, she witnesses Pakistani militias harassing Hindu passengers who are marked by their absence of burkhas and topis.[15] She chastises the men on the train for being silent as a Hindu woman is dragged away.[16] An indignant Bilqis takes off her own burkha to show the simple printed cotton sari, a trademark of Bengali women activists to this day, and her long black hair streaming down her back. She leans out of the train for air looking out to the horizon. It is from this point on that we witness a gradual shift in Bilqis' appearance and disposition. From the defiant activist traversing the city, she gradually transforms to a listless, disheveled, and unbalanced (thirsty, having hallucinations and frequent flashbacks) figure – resembling the trope of the ghostly absent-present Birangona[17] as noted in the work of Nayanika Mookherjee (2015). The word *Birangona* means brave woman or war heroine. Following independence, the term *Birangona* was bestowed on the survivors of sexual violence by the government of Bangladesh in order to honor the women for their role in the freedom struggle. The label frequently served to further ostracize the women as reintegration into society was difficult and remained incomplete. Cinematic representations of Birangona women have systematically contributed to further erasure or instrumental invoking of women's suffering (Chowdhury, 2017).

The film ends with Bilqis taking her own life – after learning of the death of her freedom fighter brother, Khokon, finding his body and attempting to give it a proper burial (Antigone style),[18] and getting captured by the Pakistani army. In a dramatic scene, as Bilqis comes to resemble more and more the figure of the madwoman or the iconic representation of the ghostly Birangona, she prevents her own rape by a Pakistani general by detonating a hand grenade she finds in the room, killing both herself and the enemy. Hence the film ends with the exit of the woman combatant (a familiar trope in *Muktijuddho* films where the exit of Birangona occurs by suicide) where death is seen preferable to rape. The assailant here, General Shamshad Khan, interestingly is played by the same actor (Shatabdi Wadud) who played the role of General Sarfraz Khan killed by freedom fighters earlier in the film, thus noting that the villainous Pakistani army officers are interchangeable. The credits roll to Kazi Nazrul Islam's Bidrohi,[19] composed by Altaf Mahmud, vocals by Chandan Chowdhury, and the following postscript runs across the screen: "On 16 December finally Bangladesh was liberated [sic]. Syeda Bilkis Banu is one of those three million martyrs who gave their life for the independence of Bangladesh in 1971." Significantly, Bilqis is recognized as a martyr who sacrificed her life for the freedom struggle but also preferred self-annihilation to rape, which is perceived as surrender.

Throughout the film, we see a play on the title *Guerilla* where presumably an innocent and docile Bengali woman is capable of acting as an insurgent in the face of personal, communal, and national threat. Her rebellious and passionate nature is the flipside to her soft femininity. The motif of agency in death and sacrifice is ultimately embraced while the question of women's place and integration in the independent nation remains unclear.

While *Guerilla* doesn't quite fit into the genre of women's cinema since it is directed by a man, its intention is to glorify the history of the *Muktijuddho* and to solidify its heroic image, through a disruptive yet acquiescent narrative of female resistance. Despite having a woman freedom fighter as its heroine, female agency is framed within patriarchal norms. Nevertheless, the question of women's belonging to the nation is of feminist concern. Literary scholar Sally McWilliams (2009) provides a useful analysis of narrative strategies employed in fiction and film to examine a specific feminist representation of the politics of reading women's positionality and agency within trauma narratives. Arguably, what Yousuff achieves is a woman-centered narrative that presents a woman's awakening within a metanarrative of patriarchy. His narrative strategies create new envisionings as they challenge hegemonic narratives of masculine agency, identity, and nationalism. *Guerilla* marks a departure from previous nationalist cinema by centralizing Bilqis Banu's coming into consciousness and participation in the Liberation War without solely making her story about the usual entry point of women in war films: sexual violence. That singular act of violence does not define women's participation in the war in *Guerilla*, rather we see the development of Bilqis' character as more multidimensional – a wife, daughter-in-law, sister, comrade, insurgent, and the most valued: martyr. With regard to the last motif, however, Bilqis is an insurgent in war as well as against patriarchal social norms. She resists Pakistani occupation and defies the societal, familial, and cultural constraints that limit women's agency.

The film decenters masculinist power by integrating the marginalized Other as integral to the construction of historical and cultural knowledge. In so doing, Yousuff provides a space of new possibilities. Further, Yousuff's film acts as an interventionist film, one in which patriarchal, nationalistic discourses are disrupted not subverted. At the same time, however, the film is unable to escape patriarchal gender norms that transcend wartime – the female combatant cannot coexist with the nation, just as the Birangona, because such a role real or perceived has not been imagined. Even in this genre-bending film, the female combatants are simultaneously mothers (Mrs Khan who calls out for her son at the moment of death, another comrade transports spools in her baby's stroller,) and/or wives and sisters (Bilqis searching for her husband Hasan and attempting to give proper burial to her brother Khokon when she is captured).

This brings me back to the question, "What are the conditions in which a woman could be perceived as combatant, survivor, and full citizen?" Here the work of African American feminist scholar Patricia Hill Collins is pertinent: speaking to the historic oppression of blacks from slavery to the present, Collins posits that in feminist contexts, sexuality represents a central site of the oppression of women with rape as its dominant narrative trope (Collins, 2004). In anti-racist discourses, where sexuality is also a central site, the lynching of blacks has embodied the trope. The spectacle of lynching to maintain control over the black population had a visible public dimension whereas rape of black women remained more of a private suffering. The failure of black men to protect black women from rape was further emasculating to black men's diminished sense of self. Rather than conceptualizing lynching and rape as either race- or gender-specific mechanisms of social control, Collins approaches institutionalized rape and lynching as different expressions of the same type of social control – that of oppression and dehumanization of black people.

In a similar vein, *Muktijuddho* was conceptualized through gendered tropes of the heroic male freedom fighter and the victimized woman (Birangona), whereas the public sacrifice of the former has been valorized to the private covering of the latter. Here, I do want to acknowledge Mookherjee's (2015) important work arguing that the rape of women has not been erased or silenced so much so as censored and instrumentally utilized in human rights, state, and cultural memorialization purposes. Yet the relegation of feminine suffering to shame and secrecy has not given voice to the multifaceted struggles of women during war. Even when *Guerilla* defies the dominant narrative by focusing on a female combatant, she cannot remain in the independent nation as a hero or a citizen. For that to occur, Collins' gender ideology would have been integrated into the film so that the violence against *Muktijoddhas* (men and women) were articulated as different expressions of social control and systematic repression of the Bengali populace. Here, too, failure to "protect" women (and nation) is a sign of failure to enact hegemonic masculinity, which was denied to Bengali men as racialized inferiors. There are comments about Bengali freedom fighters as "pygmy *Muktijoddhas*" by the Pakistani generals in the film referring to their smaller size and darker skin shade. Conceptualizing women's roles as not only sacrificial to the war, and men's as categorically heroic, but both as sites of social and political repression would open up ways to rethink the *Muktijud-dho* gender ideology, which render women's struggle insufficiently admissible and visible.

Further, borrowing from transnational feminist insights, I draw upon the work of sociologist Jyoti Puri (2016), who offers juxtaposition of dissimilar contexts as a methodology to illuminate the working of power. Juxtaposing the two instantiations of anti-black and anti-Bengali racism/oppression allows us to see how one illuminates the other. In a recent article titled, "Juxtaposing 'Antipolice' Rhetorics: Policing, Race, Gender, and Sexuality across Southern Contexts," Jyoti Puri has illustrated that unlike a simple unproblematic comparison, juxtaposition as a concept can also serve as an epistemological device. Juxtaposition, she suggests, "does not rest on establishing a common yardstick between the two cases. It also does not necessitate papering over differences in order to establish comparability of cases. Instead, juxtaposition entails exploring how each case is supplemented by being placed in thoughtful relation to the other" (2016, p. 4). Puri contrasts anti-police targeting of Hijra[20] communities in India to anti-black police responses in the US. She states, "Juxtaposition offers the possibility of thinking across these two distinct moments [in this case, the perceived distinct categories Black and Bengali Muslim] and two dissimilar settings [in this case, trajectories] to deepen understandings of how institutional racism continues to imperil and devalue the lives of some while being rationalized as necessary" (p. 6).

This methodological tool of juxtaposition helps in understanding the workings of power in dissimilar contexts while putting the oppression of racialized/variously Othered populations in a transnational frame. The work of feminist philosopher Erinn Cunniff Gilson is useful in tracing the theoretical interventions around gender, vulnerability, and agency throughout the film. Gilson takes up the complicated nature of vulnerability in sexual violence discourse to demonstrate how it is associated both with femininity and with weakness and dependency (2016). As a feminized concept its association with femininity is made more problematic by assigning it inferior status. Bilqis' death by suicide has meaning only in terms of the dominant script of *Muktijuddho* gender ideology where women represent vulnerability and thus Bilqis exercises limited agency but at the cost of her own self-annihilation. Interestingly, while the on-screen debauchery of Shamshad (the Pakistani army general) is in full view, the simultaneous assault on Shiraj, a freedom fighter whom Bilqis claims as her younger brother, who the soldiers discover as Hindu (because of his uncircumcised penis) – happens off-screen. Here, both Bilqis' and Shiraj's vulnerability are feminized as gendered and racialized Others to the hegemonic Pakistani Muslim male military figure. Bilqis hears his tortured screams as she fends off her assailant. If vulnerability, as Murphy (2011) argues, is tantamount to violability, she is vulnerable by nature, and she must take responsibility for protecting herself – and her agency in *Guerilla* comes from taking this responsibility and choosing self-annihilation over rape, which is a violation of the body. A woman who has been violated cannot be a martyr or celebrated in life as a freedom fighter, and nor can the violation of a male freedom fighter be publicly depicted as these roles have not been imagined. As Gilson notes,

> inferior strength and sexualization – comprise the specificity of feminine vulnerability and constitute it as a dualist, reductively negative form of vulnerability: one is vulnerable because one's body is the kind of object on which others, active male subjects, seek to act and because one cannot prevent them from doing so. Given hegemonic perceptions of gender and sexuality, to be a woman is to inhabit the kind of body that is perceived as inciting lust and thus as inviting sexual attention, whether desired or not. Conceived in this reductive way, women's vulnerability is not just susceptibility to any kind of harm but rather is thought of in terms of a particularly sexual vulnerability.
>
> (2016, pp. 75–76)

Due to the physical presumption of vulnerability, woman is read as victim in the context of violent conflict and thus it becomes difficult to reimagine how gender can interact with war in a more nuanced and multifaceted way. While *Mukitjuddho* stretches the boundaries of woman as victim, the heroine's bravery and glory is ultimately tied to her decision to kill herself rather than be raped. By being female-bodied, Bilqis opens herself up to violent temptation and violation, her vulnerability is portrayed as embedded within her physicality and thus impossible to shed.

Gilson reminds us,

> The conventional concept of victimization comprises a set of norms that operate as criteria delimiting who will be socially recognized as a victim and who will not be. These norms require victims to fit a particular profile to count, that is, to be convincing... (to be) a "true" victim... one must be vulnerable in culturally appropriate ways.
>
> (2016, p. 80)

An illustrative example of a victim who didn't "behave" as a victim in the socially accepted way is the character Neela, from the *Muktijuddho* film *Meherjaan*. Neela, who demonstrates female sexual expressivity, has been decried widely as wanton, sexualized, and not worthy of sympathy nor recognizable as a victim, despite similar violations experienced by other valorized Birangona.

The themes of agency, healing, and trauma are centrally represented in director Rubaiyat Hossain's controversial woman-centered film, *Meherjaan*. Hossain (2011) describes her debut feature film, *Meherjaan*, as a "women's 'feminine' re-visiting of the Bangladesh national liberation." Released only a few months prior to *Guerilla*, the film was pulled from theaters because of massive protests, including threats to its director and crew.

Perhaps the single most damning criticism of *Meherjaan* has been that the film obscures the trauma of 1971 and trivializes the suffering of women, despite the director's insistence that it is a feminist and even a nationalist film. Commentators who are otherwise open to critical perspectives of 1971 took issue with the depiction of Neela, a Birangona. In a public debate about the film organized by the Dhaka Arts Council, filmmaker and freedom fighter Morshedul Islam calls for a stricter adherence to a conventional narrative of 1971. He expresses grave discomfort with the depiction of Bengali men as weak, and Birangona women, Neela in particular, as wayward. Islam accuses the director of diverging from a patriotic rendition of 1971.

> As an audience member, I did not feel an ounce of sympathy or respect for that character [Neela, "the raped woman"] – as a Birangona. The way she carried on, her dressing, everything. Perhaps, the next generation will defend this portrayal by saying that they want to depict a Birangona as a strong woman. She also says that it is not the first time that she experienced rape. What is the meaning of this? Why include such a storyline? What this did was soften the issue of rape by Pakistani army. As a result, that character did not move us. The director misrepresented the Birangona and trivialized their experience.
>
> (Boithok, 2011)

Not only the "spirit of 1971" (*shadhinotar chetona*), but these comments illuminate that in *Muktijuddho* cinema a particular gender ideology is equally sacred. Representation of martyrs and Birangona are delimited and hierarchical. It is striking that this freedom fighter and filmmaker cannot muster up any sympathy for Neela because she dares to speak aloud not only about rape by Pakistani soldiers but violence against women in non-wartime. This reaction is especially intense because the film portrays the diminished masculinity of Bengali men, and also fails to present a categorical and obvious enemy "Other" who kills, rapes, and pillages. Moreover, the audience is upset by Neela's "inappropriate" dress and demeanor and finds this insulting to women who fought in the war. In an article jointly written by academics from the University of Dhaka along with Ferdousi Priyobhashini, one of the few survivors of sexual violence in 1971 to speak publicly of her rape by Pakistani soldiers, there is strong criticism of the film as a betrayal to the history of the Liberation War and an insult to all freedom fighters and Birangonas. They were particularly offended by the depiction of the three main female characters as "sex symbols" and specifically Neela as "sexy" and "wanton" in male company (Ferdaus et al., 2011).

Anthropologist Nayanika Mookherjee argues that women's wartime experiences have been memorialized in the public discourse in Bangladesh in certain elite class-coded ways (Mookherjee, 2015). For instance, while secular Bengali resistance (women's participation in nationalist song and theater troupes wearing sari and *teep*, a particular aesthetic which was coded as ethnically Bengali yet Muslim) is a source of pride, women's sexual suffering is met with shameful silence or metaphorized as the plunder of the motherland. She points out that when women speak out about sexual violence in Bangladesh it challenges both the aesthetic and political memorialization of the war. Mookherjee documents how the narrative of Birangona's horrific history of rape is told, not forgotten or silenced, even as the complexities of her life story are occluded from the prevalent discourse of the war. It is not the knowledge of rape that brings social sanction but the speaking of it in public. The critical question is how to reconcile the private suffering of women with public national suffering and women's embodiment of it.

An ethical recognition of gendered vulnerability in *Muktijuddho* narratives entails, as Gilson suggests, recognizing the in-betweenness and intertwined spaces of what appears to be diametrically oppositional ways of being or terms like strength and weakness, activity and passivity, agency and the absence of capacity to act. Gilson contends,

> Vulnerability itself is the condition that enables one to deal with and heal from exploitation. It is therapeutically necessary insofar as to heal is not to secure oneself so as to be invulnerable and inviolable but rather to come to be able to experience one's vulnerability with some semblance of safety (Brown 2012).
>
> (p. 92)

The question is, can *Muktijuddho* films accommodate such in-betweenness and complexities of women's experiences, and struggles?

Woman in/and the nation: looking ahead

Nayanika Mookherjee's recent book (2015) argues that in Bangladesh the issue of wartime rape is not invisible or simply a public secret. The use of the word "Birangona" by Sheikh Mujib, the first president of Bangladesh, created the space for these women to be publicly viewed as citizens who had been wronged and whom the nation owed an ethical debt. Nevertheless, their post-war lives exemplify the fact that they continue to be a "spectral wound" on the nation's body. Even if they are reconciled with their families, as Mookherjee argues, *"khota"* (scorn) is part of their ordinary mode of being and living after the event (Mookherjee, 2015). Yasmin Saikia's *Women, War and the Making of Bangladesh* offers an insight into violence experienced by Bengali and Bihari women during the war (Saikia, 2011). Her research juxtaposes memories of both victim and perpetrator during the war, taking her to both Bangladesh and Pakistan. Saikia states:

> What is of real concern to women is to consider and question how their lack of recognition as human is made possible. The power of nation and masculinity in 1971 became impervious to the responsibility of

protecting, but became the force of terror. There is thus a profound connection between the person acting or being acted upon, and the realm of structures created by human power and need, which turns against humanity time and again. Women's testimonies question how power endowed to institutions triumphed over human beings who created it.

(p. 112)

Both these scholars are referring to the various complex processes which actively in/visibilize Birangona women in and from nationalist memorializations of history and war – they appear but only as spectral wound or to provide testimony to the trope of plunder. As an appendage to the project of nation building, national cinema, too, has deployed similar gender imagery. However, recently, few films have attempted to probe these difficult questions.

In addition to creating an alternative archive of 1971 with complex and diverse gender representation, together these newer films explore the possibility of healing and reconciliation within the realm of intimate and interpersonal relations. In conjunction, these films urge a reconceptualization of how women are depicted in wartime cinema. In *Meherjaan*, Hossain encourages a woman-centered vision of healing and reconciliation. In *Ekattor er Shongram* a Hindu woman is the Birangona whose progeny, a child of war, symbolizes the hope to rehabilitate a devastated *Muktijoddha* (male freedom fighter). Nevertheless, this same Birangona of *Ekattor er Shongram* cannot return to her village in an independent Bangladesh with the same *Muktijoddha*, Karim. *Guerilla*, the first film to narrate the story of a woman combatant, ends with the protagonist's self-annihilation. The latter two have limited success in disrupting the *Muktijuddho* ideology, whereas *Meherjaan* has faced such vehement criticism and protest, it cannot be screened in public theaters in Bangladesh. One can surmise that gender ideology is most sacred in sites relating to *Muktijuddho* – the defining event for national identity, and as such national cinema, as its cultural analogue is bound by its normative memorialization.

Women of color theorists, such as Treva Lindsey and Jennifer Nash, have engaged with the historical sexual subjugation of black women during slavery and the powerful legacies it left behind. Lindsey argues that "politics of respectability" influence how black women and African American communities delineate what constitutes objectification and hypersexuality and that contemporary films in the US provide unique sites to dissect such renderings of women's subjugation and sexuality. She asks whether the historical legacy of silencing or sexual conservatism (a term used by Jennifer Nash) forecloses transgressive possibilities of reclaiming a more nuanced female sexual expressivity (Lindsey, 2013; Nash, 2008).

Like Nash and Lindsey, I argue that filmic representations of women's sexual subjugation during the Bangladeshi Independence War have been normatively depicted in commercial cinema highlighting their victimization, erasure by death or suicide, shame, or mental instability. In contrast, some newer films, such as *Meherjaan* (and *Itihaash Konna*), prioritize women's narratives as the primary vehicle for reconstructing this normalized circulation of women's history. Feminist scholar Kavita Daiya has illustrated how within partition narratives, the female body comes to be symbolically overlaid with the project of nationalism to the extent that it serves as a metaphor for their perceived Otherness (Daiya, 2008). In Bangladeshi films, the methodical reproduction of the "authentic Birangona" reifies the Otherness through similar iconic imagery (Mookherjee, 2015).

Jennifer Nash reminds us that black feminism has functioned as a "critical social theory" in its engagement with visual culture, with the (re)production of what Patricia Hill Collins terms "controlling images," which Nash defines as "dominant representations that produce and entrench racial-sexual mythologies." The social purpose of controlling images is "to provide a justification for the state's continued disciplining of the black female body." It is a useful term to deploy in the case of Birangonas where arguably controlling images of the Birangonas illustrates the ideological power of these images in securing conceptions of their sexual subjugation. Like the regulation of the black female body by the state, the regulation of the Birangonas has also rendered it a public site, "a space onto which social debates and collective anxieties about morality, religion, policy and the state are inscribed" (Nash, 2008, p. 97). This representation becomes normative rather than analytical and is at the expense of women's sexual heterogeneity, multiplicity, and diversity. Against such normative production, Nash urges feminist scholars to ask how objectification is mobilized in specific historical contexts and what could be alternative reading practices – a representational space for women to view themselves and each other as sexual subjects. *Meherjaan* attempts this but with very limited success, whereas *Guerilla* resists but cannot subvert. The question remains, to what extent can an ethical reckoning with masculinist narrations of war, vulnerability, and agency be accommodated within the frames of nationalist and/or human rights cinema?

Discussion questions

1   What are the intersections of film, human rights, and advocacy? In what ways are varied histories of struggles in the South Asian region communicated through film? What roles do/can films play in social and political mobilization, transformation, and activism around questions of justice and human rights?

2   Reflect on how gender ideologies come to shape human rights representations, historical memorializations, and social and political mobilizations.

3   Can you imagine a gender ideology that transcends the feminization of vulnerability? What would such a landscape look like? What would it enable us to do in human rights advocacy arenas?

Notes

1 The Liberation War of Bangladesh (Bengali: *Muktijuddho*) is the revolutionary Independence War of Bangladesh (formerly East Pakistan) from its colonial rule by West Pakistan. The nine-month struggle was notably one of the most terrible humanitarian crises of the 20th century. It started on March 25, 1971 with Operation Searchlight, a planned military attack on unarmed Bengali civilians by the then Pakistani government. The mass political uprising of the Bengali nationalist movement turned into a genocide that continued even after the end of the war on December 16, 1971. Official estimates suggest 3 million people were killed; 200,000 women systematically raped, and 10 million people were displaced.

2 In 1947, after 300 years of colonial rule, the British finally relinquished their control of India. On August 14–15 of that year the Indian subcontinent was partitioned into two independent nations: Hindu-majority India and Muslim-majority Pakistan. This triggered the displacement of 15 million people along religious lines and riots and mass violence ensued. In 1971, the new state of Pakistan, which had been divided into two halves, separated by 2,000 kilometers of Indian territory, was reconfigured once again and East Pakistan became the independent nation of Bangladesh.

3 From 1975 to 1990, Bangladesh was governed by two military dictators. Ziaur Rahman ruled the country from 1975 to 1981 and Hussain Mohammed Ershad from 1982 to 1990. This 15-year period of military rule started after the first president of Bangladesh, Sheikh Mujibur Rahman, was assassinated in 1975. Since then, the parliamentary representative democratic republic of Bangladesh has undergone several military coups and the legislative and judiciary branches were hostage to the military-controlled executive power. It severely curtailed the civil rights of the citizens of Bangladesh and by the end of 1990, a cross-country anti-dictatorship movement dislodged the military rule and Bangladesh returned to parliamentary democracy.

4 In January 1992 the Committee for Resisting Killers and Collaborators of Bangladesh Liberation War of 71 (Ekattorer Ghatak Dalal Nirmul Committee) was formed. An unofficial Peoples' Tribunal was created in Dhaka by the National Coordinating Committee for the Realization of Bangladesh Liberation War Ideals and trial of Bangladesh war criminals of 1971. Led by Jahanara Imam, writer, political activist, and mother of martyred student leader Shafi Imam Rumi, many veteran activists and 200,000 participants from all over the country campaigned for justice and conducted a mock trial of several leading Liberation War criminals. In the absence of state patronage, this symbolic trial is seen as a landmark public uprising that was particularly inspirational to the younger generations of Bangladesh.

5 The International Crimes Tribunal (ICT) in Bangladesh is a domestic war crimes tribunal set up in 2009 to investigate and prosecute suspects for the genocide committed in 1971 by the Pakistan Army and local collaborators. During the 2008 general election, the Awami League pledged to try war criminals. The government set up the tribunal after the Awami League won the general election in December 2008. According to the International Crimes (Tribunals) Act 1973 and subsequent 2009 Amendment, the ICT in Bangladesh has "the power to try and punish any individual or group of individuals, or any member of any armed, defense or auxiliary forces, irrespective of his nationality, who commits or has committed, in the territory of Bangladesh, whether before or after commencement of this Act, any crimes mentioned in sub section [2] of section 3 of the Act" (article 3.1). On July 26, 2010, after the first hearing, the ICT issued arrest warrants against several of the accused for crimes against humanity and established a second tribunal (ICT 2) on March 22, 2012.

6 The Awami League Government of Bangladesh is constituted by one of the largest three political parties of Bangladesh and has governed the country several

times (1996–2001, 2009–2014, and 2014–present). It is the political party associated with the founding of the nation, Bengali nationalism, its first president
Sheikh Mujibur Rahman and at present prime minister Sheikh Hasina, daughter
of Mujib.

7 A freedom fighter (Bengali: *Muktijoddha* or *Mukti Bahini*) is a member of the liberation army or guerilla force of Bangladesh who fought against the Pakistani
army during the Liberation War of 1971. According to the Bangladesh Genocide
Archive, the estimated grand total of freedom fighters is 105,000. Using guerrilla
warfare tactics, a popular resistance movement by the freedom fighters secured
control over large parts of the Bengali countryside.

8 Bengali Muslims are an ethnic, linguistic, and religious population who make up
the majority of Bangladesh's citizens. The Bengali Muslim population emerged as
a synthesis of Islamic and Bengali cultures. After the Partition of India in 1947,
they were the majority group in Pakistan until the independence of East Pakistan
in 1971. The ethnolinguistic and religious components of this identity have been
seen as contradictory to one another, and have frequently been mobilized for
political gains.

   The trajectory of middle-class Bengali Muslim women's identity integrates the
socio-cultural, economic, political, religious, and chronological histories of the
Muslim population in Bengal. In the 20th century, it can be traced to 1918 with
the founding of *Sougat* – a liberal reformist periodical which pioneered the
women's weekly *Begum*, a few weeks before the Partition of India in 1947. More
can be found in Sonia Nishat Amin's comprehensive discussion of Muslim
women. See, Amin, 1996.

9 "Operation Searchlight" was a planned military operation carried out by the Pakistan Army to curb the Bengali nationalist movement in East Pakistan in March 1971.
It aimed to crush all political and military opposition in the eastern wing of Pakistan.
The violence resulting from "Operation Searchlight" led to the War of Liberation
by the *Mukti Bahini* against Pakistani "occupation" forces in Bangladesh.

10 Sheikh Mujib is the popularly shortened name of Sheikh Mujibur Rahman, a Bengali nationalist politician and the founding leader of the People's Republic of Bangladesh. He was the leader of the Awami League and served as the first president of
Bangladesh and later became prime minister. He is popularly known as *Bongobondhu*
(friend of Bengal) and achieved the honorary title of "Father of the Nation" for
leading the Independence struggle of Bangladesh. He was assassinated in 1975 and his
eldest daughter Sheikh Hasina is the current prime minister of Bangladesh.

11 Ziaur Rahman (January 9, 1936–May 30, 1981) was the 7th president of Bangladesh from 1977 to 1981. During the Liberation War of Bangladesh he was the
sector commander of sector 1, later sector 11, and the brigade commander of Z
force. After the assassination of Sheikh Mujibur Rahman, being a deputy army
chief of staff major general, he acted behind dissolving the parliament and instituting a state of emergency under martial law. He later founded the Bangladesh
Nationalist Party. He was assassinated in 1981. His widow, Begum Khaleda Zia
became the first woman prime minister of Bangladesh in 1991 after the Bangladesh Nationalist Party won the general election.

12 Altaf Mahmud was a musician, cultural activist, and martyred freedom fighter of
the Bangladesh Liberation War. He was also an activist of the Language Movement and composer of "Amar Bhaier Rokte Rangano," a famous song written to
commemorate the event.

13 *Shadhin Bangla Betar Kendro*, or Independent Bengal Radio Center, was the clandestine radio station, located in Kalurghat, north of the city of Chittagong, Bangladesh. Soon after the overtake of Dacca Radio Center by the Pakistani army on
March 26, 1971 the freedom fighters of Bangladesh started broadcasting and it
became the broadcasting center of the Bengali nationalist force. The station

transmitted the Declaration of Independence of Bangladesh and played a vital role in the Liberation War.

14 Burkha is an outer garment worn by women coming from some Islamic communities. The garment covers the body and the face in public and is worn throughout Asia, Africa, Europe, and the Middle East.

15 Hats akin to skullcaps that are associated with Islamic dress in the subcontinent.

16 Hindus are the followers of Hinduism. There are over 1.03 billion Hindus worldwide. They adhere to a wide array of belief and practice.

17 The word *Birangona* means brave woman or war heroine. Following independence, the term *Birangona* was bestowed on the survivors of sexual violence by the government of Bangladesh in order to honor the women for their role in the freedom struggle. The label frequently served to further ostracize the women as reintegration into society remained incomplete. On October 23, 2015 Bangladesh government for the first time declared 43 *Birangona* as freedom fighters recognizing the proposal of the parliament of Bangladesh on January 2015.

18 A proper burial (Antigone style) is a burial rite in Greek culture where the concept of the physical body has the political economy of prosperity after death. With public mourning, funeral, offering rituals, and many other memorial services are performed and then the body is buried. Sophocles' Antigone c. 441 BC exemplifies the importance of the customs and culture of honoring the deceased. In Guerilla, Bilqis' attempt to give Khokon, her deceased freedom fighter brother, a proper Islamic burial is akin to honoring the deceased in the face of Pakistani cultural and military oppression.

19 Published in 1922 in the *Bijli* (Lightning) magazine, Kazi Nazrul Islam's *Bidrohi* (The Rebel) is his most famous work. He criticized the British Raj and called for revolution through this famous poem. Nazrul is the national poet of Bangladesh and is acclaimed as the rebel poet historically after the title of this poem.

20 The term *hijra* refers to the transgender or intersex or third-gender people in South Asian countries. The government of Bangladesh legally recognized hijra as the third gender in 2013. Despite the legal recognition as third gender in several South Asian countries, *hijras* continue to struggle for their rights as citizens.

References

Amin, S.N. (1996). *The world of Muslim women in colonial Bengal, 1876–1939*. Leiden: Brill.

Boithok, A. (2011). Meherjaan debate 1 (Meherjaan Bitorko, Kisti Ek). Available at: https://arts.bdnews24.com/?p=3417 [Accessed February 27, 2017].

Chowdhury, E.H. (2017). Ethical encounters: Friendship, reckoning and healing in Shameem Akhtar's *Daughters of History* (1999). In A. Kurian and S. Jha, eds, *New feminisms in South Asia: Disrupting the discourse through social media, film and literature*. New York: Routledge, pp. 238–253.

Collins, P.H. (2004). *Black sexual politics: African Americans, gender, and the new racism*. New York: Routledge.

Dabashi, H., ed. (2006). *Dreams of a nation: On Palestinian cinema*. London: Verso.

Daiya, K. (2008). *Violent belongings: partition, gender, and national culture in postcolonial India*. Philadelphia, PA: Temple University Press.

Ferdaus, R., Babu, M., Gayn, K., and Priyobhashini, F. (2011). Meherjaan: An insult to the Liberation War and women. *Prothom Alo*, January 26. Available at: www.prothom-alo.com/detail/date/2011-01-26/news/126403

Gayen, K. (2013). *Construction of women in the war films of Bangladesh (Muktizuddher Cholochchitre Naree Nirman)*. Dhaka: Bengal Publications.

Gilson, E.C. (2016). Vulnerability and victimization: Rethinking key concepts in feminist discourses on sexual violence. *Signs: Journal of Women in Culture and Society*, 42(1), pp. 71–98.

Goldberg, E.S. (2007). *Beyond terror: Gender, narrative, human rights.* New Brunswick, NJ: Rutgers University Press.

Hossain, R. (2011). Meherjaan press kit. Available at: https://rubaiyat-hossain.com/m eherjaan/ [Accessed February 28, 2018].

Itihaash Konna (1999). Film. Directed by Shameem Akhtar. Bangladesh: Mrittika Productions.

Lindsey, T.B. (2013). Complicated crossroads: Black feminisms, sex positivism, and popular culture. *African and Black Diaspora: An International Journal*, 6(1), pp. 55–65.

Masud, M. (2017). They are not the result of anyone's sin (Ora karo paaper foshol na). *Prothom Alo*. Available at: www.prothomalo.com/entertainment/article/1387871/% E2%80%98%E0%A6%93%E0%A6%B0%E0%A6%BE-%E0%A6%95%E0% A6%BE%E0%A6%B0%E0%A6%93-%E0%A6%AA%E0%A6%BE%E0%A6% AA%E0%A7%87%E0%A6%B0-%E0%A6%AB%E0%A6%B8%E0% A6%B2-% E0%A6%A8%E0%A6%BE%E2%80%99%3E [Accessed December 16, 2018].

McWilliams, S.E. (2009). Intervening in trauma: Bodies, violence, and interpretive possibilities in Vyvyane Loh's *Breaking the Tongue*. *Tulsa Studies in Women's Literature*, 28(1), pp. 141–163.

Meherjaan (2011). Film. Directed by Rubaiyat Hossain. Bangladesh: Era Motion Picture.

Mookherjee, N. (2015). *The spectral wound: Sexual violence, public memories, and the Bangladesh war of 1971.* Durham, NC: Duke University Press.

Murphy, A.V. (2011). Corporeal vulnerability and the new humanism. *Hypatia*, 26(3), pp. 575–590.

Nash, J.C. (2008). Strange bedfellows: Black feminism and antipornography feminism. *Social Text*, 26(4), pp. 51–76.

Puri, J. (2016). Juxtaposing "antipolice" rhetorics: Policing, race, gender, and sexuality across southern contexts. In: *National Women's Studies Association Annual Conference: Decoloniality*. Montreal, pp. 10–13.

Raju, Z.H. (2015). *Bangladesh cinema and national identity: In search of the modern?* London: Routledge.

Saikia, Y. (2011). *Women, war, and the making of Bangladesh: Remembering 1971.* Durham, NC: Duke University Press.

Shongram 71 (2014). Film. Directed by Munsr Ali. United Kingdom: Spotlight UK.

Further reading

Chowdhury, E.H. (2016). War healing and trauma: Reading the feminine aesthetics and politics in Rubaiyat Hossain's *Meherjaan*. *Feminist Formations*, 28(3), pp. 27–45.

D'Costa, B. (2013). *Nationbuilding and war crimes in South Asia.* London: Routledge.

Mookherjee, N. (2015). *The spectral wound: Sexual violence, public memories, and the Bangladesh war of 1971.* Durham, NC: Duke University Press.

Raju, Z.H. (2015). *Bangladesh cinema and national identity: In search of the modern?* London: Routledge.

Saikia, Y. (2011). *Women, war, and the making of Bangladesh: Remembering 1971.* Durham, NC: Duke University Press.

16 Right now in no place with strangers

Eudora Welty's queer love

Avak Hasratian

It may seem perverse to examine select fictional and non-fictional works of a southern American woman writer, Eudora Welty, to draw out lessons for such global and complex social and legal subjects as sexuality, much less sexuality *and* human rights. To do so, one would have to be able to come to some agreement on a working definition of *both* – such is a global and heterogeneous undertaking encompassing multiple interdisciplinary approaches indeed. Happily, the compendium to hand addresses many aspects of that large-scale work.

Discipline and context

I prefer to work in smaller scales. But before I do, I would like to reflect on disciplinary methods within literary studies today; how they relate to human rights; and why Eudora Welty is well suited to both bridging and "queering" the two. To do so, I ask to be permitted a few general observations. Human rights discourse – including the subsets characterizing issues of sexual subjectivity, broadly construed – is structured around a series of such oppositions as the universal and the particular; the global and the local; the abstract and the concrete; and the generic "human" and the specifics of human individuals. These oppositions are historically necessary and vital because they emerge from the very systems bent on placing an injured minority group into the latter set of terms and in so doing, denying their larger humanity. As a result, critics and activists working in human rights and the rights of sexual minorities take up and use that very minority status to make claims to the broader, first set of terms, without giving up on the uneven and often tragic histories that have placed minorities within the latter set.

As Joseph North shows in his important new book, *Literary criticism: A concise political history* (2017), much of the literary criticism that supplanted the New Critics' privileged abrogation of history and particularity has also been a dialectical mix of and debate between just such terms, whether of the Marxist/materialist variety or of the New Historicist variety. In this key respect, literary criticism and human rights discourse have mirrored one another. Far from trying to rescue the rightfully discarded vestiges of the

New Critics' belief in the ahistorical and disinterested purity of art, North shows that we can attend to the aesthetic dimension of art without reducing it to a diagnostic tool by means of which to critique cultural logics and thus save injured groups through the *noblesse oblige* implicit in such critique. To his way of thinking, attending to how we feel about art and how art makes us feel is as important as the histories and cultures from which such art emerges. So attending prevents us from falling into the dominant neoliberal and politically futile trap in which, North shows, so many otherwise well-meaning literary critics have become rather stuck.

Eudora Welty is especially useful as she harnesses affect to drive a minor wedge into this major and ongoing debate within human rights and literary studies alike. This is because, as I hope to show by the end of this essay, her theories of writing and her writing itself deliberately and very intentionally render the above oppositions inoperative. To her, art is a memory of its moment, much like a photograph – Welty was an avid photographer as well – and we can, in reactivating such moments, suspend rather than reify the terms that would force us to divide those moments into easily identifiable and opposed pieces. Thus, Welty rejects the dualist thinking defining a good deal of human rights and literary discourse alike and asks us instead – much like the queer theorists and philosophers with whom I place her in conversation – to focus on "love," or the capacity for humans to connect meaningfully in the moment and at the level of unique complex individuals whose individuality is not opposed to but the grounds for their universality. Welty uses love to suspend the difference between such oppositions, just for a moment of stillness, when and wherein humans can be impervious to the world and its categories, even as she acknowledges that we must return to such categories. How she accomplishes at least a *rapprochement* between if not a total overcoming of such terms will emerge in what follows.

Queer time and place

With a bit of help from Lloyd Pratt, we can begin. His essay, "Close reading the present: Eudora Welty's queer politics," claims that close reading *is* the practice of attention to specificity and allows Welty to queer time itself. The "project of close reading," Pratt argues, "stems from queer theory's (often disavowed) literary-critical origins [and] is… its greatest source of strength" (2011, p. 183). Such a project prevents grounding human beings and art in a potentially deadly and nostalgic attachment to or even fetishism for the past that disallows new forms of being – including queer ones, separate and apart from marriage, monogamy, and children – from becoming.[1] Welty frees one from being only or primarily defined by links to the past – albeit temporarily. This provides an opening for potential outcomes otherwise closed to someone who lives within the past. Pratt deploys a quote by Eudora Welty to claim that the past is a time that troubles William Faulkner's work. He writes that

[i]n a pointed response to William Faulkner, the climax of [Welty's novel] *The Optimist's Daughter* centers on the following realization, which, like most of the novel, points to the present as our only resource: "The past is no more open to help or hurt than was Father in his coffin. The past is like him, impervious, and can never be awakened." Nostalgia is a tapped-out resource and futural optimism is a false promise.

(Welty, p. 179, cited in Pratt, 2011, pp. 184–185)

Readers and critics of Faulkner might immediately recognize that here, Welty (and Pratt) is criticizing Faulkner's attachment to places where and times when the difference between such identities as white and black, men and women, and finding oneself within a well-defined and utterly patriarchal system of kinship was rather absolute.[2]

What, then, is Welty's solution to the problem of such past history as the privileged time of white heterosexual masculinity – a problem shared by the history of human rights, emerging, as it does, from the (white, straight, male subject of) European Enlightenment? In a series of seminars that Welty presented on time, one of which is called, "On Faulknerian time" (1965b), Welty somewhat ambivalently notes that Faulkner's obsession "not [with] chronology," but with time as such (p. 57) may be the very means of undoing the forms of static time that move us nowhere fast. Put another way, Welty uses Faulkner against himself. Her implicit reply to Faulkner, in *The optimist's daughter* (1969), as cited by Pratt, is that Faulkner's patriarchal fathers are dead, their time is up, and she queers time accordingly.

How? Pratt claims that, "[t]o a significant degree, and to its credit, queer theory" – much like Eudora Welty – "has resisted the forms of rote historicism that have proven themselves to be inimical to the project of working on and in the present" (2011, p. 183).[3] Indeed, even if a present moment is one we're taking from a specific past, it is in the event of reading that moment when new possibilities, and possibly optimistic, futures arise. After Laurel's father, who, as Judge McKelva, we might interpret as the beneficent patriarch and father – much like a modern liberal democratic nation – dies, Laurel and her stepmother Fay fight over an object that they both want (a breadboard). Here I pick up Welty from just before Pratt's own citation of Welty's text:

"What do you see in that thing?" asked Fay.
"The whole story, Fay. The whole solid past," said Laurel.
"Whose story? Whose past? Not mine," said Fay.
"The past isn't a thing to me. I belong to the future, didn't you know that?"
… The memory [of the past] can be hurt, time and again – but in that may be its final mercy. As long as its vulnerable to the living moment, it lives for us, and while it lives, and while we are able, we can give it up its due.

(Welty, 1969, pp. 178–179)

Laurel then proceeds to say "never mind," and, "laying the breadboard down on the table," declares to Fay, in a final parting, "'I think I can get along without that too.' Memory lived not in initial possession but in the freed hands, pardoned and freed, and in the heart that can empty but fill again, in the patterns restored by dreams" (Welty, 1969, p. 179). We can explore and appreciate the past by letting it go, by decathecting from it. Doing so allows us to step into a potential – and only potential, that is, unrealized – future. Such a future isn't reified, unlike "'the whole solid past... which isn't a thing'" to Laurel. She will not be distracted from the now.

What this unleashes for sexuality and human rights discourse is the ability to think seriously about how who and what we have lost is the condition for becoming who and what we are. Put another way, to gain legal rights we lose certain, possibly extra-legal, freedoms. What have we given up to get married? What potential forms of being have we occluded to define ourselves and exist as only this or that type of sexual minority? What deeply inflected and interior psychic objects dwell within our memories and in our hearts, even if we deny they are part of us? Such objects are no less "material" for being psychic any more than art is immaterial for being purposelessly beautiful. Yet this is neither apolitical nor ahistorical; Welty's art is a form of memorialization that unites past with an openness to the future in terms of examining our moment. She helps us to think about same-sex marriage rights in the US in terms of what such rights want us to *forget*, namely, the forms of coupling other than marriage or marriage-like coupling that have been long treated as illegitimate and that are illegal and indeed under siege in the US today.[4] What would it look like if married gay couples began using their newfound political power to advocate affirmatively for sex workers in the US and beyond, heterosexual married men who have sex with men, or female adulterers in a global context, each of whom is treated as the negation of marriage itself?[5]

We must be careful not to tack too quickly into the winds of political futurism, especially a neoliberal and happily married one. Doing so would result in what Lauren Berlant calls "cruel optimism." That is, attainment of the object of desire must remain on a forever-futural horizon, because actually attaining it leads to the horrible "realization [that doing so] is discovered either to be impossible, sheer fantasy, or too possible, and toxic" (Berlant, 2011 p. 24). "Cruel optimism," she continues, "provides... the continuity of the subject's sense of what it means to keep on living and to look forward to being in the world." The condition that would result from attaining the object "will defeat the capacity to have any hope about anything," because the mere "threat of the loss of x in the scope of one's attachment... can feel like a threat to living on itself" (p. 24). To queer time, we must attach the past *and* the future to the present if we are to read and therefore do anything good about both – *beside and outside* of our own present.

The historical impulse – shared by literary criticism and human rights discourse – to situate every present within and emerging from an endlessly resurrected past induces one to target and politicize what yokes the present to that past and then use it to attack the present as – oddly enough – *insufficiently futuristic*, that is, as insufficiently advanced or progressive – because fatally attached to and unable to mourn a "bad past." Such reads as a form of melancholia. The related tendency, also using the historical impulse but that goes in the opposite direction, is to fall into a future-nostalgia, a future-sickness, that is, to use the past to imagine an *overly optimistic*, impossible yet-to-be – because such imaginings must always be prepared to lose that "good future," a future that will never arrive and thus is always ready to become lost. This is not melancholia but something rather different since the lost object never arrives and is therefore more akin to a perpetual preparedness for mourning. To combine Pratt and Berlant, we might say that in the moment and event of reading, the specific history of characters as well as the futures they initiate slip under yet inform the affective pull they exert on us right now.

Welty shows how history and the future nuances our experience of the present, and such a present-oriented nuance is fruitful for queer sexuality's access to human rights. Her writing about fiction is not separate, in my view, from the aesthetic, affective, ethical, and political investment in rights – albeit in her own terms. Welty's timeliness for human rights emerges from her claim that "[t]he challenge to writers today... is not to disown any part of our heritage. Whatever our theme in writing, it is old and tried. Whatever our place, it has been visited by the stranger, it will never be new again. It is only the vision that can be new" (Welty, 1956, p. 59). This is a strange formula. It is contradictory: We are where we are from but we are not (bound to) where we are from; our theme is old especially when we think it to be new; our place, our home, what is most familiar to us, has been peopled by strangers and is therefore uncanny. Which is it: place or non-place, old or new, the familiar and homey or the strange and uncanny – and, I would add, the particular or the universal? What does she mean that the "vision" of most such terms, *rendered in fiction*, "can be new?" How do we achieve such "newness" without falling into the trap of either a too-limiting specificity or a too-broad universality? How can one be neither pathologically attached to one's past nor totally unmoored from it to the point of floating glossy-eyed about a future that blinds us from the present?

Welty, in her essay "Must the novelist crusade?" (1965a), uses Faulkner and slams identity politics to answer these questions. She shows how to make a present that suspends such politics' past and future, a present that therefore takes the place and time of past and future. Faulkner, she recounts, had been unfairly attacked "in some respectable press" by a "journalist" who claims that Faulkner couldn't possibly "know... what he was writing about in his life's work" because "he was" – and here she quotes the journalist –"'after all, only a white Mississippian'" (p. 74). Welty does not believe that – despite her knowledge as well as the journalist's knowledge of Faulkner's specific identity – his art can be reduced to identity. Thus she demolishes those who would see Faulkner (or her) as limited to what is supposedly the writer's race and place – and, we might add, gender – as the only epistemological basis on which she or he can write about anything. That may work for journalists, but not for fiction writers. Welty destroys this unidentified journalist's claim even though she disagrees with Faulkner's use of an often bleak past temporality and herself uses the south as the set-ting for much of her fiction.

Indeed, in her essay, "Place in fiction," she believes that one's particular place is of absolutely crucial importance: "art that speaks most clearly, explicitly, directly and passionately from its place of origin will remain the longest understood" (1956, p. 59). However, she immediately and cleverly adds that "[i]t is through place that we put our roots, *wherever birth, chance, fate, or our traveling sets us down*" (emphasis added, p. 59). Therefore, one's "roots" are entirely an aleatory matter and in fact can change, can "reach toward... America, England, or Timbuktu" (p. 59). While it is easy to con-clude that she uses "Timbuktu" in the common American sense of an exotic place so far, far away as to be unreachable, something tells me that Welty knew it is a city in Mali or didn't care because one always writes from where one is and from there can stretch into other places. Her rhetorical point remains the same either way: she makes the writer's "roots" into something much more like Gilles Deleuze's notion of the "rhizome," which can grow and reach out in most any direction, guided more by circumstance and chance than by family bonds and static laws.[6]

Welty's sense of the present is based in a liberatory human impulse to travel and spread and act on a whim rather than dig into "its own" ground, be tied down, and then grow up. Here, it is important to note the work of Kathryn Bond Stockton, whose book, *The queer child, or Growing sideways in the twentieth century* (2009), is clearly influenced by Deleuze's notion of the rhizome. Stockton describes forms of sexuality and childhood and child-like adulthood that refuse the dominant terms by which society dictates that queers must grow up. Interestingly, Welty peoples some of her fiction with characters like those Stockton describes. In Welty's short story, "The hitch-hikers," the protagonist, Harris, is a sexually ambiguous, unmarried, traveling, and rootless salesman. For him,

> the recurring sight of hitch-hikers waiting against the sky gave him the flash of a sensation he had known as a child: standing still, with nothing to touch him, feeling tall and having the world come all at once into its round shape underfoot and rush and turn through space and make his stand very precarious and lonely.
>
> (Welty, 1941a, p. 62)

He is the image of a still and silent child, and acts as such throughout the story. Indeed, there's some evidence to suggest that this childlike feeling of fullness is related to an equally childlike impulse to be drawn, inexorably, towards one of the two hitch-hikers, as if in proto-desire for intimacy not only with another man, but a stranger as well. And in the story, "Why I live at the P.O.," about a tomboy of a girl who refuses to grow up in terms her family prescribes, there is a character, "Uncle Rondo," who is much like an adult adolescent, which is one of the ways that Stockton describes queers – especially gay men – as being portrayed in fiction and film. Welty affirmatively enjoys such characterizations, making of them, as she does, pure camp: Uncle Rondo drinks a bottle of narcotics or some such deliriant, available to him as he is a pharmacist, dresses up in one of his niece's "flesh-colored kimonos," calls the protagonist "Sister," and in so doing, plays the part of the flamboyant queen (Welty, 1941b, p. 47). As a matter of biographical and historical curiosity, Welty had deep friendships with gay men in the arts (one of whom was murdered) and remained unburdened by marriage or children.

Freeing oneself from an attachment to, say, marriage – including same-sex marriage – or to a city for only one or another race (here, one thinks, as Welty does, of the extreme heterogeneity of New Orleans), or freeing oneself from an attachment to, say, only one kind of sexuality or sexual identity, or moving as far away as possible from one kind of being grown-up – the married, monogamous, often child-bearing kind, who would never commit adultery, especially female adultery – is of keen interest to Welty, as we will see in her aptly titled short story, "No place for you, my love" (1955). Doing the work of such freeing, she suggests, is only possible on grounds that the *hic et nunc* – rather than constantly renegotiating the past – unleashes at least the potential of shareable places and moments, even those that aren't "our own" or "proper" to "us," much less "our property" in "our time." No matter how ancient, rooted in the past, or primal the claim – in both the physical and psychic senses – now is the place and time to be and it belongs to no one.

Right writing

It is clear that Welty's concerns about how to write fiction – and the contradictions or at least opposed sets of terms generated thereby – are not unlike those generated by human rights discourse. As Wendy Brown has shown, recognition of a group's historical injury or exclusion is necessary for such a people's injury to be redressed by rights. Indeed, identification of such individuals *with* their historical injury or exclusion based on or related strongly to minority sexual identity (or another injured minority status) is a condition for such redress. Brown critiques what she calls "politicized identities" because they are shot through with political power and therefore destroy the forms of desire, love, and kindness that people can share *regardless* of their particular status yet without recourse to a naïve universalism either (1995a, p. 96). In her chapter, "Rights and losses," Brown suggests that it is difficult "to deploy rights on behalf of identities that aim to confound the humanist conceit" of universalism (p. 96). She tries to move beyond the "universal-local paradox of rights" (p. 98) by postulating a question that I would call a Weltyan theory of writing rights in the present, as I have been describing it: Brown asks, "[w]hat if the value of rights discourse for a radical democratic project lies not in... [being] a remedy to social injury, but in the (*fictional*) egalitarian imaginary this discourse could engender... most effectively... [as] '*pre-political*' struggles for membership or *post-political dreams* of radical equality" (emphases added, p. 133)? Long before Brown's inquiry, Welty forewent the problems generated by liberalism's identities politicized in and by past resentments towards the present and future by collapsing both into the present. Instead, she favors something much like Brown's "(fictional) egalitarian imaginary," situated in a *changeable present* and thus hopes for what might be or become a better human future (p. 133).[7]

To glimpse such possibilities, let us draw on Sophia A. McClennen and Alexandra Schultheis Moore's "Introduction: Aporia and affirmative critique: Mapping the landscape of literary approaches to human rights research" to *The Routledge companion to literature and human rights* and claim that literary humanists should interrogate assumptions about "who counts as a bearer of rights and by whom" (2015, p. 16). Article 16 of the United Nations' *Universal Declaration of Human Rights* (1948) enshrines heterosexual marriage as normal and natural even though it is neither. As Greg A. Mullins – a contributor to the *Routledge companion* – declares in his essay "Queer rights?," we must have "a critical understanding of the cultural formations of specific genders and sexualities. Only the most unreconstructed universalist would attempt to impose a single meaning of gender or of sexuality on all the world's cultures. The demand for cultural specificity is axiomatic" (2015, p. 55). "However," he continues, "this same demand poses the danger of placing upon gender and sexuality (and literature) the burden of bearing culture as such," which would be a bit imperious (p. 55).

The real problem leading from the specific-universal, or culture-Culture oppositions, Mullins shows, is that when a sexual minority argues that "international standards trump local culture," it leads to the reverse argument by other elements of such local culture, some of whom might view trans women's freedom or male same-sex sexuality as an imported Western imperialist pollutant rather than something strange but that has long existed within and is therefore *strangely familiar* to a specific culture or indeed an entire nation (2015, p. 55).[8] Mullins' resolution to this false opposition, then, resides in a statement quite similar to Welty's notion of writing about place: namely, Mullins claims we must "insist that culture is neither static nor monolithic, [and] contend that conservatives are not gatekeepers of culture, and point out that in any given culture, fairness and justice trump prejudice and hatefulness" (p. 56). In other words, we should appeal to how one can be a bit of an outsider to or a stranger to one's culture without, as Welty suggests, "disown[ing]... [one's] heritage" and in so doing, one can have a "vision that can be new" (Welty, 1956, p. 59). Such a new vision might be as simple as taking someone who has been a stranger to a familiar place, or who is familiar somehow yet in a stranger's place, and letting them in – fully *recognizing* them, even if one disagrees with or dislikes them – without further question or qualification.

This is not power-free: the "we" who let "others" or even otherness itself in, are in a position of privilege to adjudicate whether, where, and for how long to do so, and in almost all imaginable cases, so doing is temporary. It may not be grounded in reciprocity, or may come with expectations and obligations, thus subject to abuse. Viewed thus, Welty's task for writing is not so easy when applied to real life: "[T]o try to enter into the mind, heart, and skin of a human being who is not myself," regardless of "[w]hether this happens to be a man or a woman, old or young, with skin black or white," may be the job of a good fiction writer (Welty, 1980, p. xi). But to do this job outside fiction, as a good human being, with a particular combination of skin, gender, sexuality, and age (among other variables), in relation to a differently situated human, is another task altogether. How can we accept radical difference when we cannot provide it refuge in our minds and hearts for very long? The answer, Welty suggests, is to refuse to believe that real life and fiction are opposed. This is also the task for literary criticism now, and for its potential future, as Joseph North and queer theory sees it. If one begins to think that reality is made up and that what we make up impacts reality, then forthcoming may be a time when the boundary between the "us" and the "them" we only occasionally, if ever, allow into our real lives but frequently allow into our imaginations, might fall away.

Everybody's like "us," even if we don't like "them"

However, if differences don't matter because we can imagine being different, then what's the point in becoming-different in the first place? Welty's answer is to use difference as that which overcomes itself; she negates her own negation of difference, and so can we. Her broadly humanist concerns invite her readers to enjoy if not practice a similar tautology: namely, that there is no difference between differences except for difference itself. The specific and the local *is* the universal of each group of individuals, and each group of individuals' universality *is* their specific situation. Welty uses the particular aspects of highly individualizing character development in order to make quite general claims for and about affective and living human beings as such:[9] Her aim as a fiction writer is to show that

> People are not Right and Wrong, Good and Bad, Black and White personified... Fiction writers cannot be tempted to make the mistake of looking at people in the generality – that is to say, of seeing people as not at all *like us*. If human beings are to be comprehended as real, then they have to be treated as real, with minds, hearts, memories, habits,

hopes, with passions and capacities like ours. This is why [fiction writers] begin the study of people from within.

The first act of insight is *throw away the labels*. In fiction, while we do not necessarily write about ourselves, we write out of ourselves, using ourselves; what we learn from, what we are sensitive to, what we feel strongly about – these become our characters and go to make our plots. Characters in fiction are conceived from within, and they have, accordingly, their own interior life; *they are individuals every time*. The character we care about in [fiction] *we may not approve of or agree with – that's beside the point*. But he has got to seem alive. Then and only then, when we read, we experience or surmise things about life itself that are deeper and more lasting and less destructive to understanding than approval or disapproval

(first emphasis in original; latter emphases added, Welty, 1965a, p. 79).

Welty undoes every opposition she creates, or renders each so circular that it turns and returns as a self-devouring ouroboros: the "deeper and more lasting" aspects that "we experience or surmise about life itself" and in general are shareable across differences that emerge from specific, historically situated individuals whose lives deeply matter but whose differences don't matter, except insofar as those very same differences are necessary to give us access to the "deeper and more lasting" aspects of humanity. When Welty, in the same essay, suggests that "we are all agreed upon the most important point: that morality as shown through human relationships is the whole heart of fiction, and the serious writer has never lived who has dealt with anything else" (1965a, p. 76), is she negating her own negation of "approval or disapproval" as "destructive to understanding" (p. 79)? Is she, then, really an overweening moralist?

What Welty means by morality is an absolute kindness and indeed hospitality towards people, even those we don't like, especially strangers. In this key respect, she stands in stark contrast to another southern American woman writer, Flannery O'Connor, who divides love into "divine, natural, & perverted" (2013, p. 30). O'Conner's disgust with physical love as opposed to "supernatural" love and her association of the former with homosexuality, which she considered sexual deviance (along with most any physical sexual act at all), "Hell" and "Satan" are indications of her own grotesque religious and literary struggles (pp. 30–31).[10] The questions should instead be: what does Welty mean by "morality *as shown through human relationships*" (emphasis added, p. 76)? What does she mean by "human relationships?"

She answers these questions by using odd words, words that are placeholders and time spaces for anything that might transpire between individuals so as to be called "human relationships" or just relations between humans. She accomplishes this feat of imagination by using the point where everything specific converges into the general and everything general is concentrated and communicated by virtue of its specificity. Regardless of where and when they are from, or what their identity may be, then, for writers and their human characters, Welty claims that "[s]ituation itself always exists; it is whatever life," and no matter what makes it this or that type or category of human life, it "is up to here and now, it is the living and present moment. It is transient, and it fluctuates" (1965a, p. 78). This is a moment where the difference between who and where one is in relation to other forms of difference gives way to a transition and fluctuation within, rather than opposition between, ontologies of identity, difference, and time itself.[11] What confounds identity secures individual singularity as one's universality in a moment that cannot last but is neither lost nor refuses reappearance.

An entire cadre of contemporary Continental European philosophers – and many American literary critics and queer theorists, too – who have been in an ongoing discussion with each other in order to imagine a future free from the constraints of liberal individualism, universalism, identity, and difference, could not have – and have not – created a clearer or more apt formula for describing what life is and what human relationships are than has Eudora Welty. Long before Giorgio Agamben – to take an exemplary figure from such philosophers – began his life's work to render inoperative the difference between the individual and universal, and between dualist terms that divide some from other humans (and humans from animals), Welty was doing just that in her life's work. It is worth noting the odd accord between them across time (decades), distance (the Atlantic), and language (southern American English; Italian): Agamben's 2007 essay, "Whatever," in his book, *The coming community*, suggests that to live truly in the now so as to make possible a better future, "the Whatever in question here relates to singularity not in its indifference with respect to a common property (… being… French, being Muslim), but only in its being *such as it is*. Singularity is thus freed from the false dilemma that obliges knowledge to choose between the ineffability of the individual and the intelligibility of the universal" (emphasis in original, p. 1). And this "being-*such*," whatever such may be, "is whatever you *want*, that is, lovable" (emphases in original, p. 2).

With this emerging theory of love in mind, and if I may take the liberty, I would like to rewrite the conclusion that Pratt draws from this key aspect of Welty's (theory of) writing by refracting it through Agamben's theory that one's singular quiddity is the condition of universal lovability. Pratt writes that "[f]or Welty, attending to the present requires a level of inattention to the future (and the past) that prohibits the crusade" (2011, p. 203). Instead, I would write that for Welty, attending to the present requires an inattention to identity's attachments to the past and future, because individuals live in moments that are such complex yet singular quiddities they confound and therefore are foundational to an understanding of what humans share, even in their strangeness one to another.

"Stranger loving"

I borrow this section heading from Tim Dean's chapter, "Cruising as a way of life," in his book, *Unlimited intimacy: Reflections on the subculture of bare-backing* (2009, p. 177). Therein, he describes a Weltyan way of life – albeit in his case, between gay men and MSMs (men who have sex with men) – as follows: "The kind of contact that I'm trying to delineate, though often we seek it through sex, remains irreducible to genital contact. That is to say, erotic encounters represent not just an instance of but also, perhaps more significantly, a metaphor for contact with otherness... [as] *contact with strangers*" (emphasis in original, p. 181). Dean begins his chapter with a question, "taken from gay leatherman Scott Tucker's critique of antipornography rhetoric," and that question – equally applicable to most any human being – is: "*Why should strangers not be lovers*" and ends his chapter with an even more intriguing question: "Why should strangers not be lovers and yet remain strangers" (emphasis in original, p. 176 and p. 212, respectively)? Furthermore, and perhaps more radically than Tim Dean's account of stranger loving (though Dean does talk about the role of not talking), Jacques Derrida, in his work, *Of hospitality*, "wonder[s] whether... absolute hospitality doesn't consist in suspending language, and even the address to the other. Shouldn't we also submit to a sort of holding back of the temptation to ask the other who he is, what his name is, where he comes from, etc.?" (2000, p. 135). This is a more intense version of letting in and even loving contact with the stranger than one conditioned on questions of law.

Welty doesn't explicitly address either sexuality or human rights in her fiction as we think of them today, that is, politically in terms of the rights of sexual minorities who are subjects of various social and legal discourses, disciplines, and punishments, among others. But she does move into the non-terrain of otherness and love between strangers that suspends the terms by which humans are divided into those who bear and those unworthy of rights. As McMahand and Murphy remind us, Welty not only was friends with many gay men, but also heard of and knew about "violence against queer [male] bodies" in her Mississippian hometown and state (2014, p. 78). They demonstrate how Welty actually mourned and commemorated the suicide, murder, and death, thus loss of queer lives – much as she did for black lives – with "enormous force" in her work (p. 70). They recall for us that "biographers, historians, and literary critics... [have shown that] Eudora Welty's friendships with gay men and her apparent knowledge of the functions and stresses of the closet" have gone underthought "with her representation of it in her fiction" (p. 69). They correct that elision. One of Welty's closest friends, for whom she wrote a difficult memorialization and commemoration, was "Frank Hains, whose homosexuality and love of arts had been implicitly linked to his murder" in 1975 (p. 69).[12] Thus we might call what Welty achieves through silence to be a form of both personally and politically motivated cruising and contact with us as readers, closeted in fiction. When Welty's fiction goes in a direction oblique to open advocacy and instead in the direction of both Dean's and the Derridean sense of remaining strangers, remaining silent, even closeted, *her* apparent silence is very loud indeed.[13]

Welty's short story, "No place for you, my love," is exemplary in rendering in aesthetic feeling a sense of closeted cruising and silent contact. The first sentence is: "They were strangers to each other, both fairly well strangers to the place, now seated side by side at luncheon" (1955, p. 465). Yes, this is a man and a woman, but I would remind you that Welty demands that we toss out labels. Theoretically, anyone can identify with the desire of the other, regardless of the other's identity.

He, a married man, and she, most likely a married woman, each from different places, meet as strangers in New Orleans and travel to both a real "no place" and a sensual "no place," where stranger loving can take place nearly outside of time. As with Derrida's sense of radical hospitality (and Dean's sense of cruising contact), neither character is named in the text and both spend the entire day and evening in near silence. They do not ask one another's names. But they have a silent way of coming together: "Of all human moods," the text reads, "deliberate imperviousness may be the most quickly communicated – it may be the most successful, most fatal signal of all. And two people can indulge in imperviousness as well as in anything else" (1955, p. 466). The absolute impenetrability of the strangers is made all the more acute in light of their silent agreement and silent drive out of the luncheon, out of New Orleans to nearby Arabi, onto a ferry across the Mississippi, and down as far south and east as the road can take them until it ends in Venice, a city on and somewhat in water.[14] Every situation and setting is at the threshold between land and water, in "a strange land, amphibious" (p. 479). This is no ordinary affair. Like Dean's stranger loving, it is about contact; like Derrida's radical hospitality, it is about not even addressing the other as such.

At every moment others who aren't addressed as others but parts of the place, come into place between the two, making them always at a threshold: the wetness, swarms of insects, shells, catfish, cows, a pet-like alligator, a dog, a goose, shrimp and shrimpers, cooks, a half-nude parish priest, and omnipresent running, playful, and in some cases gambling, children. The text only openly indicates that there is a different presence when the man thinks to himself, "[w]hatever people liked to think, situations (if not scenes) were usually three-way – there was somebody else always. The one who didn't – couldn't – understand the two made the formidable third" (1955, p. 471). But in this situation, there is nothing but the present and presence of movement and transience and figures of being in-between, which is one way of describing the place of the present. Recalling Welty's refusal of the past's hold on the present, the text describes their fast drive through a graveyard on a "track... with only a few inches to spare" between tombstones: "Names took their places on the walls... at a level with the eye, names as near as the eyes of a person stopping in conversation, and as far away in origin, and in all their music and dead longing, as Spain" (p. 472). Then a list of flowers follows, a deliberate non-sequitur or refocus on what lives now rather than on the names of others in some Faulknerian then-time.

On reaching the road's terminus, they enter a food, drink, gambling, and gathering shack named "Baba's Place" (p. 475). Once "[t]he evening was at the threshold," the strangers "danced gratefully" until "they began moving together too well" (p. 477). "They danced on still as the record changed, after standing wordless and motionless, linked together in the middle of the room, for the moment between" (pp. 477–478). Here, as with the parts of the place enveloping the strangers, which includes non-speaking but ever present animal life, we see that Welty unites the specifics of location and context with rather than in opposition to an arguably universal formula for stranger loving: People who don't know one another somehow, with barely a word exchanged, fall into a singularity much like Agamben describes as the non-space time that unites the individual with the universal into "whatever you *want*, that is, lovable" (emphases in original, p. 2). As they continue to dance, we read that

> [s]urely even those immune from the world, for the time being, need the touch of one another, or all is lost. Their arms encircling each other, their bodies circling in the odorous, just-nailed-down floor, they were, at last, imperviousness in motion. They had found it, and had almost missed it: they had had to dance. They were what their separate hearts desired that day, for themselves and for each other.
>
> (Welty, 1955, p. 478)

They reach a point where the "it" that "[t]hey had found" is an inalienable yet totally strange other-than-themselves. This is why, following their dance, they "dared not think the words 'happy' or 'unhappy,' which might strike them... like lightning" (p. 478). No such terms of reductive affect can capture their it-ness any more than in this place, the law could find, much less define them, as adulterers. They are not merely outside law; they are outside space and time.

They lose difference and in so doing, gain a Weltyan new vision for what stranger loving is and can be: before they hit the road back to New Orleans, they kiss, and "[i]t was the loss of that distinction" between whose face, body, arm, shoulder, was whose, "that told him this was now" (p. 479). Most importantly, they share an unspoken and absolute agreement: as they begin to uncouple and return to something like their individual selves, "[f]or their different reasons... neither of them would tell this... that, strangers, they had ridden down into a strange land together and were getting safely back" (p. 480). When the man and woman have an intimate encounter, it was at a time when and place where female adultery could have resulted in bad consequences for her but not her putative husband. This is without considering the complications that cross-racial encounters might have caused. And even though Welty wants the reader to imagine identifying with the two characters, if they had been two men or two women in the deep south in the 1950s, they would very likely have been kicked out of "Baba's Place"—or far worse. So while singular love cannot continuously transcend historical moments/time and place/location, Welty does want us to imagine identifying with the characters in fiction even if we cannot enact what they do in our real lives. That's why she sets up the structure for a non-place of a potential future for those who couldn't fit into her present and place – or perhaps yet cannot fit into ours.

To set up such a structure, individuals, and their heritage – and therefore where they come from and who they are – is, paradoxically, key to the encounters. Such specificity is temporarily suspended in moments of moving stillness as defined by a dance, but then people who are different (must) go back to their differences. The paradox is in being able to experience love across differences *both because of and despite* those differences, as they are held still in the moment of encounter. This is why, like her characters, Welty wants us to think in "closeted" and furtive terms to experience risking our safety, especially the safety so deeply embedded within sexuality and human rights in the contemporary US: the safety to be and remain in domestic, liberal, monogamous, married households; the safety to speak and act without fear – much like some of her gay friends did, even at the cost of their very lives.

Her characters are erotic and public exhibitionists on a dance floor, and "[t]hey were so good together that once she looked up and half smiled" and, in a rare moment of speaking, remarks, "For whose benefit did we have to show off?" (1955, p. 478). In Albert Devlin's terms, "'No place for you, my love' is the one [story] that carries the author's greatest self-awareness of having written 'on the sharp edge of experiment'" and its purpose "is to isolate the curious substrate of emotion that travels with the couple into a mythical land that is pure exposure" (2002, p. 395). What would it mean to be so sensuously and indeed sexually free as to be able to expose oneself to stranger loving anywhere at any time without fear of moral much less legal reprisal? Like Tim Dean, I am talking about contact that may be prurient, but is irreducible to the physical. Such contact may be a form of psychic concupiscence and thus shareable. Must stranger loving always be and remain untold in order to avoid the law of hospitality as opposed to unconditional hospitality? It should be noted that only one person in "Baba's Place," a man, makes an unspecified comment about the woman's potentially morally opprobrious status. *He* is mocked and shamed, not the stranger lovers. No one else – not the gambling children nor the gambling adults, any more than the dog and the goose that call Baba's home and speak most by saying little to nothing – cares at all, except either to ignore or to enjoy the scene.

Welty's fiction as well as – and arguably more-so – her non-fiction writing about writing, create the structural conditions of human connection and kindness that are imbued with many of the same key terms and ways of thinking as we find in struggles over sexuality and human rights, including those that would exclude the form of stranger loving we see in "No place for you, my love." That title itself places the characters in exile before and after they find refuge in the singularity they form. The difference is that after they've formed it, they will always be able to keep it, not as a reminder of the past, but of a present that never leaves and will always live, as the last line reads, "as the lilt and expectation of love" (Welty, 1955, p. 481). Welty's aesthetic preoccupation with the obliquity of desire makes her writing a refuge for humans who connect through such desire and sexuality. In this key respect – to use Welty's own rather sensual words about writing, "inherent in [writing] is the possibility of a shared act between its writer and its reader" (1965a, p. 76). She creates such acts as forms of love, sexuality, and radical hospitality that connect beings who are otherwise strangers one to another.[15] She imagines points of contact between parties that would otherwise not meet and needn't even reconcile their differences because their unknowability as such produces love.

Welty reveals the singularity of stranger loving to be a humanizing and affirmatively depersonalizing quiddity; its feeling and the feeling it gives us equips us to enjoy others' enjoyment, to desire as others desire, to feel and sense our way into people different from and strangers to ourselves. Welty peoples our imagination with intimate and anonymous and often nearly silent points of contact, and thus leaves open many positions we might want to take. In doing so without any further identifiers – or even speech – her readers can become momentarily and quietly queer.

In Welty's mid-20th century, as much as now, one can therefore pick a "type" of such humans as are considered dangerous to the body politic *outside* of fiction – female adulterers, unmarried and/or non-monogamous men who share intimacies with other men outside the "gay/straight" binary – and *within* fiction, love every one. And in claiming that the work of writing is about "the individual... every time," whose experience "affirms... by the nature of itself. It says what people are like. It doesn't, and doesn't know how to, describe what they are *not* like, and it would waste its time if it told us what we ought to be like, since we already know that, don't we?," Welty frees us from a human rights triple bind in one stroke (emphasis in original, 1965a, pp. 79 and 81, respectively). That is, she sees no contradiction between and is therefore able to unite the *generally* human good to the *individually* structured case in point; and she liberates us both from prescriptions of the future "ought" and prohibitions of the past "not." People are what they are and want what they want. Fully taking in the "what-ness" of those wants – or what, as we have seen, she calls the "whatever life" of "whatever theme" from "whatever place" – is to allow ourselves to be "visited by the stranger" (1956, p. 59). And in so doing, without reprisal or retaliation, we open and make room for loving kindness. This is the right she writes.

Feeling learning

Developing one's sense of the presence in time and place of oneself, others, and the textual event itself is, I believe, as indispensable to Welty's fiction and non-fiction as it is to human rights. So developing accords not only with Pratt's approach but also with one of the primary inquiries and aims of Welty, which happens to be shared by Joseph North's book about the history of literary studies as a discipline in the English-speaking world: namely, "the question of how and to what extent the societies in which we live allow us to cultivate deeper modes of life" (North, 2017, p. vii). To North, "political concerns" within English-speaking liberal societies demand that

> there is much at stake here for the left. For the struggle is being fought, must be fought, on the terrain of sensibility. Not on sensibility alone, of course – a mistake that keeps being made – but never entirely outside it. If we continue to surrender our ability to fight on that ground, we cannot win.
>
> (p. xi)

From closely reading and examining select aspects of the writings of one author, of one gender, from one region, of one country, in one language, we have come to some specifically aesthetic, ethical, and indeed political generalizations – that do not negate specific cultural moments and places but *are* those moments and places – about what we mean by sexuality and human rights and how we can attune our sensibilities to dwell within, be kind to, and therefore improve the present and others within it as a result.

The stakes in doing so are shareable: we can use the fictional and in some cases non-fictional literary texts, on the one hand, to point us toward specific samples of and data from the literature by and about those working on the complex of sexuality and human rights, on the other hand. Thereby we suture a small contributory thread into that complex. The suture itself – where people touch in Welty's stories – is itself comprised of multiple staple fibers that couple, uncouple, and recouple, but never stay together for too long; it gives off pilings and fuzzies; it doesn't remain continuous. To put it in Welty's terms, "[t]here was a touch at her arm – his, accidental" (1955, p. 474). Whose arm is whose? This intimacy between beings emerges from the gap within human rights – stranger loving, accidental touching – that is implicitly sexual, at least sensual, deeply affective, and a queer experience impervious to laws and interdictions. These moments in now-time and no place cannot be captured except in moments of moving stillness such as Welty depicts. They render inoperative the previous and next moments from which we gain a sense of self.

Welty allows us to keep and be affected by (the memories of) strangers and otherness by virtue of the suspension and deliberate "letting go," just temporarily, of the past, future, and security of "our" place. Such markers of self as the name of a person with whom we share intimacy is both vital – as place holders – and irrelevant – as it is up to us to fill them with contents. Such is Welty's way of thinking about time, place, writing, strangers, and love. It enables her and "us" to feel into people who are unlike her and "us." The basic queering of human rights that she enacts in and about her writing – and that she shares with select queer theorists and European philosophers – is to suggest that one can identify with the desire of the other and even the desire to become the other both without regard to the other's individuality and heritage, and because of it. This is impersonal personalization.[16] Welty is the weighbridge between such terms that make sexuality and human rights so heavy a topic; we can assess the relative mass and importance of the historical and specific contents of sexuality and human rights in relation to moments of love impervious to alienation and division, using the scales she develops in her writing.

As a political project, this may not be sustainable, at least not in traditional terms.[17] But I believe that just such moments are meaningful for sexuality and human rights outside their normative, spoken, and legal dimensions – because both can change over time and with specific historical contents. To make stranger love into livable moments worth remembering, Welty invites us to do in life what she does in writing – which is her life, thus real. This may be a luxury afforded to literate readers of American fiction. But for that very same group, an *ästhetische Bildung* is desperately needed for the development of a sensible and sensitive consciousness and therefore potentially more just relations between humans.

Discussion questions

1 Do you think that you can maintain your sense of personal heritage while not being averse to the possibility of its loss?

2 Do you think your personal heritage is the ground on which to found your future?

3 What do you think would happen to you if you were to break from your personal heritage? Would you lose your sense of individual uniqueness? Would you turn into someone else? What would such a "break" look like, and what, if anything, might it make possible?

4 Do you ever find yourself imagining living as someone else, as someone other than who you are?

5 How often do you encounter people you do not know? Where? When? How do such encounters make you feel?

6 Have you ever been a hitch-hiker? Have you ever picked up a hitch-hiker? What was the experience like?

7 Would you allow a complete stranger into your private home? If so, under what, if any, conditions? If not, why not?

8 Would you ever consider having intimate, even erotic or sensual, contact with someone whom you do not know – perhaps without even

speaking or exchanging names? If so, under what, if any, conditions? If not, why not?

9 Do you think you could, using fiction and/or film, feel your way into the time and place of someone else, someone who does not share your gender and/or sexuality?

10 Can you imagine yourself empathizing with someone you do not like, indeed whom you strongly dislike?

Notes

1 For a critique of modern liberalism's promise of a rights-bearing subject as based on perpetual pain, self-subjection, and disappointment, see Brown, 1995b. See also her work on the past as opposed to the future and present (2001), especially the chapter titled "Futures," pp. 138–73.

2 With few exceptions, notably *Light in August*, most of Faulkner's work is obsessed with placing humans within definable racialized and gendered kinship systems emerging from and inexorably tied to a past that returns or indeed never passed. Even Walter Benn Michaels, who, despite being a leading Americanist critic of identity politics, cannot see a way out of Faulkner's obsession. See, e.g., his essay, "*Absalom, Absalom!*: The difference between white men and white men" (2003). Benn Michaels shares Welty's impulse to mistrust identity as the primary indicator of who one is and what one should believe and do. See, e.g., Benn Michaels, 2006.

3 I'm sure the irony of Pratt's claim is not lost on him, considering that his latest work, *The strangers book: The human of African American literature* (2016), required an immense amount of painstaking historical and archival research, notably at "the American Antiquarian Society... the Amistad Research Center at Tulane University, the Boston Athenaeum, the Historic New Orleans Collection, the Library Company of Philadelphia, the Nantucket Atheneum, the Nantucket Historical Association, the New Orleans Public Library's City Archives, the Providence Athenaeum, the Vere Harmsworth Library at the University of Oxford, and Xavier University of Louisiana's Archives and Special Collections" (p. 183). This being the case, his claim stands, since *The strangers book* is a *tour de force* of close readings of "Frederick Douglass's editorials, correspondence, addresses, lectures, and autobiographies" together with "the antebellum criticism and poetry of a circle of francophone free men of color who wrote in New Orleans" in order to show how they "were part of a political-aesthetic project" that is "both rhetorical and material" (pp. 1–2). Pratt's avowedly humanist and democratic and presentist aim – the book's dedication is "For the Katrina people (those who made it, those who did not)" (p. v) – is to show that being human is a strange condition, and that such strangeness should be accepted as difference rather than "appropriate[d] or penetrate[d]" into identity much less rejected as the absolute unlike (p. 2). In this key respect, Pratt's aim is formally in solidarity with Joseph North's even though their content couldn't be more different.

4 Lee Edelman makes the case (2007) that with the rise and normalization of same-sex relationships, those who fall outside such a new normal will become outcast queers. My own brilliant colleague, Holly Jackson, warns against this as well (2014). She writes, "Who will be next on the wrong side of the line between 'us' and 'them,' guarded in the name of the American family?"

5 David M. Halperin's "Introduction" to *The war on sex* (2017) documents and contextualizes the draconian measures recently taken against sex workers. See endnote 10.

6 See Deleuze and Guattari, 1987.

7   Despite Wendy Brown's critique of the subject who subjects itself to power in liberal societies as a problem inherent to the individual, I fully agree with Rajini Srikanth and, like her, "refuse to abandon the individual as a valuable terrain of analysis: private feeling is worthless only if treated as isolated and discrete" (2012, p. 4). I would add that Srikanth's notion of the feeling individual comports with Welty's notion that individual life and feeling are and should be shareable in deeply meaningful ways, as we will see. Srikanth's is also an excellent definition of character in fiction and real life alike: what would we read and who would we be without deep and shareable feeling?

8   The notion that there needn't be a constant conflict between so-called Western deviant sexual imports that dare to claim to be universal and local practices that are in fact queer is the focal point of the troubling yet optimistic documentary, by Masood Khan, *How gay is Pakistan?* He follows the lives of Pakistani trans women and men who have sexual contact with men. Both are very familiar and have long histories in Pakistan. Only when they manifest as "too Western" are they met with legal sanction or worse (beatings, torture, death). The irony is that Western-style laws, first imposed by Imperial Britain, are sometimes the very ones used against such trans women and MSMs (men who have sex with men). See also, for the case of Iran, Najambadi (2013).

9   See note 7.

10 Such a destructive moralism would seem to have been overcome by the legalization of same-sex marriage, first piecemeal, then by virtue of its being federally incorporated against the states as a result of the Supreme Court's decision in *Obergefell* v *Hodges*; and by the massive and rapid decline in homophobia in the US. However, before we celebrate our nuptials, let's be aware of the massive and sustained backlash against queerness taking place in the US and indeed being exported from the US. Such is documented in David M. Halperin and Trevor Hoppe's co-edited and timely (2017) book, *The war on sex*. From state-by-state religious liberty bills to wars against sex workers and pornography, they and their contributors show that there is more rather than less work to be done. The domestication and thus normalization of same-sex couples, while salutary, can have the effect if not intent of disavowing the affected new queer subjected populations. See also Warner, 2000. See note 5.

11 For further philosophical explanations of how this process works in both theoretical and arguably real-life terms (the two aren't necessarily opposed), see Seshadri (2011).

12 Details of Welty's response to her friend's murder can be found in Marrs, 2005. See also Nissen, 2003 and Richards, 2018.

13 In "Must the novelist crusade?" she deliberately eschews the notion that the novelist or fiction writer ought to bend her or his work toward a political goal, or that aesthetics as such should even be political – creative fiction is, in her words and after all, "taking life as it already exists, not to report it but to make an object, toward the end that the finished work might contain this life inside it, of offer it to the reader" (p. 75). Put another way, aesthetic and political objects bear a queer and oblique relationship to the realities that they transform, even as both bear strongly on human life – on its ability to be left to live as it is, want what it wants, and love what it loves. Welty is not wholly un- or apolitical. In 1963, in Welty's own hometown of Jackson, Mississippi, the black civil rights activist Medgar Evers was assassinated by a white supremacist Klansman. In "'The southern imagination': An interview with Eudora Welty and Walker Percy," conducted by the conservative William F. Buckley, Jr., Welty was asked about this event. She replied that "I was writing a novel at the time" and that "what I was writing about was human beings," but "when Medgar Evers was assassinated here – that night, it just pushed up to what I was doing. I thought to myself, 'I've

lived here all my life. I know the kind of mind that does this' – this was before anyone was caught. So I wrote a story in the first person as the murderer, because I thought, 'I am in a position where I know. I know what this man must feel like. I have lived with this kind of thing'" (Buckley, 1984, p. 100). See also *Eudora Welty and politics: Did the writer crusade?*, a collection of essays edited by Harriet Pollack and Welty's best biographer, Suzanne Marrs (2001a). It reveals that Welty the person, photographer, and writer may have been a bit more politically inclined (towards progressive causes) than she was willing to admit. See especially Pollack and Marrs, 2001b.

14 Venice, Louisiana, is the terminal point for the final road on the southernmost point reachable by car on the Mississippi river.

15 For a study of how such love works in queer theory itself, see Restuccia, 2006.

16 For an unsurpassed theory of depersonalization as it relates to gay men, see Bersani, 1995.

17 There is an effort to change this by using stories to build peace. See http://guest bookproject.org/

References

Agamben, G. (2007). Whatever. In: *The coming community*. 6th ed. Translated by M. Hardt. Minneapolis, MN: University of Minnesota Press, pp. 1–3.

Berlant, L. (2011). *Cruel optimism*. Durham, NC: Duke University Press.

Bersani, L. (1995). *Homos*. Cambridge, MA: Harvard University Press.

Brown, W. (1995a). Rights and losses. In: *States of injury: Power and freedom in late modernity*. Princeton, NJ: Princeton University Press, pp. 96–134.

Brown, W. (1995b). Wounded attachments. In: *States of injury: Power and freedom in late modernity*. Princeton, NJ: Princeton University Press, pp. 52–76.

Brown, W. (2001). *Politics out of history*. Princeton, NJ: Princeton University Press.

Buckley, Jr., W. (1984). "The southern imagination": An interview with Eudora Welty and Walker Percy." In: P. Whitman Prenshaw, ed., *Conversations with Eudora Welty*. Jackson, MI: University Press of Mississippi, pp. 92–114.

Dean, T. (2009). Cruising as a way of life. In: *Unlimited intimacy: Reflections on the subculture of barebacking*. Chicago, IL: University of Chicago Press, pp. 176–212.

Deleuze, G. and Guattari, F. (1987). Introduction: Rhizome. In: *A thousand plateaus: Capitalism and schizophrenia*. Minneapolis, MN: University of Minnesota Press, pp. 3–25.

Derrida, J. (2000). *Of hospitality: Anne Dufourmantelle invites Jacques Derrida to respond*. Stanford, CA: Stanford University Press.

Devlin, A. (2002). Eudora Welty. In: C. Perry and M. Weaks, eds, *The history of southern women's literature*. Baton Rouge, LA: Louisiana State University Press, pp. 391–398.

Edelman, L. (2007). *No future: Queer theory and the death drive*. Durham, NC: Duke University Press.

Halperin, D. (2017). Introduction: The war on sex. In: D. Halperin and T. Hoppe, eds, *The war on sex*. Durham, NC: Duke University Press, pp. 1–61.

Halperin, D. and Hoppe, T., eds (2017). *The war on sex*. Durham, NC: Duke University Press.

How gay is Pakistan? (2015). Film. Directed by K. Masood. England and Pakistan: BBC and Netflix.

Jackson, H. (2014). *The death of "family values"? Let's hope*. Available at: www.wbur.org/cognoscenti/2014/10/09/family-values-scotus-gay-marriage-holly-jackson [Accessed March 1, 2018].

Marrs, S. (2005). "The strong present tense": On and off the road 1974–1980. In: *Eudora Welty: A biography*. Orlando, FL: Harcourt, pp. 396–445.

McClennen, S. and Schultheis Moore, A. (2015). Introduction: Aporia and affirmative critique: Mapping the landscape of literary approaches to human rights research. In: S. McClennen and A. Schultheis Moore, eds, *The Routledge companion to literature and human rights*. New York: Routledge, pp. 1–19.

McMahand, D. and Murphy, K. (2014). "Remember right": Disenfranchised grief and the commemoration of queer bodies in Welty's fiction and life. *Eudora Welty Review*, 6(1), pp. 69–82.

Michaels, W.B. (2003). Absalom, Absalom! The difference between white men and white men. In: R. Hamblin and A. Abadie, eds. *Faulkner in the twenty-first century: Faulkner and Yoknapatawpha, 2000*. Jackson, MI: University Press of Mississippi, pp. 137–153.

Michaels, W.B. (2006). *The trouble with diversity: How we learned to love identity and ignore inequality*. New York: Picador.

Mullins, G. (2015). Queer rights? In: S. McClennen and A. Schultheis Moore, eds, *The Routledge companion to literature and human rights*. New York: Routledge, pp. 53–59.

Najambadi, A. (2013). *Professing selves: Transsexuality and same-sex desire in contemporary Iran*. Durham, NC: Duke University Press.

Nissen, A. (2003). Queer Welty, camp Welty. *Mississippi Quarterly*, 56(2), pp. 209–230.

North, J. (2017). *Literary criticism: A concise political history*. Cambridge, MA: Harvard University Press.

O'Connor, F. (2013). *A prayer journal*. New York: Farrar, Straus and Giroux.

Pollack, H. and Marrs, S., eds (2001a). *Eudora Welty and politics: Did the writer crusade?* Baton Rouge, LA: Louisiana State University Press.

Pollack, H. and Marrs, S. (2001b). Seeing Welty's political vision in her photographs. In: H. Pollack and S. Marrs, eds, *Eudora Welty and politics: Did the writer crusade?* Baton Rouge, LA: Louisiana State University Press, pp. 223–251.

Pratt, L. (2011). Close reading the present: Eudora Welty's Queer Politics. In: E. McCallum and M. Tuhkanen, eds, *Queer times, queer becomings*. Albany, NY: State University of New York Press, pp. 183–204.

Pratt, L. (2016). *The strangers book: The human of African American literature*. Philadelphia, PA: University of Pennsylvania Press.

Rahita Seshadri, K. (2011). The time of hospitality – again. In: R. Kearney and K. Semonovitch, eds, *Phenomenologies of the stranger: Between hostility and hospitality*. New York: Fordham University Press, pp. 126–141.

Restuccia, F.L. (2006). *Amorous acts: Lacanian ethics in modernism, film, and queer theory*. Stanford, CA: Stanford University Press.

Richards, G. (2018). Queering Welty's male bodies in the undergraduate classroom. In: M. Miller Claxton and J. Eichelberger, eds, *Teaching the works of Eudora Welty: Twenty-first century approaches*. Jackson, MI: University Press of Mississippi, pp. 109–114.

Srikanth, R. (2012). Introduction: The landscape of empathy. In: *Constructing the enemy: Empathy/antipathy in US literature and law*. Philadelphia, PA: Temple University Press, pp. 1–40.

Stockton, K.B. (2009). *The queer child, or growing sideways in the twentieth century*. Durham, NC: Duke University Press.

Warner, M. (2000). *The trouble with normal: Sex, politics, and the ethics of queer life.* Cambridge, MA: Harvard University Press.

Welty, E. (1941a). The hitch-hikers. In: *Collected stories of Eudora Welty.* Orlando, FL: Harcourt, 1980, pp. 62–74.

Welty, E. (1941b). Why I live at the P.O. In: *Collected stories of Eudora Welty.* Orlando, FL: Harcourt, 1980, pp. 46–56.

Welty, E. (1955). No place for you, my love. In *Collected stories of Eudora Welty.* Orlando, FL: Harcourt, 1980, pp. 465–481.

Welty, E. (1956). Place in fiction. In *On writing.* New York: Modern Library, 2002, pp. 39–59.

Welty, E. (1965a). Must the novelist crusade? In: *On writing.* New York: Modern Library, 2002, pp. 74–88.

Welty, E. (1965b). On Faulknerian time. In *On William Faulkner.* Jackson, MI: University Press of Mississippi, 2003, pp. 57–62.

Welty, E. (1969). *The optimist's daughter.* New York: Vintage, 1990.

Welty, E. (1980). Preface. In *Collected stories of Eudora Welty.* Orlando, FL: Harcourt, pp. ix–xi.

Further reading

Bibler, M. (2009). *Cotton's queer relations: Same-sex intimacy and the literature of the southern plantation, 1936–1968.* Charlottesville, VA: University of Virginia Press.

Brown, C. (2012). The 1960s: Personal and political unrest. In: *A daring life: A biography of Eudora Welty.* Jackson, MI: University Press of Mississippi, pp. 59–66.

Critchley, S. (2011). The null basis-being of a nullity, or between two nothings: Heidegger's uncanniness. In: R. Kearney and K. Semonovitch, eds, *Phenomenologies of the stranger: Between hostility and hospitality.* New York: Fordham University Press, pp. 145–154.

Dawes, J. (2015). Human rights, literature, and empathy. In: S. McClennen and A. Schultheis Moore, eds, *The Routledge companion to literature and human rights.* New York: Routledge, pp. 427–432.

Fried, S. (2004). Sexuality and human rights. *Health and Human Rights*, 7(2), pp. 273–304.

Hasratian, A. (2007). The death of difference in Light in August. *Criticism: A Quarterly for Literature and the Arts*, 49(1), pp. 55–84.

Hoppe, T. (2017). Forward: Thinking sex and justice. In: D. Halperin and T. Hoppe, eds, *The war on sex.* Durham, NC: Duke University Press, pp. ix–xi.

Howard, J. (1999). *Men like that: A southern queer history.* Chicago, IL: University of Chicago Press.

Kearney, R. and Semonovitch, K. (2011). At the threshold: Foreigners, strangers, others. In: R. Kearney and K. Semonovitch, eds, *Phenomenologies of the stranger: Between hostility and hospitality.* New York: Fordham University Press, pp. 3–29.

Kreyling, M. (2004). Free Eudora! *American Literary History*, 16(4). pp. 758–768.

Muñoz, J.E. (2009). *Cruising utopia: The then and there of queer futurity.* New York: New York University Press.

Nussbaum, M. (2013). *Political emotions: Why love matters for justice.* Cambridge, MA: Harvard University Press.

Pitavy-Souques, D. (2014). "Moments of truth": Eudora Welty's humanism. *Eudora Welty Review*, 6(1), pp. 9–26.

Project, G. (2018). Home. Guestbook project. Available at: http://guestbookproject. org/ [Accessed March 1, 2018].

Pugh, T. (2016). *Precious perversions: Humor, homosexuality, and the southern literary canon.* Baton Rouge, LA: Louisiana State University Press.

Sedgwick, E.K. (2003). *Touching feeling: Affect, pedagogy, performativity.* Durham, NC: Duke University Press.

Sessums, K. (2007). Skeeter Davis, Noël Coward, and Eudora Welty. In: *Mississippi sissy.* New York: Picador, pp 27–39.

Traber, D. (2007). (Silenced) transgression in Eudora Welty's The Optimist's Daughter . *Critique,* 48(2), pp. 184–196.

Treanor, B. (2011). Putting hospitality in its place. In: R. Kearney and K. Semonovitch, eds, *Phenomenologies of the stranger: Between hostility and hospitality.* New York: Fordham University Press, pp. 49–66.

Welty, E. (1984). *One writer's beginnings.* Cambridge, MA: Harvard University Press.

17 On the human right to peace in times of contemporary colonial power

Adriana Rincón Villegas

Introduction

Over the last few decades, international organizations such as the United Nations (UN) have opened the debate on giving peace the status of a human right. Scholars who theorize about the right to peace classify it as a *third-generation* right.[1] Third-generation rights, also called *collective* or *solidarity* rights, refer to protection from threats such as "gross material disparity, massive environmental degradation, and global war" (Woods, 2013, p. 194). In December 2016, the UN General Assembly (UNGA) adopted the "Declaration on the Right to Peace". Although this right has not yet been codified in any legally binding international body of law, the categorization of peace as a right and its inclusion in the international legal system has been a topic of debate for decades. More importantly, this debate has evolved in parallel with the process of global human rights propagation. As peace is linked to the rights to life and dignity, advocates of the right to peace have claimed that peace is the foundation of all other rights.

In spite of the massive proliferation of human rights in the international legal system of the last few decades – including the right to peace – egregious human rights violations continue to happen globally, on a daily basis. What would be the added value the conceptualization of peace as a human right brings to the international human rights legal system? What are the values the right to peace aims to protect and to guarantee? Does legally protecting the right to peace include fighting social injustice? Or, on the contrary, could the right to peace be a rhetoric statement that aims to appease the struggle for social justice?

The goal of this paper is twofold. First, I aim to critically engage the notion of peace as a human right from a decolonial theory perspective, by analyzing its ineffectiveness in fighting social injustice, and its claimed but unfulfilled promise of universality. I argue that the discourse of human rights has proven to be not only insufficient to protect the rights of the marginalized, but also complicit to the continuity of structural violence and social inequality. I also explore how the idea of "the human" in human rights is conceived under the logics of the coloniality of power that comes back from the conquest of America and persists today. Second, I aim to explore the legal conceptualization of the right to peace through the case of Colombia, which is one of the few examples where peace is explicitly defined as a human right in their national constitution.

For that purpose, this paper is divided into four parts. First, I explain the concept of coloniality of power and how it works to produce a discourse of human rights whose full benefits are dependent on factors of race, gender, and other systems of oppression. Second, I present an analysis from critical peace studies of the indetermination and vagueness of the notion of peace, and describe how peace has been coopted by the discourse of liberal democracy. Third, I analyze selected UNGA resolutions, in order to understand the origins of the conceptualization of peace as a human right in the international community, based on the theoretical framework presented in the two previous sections. Finally, I analyze the case of peace as a human right in Colombia, and raise questions about what it specifically means for a war-torn country to constitutionally protect the right to peace. I will conclude summarizing the main points of the paper and raising some questions for further debate. This article is part of a larger research project in the process of completion, and it presents reflections based on my pre-dissertation research in Colombia during the summer of 2017.[2]

Coloniality of power and human rights

Decolonial theory aims to unveil the colonial power that is present in and pervasive of modernity. Along with postcolonial theory, it departs from the idea that the end of colonialism as a geopolitical institution has not translated into a real eradication of colonial oppression.

> On the contrary, what has happened is a transformation from modern to global colonialism, which has been possible thanks to global capitalist institutions such as the World Bank and the International Monetary Fund, as well as military institutions such as NATO, intelligence agencies such as the Pentagon, and international cooperation from the North. In short, what have changed are the types of domination, not the structure of the center-periphery relation.
>
> (Curiel, 2014, p. 49, my translation)

Quijano (2000, 2007) proposes that the conquest and colonization of America triggered a radical and definitive change in the configuration of social and political power. Race, as an essential instrument of oppression, determined labor, economic, domestic, and political relations. Racialization brought by the imperial colonial power established a system of privilege that, ultimately, denied the essence of humanness to entire conquered populations, and by dispossessing them from their history, religion, and resources, they excluded them from the category of "humans." He calls this configuration of power the *coloniality of power*. For Quijano:

That specific basic element of the new pattern of world power that was based on the idea of "race" and in the "racial" social classification of world population – expressed in the "racial" distribution of work, in the imposition of new "racial" geocultural identities, in the concentration of the control of productive resources and capital, as social relations, including salary, as a privilege of "Whiteness" – is what basically is referred to in the category of coloniality of power.

(2000, p. 128)

This configuration of power did not disappear in modernity, but it was essential to its development and it persists in the present, as the ideas of superiority and inferiority derived from this racialized pattern of world power became naturalized in society. They dictate relations of production, (racialized and gendered) division of work, assumptions on capability and merit, and knowledge production. In short, the very existence of modernity is structured and determined by the coloniality of power, of knowing, and of being (Maldonado-Torres 2017, p. 118). In the case of Latin America in particular, the colonial legacy dating from the conquest in the 15th century persists in the present. As Mignolo (2011) states, today, the so-called Global South is at the receiving end of globalization, and it is the site where the consequences of its flaws are reflected in the limited access and in the permanent violation of human rights.

Far from being neutral and value-free postulates, the discourse of rights and the ideal of the human are embedded in the discourse of liberal democracy. Why is this problematic? First, the market economy is based on accumulation of capital, which has trigged an unprecedented landscape of exploitation, inequality, environmental degradation, violence, poverty, and hunger. Liberal democracy not only does not challenge the foundations of capitalism, but it promotes them under the flags of people's protection from fear and want. Second, the discourse of human rights was originally conceived on a particular understanding of who its beneficiaries were supposed to be. "From the sixteenth century to the Universal Declaration of Human Rights, He who speaks for the human is an actor embodying the Western ideal of being Christian, being man and being human" (Mignolo, 2009, p. 10). In consequence, everyone who did (and does) not match this idealized figure (for reasons of gender, race, class, sexuality, ability, religion, etc.) ended up excluded from the benefits derived from the full enjoyment of human rights.

Echoing Mignolo (2009) I ask, how accessible and universal is the notion of "human" in human rights? Since the coloniality of power is based on particular understandings of human superiority and inferiority, the discourse of human rights is certainly part and parcel of the construction of the idea of "the human" conceived in modernity. As Maldonado-Torres (2017, p. 117) points out, "the universality of human rights is delimited by what is considered to effectively constitute the state of being human in the first place." Critical human rights scholars such as Hunt (2007) and Mignolo

(2009) complicate these assumptions of human rights' universality and neutrality. They argue that the ideas of human and humanity are not originally conceived as all-inclusive as the human rights legal documents claim. In the 18th century, Hunt (2007, p. 18) points out, the multiple references to the equality of "all men" were only directed to a privileged white male elite, excluding "those without property, slaves, free blacks, in some cases religious minorities, and always and everywhere, women." In short, despite the multiple formal international instruments that create an increasing number of rights and liberties for "all people," the basis in which the human rights discourse is created grants privilege to certain groups over others. Can we sustain theoretically or empirically that the access to freedom of speech is the same for a white male in Canada as for an indigenous queer woman in Colombia? Is the access to an inclusive, non-racist education a feasible goal in all countries of the world? If peace is a human right, does everybody benefit the same way from it?

Liberal peace as universal peace

The criticism to the right to peace does not refer only to its pretension of universality but to the indetermination of the very notion of peace. Innumerable references to peace are present in national and international legal instruments, yet peace as a concept is usually not defined or questioned. Critical peace scholars such as Richmond (2005), Roy (2006), and Ross (2011) emphasize the need for decolonizing global (liberal) conceptualizations of peace, as these narratives support the agenda of global liberalism that directly produces and perpetuates social inequality.

Richmond (2005, 2010, 2012, 2014) focuses specifically on the task of engaging the concept of peace as problematic. He departs from the assumption that peace is not a universal, homogeneous concept but a multiple set of discourses, and he calls for types of research that "examine competing concepts and discourses of peace, as opposed to accepting as unproblematic the orthodoxy that involves starting with a conception of peace as an ideal form and then exporting it through the forms of intervention inherent to peace-building approaches into conflict environments" (Richmond, 2005, p. 6.) For him, the UN discourse of peace (what critical peace scholarship calls *liberal* peace) is instrumental to the market economy system, which makes it complicit to the normalized structural violence of capitalism that includes inequality, poverty, and social injustice.

Roy (2006) and Ross (2011) also problematize liberal peace. For Ross (2011, p. 198), peace is not only a concept in need of definition, but it is often a discourse co-opted by those in power: "The power to advocate for peace has often been appropriated by the winners of social conflict as a means of forcing the losers to shut-up and stop struggling." In the same vein, Roy (2006) coined the term "putative peace" in order to define this hegemonic and imposed peace that perpetuates marginalization and inequality.

This article answers Ross, Roy, and Richmond's call for analyzing peace through critical lenses. Although several measures are created, revised, and modified in different legal instances, the notions of peace embedded in those initiatives are rarely explored or problematized.

Peace as a human right: the United Nations General Assembly

The goal of this section is to explore the origins, meaning, and scope of the right to peace. For that purpose, I chose UNGA resolutions for my critical discourse analysis, in order to trace the evolution of the notion of peace in the international legal system. Particularly, I am interested in answering the following questions: what kind of peace does the internationally recognized "right to peace" refer to? Does the right to peace claim to guarantee the absence of physical violence, liberal democracy, or social justice? In order to understand how the UN has defined peace, I conducted critical discourse analysis on selected UNGA resolutions of its 72 regular sessions, from 1946 to 2017. I found important variations to the idea of peace through this time frame.

Before 1978, the UNGA did not explicitly define peace as a human right. Most mentions of peace in resolutions from sessions 1 to 32 referred to negative peace[3] (the mere absence of physical violence), as they created measures of weapons and nuclear power control. However, some resolutions did establish direct links between peace and human rights. A/RES/5/381 (1950) and A/RES/9/819 (1954) declare that peace is only possible when freedom of speech and access to information (first-generation rights) are protected. Further, A/RES/4/290 (1949) establishes the "Essentials of Peace" or basic principles of peace among nations. It establishes the promotion of international cooperation, protection of the Universal Declaration of Human Rights, and the prohibition of violating the UN Charter (1945). Interestingly, these two resolutions define peace beyond mere absence of violence but as inextricably linked with human rights protection.

It was not until 1978 that the UNGA explicitly proclaimed that all individuals and nations had the inherent right to live in peace. A/RES/33/73 established the "Declaration on the Preparation of Societies for Life in Peace," where it reaffirms "the right of individuals, states, and all mankind to life in peace" through the observance of eight principles as preconditions for protecting the right to life in peace, which include negative peace measures such as weapon control and positive (liberal) peace measures such as international cooperation. In 1984, the UNGA established the "Declaration of the Right of Peoples to Peace" (A/RES/39/11), which mostly refers to weapon control measures and the prevention of nuclear war.

Following Galtung's categorization, I found that most of the resolutions prior to 1990 conceptualize peace as the mere absence of physical violence, as they focus exclusively on measures related to weapon control and prevention of war. Structural and socio-economic violence were not included or conceptualized within the realm of the right to peace. An interesting shift happened in 1990, when the UNGA established that the right of peoples to peace implied protection of other first-generation rights such as sovereign equality, political independence and territorial integrity, non-intervention, peaceful dispute settlement, equal rights and self-determination of peoples, respect of human rights, and international cooperation (A/RES/45/14).

This conceptualization of peace (what critical peace scholars would call *liberal peace*) remains constant in subsequent resolutions. In 1999, A/RES/54/ 54 established that measures of arms control and disarmament, demobiliza-tion, and reintegration mechanisms were prerequisites for social and eco-nomic development, which were essential for consolidating peace. This narrative introduces a direct link between development and peace. In its 58th session (A/RES/58/192, 2003), the UNGA established peace as a vital requirement for the promotion and protection of other rights, including the *right to development*. For the first time development was declared a human right, and interestingly, the link between the rights to peace and develop-ment continues to permeate the narrative today. In 2005, A/RES/60/163 explicitly declared that, "The deep fault line that divides human society between the rich and the poor, and the ever-increasing gap between the developed and the developing worlds pose a major threat to global prosperity, peace and security, and stability" (no. 2).

This new perspective on the right to peace has been broadly discussed over the last five years in the regular sessions of the UNGA. Also, the Human Rights Council, in Resolution 20/15, established a working group in order to draft a UNGA resolution on the right to peace. Finally, in 2017, the UNGA launched the "Declaration on the Right to Peace" (A/RES/71/189) which defined peace as follows: "Peace is not only the absence of conflict but also requires a positive, dynamic, participatory process, where dialogue is encouraged and conflicts are solved in a spirit of mutual understanding and cooperation, and socioeconomic development is ensured" (p. 3).

The notion of peace has shifted in the international legal system of human rights from referring merely to the establishment of limits to war, to being determined by the pursuit of socio-economic development, international cooperation, and liberal democracy. In short, peace is only possible when "socio-economic development is ensured." Peace *becomes* development. In consequence, peace becomes complicit to – if not a direct site of – the maladies of the market economy, and importantly, to the inclusion and exclusion from its benefits.

Social injustice in times of "the right to peace": the case of Colombia

This section aims to raise the question on the beneficiaries of peace. Who are the "humans" imagined by the "human right to peace"? For that purpose, I explore the specific case of Colombia, as one of the few examples of the categorization of peace as a human right in its legal system. I ask, in a country that faced more than five decades of armed conflict, what does it mean to legalize (in this case, to constitutionalize) the right to peace? Colombia was the first Latin American state (and one of the few worldwide) that explicitly included the right to peace in its national constitution. Although some other Latin American constitutions include peace as a state goal, they do not give peace the constitutional status of a human right. This process was triggered both by the influence of social movements in the country in the 1980s, certain peace processes in the 1980s and early 1990s, and the global shift towards human rights that importantly impacted legal systems in Latin America.

After decades of violent conflict, the 1990s marked the beginning of a new peace process with guerrilla groups, and the adoption of a new constitution in Colombia. Guerrilla groups such as the April 19th Movement, the Popular Liberation Movement, and the *Campesino Indígena Quintín Lame* movement signed peace agreements in 1990 and 1991. As a result of these peace negotiations, the national constitution of 1886 was replaced with a new one, which explicitly established peace as a foundational pillar of the nation. Indeed, the 1991 Constitution was known as "La Constitución de la Paz" (the Peace Constitution). For the first time in the country's history, the Colombian legal system granted peace the status of *a constitutional right*. However, it was never clear how to operationalize the right to peace, what its scope was, or how to access it. Lemaitre (2011, p. 12) argues that the members of the 1991 Assembly had different conceptualizations in mind on what they called the right to peace: "Peace as distributive justice, peace as human rights protection, peace as absence of war, or peace as order and respect to the rule of law." As a consequence, Lemaitre observes,

> The word *peace*, repeated infinitely from the first to the last day of the Assembly debates, arrived to the fourth of July of 1991[4] transformed into the most intangible of all rights. The right to peace of art.22 was the most emblematic example of how a right, all rights, can mean nothing and can generate empty agreements between political enemies and contested ideologies.
>
> (p. 17, my translation)

As innovative and ambitious as it was, this constitutional inclusion did not prevent Colombia from the intensification of war in the upcoming years. The groups who did not demobilize in the early 1990s expanded their territorial control and exponentially strengthened their military capability. As a consequence, millions of Colombians suffered mass violence in many parts of the country throughout the 1990s up to the present. Between January 1, 1985 and September 1, 2018, illegal armed groups assassinated 267,658 people, expelled 7,434,999 people from their homes, kidnapped 32,695 people, and committed sexual crimes against 26,374 individuals (Unidad para la Atención y Reparación Integral a las Víctimas, 2018). Women are significantly and uniquely affected by war in Colombia, but they – especially those women who are especially marginalized because of their race, class, or sexual orientation – have little voice in the decision-making processes related to peace in Colombia (Meertens, 2016; Chaparro and Martínez, 2016). LGTBQ+ individuals from rural areas were often targeted and suffered brutal violence during the Colombian conflict, yet they were given few opportunities to participate in the writing and consolidation of the peace accords. The voices of indigenous people who were also disproportionately affected by violence and displacement were often excluded and their participation was limited to the final stages of the agreement (El Tiempo, 2016). This raises important but unaddressed questions as to what these peace initiatives mean for the historically marginalized communities in the country.

On September 26, 2016, with the assistance of a UN verification mission, the Revolutionary Armed Forces of Colombia (FARC) and the national government of Colombia signed a peace agreement. After reaching a consensus on the accords, the parties proposed a referendum for citizen approval of the peace agreement. However, in October 2016, Colombian citizens voted NO in that referendum. Scholars and analysts have explained this negative outcome in a variety of ways – from extreme weather that impacted voting to a strong and politicized campaign against the peace accords from the Colombian right wing. A revised version of the agreement was eventually signed on November 24, 2016. However, despite the approval of the agreement, violence is still happening systematically in the country, especially against social leaders. According to the Colombian non-governmental organization Indepaz, from 2016 to 2017, 289 social leaders were killed, 116 in 2016 and 173 in 2017 (González Perafán and Delgado Bolaños, 2018, p. 4).

Peace has been a constitutional right in Colombia since 1991, and it has maintained a territorial, localized approach since 2016. For the Colombian legal system, this means that the whole legal architecture of the state has to be aligned with/built around the protection and guarantee of the right to peace. However, while peace is one of the constitutional goals, principles, values, and rights of the state, it seems as though the institutional design of peace has not been enough to prevent the country from experiencing the intensification and brutality of war. In that sense, what would be the added value the conceptualization of peace as a human right brings to the Colombian legal system? What are the values the right to peace aims to protect and to guarantee in Colombia? Is the right to peace a rhetoric mechanism that aims to appease the struggle for social justice in Colombia?

Conclusion

In this article, I have explored the idea of peace as a human right both theoretically and in two specific legal settings: UNGA resolutions and the Colombian legal system. First, I critically engaged the notion of peace as a human right from a decolonial perspective. I joined decolonial theory scholars when they point out how "the human" in human rights is conceived under the logics of exclusion inherited from colonial power. With that framework in mind, I traced the origins of the right to peace through selected UNGA resolutions. I collected and analyzed selected UNGA resolutions from its regular sessions from 1946 to 2017, which allowed me to understand the variations on the UN's notions of peace through time. I concluded that the current notion of the right to peace alludes to the right to *liberal* peace, that is, a conceptualization of peace linked to the values – and flaws – of liberal democracy and the market economy. I pointed out how this narrow interpretation of peace is problematic. First, its claim of universality may justify imposing Western values – such as liberal peace – to non-Western communities with no regard to their own interpretations of what peace should look like. As Mutua states, "human rights represent the attempted diffusion and further development at the international level of the liberal political tradition" (Mutua, 2001, p. 592). The coloniality of power in liberal peace raises questions on who its beneficiaries are, as this kind of peace does not challenge unequal configurations of power and structural violence. Second, through abiding to liberal democracy, liberal peace becomes complicit – or compatible at the very least – with the social injustice and inequality that liberalism produces.

This article raised questions about the case of the right to peace in Colombia. The right to peace was included in the 1991 Colombian national constitution. This constitutional inclusion did not prevent the country from the intensification of war in the upcoming years. As a consequence, millions of Colombians, especially those who have been historically marginalized, suffered mass violence in many parts of the country throughout the 1990s to the present. The Colombian government led multiple transitional justice initiatives, and also led a peace process that concluded with the peace accords of 2016. However, these processes raise questions regarding who got included and excluded from the decision-making process, as well as who will benefit from it. How does the inclusion of peace as a human right actually contribute to peace in Colombia? Who is included and who is marginalized from the benefits that stem from legalizing peace as a human right?

It is undeniable that peace as a human right is a magnetic idea. In theory, it implies that peace does not exist as a concession by the powerful but as a given, as an innate, sacred feature of human existence. However, I argue that it is necessary to unpack the meanings, scope, and assumptions of the right to peace in order to determine its flaws and unfulfilled promises. As Freeman (2011) states, "There is obviously a wide gap between the promises of the 1948 Declaration and the real world of human-rights violations" (p. 5).

Discussion questions

1   What would be the importance of formally recognizing the right to peace in national and international bodies of law? What difference – if any – would this categorization make?

2   What is the relationship between the right to peace and social justice? Does achieving peace necessarily mean achieving a more equal and inclusive society?

3   What would be the role of gender oppression in the configuration of power of modernity –what Quijano calls the "coloniality of power"?

Notes

1 Scholars classify human rights in *generations* (depending on their chronological appearance – not its hierarchy). According to Woods (2013, p. 193), "while first-generation Lockean rights sought to protect the individual from the emerging public power, the territorial state, second-generation economic, social, and cultural rights reacted to the devastating impact of industrial capitalism on the individual's ability to satisfy basic needs, i.e., the interplay of public and private power."

2 My preliminary research was assisted by participation in the University of Massachusetts Boston-SSRC Transdisciplinary Dissertation Proposal Development Program with funds provided by the Andrew W. Mellon Foundation.

3 Galtung (1969) categorizes the meaning of peace into two groups: negative peace (i.e., mere absence of physical violence,) and positive peace (i.e., the absence of structural violence).

4 This was the day the 1991 constitution entered into force.

References

Chaparro, N. and Martínez, M. (2016). Negociando desde los márgenes: La participación política de las mujeres en los procesos de paz en Colombia (1982–2016). Documentos 29, Ideas para Construir la Paz. Bogotá: DeJusticia.

Curiel, O. (2014). Construyendo metodologías feministas desde el feminismo decolonial. Otras formas de (re)conocer. In: I.M. Azkue, M. Luxán, M. Legarreta, G. Guzmán, I. Zirion, J. Carballo, ed., *Reflexiones, herramientas y aplicaciones desde la investigación feminista*. Donostia-San Sebastian: Hegoa.

El Tiempo (2016). Indígenas visitan a las delegaciones de paz. Available at: www.eltiempo.com/archivo/documento/CMS-16630582 [Accessed May 13, 2018].

Freeman, M. (2011). *Human rights: An interdisciplinary approach*. Boston, MA: Polity.

Galtung, J. (1969). Violence, peace, and peace research. *Journal of Peace Research*, 6(3), pp. 167–191.

González Perafán, L. and Delgado Bolaños, C. (2018). Homicidio de defensores y defensoras de paz: Una tragedia que no se detiene. *INDEPAZ, Ideas Verdes, Análisis Político*, 6, pp. 1–10.

Hunt, L. (2007). *Inventing human rights*. New York: W.W. Norton & Company.

Lemaitre Ripoll, J. (2011). *La paz en cuestion: La guerra y la paz en la Asamblea Constituyente de 1991*. Bogotá: Universidad de los Andes.

Maldonado-Torres, N. (2017). On the coloniality of human rights. *Revista Crítica de Ciências Sociais*, 114, pp. 117–136.

Meertens, D. (2016). Justicia de género y tierras en Colombia: Desafíos para la era del "pos-acuerdo." *European Review of Latin American and Caribbean Studies*, 102, pp. 89–100.

Mignolo, W. (2009). Who speaks for the "human" in human rights? *Hispanic Issues On Line*, 5(1), pp. 7–24.

Mignolo, W. (2011). The Global South and world dis/order. *Journal of Anthropological Research*, 67(2), pp. 165–188.

Mutua, M. (2001). Savages, victims, and saviors: The metaphor of human rights. *Harvard International Law Journal*, 42(1), pp. 201–245.

OHCHR (2012). Resolution A/HRC/20/15. Available at: www.ohchr.org/EN/NewsE vents/Pages/DisplayNews.aspx?NewsID=20252&LangID=E#sthash.QIuCHKaN.dp uf [Accessed February 13, 2018].

Quijano, A. (2000). Coloniality of power and eurocentrism in Latin America. *International Sociology*, 15(2), pp. 215–232.

Quijano, A. (2007). Coloniality and modernity/rationality. *Cultural Studies*, 21(2–3), pp. 168–178.

Richmond, O.P. (2005). *The transformation of peace*. Basingstoke: Palgrave Macmillan.

Richmond, O.P. (2010). Resistance and the post-liberal peace. *Millennium*, 38(3), pp. 665–692.

Richmond, O.P. (2012). *A post-liberal peace*. New York: Routledge.

Richmond, O.P. (2014). *Peace: A very short introduction*. Oxford: Oxford University Press.

Ross, A. (2011). Neo-missionaries and the polemics of helping. *Expositions: An Interdisciplinary Journal of the Humanities*, 5(2), pp. 103–110.

Roy, A. (2006). *Ordinary person's guide to empire*. New Delhi: Penguin Books India.

UN General Assembly (1948). Universal Declaration of Human Rights, 10 December, 217 A (III). Available at: www.refworld.org/docid/3ae6b3712c.html [Accessed January 11, 2018].

UN General Assembly (1950). Resolution 5/381, Condemnation of propaganda against peace, A/RES/5/381. Available at: undocs.org/A/RES/5/381 [Accessed February 4, 2018].

UN General Assembly (1954). Resolution 9/819, Strengthening of peace through the removal of barriers to free exchange of information and ideas, A/RES/9/819. Available at: undocs.org/A/RES/9/819 [Accessed February 4, 2018].

UN General Assembly (1978). Resolution 33/73, Declaration on the preparation of societies for life in peace, A/RES/33/73. Available at: undocs.org/A/RES/33/73 [Accessed February 4, 2018].

UN General Assembly (1984). Resolution 40/11, The Right of Peoples to peace, A/RES/41/10. Available at: undocs.org/A/RES/40/11 [Accessed February 4, 2018].

UN General Assembly (1986). Resolution 39/11, Declaration of the Rights of peoples to peace, A/RES/39/11 Available at: undocs.org/A/RES/39/11 [Accessed February 4, 2018].

UN General Assembly (1986). Resolution 41/10, Right of Peoples to peace, A/RES/41/10. Available at: undocs.org/A/RES/41/10 [Accessed February 4, 2018].

UN General Assembly (1990). Resolution 45/14, Implementation of the Declaration on the Right of Peoples to Peace, A/RES/45/14. Available at: undocs.org/A/RES/45/14 [Accessed February 4, 2018].

UN General Assembly (1999). Resolution 54/54, Consolidation of Peace through practical disarmament measures, A/RES/54/54. Available at: undocs.org/A/RES/54/54 [Accessed February 4, 2018].

UN General Assembly (2003). Resolution 58/192, Promotion of peace as a vital requirement for the full enjoyment of all human rights by all, A/RES/58/192. Available at: undocs.org/A/RES/58/192 [Accessed February 4, 2018].

UN General Assembly (2005). Resolution 60/163, Promotion of peace as a vital requirement for the full enjoyment of all human rights by all, A/RES/60/163. Available at: undocs.org/A/RES/60/163 [Accessed February 4, 2018].

UN General Assembly (2017). Resolution 71/189, Declaration on the right to peace, A/RES/71/189. Available at: undocs.org/A/RES/71/189 [Accessed February 4, 2018].

Unidad para la Atención y Reparación Integral a las Víctimas (2018). Registro Único de Víctimas (RUV). Available at: https://www.unidadvictimas.gov.co/es/regis tro-unico-de-victimas-ruv/37394 [Accessed September 16, 2018].

United Nations (1945). Charter of the United Nations, 24 October 1945, 1 UNTS XVI. Available at: www.refworld.org/docid/3ae6b3930.html [Accessed January 11, 2018].

Woods, J. (2013). Theorizing peace as a human right. In: *Human Rights and International Legal Discourse*, 7. New Orleans: Loyola University New Orleans College of Law Legal Studies Research Paper 2014–2002, pp. 178–236 Available at: https:// ssrn.com/abstract=2419109 [Accessed February 5, 2018].

Further reading

Barreto, J.M., ed. (2013). *Human rights from a third world perspective: Critique, history and international law*. Newcastle: Cambridge Scholars Publishing.

Escobar, A. (1995). *Encountering development: The making and unmaking of the third world*. Princeton, NJ: Princeton University Press.

Maldonado-Torres, N. (2007). On the coloniality of being: Contributions to the development of a concept. *Cultural Studies* 21(2–3), pp. 240–270.

18 Beyond dignity

A case study of the mis/use of human rights discourse in development campaigns

Chris Bobel

"Dignity can't wait"

These three words are framed and on display in the Kampala offices of Days for Girls (DfG) Uganda, part of a global network that provides cloth menstrual pads and health education to girls in need in the Global South (Days for Girls, 2016). DfG was founded in 2008 by Celeste Mergens when she was working for a non-governmental organization (NGO) running a Kenyan orphanage. One night she woke up with a start, wondering how the girls dealt with their periods. The answer stunned Mergens: They remained in their dormitory room and bled on cardboard scraps. She established DfG to meet what she regarded as a desperate need – menstrual products (www.daysfor girls.org). For DfG, girls' dignity hinges on their access to menstrual pads.

DfG is part of a rapidly growing development subsector known as Menstrual Hygiene Management (MHM) which arose out efforts to close the education gap for girls in low- and middle-income countries, initially spearheaded by those working in the water sanitation and hygiene (WASH) sector. Today, MHM cuts across many development agendas and is gaining traction in public health research and advocacy (Sommer et al., 2015). Across the globe, I/NGOs and social enterprises, United Nations (UN) agencies, donors, academics, and corporations are shining an unprecedented light on menstruation – an experience shared by nearly all females[1] and yet one that is poorly understood and generally shrouded in shame (Johnston-Robledo and Chrisler, 2013; Bobel, 2010). The most widely circulated definition of MHM is:

> Women & adolescent girls are using a clean menstrual management material to absorb or collect blood that can be changed in privacy as often as necessary for the duration of the menstrual period, using soap and water for washing the body as required, and having access to facilities to dispose of used menstrual management materials.
>
> (Sommer and Sahin, 2013, p. 1557)[2]

Consistent with this definition, the lion's share of MHM initiatives are focused on providing access to menstrual care materials, though some provide puberty and/or menstrual health education, advocate for menstrual-friendly policies, and/or address infrastructure needs, such as access to water and latrines. By my count, approximately 130 MHM campaigns are active in 36 countries of the Global South.[3] About 75 percent are NGOs, like DfG, while the remaining fourth are social enterprises, such as Rwanda-based Sustainable Health Enterprises who uses a microfinance model to provide small grants to local women to manufacture and sell single-use pads. Notably, 42 percent of these organizations are founded and/or led by Westerners. MHM, together with many development efforts, draws on discourses of human rights to compellingly articulate issues and a call for urgent action. But in some limited cases, their invocation can misdirect intervention. In this chapter, I consider such a case through a critique of the ways MHM deploys the key human rights frame of *dignity*.

My analysis draws on textual analysis of 45 MHM organizations' online materials, participant observation with eight of these organizations in the field, and in-depth interviews with 70 individuals doing MHM work. I analyzed this data using feminist critical discourse analysis, a hybrid method combining feminist studies and critical discourse analysis "with the aim of advancing rich and nuanced analyses of the complex workings of powers and ideology in discourse in sustaining (hierarchically) gendered social orders" (Lazar, 2007, p. 141).

Bridging MHM to human rights

As American political theorist Charles Beitz (2013) asserts, "The idea of human dignity is ubiquitous in the contemporary discourse of Human Rights" (p. 259), and legal scholar Oscar Schachter (1983) once wrote, "No other ideal seems so clearly accepted as a social good" (p. 849). Dignity appears in the Preamble of the Charter of the UN as well as the Universal Declaration of 1948 in the first line of the Preamble: "Whereas recognition of the inherent dignity and of the equal and inalienable rights of all members of the human family is the foundation of freedom, justice and peace in the world." And it appears in the first article of the same document:

> Article 1.
> All human beings are born free and equal in dignity and rights. They are endowed with reason and conscience and should act towards one another in a spirit of brotherhood.

Many MHM advocates make the link to human rights by explicit referral to the Sustainable Development Goals (SDGs) – 17 targets that set the global development agenda. MHM is implicated in goals 3, 4, 5, 6, 8, and 12, or the rights to good health and wellbeing, quality education, gender equality, clean water and sanitation, decent work and economic growth, and responsible consumption and production, respectively. The goals are often linked to what feminist critical development scholars have dubbed "the girling of development"

(Hayhurst, 2011), or strategic efforts to focus on girls as economic levers of change.[4] MHM advocates fixate on how evidence of menstruation prevents the achievement of rights because it separates women from the world of men. That is, menstruation, or more precisely, the public disclosure of menstruation, presents a barrier to girls. This logic tethers human rights discourse to MHM, a process social movement scholars refer to as "frame bridging" or "linking of two or more ideologically congruent but structurally unconnected frames regarding a particular issue or problem" (Benford and Snow, 2000, p. 624). Tying MHM to human rights has enabled UN agencies, such as UNICEF and the Water Sanitation Supply Coordinating Council, to gain attention, currency, and, above all, urgency. This is an important move as menstruation, riddled with stigma and shame, is difficult to engage. Tapping into human rights discourse vis-à-vis the trope of dignity is a way to elevate the topic, to make it possible to talk about periods without actually talking about blood. This frame presents a curious paradox. While MHM advocates persistently challenge the stigma of menstruation through sloganeering such as "break the silence" and "smash the shame," they advocate concrete interventions focused on keeping menstruation hidden through "upgraded" menstrual care materials.[5] These strategies are typically neither indigenous nor traditional, often favoring Western-style single-use pads, cups, or cloth pads designed expressly for menstruation. Advocates claim that current means of menstrual management are unsafe and unhygienic despite a dearth of evidence to support this claim.[6]

My complaint is not with this general deployment of the human rights frame. Rather, I grow uneasy with how MHM discourse uses human rights discourse to accommodate stigma. MHM's focus on managing the menstrual body so that no evidence of menstruation is detected reifies the menstrual mandate of shame, silence, and secrecy. MHM, then, serves as a user's manual for disciplined embodiment, rather than a program for instituting the attitudinal change necessary to normalize menstruation. Below, I support this argument through selections of MHM's discourse of dignity in two categories – in the voices of NGOs and social business and even researchers.

MHM discourses of dignity

"Keeping dignity intact": NGOs and social businesses

Aakar Innovations (www.aakarinnovations.com), an Indian social business producing and selling what they claim is a 100 percent compostable single-use pad (the Anandi Pad), tweeted the following:

> AakarInnovations@aakarinnovation
> Aakar's 100% Compostable Menstrual hygiene Solution. Support us to empower every woman to live with dignity.
>
> (September 26, 2015)

Here, menstruator dignity hinges on access to an eco-friendly single-use commercial pad designed to replace the freely available repurposed cloth that Indian menstruators living in slums – Aakar's stated target group – typically use. As evidence, they include a poorly sourced claim on their homepage: "Today, only 12% of India's 335 million menstruating women use sanitary napkins to manage their menses (www.aakarinnovations.com)."[7]

Similarly, Be Girl (makers of a panty with a mesh pocket to hold a range of absorbents) clearly makes the dignity and product connection here: "We believe that every person has the right to own and feel pride in products that directly impact dignity... Fostering equality within gender is fundamental to achieving gender equality. Financial or social status should not dictate quality for menstrual products, which are intrinsically tied to self-worth and self-efficacy" (Be Girl, 2017).

Another example comes from Subz Pants and Pad, a South African effort that produces and distributes reusable cloth pads and panties. Its charity arm, "Project Dignity," explains on its website: "Through Project Dignity we give the girls their basic education they deserve. Their dignity is kept intact and we empower them to be the best they can" (Project Dignity-Subz Pads, 2017).

Finally, EcoFemme, a progressive social enterprise in the Indian state of Tamil Nadu that has been manufacturing cloth pads since 2010 and pairing the for-profit side of the business with its NGO arm, "Pad for Pad," which distributes free pads and menstrual health education to adolescent girls. In a July 2017 newsletter describing Pad for Pad's curriculum, they write: "Sessions are designed to give girls the skills to manage their periods hygienically and with dignity, and the chance to relate to menstruation as a normal, healthy experience" (EcoFemme, 2017). This last example is telling in the way it makes apparent a contradiction embedded in the MHM discourses of dignity. If menstruation is normal and healthy, why must it be *managed* to ensure dignity? The answer is simple – dignity depends on keeping menstruation private.

Advancing the goal of discrete management: the grey and scholarly literature

Those generating knowledge about MHM similarly use the dignity frame.[8] For example, PMA2020, a project that uses mobile technology to collect data and monitor key indicators for a number of health and development issues, including MHM. In partnership with Johns Hopkins researchers, PMA2020 is the first to provide data regarding MHM indicators on a large scale. To date, they have generated one-page briefs on a number of national, state, and urban settings in the Global South, each leading with this boilerplate statement: "Globally, many women and girls face challenges when managing their menstruation. Failure to address the menstrual hygiene needs of women and girls can have far-reaching consequences, including affecting progress toward achieving the SDG goal of gender equality" (Johns Hopkins, 2017).

Here, the risk of *not* attending to MHM is foregrounded with direct reference to SDG goal 5. In this frame, MHM has the power to challenge sexism. So, what does addressing "the menstrual hygiene needs of women and girls" actually mean? The next paragraph explains: "Menstrual Hygiene Management (MHM) refers to the practice of using clean materials to absorb menstrual blood that can be changed privately, safely, hygienically, and as often as needed for the duration of the menstrual cycle" (Johns Hopkins, 2017). The sparsity of this definition is striking; it makes clear that the key to dignity is to avoid menstrual disclosure.[9]

Robin Boosey and Emily Wilson's 2014 analysis of key international human rights treaties and related reports is also illustrative. The authors searched these documents for references and allusions to menstruation. They found, "menstruation is not at all addressed... If it is discussed, it is only in a limited way, through ambiguous allusions or brief clear references that omit crucial details" (p. 61). They assert that these conspicuous omissions reflect a clear androcentrism at work, a bias that undermines human rights claims of universality. They also point to the lack of menstrual engagement in these documents as indicative of the global cultural silence regarding menstruation that gets reproduced in a discursive loop of silence breeding more silence ad infinitum. They write: "The menstruation taboo is formed in a cyclical process; when its demands for silence are satisfied, its taboo status and negative impact on the fulfilment of the human rights of women and girls are reinforced" (p. 62). To their credit, Boosey and Wilson offer a sophisticated critique of the relationship between menstruation and privacy when they offer this analysis:

> Through (re)articulation, a web of meaning surrounding menstruation has been created, as it has been associated with the less valued, feminine halves of binary pairs, such as honour/shame, rational/emotional, and public/private, which are themselves inter-related. Shame, for example, is closely associated with privacy as shameful matters should be hidden from public view. Although articulations appear logical, they are marked with contradictions, which draw attention to their constructed nature... The fact that articulations between menstruation and shame or privacy appear natural, despite their contradictions, highlights the power relations at work under the surface in the process of drawing up boundaries.
>
> (p. 58)

I could not agree more, but concurrently, the authors seem unable to transcend the established criteria for "good" MHM, which depends on dignity through privacy. Earlier in the paper, they use World Health Organization and UNICEF (2012, p. 16) definitions to establish good MHM, wherein privacy as precondition figures quite prominently. They state these requirements:

Access to necessary resources (e.g. menstrual materials to absorb or collect menstrual blood effectively, soap and water), facilities (a private place to wash, change and dry re-usable menstrual materials in privacy during menstruation, and an adequate disposal system for menstrual materials, from collection point to final disposal point), and education about MHM for males and females.

It is tempting, therefore, to see their analysis set against both their call to action and definitions of MHM as curiously paradoxical: Break the silence to enable menstruators to silence their menstruation.

Similarly, Inga Winkler and Virginia Roaf (2014), who both served as consultants to the first UN Special Rapporteur on the Right to Safe Drinking Water and Sanitation, endeavor to make the human rights case for menstrual hygiene. They believe that a human rights framework can shine a light and instigate action (pp. 6–7). More precisely, they assert:

> The contribution of the human rights framework lies in drawing attention to the plight of women and girls who are not able to manage their menstruation adequately by highlighting States' and other actors' obligations and responsibilities with respect to menstruation and its hygienic management… Considering menstruation as what it is – a fact of life – and integrating this view at all levels, will contribute to enabling women and girls to manage their menstruation adequately, without shame and embarrassment – with *dignity*.
>
> (p. 2, emphasis mine)

While Winkler and Roaf's aim is to normalize menstruation as a "fact of life," they undermine this claim when they assert that menstruation must be managed to avoid shame, embarrassment, and the loss of human dignity. The enabling environment they advocate is necessary because, "Human dignity is closely related to the right to privacy" (p. 19). They summarize the centrality of dignity and privacy: "It be may be in the aspects of dignity, privacy, and gender equality where the human rights perspective helps most to develop the understanding of what is needed for women and girls to be able to manage their menstruation adequately and make menstrual hygiene a priority for decision-makers" (p. 14). Management, in this conceptualization – one shared across MHM organizations – refers to the capacity to conceal menstruation even while the same organizations assertively denounce menstrual shame, stigma, and silence.

To be fair, Winkler and Roaf – and most other MHM advocates – do not focus *only* on menstrual management per se. For example, some are critical of cultural and religious practices that marginalize menstruators. Winkler and Roaf mention mandated separate sleeping and eating, bans on cooking and access to usual water sources and/or toilets, and dietary restrictions. These, too, undermine human rights, as they deny menstruators their agency and free will. But the primary focus here, as elsewhere, is on the concealment of menstruation – perhaps a less egregious set of expectations, but expectations nonetheless.

What's private is a cultural construction and it is tied, in the case of menstruation, to norms of femininity. Winkler and Roaf take this up in their article when they entertain the origins of the menstrual taboo. For them, menstruation is a foil to femininity. They write, "Despite being an integral part of being female, menstruation goes against 'feminine' attributes, with such attributes being deeply influenced by gender stereotypes... One such stereotype is that women should be beautiful and beautified" (2014, p. 4). And yet, they still rely on the privacy→dignity calculus, which tees up product-focused interventions. The following passage makes this clear:

> Dignity is difficult to maintain for women and girls when one of the signifiers of being female is a source of embarrassment and shame. For women who do not have the means to manage their menstruation discreetly, there is a constant fear of smelling, leaking, or staining. Dignity is also difficult to maintain when menstruating women and girls use damp and soiled materials that cause discomfort, itching, and even infections. When menstruating women and girls are ostracized and face restrictions in their everyday life, based on beliefs that menstruation is impure and unclean, this adds further to feelings of embarrassment and shame.
>
> (p. 13)

What compromises women's and girls' dignity is the inability to "manage their menstruation discreetly," when, in fact, the barrier to dignity is the social construction of menstruation as taboo built upon the foundational assumption of women's inferiority – an artifact of the sexist perception of women's bodies as unstable, dysfunctional, and undisciplined.

Winkler and Roaf are not blind to the complexities in play here. They call for action that at once guarantees privacy and challenges menstrual taboos. But I find it hard to square how both can be addressed at once. Some might argue that there is no contradiction here. Breaking the silence means talking openly about menstruation, while management refers, quite specifically, to a set of behaviors tied directly to caring for the menstruating body. But how sincere, how transformative, is a social change agenda that promotes transparency *only* in the realm of talk? The actual reality of menstruation – the blood on skirts, hands, in the latrine, the pads, the bins with discarded products – must remain hidden, a private matter.

Still another and more recent theoretical paper was drafted and circulated in conjunction with the 2016 Menstrual Hygiene Day. The authors – Hannah Neumeyer, head of the Human Rights Team at WASH United, and Amanda Klasing, senior researcher with Human Rights Watch – primarily address development practitioners working on MHM in an attempt, it appears, to help this audience more knowledgably and strategically deploy the language of human rights to advance their MHM agendas (2016). In aligning menstruation, MHM, and human rights, they write: "Women and girls encounter difficulties in managing hygiene during menstruation when they lack the enabling environment to do so" (p. 7). Here, as in nearly all MHM discourse, MHM is collapsed to include only menstruation – the three–seven-day period of shedding the uterine lining – and the support necessary to keep this process invisible.

What the paper does well is draw the connections between MHM and pre-established related human rights that have developed as development sectors: the rights to water and sanitation, health, education, work, and gender equality. The unifying claim is poor MHM (read: failure to conceal menstruation as it happens) undermines the capacity of girls and women to realize their full participation in society, to be good (bio)citizens, as I argued earlier. MHM advocates consistently assert that without good MHM, other human rights are in jeopardy.

Ilana Cohen's sophisticated analysis of these same three papers is useful. She identifies the particularly Western view of menstruation, as consistent with conceptualizations of womanhood as closer to nature, the lesser half of the nature/culture duality. She writes, "The theoretical perspective underlying these papers holds that women must control the 'nature' in themselves so as to enter the valued cultural world and be considered members of society" (2016, p. 9). The end game, finds Cohen, is for the "metaphorical and literal movement of women into men's spaces rather than to rights being fulfilled regardless of gender" (p. 3).

Cohen deepens her critique of MHM's use of the human rights frame by challenging the assumption that menstrual management will enable gender equality. If we consider South Asian gender theory, concealment is a less obvious standard. For some, menstrual rituals and even restrictions publicly signal when a woman or girl is menstruating (see, for example, Nagarajan, 2007; Bean, 1981). Menarche, in some regions, is still regarded as the maturational event it was once in the West (Brumberg, 1997). For instance, in both Tamil Nadu and Karnataka India, a girl's first menstrual cycle is celebrated with multi-day ceremonies (Bhattacharyya, 1997). Clearly, menstruation is *not* universally regarded as something best obscured; cultural differences do exist. But the human rights frame drawing on dignity and privacy fails to capture this diversity and, instead, accommodates a Western view.

The raced and gendered "hygienic" body in crisis

As these examples illustrate, in MHM, dignity is dependent on menstrual invisibility, a goal achieved through what Vostral (2008) terms "technologies of passing." While Vostral developed this concept about mass-produced menstrual care introduced in the 20th-century United States, the concept is easily applied to the case of MHM in the Global South. Often the campaigns

convey how urgent it is to enable "passing" as non-menstruators. US historian Brumberg dubbed menstruation a "hygienic crisis" (1997, p.31) – a
view now being aggressively exported around the globe. The focus on *hygiene*
is important, especially as it is inflected with racialized and gendered understandings of embodiment.

According to Goldenberg and Roberts (2004), menstruation, as a female
bodily process, is animalistic because it positions women as close to nature.
The social mandate, then, is to contain the creaturely to meet the standards
of human (read: male) embodiment. Thus, if women are to gain access to the
public sphere, their creaturely selves must be contained, a view that comes
through in the MHM discourse discussed above. Earlier, Sandra Bartky
(1990) drew upon Foucault's (1977) theory of the body disciplined through a
self-surveillance to reveal the various ways that women contain the body in
pursuit of hegemonic femininity, locked in constant struggle to control "the
body's size and contours, its appetite, posture, gestures, and general com-
portment in space and the appearance of each of its visible parts" (p. 80).
One feature of women's bodies that must remain *invisible*, of course, is
menstruation. It is a menstruator's job to transcend nature. And so, we
circle back to the concept of dignity as enshrined in human rights doctrine.
The dignified body is the body that effectively disciplines itself to obscure
menstruation.

The notion of the gendered hygienic body is also deeply racialized. Timothy
Burke's (1996) interdisciplinary study of the complicated marriage of global
capitalism, colonialism, consumerism, and commodification shows certain
values of bodily presentation and care signaled growing tensions between the
traditional and the modern and the African and the European, and opened
the door to multinational corporations who ingeniously created markets for
products like soap. Consumer culture, Burke shows, rose on the back of a
racialized understanding of the hygienic body – one intimately imbricated in
the commodification of the body held to a white, Western standard. This
raises the obvious question: How might the history of consumer demand for
menstrual products follow a similar trajectory, shaped by the same racial politics that cast the body of color as "unwashed" and in need of intervention?

Following Burke, Sanyu Mojola's qualitative study of Kenyan schoolgirls
demonstrates how Western ideals of modernity, gender, and race shape
girls' relational and consuming behaviors. Framing her work in the tradition
of other studies connecting beauty products with ideals of modern femininity (see, for example, Weinbaum et al., 2008), she shows how contemporary
girls use romance and sex to negotiate access to the products they are
socialized to "need." "Consuming femininity," as Mojola calls it, is not new
(and not limited to those with means; it is an ideal, an aspiration), "what has
shifted, however, are the scripts that are used to bind modern femininity and
consumption together... Pursuing racial respectability and Westernized
sophistication in part underlay African women consumers' motivations"
(2015, p. 3). Here, as elsewhere, the project of disciplining the body is

intersectional; it is a gendered ideal pinned to the dominance of Western (read: white and middle-class) hegemony that privileges bodies shaped by the market. This is the backdrop against which MHM successfully frames MHM as a hygienic crisis that must be resolved through engagement with consumer culture.

This, of course, is not a new story. NGOs, social businesses, and corporate social responsibility initiatives are known to introduce product-based solutions in low-income regions. Rayvon Fouché's (2012) analysis of "One Laptop per Child" (OLPC), an initiative to provide low-cost, low-power machines to children in the Global South, is a powerful case study. Fouché shows how OLPC failed to deliver on its "dream of creating a non-geographically-bound digital technological citizen from a clean slate of third-world children" (p. 77), largely because the software designed to run on the computers was inadequate. The discourse of the OLPC program, infused with what Fouché calls a "racial politics of technology," is linked "to a troubled history of Western 'advanced' technology and its deliverers as saviors" (p. 73). Simultaneously, the conditions that created the on-the-ground conditions of poverty are sidestepped because:

> At worst they are ignored because the bringers of the artifact believe that technology and computing will build a direct path to a Western-style promised land. These programs driven by the "if only they had…" mantra, sadly, though not purposefully, construct receivers of these technological tools as empty vessels into which Western technological knowledge must be poured.
>
> (p. 73)

To summarize, the deployment of human rights discourse of dignity and privacy in the emerging movement of MHM produces a complicated picture. It effectively arrests attention, bridges issues, and situates itself as a legitimate issue of development while simultaneously constructing the body as a problem in need of solution. Instead of troubling the pervasively negative view of menstruation, MHM promotes "management" through disciplining the (racialized and gendered) body. Hence, the "good period" is the one we don't know about; the "good girl" is the one who hides her menstruation, thus burdening girls with the sole responsibility of "managing" menstruation. It is ultimately this hyper-regulation that makes girls perfect economic targets and situates MHM as an incentive to create and sustain a consumerist path to modernity rather than a program for progressive social change.

Discussion questions

1   Body hair removal, such as shaving, is another body management practice. How could Bobel's analysis apply here? How are norms surrounding body hair gendered, raced, and classed? What other body management

practices can you think of that also reflect hegemonic standards of embodiment in particular social contexts?

2　What might be other unintended negative consequences of MHM, especially for campaigns that introduce single-use (disposable) products into communities? How can these impacts be productively addressed?

3　Bobel mentions MHM advocates' claim that cloth can cause health problems is not supported in the research literature. Why, then, might they assert this claim? What assumptions likely undergird this view?

Notes

1　I intentionally use the word female here to signal that menstruation, while deeply imbued with gendered social meanings, is not unique to women and girls. Indeed, not only women menstruate as some transmen and non-binary individuals do as well.

2　This definition is used by key MHM thought leaders including UNICEF, the United Nations, Menstrual Hygiene Day, and WaterAid. It also appears in a number of peer-reviewed articles, the *Routledge Handbook of Water and Health*, and on *Wikipedia*.

3　The countries include: Ethiopia, Kenya, Madagscar, Malawi, Mozambique, Rwanda, Somalia, South Sudan, Tanzania, Uganda, Zimbabwe, Cameroon, Namibia, South Africa, Burkina Faso, Ghana, Liberia, Nigeria, Senegal, Sierra Leone, Haiti, Guatemala, Honduras, Mexico, Nicaragua, Bolivia, Columbia, Paraguay, Peru, Cambodia, Malaysia, Vietnam, Bangladesh, India, Nepal, and Pakistan.

4　Voluminous data make clear that, compared to boys, girls are disproportionately likely to drop out of school, experience gender-based violence including sex trafficking, early marriage, and contract HIV. Girl-centered development discourse surfaces a tension, especially for those who promote so-called empowerment and freedom. Nike's foundation "The Girl Effect," a self-described "movement" to raise awareness of the unmet needs of girls, brings us to the heart of the matter: "Girls are a smart investment to accelerate change. This isn't a social issue; it's smart economics" (Eitel, 2012).

5　Most menstruators in the Global South use pieces of cloth as menstrual absorbents, often repeatedly washing and reusing the same material (Sumpter and Torondel 2013; van Eijk et al., 2016). This was the same strategy commonly used by women and girls in the West until commercial, single-use products were introduced in the late 1800s (pads) and 1920s (tampons) and, over time, replaced cloth as the conventional means of menstrual care.

6　The data, so far, do *not* establish a clear causal link between how menstruators manage their menses and rates of infection. A study of relationship between menstrual hygiene practices, WASH access, and the risk of urogenital infections, both urinary tract infections and bacterial vaginosis, revealed that some menstrual care practices, including type of menstrual absorbent, can raise the risks of infections, but wealth and the place where a woman changes her pad are contributing factors (Das et al., 2015, p. 12). A systematic review of 14 articles that examined health outcomes associated with menstrual hygiene practices found that while a relationship between RTIs and poor MHM was reported in several of the studies, "the methodological shortcomings of the health research were many" (Sumpter and Torondel, 2013, p. 13), thus leading them to refrain from asserting a clear causal link between MHM and health outcomes.

7 This data point, while unreferenced, is pulled from an unpublished, poorly designed study conducted by A.C. Nielsen and commissioned by Plan India in 2012. The only available study report is a PowerPoint presentation labeled "proprietary and confidential."

8 Grey literature refers to materials, including research, typically produced by organizations outside of commercial or academic publishing channels. Research reports, working papers, white papers, and assorted government documents are examples of grey literature sources. They tend to be less accessible than papers published by traditional presses.

9 Elsewhere, I argue what a truly comprehensive, sustainable, and transformative definition of MHM must embrace. A reorientation to contextualized menstrual literacy, I assert, sets in motion a lifelong authentic engagement with the body. Menstruation, after all, given the age at which it begins, offers a rich opportunity – a gateway to engendering an embodied relationship that is healthy, direct, and agentic. But if MHM is reduced to finding something to bleed on, this opportunity is missed (Bobel, 2015).

References

Bartky, S.L. (1990). *Femininity and domination: Studies in the phenomenology of oppression*. New York: Routledge.

Be Girl (2017). About Be Girl. Available at: www.begirl.org/pages/about-be-girl [Accessed August 7, 2017].

Bean, S. (1981). Toward a semiotics of "purity" and "pollution" in India. *American Ethnologist*, 8, pp. 575–595.

Beitz, C. (2013). Human dignity in the theory of human rights: Nothing but a phrase? *Philosophy and Public Affairs*, 41(3), pp. 259–290.

Benford, R.D. and Snow, D.A. (2000). Framing processes and social movements: An overview and assessment. *Annual Review of Sociology*, 26, pp. 611–639.

Bhattacharyya, G. (1997). Menstruation and alleged pollution of women: Ghurye's ideas on women's dignity. *Indian Anthropological Society*, 31(1), pp. 55–64.

Bobel, C. (2010). *New blood: Third-wave feminism and the politics of menstruation*. New Brunswick, NJ: Rutgers University Press.

Bobel, C. (2015). Finding problems with simple solutions: Ethnographic insights into development campaigns to support menstruating girls. National Women's Studies Association Annual Conference. Milwaukee, WI.

Boosey, R. and Wilson, E. (2014). A vicious cycle of silence: What are the implications of the menstruation taboo for the fulfilment of women and girls' human rights and, to what extent is the menstruation taboo addressed by international human rights law and human rights bodies? Research report. ScHARR report series (29). Sheffield: School of Health Related Research, University of Sheffield.

Brumberg, J.J. (1997). *The body project*. New York: Random House.

Burke, T. (1996). *Lifebuoy men, lux women: Commodification, consumption, and cleanliness in modern Zimbabwe*. Durham, NC: Duke University Press.

Cohen, I. (2016). The right to manage, the right to hide: Unpacking the menstrual hygiene management, human rights and gender equality discourse. Unpublished manuscript.

Das, P., Baker, K., and Dutta, A. et al. (2015). Menstrual hygiene practices, WASH access and the risk of urogenital infection in women from Odisha, India. *PLoS ONE*, 10(6): e0130777. doi:10.1371/journal.pone.0130777

Days for Girls (2016). Annual report. Available at: www.daysforgirls.org/annual-rep ort [Accessed August 7, 2017].

EcoFemme (2017). Pad for pad newsletter. Available at: https://ecofemme.org/in-action/pad-for-pad/?utm_source=Eco+Femme+Newsletter&utm_campaign=f6a 0f99e19-EMAIL_CAMPAIGN_2017_07_07&utm_medium=email&utm_term= 0_37167feb6f-f6a0f99e19-281982321 [Accessed August 7, 2017].

Eitel, M. (2012). Family planning unleashes the girl effect. Available at: www.huffing tonpost.com/maria-eitel/family-planning-unleashes_b_1671962.html [Accessed May 14, 2018].

Foucault, M. (1977). *Discipline and punish: The birth of the prison.* New York: Pantheon Books.

Fouché, R. (2012). From black inventors to one laptop per child: Exporting a racial politics of technology. In: L. Nakamura and P.A. Chow-White, eds, *Race after the internet.* New York: Routledge, pp. 60–83.

Goldenberg, J.L. and Roberts, T.A. (2004). The beast within the beauty: An existential perspective on the objectification and condemnation of women. In: J. Greenberg, S.L. Koole, and T. Pyszcazynski, eds, *Handbook of experimental existential psychology.* New York: Guildford, pp. 71–85.

Hayhurst, L. (2011). Corporatising sport, gender and development: Postcolonial IR feminisms, transnational private governance and global corporate social engagement. *Third World Quarterly,* 32(3), pp. 223–241.

Johns Hopkins/Performance, Monitoring and Accountability 2020 (2017). *Managing menstrual hygiene briefs.* Available at: https://pma2020.org/mhm-briefs [Accessed August 7, 2017].

Johnston-Robledo, I. and Chrisler, J.C. (2013). The menstrual mark: Menstruation as social stigma. *Sex Roles: A Journal of Research,* 68(1–2), pp. 9–18.

Lazar, M. (2007). Feminist critical discourse analysis: Articulating a feminist discourse praxis. *Critical Discourse Studies,* 4(2), pp. 141–164.

Mojola, S. (2015). Material girls and material love: Consuming femininity and the contradictions of post-girl power among Kenyan schoolgirls. *Continuum,* 29(2), pp. 218–229.

Nagarajan, V.R. (2007). Threshold designs, forehead dots, and menstruation rituals: Exploring time and space in Tamil Kolams. In: T. Pintchman, ed., *Women's lives, women's rituals in the Hindu tradition.* New York: Oxford University Press, pp. 85–105.

Neumeyer, H. and Klasing, A. (2016). Menstrual hygiene management and human rights: What's it all about?! Draft paper. Available at: http://menstrualhygieneday. org/menstrual-hygiene-management-human-rights-whats/ [Accessed August 7, 2017].

Project Dignity-Subz Pads (2017). About us. Available at: www.projectdignity.org.za/a bout-us/Accessed [Accessed August 7, 2017].

Schachter, O. (1983). Human dignity as a normative concept. *American Journal of International Law,* 771983(4), pp. 848–854.

Sommer, M. and Sahin, M. (2013). Overcoming the taboo: Advancing the global agenda for menstrual hygiene management for schoolgirls. *American Journal of Public Health,* 103(9), pp. 1556–1559.

Sommer, M., Hirsh, J.S., Nathanson, C., and Parker, R. (2015). Comfortably, safely and without shame: Defining menstrual hygiene management as a public health issue. *American Journal of Public Health,* 105(7), pp. 1302–1311.

Sumpter, C. and Torondel, B. (2013). A systematic review of the health and social effects of menstrual hygiene management. *PLoS ONE*, 8(4), e62004. doi:10.1371/journal.pone.0062004

United Nations (1948). Universal Declaration of Human Rights. Available at: www.un.org/en/universal-declaration-human-rights/index.html [Accessed August 7, 2017].

van Eijk, A.M., Sivakami, M., Thakkar, M.B. et al. (2016). Menstrual hygiene management among adolescent girls in India: A systematic review and metaanalysis. *BMJ Open*, 6, e010290. doi:10.1136/ bmjopen-2015–010290

Vostral, S.L. (2008). *Under wraps: A history of menstrual hygiene technology.* Lanham, MD: Lexington Books.

Weinbaum, A.E., Thomas, I.M., Ramamurthy, P.G., Poiger, U.G., and Yue Dong, M. (2008). *The modern girl around the world: Consumption, modernity, and globalization.* Durham, NC: Duke University Press.

Winkler, I. and Roaf, V. (2014). Taking the bloody linen out of the closet: Menstrual hygiene as a priority for achieving gender equality. *Cardozo Journal of Law and Gender*, 21(1), pp. 1–37.

Further reading

On the concept of dignity in human rights discourse

Macklin, R. (2003). *Dignity is a useless concept: It means no more than respect for persons or their autonomy.* National Center for Biotechnology. Available at: www.ncbi.nlm.nih.gov/pmc/articles/PMC300789/ [Accessed May 14, 2018].

On the "girling of development'

Koffman, O. and Gill, R. (2013). "The revolution will be led by a 12-year-old girl": Girl power and global biopolitics. *Feminist Review*, 105(1), pp. 83–102.

Switzer, H. (2013). (Post)feminist development fables: The girl effect and the production of sexual subjects. *Feminist Theory*, 14(3), pp. 345–360.

On critical menstruation studies

Bobel, C. (2010). *New blood: Third wave feminism and the politics of menstruation.* New Brunswick, NJ: Rutgers University Press.

Freidenfelds, L. (2009). *The modern period menstruation in twentieth-century America.* Baltimore, MD: Johns Hopkins University Press.

Joshi, D., Buit, G., and González-Botero, D. (2015). Menstrual hygiene management: Education and empowerment for girls? *Waterlines*, 34(1), pp. 51–67.

Kissling, E.A. (2006). *Capitalizing on the curse: The business of menstruation.* Boulder, CO. Lynn Rienner.

Lahiri-Dutt, K. (2014). Medicalising menstruation: A feminist critique of the political economy of menstrual hygiene management in South Asia. *Gender, Place and Culture: A Journal of Feminist Geography.* doi:10.1080/0966369X.2014.939156

On embodiment and discipline

Bobel, C. and Kwan, S., eds (2011). *Embodied resistance: Challenging the norms, breaking the rules.* Nashville, TN: Vanderbilt University Press.

Fahs, B., Mann, A., Swank, E., and Stage, S. (2017). *Transforming contagion: Risky contacts among bodies, disciplines, and nations.* New Brunswick, NJ: Rutgers University Press.

Kwan, S. and Graves, J. (2013). *Framing fat: Competing constructions in contemporary culture.* New Brunswick, NJ: Rutgers University Press.

19 Teaching health and human rights in a psychology capstone

Cultivating connections between rights, personal wellness, and social justice

Ester Shapiro, Fernando Andino Valdez, Yasmin Bailey, Grace Furtado, Diana Lamothe, Kosar Mohammad, Mardia Pierre and Nick Wood

Introduction

This chapter offers a multi-voiced account of teacher and student co-authors' experiences in Psychology 403 Capstone/Gender, Culture, and Health Promotion, a course in human rights minor and global diversity at the University of Massachusetts (UMass) Boston exploring social determinants of health and rights as resources for achieving personal and community "wellness as fairness" (Prilleltensky, 2012). We describe our evolving learning from student-partnered inquiry during fall 2016/spring 2017 semesters through our group project "Know Your Rights." Within mainstream health psychology, strivings towards health equity are hindered by focusing on decontextualized individuals. Additionally, complicity with US biomedicalization of societal challenges, alongside overly narrow definitions of scientific research supporting "evidence-based" health interventions, help perpetuate ideologies and practices normalizing white outcomes, obscuring critical roles of unequal power and resources, while blaming inequalities on poor personal choices of "high-risk" individuals (Fine and Cross, 2016; Lyons and Chamberlain, 2005). Further, students from educationally disenfranchised communities view research as outside their interests and competencies, silencing diverse voices promoting health equity.

Yet health psychology offers rich resources for human rights education, particularly valuable at UMASS Boston, where working students, many with personal and family health and mental health concerns associated with intersecting inequalities, bring impactful knowledge from lived experiences confronting unjust barriers and mobilizing culturally meaningful resilience resources overlooked by mainstream models. Central to collaborative, transformative learning is a transdisciplinary, democratizing approach to health/mental health inquiry grounded in Paulo Freire's critical/participatory education (Baum et al., 2006) and Appadurai's (2006) accessible definition of research as a human right: "the capacity to make disciplined inquiries into those things we need to know, but do not know yet" (p. 167).

A course titled "Gender, culture, and health" enrolls a highly diverse group of students, prepared to learn about advancing health with equity from intersectional perspectives. By chance, the fall 2016 class consisted almost entirely of students of color, many immigrants or children of immigrants, with social psychology, gender, ethnic studies, or human rights minors, alongside experiences in community organizing, community-engaged services, or arts activism/artivism (Sandoval and Latorre, 2008) backgrounds. After the November 2016 presidential election results, reflecting together, we vowed to intensify our activism. These students created a critical mass for in-depth discussions of multifaceted social inequalities impacting health, relationships between health social determinants and both civil and human rights, and remedies towards achieving health with equity, connecting readings to lived experiences. Co-authoring this chapter, I appreciated how this course reflects my development through dialogues within our unique UMass Boston community of striving, resilient students, dedicated staff, and social justice-informed teachers who appreciate the vital role of education in inspiring knowledge, mobilizing personal and collective transformation, solidarity, and justice. "Know your rights" is now on the course syllabus list of continuing group projects, joining "UMass Boston student resources for educational success and wellness" and "Global mental health resilience and recovery" grounded in disabilities rights and mental health consumer/survivor perspectives (Jacobson, 2012; Pelletier et al., 2009). The course broadens definitions of who conducts health research, for whose benefit, to include reflexive personal narratives regarding knowledge, power and social locations, community action research partnerships, and research expanding human rights. I encourage students to conduct personally meaningful applied research uncovering oppressive societal/disciplinary ideologies while advancing professional development and advocacy.

Gender, culture, health promotion, and human rights education at UMass Boston

The right to an education is considered foundational to all rights promoting "full development of the personality" and supporting active, informed participation in one's community and nation (Claude, 2005). Education is one of the three critical domains of the UN's Human Development Index, along with adequate income and health status measured by longevity, access to healthcare, and to social determinants of health such as adequate nutrition, housing, and safe neighborhoods (Kickbusch, 2003; Burd-Sharps et al., 2008; McGowan et al, 2016). Human development offers an alternative economic development framework emphasizing how equitably a society's investments fulfill obligations to nurture capabilities facilitating full societal participation and wellbeing (Walker and Unterhalter, 2007). US and global health/public health literatures emphasize education, particularly for women and girls and other marginalized/targeted groups, as an especially powerful social

determinant impacting interrelated domains including employment opportunities, health literacy, quality of neighborhoods and social networks, and
empowered civic engagement, reducing health inequalities (Braveman and
Gottlieb, 2014; Hahn and Truman, 2015). Historically, US protection of
individual and collective rights has progressed through civil rights legislation
and action, identifying specific protected groups while requiring that individuals "Know their rights" and feel empowered to demand these (Hahn et al.,
2018; McGowan et al., 2016; Newman, 2017). Human rights education for
health professionals highlights knowledge of formal laws, institutional practices, and patient/practitioner relations advancing patient rights including
provider reflexivity regarding their own contributions to perpetuating
inequalities (Erdman, 2017). In health promotion education, feminist intersectional and critical race perspectives are increasingly influential in addressing inequalities emerging from multiple forms of oppression with
differential impacts across domains and settings (Bowleg, 2017; Shapiro,
2014; Viruell-Fuentes et al., 2012), themes addressed in Grace Furtado and
Diana Lamothe's Latinas/Women of Color Coalitions project. For community-engaged health equity work, participatory pedagogies incorporating
Freire's development of experientially grounded critical consciousness are
considered foundational to community partnerships mobilizing knowledge
linking personal and social change (Minkler, 2012; Shapiro and Atallah-
Gutiérrez, 2012; Wallerstein et al., 2017).

Bajaj (2011) explores goals and methods of three approaches to human
rights education useful for different settings and learners: *Human Rights
Education for Global Citizenship* emphasizes education fostering knowledge
and skills related to universal values and human rights standards, and the
accountability of nation-states in protecting these rights. As Fernando
Andino Valdez explores later in this chapter, this approach needs to be
rooted in compassionate empathy (Zembylas, 2017), alongside self-knowl-
edge of "grounded cosmopolitanism" (Appiah, 2006) or transversal recognition of solidarities emerging from deep knowledge of one's own
intersecting locations, identities, and consequences of inequalities (Shapiro,
2005). Latinx philosopher/activist Maria Lugones (2003) calls this capacity
"empathic world traveling," tempered by righteous anger providing clarity
regarding inequalities. *Human Rights Education for Coexistence* focuses on
interpersonal and intergroup aspects of rights, often associated with conflict settings emerging from ethnic or civil strife; this approach, too, highlights the value of empathic understanding of others in moving beyond
"tolerance" toward reconciliation, acceptance, and deeper sense of solidarity. African refugee students who have brought up their children in war
zones, like Somali American Kosar Mohammad, bring to our classrooms
her survivor's ingenuity and compassion alongside her moral clarity of
righteous anger needed to fight injustice. The third approach, *Human Rights
Education for Transformative Action*, consistent with Freire's critical/partici-
patory pedagogy, often involves learners marginalized within their

societies, for whom human rights education emerges from shared dialogues towards understanding shared experiences, thwarted needs, and cultural strengths. Roux (2012) argues for the importance of a narrative approach to *Human Rights Education as Inquiry*, beginning by creating "Safe spaces" allowing targeted groups to acknowledge experiences of discrimination and engage in dialogues towards appreciating barriers and enacting rights. Mardia Pierre and Yasmin Bailey, confronting racism and gender-based violence, share their poetry as public practice towards healing and activism/ advocacy (Shapiro and Alcantara, 2016).

Applying models and methods to UMass Boston: shared journeys of inquiry

Human rights education promoting active local/global citizenship challenges teachers to highlight specific processes and settings recognizing cultural contexts, encourage reflexivity and dialogues including personal self-disclosure inviting critical consciousness and empathy, and catalyze discussions of strategies connecting personal and collective change. Every UMASS Boston psychology classroom offers a unique educational space for shared, transformative "journeys of inquiry," through distinctive, diverse histories and communities informing each student's confronted, transcended challenges while animating their sense of purpose. Boston's communities of color represent global migrations from Africa, Asia, Latin America, and the Caribbean whose histories are often obscured by US global and historical ignorance and Boston's specific racialization into "Black and White" yet impact families and communities of our Haitian, Cape Verdean, Cambodian, and Somali students among many others. We know from decades of student-partnered research in mental health that many undergraduates choose psychology majors because personal histories overcoming mental health challenges inspired them towards helping professions. Working multiple jobs, often supporting families struggling with health burdens from intersecting inequalities, our students carry additional responsibilities limiting time dedicated to learning beyond fulfilling course requirements. Personal wellness time is often an unaffordable luxury. Introducing the syllabus, I share how my professional training as a transdisciplinary clinical/developmental psychologist evolved through partnerships with students and global/transnational community groups towards advancing knowledge for equity. Appreciating the power of personal narratives/testimonies in education and healing, I share my history as a Cuban/Eastern European/Jewish American immigrant, daughter of immigrants, and first in my family to graduate from college, alongside my health history experiencing life-long immune disorders and surviving breast cancer. Students often comment that introducing the course as informed by my life experiences allows them to explore their own, through written assignments or disclosure in class discussions.

Organization of the course

Part I: Connecting theoretical frameworks and personal narratives/reflexivity

Human rights education focused on health as a human right begins with the World Health Organization (WHO) definition of health as "not only the absence of illness, but the presence of well-being and the resources for its actualization." This definition immediately challenges narrow biomedical US healthcare approaches perpetuating inequalities, emphasizing WHO approaches highlighting social determinants and calling for health social movements (Marmot et al., 2008). We engage an academically demanding syllabus in three parts – social ecological theories promoting health with equity, participatory methods for research and community development, and practicing cultural proficiency in health, including the selection of group projects for final class presentations. The syllabus describes our ongoing Health Promotion Research Team projects, inviting students to pursue topics resonating with their lived experiences while supporting personal and professional aspirations.

In part I, we read critical health psychology and social ecological theories that help students conduct readings of power impacting each of us differentially, while appreciating highly specific forces in multiple domains, producing health inequalities or promoting "wellness as fairness" (Lyons and Chamberlain, 2005; Prilleltensky, 2012). Commencing, we view *Unnatural causes: Is inequality making us sick?* (California Newsreel, 2008), a film series created by public health/social medicine researcher/activists, designed to engage classrooms and communities in understanding and taking action on health inequalities. The series vividly dramatizes accessible, transdisciplinary academic accounts of health inequalities, while illuminating through storytelling how poverty and gendered racism impact opportunities for wellness. We share intimate details in the lives, neighborhoods, and employment of residents in rich, middle-class, working-poor, and desperately poor black and white families in adjoining council districts in Louisville, Kentucky, whose ladder of employment and accompanying privilege/power determining health/wellness opportunities intersect through their jobs at the local hospital. Inspired by these stories, students begin to share their own health/mental health experiences, while learning a language for intersectional understandings of power and resource rights impacting health outcomes including human rights (Braveman et al., 2011), human development (Burd-Sharps et al., 2008), WHO and US Health and Human Services health equity goals (Kickbusch, 2003; Koh et al., 2010), levels of racism (Jones, 2000), biology of stress and allostasis/allostatic load as impacting life-course health through systemic regulatory processes (McEwen and Gianaros, 2010), and intersectional perspectives on social determinants of health (Viruell-Fuentes et al., 2012). We review critiques of US healthcare (Starfield, 2000) asking "Is US health care the best in the world?" with the overwhelming evidence resoundingly *NO*, the US spends much more to achieve far worse population health outcomes due to failures of coordinated primary care and persistent economic inequalities. We study principles of reform grounded in patient-centered, systems-minded, and knowledge-based healthcare (Berwick, 2002). We read an article alongside a compelling personal narrative by anthropologist, scholar of indigenous lifecourse rituals, and bereaved mother Davis-Floyd (2001, 2003). Comparing technocratic/specialty medicine, humanistic/biopsychosocial, and holistic/cultural/spiritual approaches to healthcare as "Windows on birth and death," she illustrates how each in its time and space constructively contributed to her healthcare, psychological, and spiritual needs during her own tragic journey of shock, grief, and coping when her college-aged daughter died in a car accident.

Universally, students find Camara Jones' classic, accessible paper "Levels of racism: A gardener's tale" (2000) the semester's most impactful read, alongside a review of intersectionality and immigrant health (Viruell-Fuentes et al., 2012), demonstrating how oppression impacts the "immigrant health paradox" with initially better-than-expected outcomes generated by cultural protective factors become eroded by discrimination and heritage culture loss in subsequent generations. Jones synthesizes social ecological models to three levels of institutional, personally mediated/relationship-based, and internalized racism, illustrating each with the metaphor of the gardener who, constructing two segregated flower planters providing rich soil for one and poor for the other, attributes differential outcomes to the superiority of the "rich" and defectiveness of the "poor."

Encouraging students to shift their thinking from US-influenced, fragmented, individualistic perspectives on health towards personally grounded, activist global citizenship experiences of our immigrant and refugee students, particularly those fleeing global conflict zones, inspires empathic world traveling. Kosar Mohammad, a human rights minor who prepared our human rights overview for the fall 2016/spring 2017 course, is a Muslim Somali refugee whose personal and family health have been deeply affected by gendered experiences of violent displacement, early marriage, and responsibility for a chronically ill son, now a successful college student. Engaging in dialogues about rights with students more familiar with US civil rights, Kosar developed a more transnational/intersectional view of health inequalities, appreciating how racial oppression impacted students distinctly depending on their immigration experiences. For her and other African immigrant and refugee students, imposed racial stereotypes were one among multiple experiences of disadvantage their communities confronted and transcended with admirable resilience, though always with a price to pay for surviving nearly unimaginable challenges, including health burdens misinterpreted by individualistic/technocratic medicine. After preparing a compelling presentation on health and human rights for class, she focused her own final reflection on the importance of incorporating knowledge of social determinants of health as human rights into primary healthcare. She high-lighted work by family practice scholar Laura Gottlieb (Braveman and Gottlieb, 2014; Gottlieb, 2010), who writes:

> I diagnosed "abdominal pain" when the real problem was hunger; I confused social issues with medical problems in other patients, too. I mislabeled the hopelessness of long-term unemployment as depression and the poverty that causes patients to miss pills or appointments as noncompliance. In one older patient, I mistook the inability to read for dementia. My medical training had not prepared me for this ambush of social circumstance.

I introduce careers bridging health, mental health, and equity, illustrating ways to use academic, work, and personal/cultural/community experiences to heal personally and advance professionally.

Parts II and III: Methods promoting participatory inquiry, community organizing, and culturally/spiritually/structurally sensitive healthcare

In the second section of the course, we apply multidirectional social ecological models of change mapping social determinants of health and exploring community-engaged action research methods. Because awakening to the workings of inequality can be deeply depressing without methods for taking action, students learn critiques of decontextualized prevention science and strategies for community-partnered, accountable research "Getting to outcomes" (Wandersman, 2003), and participatory community organizing creating partnerships for change (Baum et al., 2006; Minkler, 2012). Meaningful assignments include a cultural identity inventory (Hyde, 2012) that helps students map domains of power in their dominant/non-dominant status and how to become aware of blind spots and areas of knowledge they bring to inquiry and practice in diverse community settings. In the third part of the course, students explore applications in clinical practice and applied settings by reading *Spirit catches you and you fall down* (Fadiman, 2012), a classic in cultural/spiritual/structural competence training in healthcare, analyzing the cultural proficiency continuum (Chavez et al., 2010) which moves from cultural competence to cultural humility as lifelong learning requiring self-reflection, readings of power, and accountability to justice. Building on prior readings, they explore cultural competence in healthcare multi-systemically, recognizing that individual providers cannot work sensitively without the support of organizations and intersectional policies recognizing resource rights promoting health.

Mid-semester, students identify areas of personal/professional interest and create working groups, each with an overarching theme. They work together in developing class presentations on topics viewed through the lens of course principles, including continuing projects from the Health Promotion

Research Team, "UMass Boston student resources for educational success and wellness," focused on mental health self-determination and resource rights promoting resilience and recovery (Pelletier et al., 2009). I encourage students to create personally and collectively meaningful groups supporting individual student interests and career advancement. Every class discovers meaningful topics uniquely, based on synergies in their backgrounds and interests. Fall 2016, most projects reflected impacts of a rights-oriented, participatory inquiry focused on the power of personal experience when informed by social ecological perspectives on wellness and equity. Haitian immigrant students Mona Joseph and Nerson Justine, both parents of young children, spoke to their struggles with racism and ignorance regarding Haiti and how cultural resources for resilience inspired their professional aspirations in elder care and mental health, respectively. Jasmany Beato, a Dominican American security officer planning to attend law school, explored lived experiences of undocumented immigrants and community-based programs protecting their rights. Other students, remaining anonymous to protect their privacy outside of agreed class discussions, focused on personal health challenges compounded by race, gender, immigration status, and poverty, including chronic illnesses associated with inequality and suicide prevention on campus focused on student survivor perspectives.

By the time students have created working groups for applications of course concepts, our collective efforts have brought us to inspiring final presentations often involving highly meaningful topics, including disclosures of personal strategies for overcoming health/mental health challenges, and impacts of family expressions of gendered racism through favoritism guided by colorism. Students discover avenues for professional development, appreciating their own community engagement experiences now elevated by a new understanding of theory and research informing their design. Chrislene Charles, who participated in youth development community organizing through Everett's Public Health Department, reflected on those experiences using course readings, advancing her professional knowledge and upgrading her resumé accordingly. By semester's end, students have gained a toolkit for understanding social determinants of health/mental health contributing to health disparities, basic concepts in community-partnered research for social action, cultural proficiency grounded in personal reflexivity and cultural humility, and strategies for mobilizing knowledge advancing personal, professional, and collective change.

The alchemy of gender, culture, race, and rights in classroom dialogues: student voices on health and human rights

What do human rights mean to UMASS Boston students? Planning this chapter, I invited a Psych 403 working group of human rights minors and other interested students to create projects connected to lived experiences of confronting challenges and moving towards collective action through their education. Human rights minors Yasmin Bailey and Kosar Mohammad were joined by others interested in intersections of gender, race, or immigration status impacting educational success and wellness, to explore how human rights/resource rights perspectives guiding the course could catalyze trans-formation by shifting frameworks and highlighting methods moving from struggle and self-blame to resistance and resilience. The following narratives from course assignments and chapter contributions illustrate how students reflected on these themes.

Fernando Andino Valdez on human rights education for global citizenship

Introduction

Fernando Andino Valdez enrolled in Psych 403 during fall 2016, and with Nelson Oliva began a collaborative project documenting their shared experiences as Latino students with disabilities. The following semester, both continued this evolving project using Photovoice as the method best cap-turing their experiences of physical barriers and silencing as Latino men experiencing both visible and invisible disabilities (Andino Valdez and Oliva, 2017). Fernando took *Introduction to human rights* in spring 2017, and fall 2017, after graduating, he was invited to open a student panel on the value of human rights education for global citizenship. He shares these reflections on learning for this chapter.

Fernando's reflection

To begin I would like to acknowledge the fact that UMass Boston is pri-marily a commuter school, with some residents, and even some students without homes. Students here work hard in and out of school and uphold many responsibilities, so I understand if many of you have not had the time to learn about human rights, but for whatever reason, you are here now and I thank you for your time. The human rights discourse should be applied to every major because at its core it provides us with a language and ideas to achieve social equity for all humans, regardless of identity or conflicting interests. It is essential to an undergraduate education because we should all know our human rights, lest they be taken away or infringed upon without our knowing. You want to be ready to take action in your community if you're experiencing injustice. Equally important, we the people have a role to play in defending human rights for others whenever possible because ethically, if not morally, it makes sense. Together we can be more effective at defending everyone's rights, especially from corrupt governments, of which there are many. Certainly I hope we all acknowledge there is corruption in our own government, but I would also like us to think of ourselves as global citizens because our power to effect change is not limited by our location. We cannot let identity politics and conflicting interests divide our unity on mutual goals and distract us from the real bad actors at play. Of course, even with mutual goals we should welcome different experiences, voices, perspectives, and ideas from all walks of life and countries. There are many ways to approach a problem in my experience. The pros and cons should be discussed to learn from each other and work towards creating a consensus on best practice for applying human rights education in the real world.

As a Puerto Rican who has lived most of his life in the United States, I grew up with a weird sense of privilege that my cousins in Puerto Rico did not have. My mother brought my older sister and me to the US when I was two months old because I was born with many disabilities that required specialized healthcare professionals unavailable in Puerto Rico. I experienced the privilege of technocratic healthcare, access to better education, and general accessibility for me and others with disabilities requiring mobility assistance such as wheelchairs and specialized educational technologies. Global citizenship as I define it is simply acknowledging the importance of our interconnectedness as human beings sharing Earth's resources. Spiritually, we should all strive for peaceful unity between all people, but more than that we live in a global economy where most countries are interdependent. While sadly we do not all share the wealth of resources, we certainly all bear the cost of environmental hardships caused by global warming and climate change.

To identify as a global citizen is to support what is right for the world regardless of one's affiliations or private interests. As a Puerto Rican living in the US, my global citizenship is informed by my experiences which form a foundation for compassion and solidarity with all too frequently occurring and ignored violations of human rights. Additionally, it is a commitment to stay informed, as best one can, to global current events. Though current events may seem beyond our sphere of influence, I argue we can always have some influence through informed action. The only hope for a global citizenry and advancement of justice based on universal human rights is to actively resist, through litigation and informed action, actions that violate our human rights. As my activism has evolved during my UMASS Boston education and since graduation, I have focused on the important role of journalism and communications as avenues for public education for informed social action. I have stayed involved in PHENOM activism for public higher education and in the battle to protect net neutrality. For my professional career, I am preparing to work in rehabilitation psychology, a field grounded in disabilities rights and focused on resource access and policy change beyond biomedical/technocratic solutions more typical of clinical mental health counseling.

Nick Wood on intersections of race and transgender rights impacting health

Nick, currently enrolled in a graduate social work program, training for work in the Boston public schools, began his final presentation by asking us to reflect on Chavez (2010): "In Vivian Chavez's Human Rights Framework and Primary Prevention, she states that human rights are "inherent to the human person, inalienable and universal. A human rights framework declares that all people deserve to be treated with dignity, compassion, and support." By the same token, Transgender rights are human rights that US colleges should aim strongly to protect on behalf of students. Research and evidence reveals a persistent stigma at structural, interpersonal and individual levels that pose significant health risks to transgender communities. These critical factors must be acknowledged and addressed by universities to ensure that transgender students can participate fully in their education process."

Nick's sharing his personal experience as a black transgender man growing up poor in the south, and what he learned about health and social justice from those experiences, contributed powerfully to our collective learning linking knowledge of rights, wellness as fairness, and activism.

Yasmin Bailey on experiences of racism as violations of human rights

Yasmin Bailey, a black Caribbean woman and daughter of immigrants, brought her knowledge as a human rights minor and as one of the organizers of the award-winning UMASS Boston Spoken Word student club. For her dialogue question initiating her presentation, Yasmin asked the class to reflect on this statement: "Vivian Chavez defines Human Rights as "basic standards without which people cannot survive and develop in dignity." In addition to the universities being a safe space for all students, Colleges should understand and try their hardest to demolish the normalcy of microaggressions through cultural competency. Studies show that microaggressions on college campuses have negative effects on the mental health of students of color."

As part of her course contribution, Yasmin submitted poetry accepted for presentation at a UMass Boston conference sponsored by the School for Global Inclusion and Social Development on arts and social inclusion, and performed in class:

Confronting racism with the power of spoken word

I am tired
I am exhausted and sad and angry and I am tired
I am sick and tired of having to bury more and more bodies I am sick of the same routine:

1 Unarmed black man shot by police
2 Administrative Leave
3 Brought to trial
4 Found not guilty
5 Rinse and Repeat I am tired

I am unable I am scared.
I am terrified for the lives of my brother and friends These young black
    men with targets on their backs for police to end Their lives
Are no longer considered

They don't have white faces They a scary ass nigger

I can't Let this consume me
I may be tired, but I will not snooze me There is no pause
There is no more time to rest
I must get up put this S on my chest Not all heroes wear capes
There is no place to escape They have locked us in a cage
    And it is target practice I have to go there
These words cannot stay here Brother and sisters open your eyes
You don't have to be enraged to see or realize
You don't have to be enraged to want to make this difference I am tired
    and scared
But this fuel is made up of my fear I will make this known
Help lives, change minds, feed souls I will not stand still
I don't have a target on my back and I am damn sure not easy to kill!

Mardia Pierre: confronting gender-based violence through creative arts

Mardia Pierre, US-born daughter of Haitian immigrants, shared her experiences as an adolescent survivor of gender-based violence and use of personal disclosure for healing and "artivism." Mardia transcended/transformed deeply traumatizing experiences by co-founding *More Than This*, a feminist organization within the Boston Area Rape Crisis Center (BARCC) engaging in dialogues of self-expression, healing, solidarity, and activism using creative arts. Mardia describes her work: "*More Than This* is a series of events allowing survivors of sexual violence safe spaces to share their art as it pertains to their healing journey. We work with BARCC counselors and they are present at our events to provide onsite counseling as well as resources. We have stations that allow visitors to be in the moment and reflect on their feelings through conversations or their own art. We have a meditation station with guided meditation and journaling. At the end of this segment performers sing, recite poetry, play guitar and share experiences, creating an environment that is intimate but not heavy. I believe everyone during our event feels connected to one another."

Mardia also performed at "Arts for Inclusion" and in class:

Mardia's poem (bolded sections emphasized in performance)

I spent long days trying to *understand* what it *meant to* **love myself**.
Desperately I searched for my identity through nightmares and dark places

Dehumanized and deprived of choice –
Something died inside.
No one taught this **little girl** her rights or how to *defend herself* from the terrors that roam the night – **or daylight**.
See I'd *stay* awake **obsessing**, ruminating on the –
Intuitive feeling that I **couldn't alone**.
Yearning to connect with those broken souls like my own.
Millions of dimmed eyes left objectified,
To afraid to *speak* **up** because that wasn't something we **spoke of**.
When we discuss inclusion we seldom think of **rape**.
Which in of itself causes survivors to isolate.
We **negate** thoughts of sharing our pain
To spare our loved ones this **burdened** *ache*.
Which threw me into patterns of depreciating beliefs.
It's as though I was **conditioned** to **neglect** my health, **question** my experience and **subject myself** to the social norm of silence.

Until I got **tired** of feeling shameful for something *someone* **did** *to* **ME**.

Let me **stand** in my truth – For I once **truly believed** I lacked the capacity
You see mama **forgot** to **teach me** the severity of a shaken sexual spirituality_
I was 13 years old when I **thought** *I lost my soul, I could've sworn I* **saw** *it* **snatched** *from my being.*
Only to take 8 years to realize it was **alive and inside**.

Like seed to soil, I've decided to **nurture her**,
Repeating to myself over and over again when I get blue
that **his** *objectification of* **my body** *is not* **MY TRUTH**.
I am stronger today
And to understand that this world is **not** a horrible place
Gave me the ability to **transform** *my hate*
I'm not alone.
I am not **broken** and
this **vessel** *is my* **home**.

I am **not** what happened to me_
But traces of its existence I've woven beautifully into **my healing tapestry**,
Don't get it twisted;
The hard days still come, and I've accepted it's inevitability as **reality**.
Focusing on becoming **more open** with **myself**,
Through deliberate introspection
And remaining unapologetic during my fits of depression
Has **Granted** me the ability to **stand in my mess**_
Stand here in my **vulnerability** and raise awareness

For these attacks are never just individual or simply physical they impose on our communities psychological well being
Sexual violence does not care for how old, your sex, nor for the color of your skin tone.
It crosses all borders and has had its taste in all cultures.
But despite it's grimness with love and transparency we can create spaces of solidarity and education to turn the groans of distress into healing melodies of perseverance.
Hi, my name is **Mardia**, a survivor of sexual violence.

Grace Furtado and Diana Lamothe: women of color creating coalitional identities

Fall 2016 semester, Grace and Diana LaMothe decided together to explore themes of how gendered racialization, cultural identity, and intersectionality affect their social standing and wellness as Latinas. *Grace described the project's origins*: Diana and I shared similar experiences of too often "passing for white" and having to explain or justify our Latinx identity. We discussed how this was protective when we encountered societal inequalities due to our white privilege, but a source of confusion and at times contention, when asked to justify our cultural heritage, despite being self-identifying Latinx women.

Diana shared these reflections focused on her biracial experience: "I think it is clear how much my cultural identity has a role as a driving force in why I want to bring more intersectional work to public health as well as social work. I know my bicultural experiences have formed the person I am today, and my passion for accepting people of all communities with respect and equality. The cultural inventory assignment helped me realize my search for identity is ever growing and necessary for me to do the work I wish to achieve. I think coming from such a diverse background has been the biggest blessing my family has given me. I have been able to experience all walks of life, which I think helps me relate more easily to others. I find validation in everyone's personal experiences, I find beauty in those struggles that targeted communities have had to endure. I know that strength as my own, which makes me want to work with disadvantaged communities even more, because of how resilient and brave they are. I hope my diversity will impact my research for the better, and help me become an ally. I did not experience all the benefits that came with being a white-passing American woman because of my family and community challenges, but I will use my privileges for providing back to my communities. I feel prepared for the resistance that may come, I feel ready with my patience and understanding, hopefully eventually earning trust as an ally, community member, and someone who can make a difference in communities with greatest needs."

Grace and Diana continued their project during spring 2017 semester, in a Gaston Institute/anthropology course I taught, Latino Leadership Opportunity Program Seminar. *Grace continues:* "Going further with our shared learning, we identified the importance of speaking to other Latinx that were self-identifying Women of Color. We decided to explore how other women identifying as Latinx/Women of Color deal with biculturalism and colorism in our daily lives. We worked with two self-identifying Afro-Latinx women in the program, creating a dialogue using collaborative auto-ethnography/testimonies (Espino et al., 2012) and participatory action research (Baum et al., 2006). Through classroom discussions and group dialogues we designed research questions exploring how racialization contributes to the Latinx experience, colorism in our own lives as reflecting processes within Latinx and other immigrant communities (Silvia, 2012), and development of coalitional consciousness both as Latinx women and as Women of Color (Zavella, 2017). We were subsequently invited to engage UMass Boston Women of Color through a campus-wide workshop, part of a series titled *Not My Normal*, a week with 40 hours of teach-ins on resisting oppression responding to the presidential election and resurgence of white supremacist, sexist, and anti-immigrant politics. Our workshop, *Women of Color Dialogue on Resisting Racism and Building Coalitional Consciousness*, expanded our space beyond Latinx, inviting self-identified Women of Color to participate in in-depth conversations about their experiences while exploring commonalities. These discussions helped us gain insights regarding intersecting oppressions, the common anguish and enduring harms we shared as targets, alongside the inspiring strategies for personal and collective empowerment we designed to resist and succeed."

Conclusion/continuing the conversations

These inspiring student voices demonstrate the power of human rights education within a Health Psychology course as an opportunity to construct dialogues deepening awareness of social determinants of health and rights, how these are distributed differentially in our lives and communities, and how we seek remedies and demand rights. Using participatory pedagogy and appreciation of the right to contribute to knowledge through inquiry, students learn comparatively across differences to conduct readings of power specific to domains and settings, appreciating their own dynamic intersections of privilege/oppression while building bridges towards compassionate understanding of barriers to rights of others. Knowledge of health and human rights allows students to use knowledge to transform personal, professional and collective opportunities, leveraging education as a transformative social determinant, expanding health literacy, employment, and sense of individual and community empowerment.

Discussion questions

1   How are personal narratives and reflexivity foundational to health and human rights education?
2   How do health and human rights activists use a social determinants-of-health approach to advocate for change?
3   How do you see the relationship between personal/intersectional sense of identity and global citizenship promoting health?

References

Andino Valdez, F. and Oliva, N. (2017). Latino male college students with disabilities: A Photovoice project. Gaston Institute and Health Promotion Research Team, University of Massachusetts, Boston.

Appadurai, A. (2006). The right to research. *Globalisation, Societies and Education*, 4(2), pp. 167–177.

Appiah, A. (2006). *Ethics in a world of strangers*. New York: Norton.

Bajaj, M. (2011). Human rights education: Ideology, location, and approaches. *Human Rights Quarterly*, 33(2), pp. 481–508.

Baum, F., MacDougall, C., and Smith, D. (2006). Participatory action research. *Journal of Epidemiology and Community Health*, 60(10), pp. 854–857.

Berwick, D.M. (2002). A user's manual for the IOM's "Quality Chasm" report. *Health Affairs*, 21(3), pp. 80–90.

Bowleg, L. (2017). Towards a critical health equity research stance: Why epistemology and methodology matter more than qualitative methods. *Health Education and Behavior*, 44(5), pp. 677–684.

Braveman, P. and Gottlieb, L. (2014). The social determinants of health: It's time to consider the causes of the causes. *Public Health Reports*, 129(1), pp. 19–31.

Braveman, P., Egerter, S., and Williams, D.R. (2011). The social determinants of health: coming of age. *Annual Review of Public Health*, 32, pp. 381–398.

Burd-Sharps, S., Lewis, K., and Martins, E.B. eds (2008). *The measure of America: American human development report, 2008–2009*. New York: Columbia University Press.

Chavez, V., Minkler, M., Wallerstein, N., and Spencer, M. (2010). Community organizing for health and social justice. In: L. Cohen, V. Chavez, and S. Chehimi (eds), *Prevention is primary: Strategies for community well being*. Chichester: John Wiley & Sons, pp. 87–112.

Claude, R.P. (2005). The right to education and human rights education. *Sur. Revista Internacional de Direitos Humanos*, 2(2), pp. 36–63.

Davis-Floyd, R. (2001). The technocratic, humanistic, and holistic paradigms of childbirth. *International Journal of Gynecology and Obstetrics*, 75(S1).

Davis-Floyd, R. (2003). Windows in space and time: A personal perspective on birth and death. *Birth*, 30(4), pp. 272–277.

Erdman, J.N. (2017). Human rights education in patient care. *Public Health Reviews*, 38(1), pp. 1–15.

Espino, M.M., Vega, I.I., Rendón, L.I., Ranero, J.J., and Muñiz, M.M. (2012). The process of reflexión in bridging testimonios across lived experience. *Equity and Excellence in Education*, 45(3), pp. 444–459.

Fadiman, A. (2012). *The spirit catches you and you fall down: A Hmong child, her American doctors, and the collision of two cultures*. New York: Macmillan.

Fine, M. and Cross, W. (2016). Critical race, psychology and social policy: Refusing damage, cataloguing oppression, and documenting desire. In: A. Alvarez, C. Liang, and H. Neville, eds, *The cost of racism for people of color: Contextualizing experiences of discrimination*. Washington, DC: American Psychological Association, pp. 273–294.

Hahn, R.A., Truman, B.I., and Williams, D.R. (2018). Civil rights as determinants of public health and racial and ethnic health equity: Health care, education, employment, and housing in the United States. *SSM-Population Health*, 4, pp. 17–24.

Jacobson, N. (2012). *Dignity and Health*. Nashville, TN: Vanderbilt University Press.

Jones, C.P. (2000). Levels of racism: a theoretic framework and a gardener's tale. *American Journal of Public Health*, 90(8), p. 1212.

Gottlieb, L. (2010). Funding healthy society helps cure health care. Opinion, Health Care Reform. *SFGate*. Available at: www.sfgate.com/opinion/openforum/article/Funding-healthy-society-helps-cure-health-care-3177542.php [Accessed January 15, 2018].

Hahn, R.A. and Truman, B.I. (2015). Education improves public health and promotes health equity. *International Journal of Health Services*, 45(4), pp. 657–678.

Hyde, C. (2012). Challenging ourselves: Critical reflection on power and privilege. In: M. Minkler, ed., *Community organizing for health and human services*. New Brunswick, NJ: Rutgers University Press, pp. 428–436.

Kickbusch, I. (2003). The contribution of the World Health Organization to a new public health and health promotion. *American Journal of Public Health*, 93(3), pp. 383–388.

Koh, H.K., Oppenheimer, S.C., Massin-Short, S.B., Emmons, K.M., Geller, A.C., and Viswanath, K. (2010). Translating research evidence into practice to reduce health disparities: a social determinants approach. *American Journal of Public Health*, 100(S1), pp. S72–S80.

Lugones, M. (2003). *Pilgrimages/peregrinajes: Theorizing coalition against multiple oppressions*. Lanham, MD: Rowman and Littlefield.

Lyons, A.C. and Chamberlain, K. (2005). *Health psychology: A critical introduction*. Cambridge: Cambridge University Press.

Marmot, M., Friel, S., Bell, R., Houweling, T.A., Taylor, S., and Commission on Social Determinants of Health (2008). Closing the gap in a generation: Health equity through action on the social determinants of health. *Lancet*, 372(9650), pp. 1661–1669.

McEwen, B.S. and Gianaros, P.J. (2010). Central role of the brain in stress and adaptation: Links to socioeconomic status, health, and disease. *Annals of the New York Academy of Sciences*, 1186(1), pp. 190–222.

McGowan, A.K., Lee, M.M., Meneses, C.M., Perkins, J., and Youdelman, M. (2016). Civil rights laws as tools to advance health in the twenty-first century. *Annual Review of Public Health*, 37, pp. 185–204.

Minkler, M., ed. (2012). *Community organizing for health and human services*. New Brunswick, NJ: Rutgers University Press.

Newman, O. (2017). The right to know your rights. *Polity*, 49(4), pp. 464–488.

Pelletier, J.F., Davidson, L., and Roelandt, J.L. (2009). Citizenship and recovery for everyone: A global model of public mental health. *International Journal of Mental Health Promotion*, 11(4), pp. 45–53.

Prilleltensky, I. (2012). Wellness as fairness. *American Journal of Community Psychology*, 49(1–2), pp. 1–21.

Roux, C. (2012). *Safe spaces: Human rights education in diverse contexts*. Rotterdam: Sense.

Sandoval, C. and Latorre, G. (2008). Chicana/o artivism: Judy Baca's digital work with youth of color. In: A. Everett, ed., *Learning race and ethnicity: Youth and digital media*. Cambridge, MA: MIT Press, pp. 81–108.

Shapiro, E. (2005). Because words are not enough: Transnational collaborations and Latina revisionings of health promotion for gender justice and social change. *NASW Journal*, 17(1), pp. 141–172.

Shapiro, E. (2014). Translating Latin American/US Latina frameworks and methods in gender and health equity: Linking women's health education and participatory social change. *International Quarterly of Community Health Education*, 34(1), pp. 19–36.

Shapiro, E. and Alcantara, D. (2016). Mujerista creativity: Latin@ sacred arts as life-course developmental resources. In: T. Bryant and L. Comas Diaz, eds, *Womanist and mujerista psychologies*. Washington, DC: APA, pp. 195–216.

Shapiro, E. and Atallah-Gutiérrez, C. (2012). Latina re-visionings of participatory health promotion practice: Cultural and ecosystemic perspectives linking personal and social change. *Women and Therapy*, 35(1–2), pp. 120–133.

Silvia, C.B. (2012). *But don't call me white: Mixed race women exposing nuances of privilege and oppression politics*. Rotterdam, NL: Sense Publishers.

Starfield, B. (2000). Is US health really the best in the world? *Jama*, 284(4), pp. 483–485.

Viruell-Fuentes, E.A., Miranda, P.Y., and Abdulrahim, S. (2012). More than culture: Structural racism, intersectionality theory, and immigrant health. *Social Science and Medicine*, 75(12), pp. 2099–2106.

Walker, M. and Unterhalter, E. (2007). *Amartya Sen's capability approach and social justice in education*. New York: Springer.

Wallerstein, N., Duran, B., Oetzel, J., and Minkler, M., eds (2017). *Community-based participatory research for health: advancing social and health equity*. San Francisco, CA: Jossey Bass.

Wandersman, A. (2003). Community science: Bridging the gap between science and practice with community-centered models. *American Journal of Community Psychology*, 31(3–4), pp. 227–242.

Zavella, P. (2017). Intersectional praxis in the movement for reproductive justice: The respect ABQ women campaign. *Signs: Journal of Women in Culture and Society*, 42(2), pp. 509–533.

Zembylas, M. (2017). Cultivating critical sentimental education in human rights education. *International Journal of Human Rights Education*, 1(1), pp. 1–26.

Further reading

Bajaj, M. and DasGupta, R. (2017). Editors' introduction. *International Journal of Human Rights Education*, 1(1). Available at: http://repository.usfca.edu/ijhre/vol1/iss1/1

Bajaj, M. and DasGupta, R., eds (2017). Inaugural issue. *International Journal of Human Rights Education*, 1(1). Available at: http://repository.usfca.edu/ijhre/vol1/iss1/4

Braveman, P. (2014). What is health equity; and how does a life-course approach take us further toward it? *Maternal and Child Health Journal*, 18(2), pp. 366–372.

Keet, A. (2017). Does human rights education exist? *International Journal of Human Rights Education*, 1(1). Available at: http://repository.usfca.edu/ijhre/vol1/iss1/6

Monaghan, C., Spreen, C.A., and Hillary, A. (2017). A truly transformative HRE: Facing our current challenges. *International Journal of Human Rights Education*, 1(1). Available at: http://repository.usfca.edu/ijhre/vol1/iss1/4

World Health Organization (2002). Twenty-four questions and answers on health and human rights. *Health and Human Rights Publication Series*, 1. Available at: www.who.int/hhr/NEW37871OMSOK.pdf [Accessed May 14, 2018].

Appendix

Human rights at a public urban university: the case of the University of Massachusetts Boston

Bryan Gangemi and Rita Arditti

The Human Rights Working Group (HRWG) of the University of Massachusetts (UMass) Boston is a four-year-old group composed of students,
staff, faculty, and human rights activists from the wider community.[1] One of
the greatest features of the HRWG is its diversity in gender, race/ethnicity,
age, class, occupation, and sexual orientation. Working together in such a
diverse group has widened our individual perspectives and provided the
opportunity to learn from each other in an atmosphere of respect for our
differences. As we strove for a group process that reflected our engagement
to human rights, our mission and our goals became more clear and distinct.
Based in an urban, public, non-residential, research-intensive institution, the
group is committed to a vision of the urban mission of UMass Boston that
promotes economic and social justice. Of the 13,000 [in 2005] students
enrolled at the university, 60 percent are the first in their families to gain
higher education in the US. Within this demographic, a significant portion
of the student body has overcome great economic adversities, migration
losses, the fallout from violent communities, and unfair distribution of
social resources. Our student body has a rich base of experiential knowledge
that has allowed our group to tie theory with practice in our work, making
human rights education truly relevant within our community.

The activity of the HRWG has centered in organizing educational events
on campus around various human rights issues; supporting human rights
projects and initiatives from outside organizations, collaborating with other
organizations on events and conferences (like the 2004 Boston Social
Forum); writing articles for the campus student newspaper; and developing
ideas and curricula on human rights for the UMass Boston student population. Currently the group has 20 active members who work on our various
projects with close to 80 members in the UMass Boston community who
serve as our base of support. Under the guidance and directive of four con-
secutive student chairpersons we have hosted ten major events. Events
include: "Colombia, a Human Rights Disaster," a forum held in 2001 that
featured Noam Chomsky and Germán Plata Diaz, a human rights worker
from Barracancabermeja, Colombia, and "War on Terrorism or Assault on
Human Rights: Civil Liberties, Homeland Security, and Democracy in the

Post 9/11 World," an all-day conference held in May 2003 which featured, among other scholars and activists, National Lawyers Guild president Michael Avery and legal scholar David Cole. Especially relevant to UMass Boston was the forum we organized in the fall of 2003, "Connect the Dots: Globalization, Privatization, and the Rising Cost of Higher Public Education," a forum linking tuition increases at our university to the larger global movement towards privatization. This past spring we hosted "Integrating Human Rights in Higher Education," which focused on our work with human rights education and featured Human Rights Education Associates executive director Felisa Tibbitts.

Human rights education

In the last year much of the group's work has focused on the importance of introducing an explicit perspective on education and human rights in the UMass Boston community. The active presence and participation of the UMass Boston community at our forums has served as an impetus to direct our efforts towards the development of a human rights academic program that would more fully integrate our work into the university's academic culture. Many members were eager for this vision to turn into a feasible goal. We quickly created a subcommittee that laid out a series of steps to gauge the potential and possibility of such a program. One of our first steps was connecting with faculty who had successfully implemented other academic programs that were grounded to a strong human rights philosophy. Members of the HRWG conducted interviews with the directors and founders of departments such as Women's Studies, Asian American Studies, and Labor Studies to see how these programs came to fruition. In addition to gathering insight on the success of these programs, we were exposed to a rich body of human rights content in a number of already existing courses. Wanting to engage more with faculty with a human rights perspective, we wrote a short paper to capture what we were looking for in our efforts to integrate an explicit human rights component in the university's academic body. Taking as a starting point the Universal Declaration of Human Rights we proposed that:

> A Human Rights course could be one that raises consciousness and knowledge about human rights, discusses their importance to achieve a free and just society, and stresses the need to integrate those rights into the public sphere. This can be done over a wide range of perspectives and methods, such as courses that introduce students to legal frameworks, discuss justice promotion, teach critical analysis, or explore historical roots of human rights topics. At the core, we hope there will be an intention to help build a culture of human rights, commitment to the promotion of civil society and to the values that support progressive social change,

and an understanding of the indivisibility and interdependence of human rights.[2]

Faculty across all colleges, departments, and disciplines responded with great enthusiasm, submitting dozens of syllabi, leading us to consider the following clusters of related courses in constructing our academic program:

1 Human rights: history; social construction of human rights; critical analysis of human rights rhetoric and human rights documents; legal frameworks, both at the international and local levels.
2 Actualizing human rights; social justice promotion; international and local efforts to *implement* human rights.
3 Identity and culture; indigenous rights.
4 Human rights education.
5 Case studies/new directions.

We propose using these clusters as a framework for the development of a full academic program. As faculty continued to express interest and academic departments continued to submit syllabi a picture began to emerge that many of the courses in the university had a human rights dimension that could fit well within our vision of creating an academic program. It also became clear to us that there was an immediate need for a basic interdisciplinary Introduction to Human Rights course where some of the fundamental ideas and practices regarding human rights would be analyzed and discussed. We concluded that from that base further human rights course work could then be built.

Inspired by similar work by Karen Suyemoto's course, "Introduction to Asian American Studies," and cognizant of the collective group process that had taken us to this point, we came up with the idea of a course coordinated by two faculty members: Elora Chowdhury from Women's Studies and Amy Den Ouden from Anthropology, but taught by "guest" faculty from various UMass Boston faculty and outside activists and scholars. The committee laid out the template for the syllabus building upon the clusters we created as the central units for the Introduction to Human Rights course. By using this template we wanted to fully capture the breadth and depth of the material that we would cover, while laying a foundation for the full program we envision building in the future. Over a span of four months, eight faculty members, two students, and a community activist/scholar put endless energy, time, and effort into the design of the syllabus. With trepidation, we gave ourselves a deadline, we decided that by March 2005 we would present a complete course outline to the UMass Boston faculty council! Hard to believe but true, we met our deadline, presented our course to the faculty council, and won approval for it to be offered in the spring of 2006!

In summary, the HRWG will continue to work with the UMass Boston community at large in developing an integrated vision of human rights that takes into consideration the harsh realities of life in our times. It was important to us that the course address explicitly the importance of the pedagogical process of learning about human rights in a way that leads to empathy, solidarity, development of learners into activists, and personal transformation. In addition to cognitive skills about human rights, the course puts a strong emphasis on the values at the core of human rights, such as dignity and freedom, attitude change, value clarification, and empowerment issues. It involves knowledge not just about human rights violations but also about human rights promotion and protection, a proactive approach to everyday life, and a commitment to social justice. Our approach to human rights education resonates with Paulo Freire's thinking regarding learning and social change, the relation between teacher and learner, and the development of a critical consciousness. It is our hope that a full program will come to fruition that encapsulates these core values and principles that define our work.

Notes

1 This essay first appeared in R. Arditti and B. Gangemi (2005), Human rights at a public urban university: The case of UMass Boston. *TwelveTen: US Human Rights Network Semi Annual Newsletter*, 1, pp. 5–6.
2 "A call for human rights courses at UMASS Boston," summer 2004.

Index

Note: page numbers in bold type refer to Tables.

2030 Agenda for Sustainable
    Development Goals 12, 89, 131,
    138–144, **140**; see also SDGs
    (Sustainable Development Goals)

AAF (Australian Aboriginal Fellowship)
    202–203
Aakar Innovations 299–300
Abdullah-Awad, Z.J. 191
Abernathy, Ralph 68
Aboriginal Black Power Movement 205
Aboriginal Commission 202
Aboriginal people, Australia, human
    rights history 13, 196–209
Aboriginal Tent Embassy 205
Aborigines Protection Society (APS) 203
abortion, South Africa 117
abuse 22, 24, 25, 27; and NGOs 36–37;
    see also child abuse
access to courts, South Africa 112
accountability: and the MDGs
    (Millennium Development Goals)
    136; and the SDGs (Sustainable
    Development Goals) 142–143
accumulation, of capital 51, 53,
    57, 287
action research 313, 318
activism 35; art 313, 315, 321, 322, 323;
    indigenous peoples 196, 199, 200–201,
    206; Latin America 66, 70, 72, 76;
    LGBTQ 171; women's 86, 89, 93,
    94–95
Adichie, Chimamanda Ngozi 11
adolescents 267, 297, 300, 323
adoption: same-sex 172;
    South Africa 117
adulthood 266

advocacy 135, 168, 169, 171, 200, 244,
    313, 315
aesthetic 253–254, 262, 265, 273,
    276, 277
affect, and Eudora Welty's queer love
    262, 265, 269, 274, 277
African Charter on Human and Peoples'
    Rights 42–43
African Commission on Human and
    Peoples' Rights 43
African National Congress (ANC) 113
African Women's Rights Protocol 79,
    83, 84, 89–90, 92, 94
afro-pessimism 50, 51, 52, 55, 60
Agamben, Giorgio 189, 190, 271, 274
agency 14, 302–303; and Bangladeshi
    Muktijuddho film 14, 243, 244, 249,
    251–252, 254, 256
Ahmadinejad, Mahmoud 3
Ahsan, Joya 246
AI see Amnesty International (AI)
Alfaragi, Saad 133
Ali, Nada Mustafa 11, 79–97
alQaws 175
Alston, P. 43, 144
Althusser, Louis 50–51
American Anti-Imperialist League 66
American Convention on Human
    Rights, 1969 42
American Declaration of the Rights and
    Duties of Man, 1948 42
Amnesty International (AI) 68, 69,
    70–73, 236; and LGBTQ rights 168
An-Na'im, Abdullahi Ahmed 20, 23,
    45, 80
ANC (African National Congress) 113
Andrews, Shirley 203

anthropocentrism 5
anthropology 6, 9, 23, 80, 253, 317; and
    experiences of human rights work in
    Haiti 215, 217, 220, 226; methods 217
anti-blackness 50–52, 53, 54, 60, 251
anti-humanism 50–51, 52
anti-imperialism 11, 65, 66, 75
anti-sodomy laws, India 175
Appadurai, A. 312
Appiah, A, 22, 186
APS (Aborigines Protection Society) 203
Arc International 168
Arditti, Rita 6, 331–334
Arendt, Hannah 26, 29, 54, 57, 58–59,
    98, 101
Arizona 105
art 91, 262, 264, 265–266, 323;
    see also creative arts
Asian migrants to US 102–103
ästhetische Bildung 278
Astraea Lesbian Foundation for
    Justice 171
asylum seekers 29, 30; *see also* refugees
Australia: 1967 Constitutional
    Referendum 204; indigenous people,
    human rights history 13, 196–209;
    nuclear weapons testing 200–201
Australian Aboriginal Fellowship (AAF)
    202–203
Australian People's Assembly for
    Human Rights 202
Avery, Michael 332
Awami League 245, 246, 247

Baartman, Sarah 91
Bahrain 236–237; *see also* GCC (Gulf
    Cooperation Council) states (Bahrain,
    Kuwait, Oman, Qatar, Saudi Arabia,
    United Arab Emirates)
Bailey, Yasmin 14–15, 315, 320, 322–323
Bajaj, M. 314
Balibar, E. 26
Ban Ki-Moon 134
Bandler, Faith 202
Bangladesh Independence War 255
Bangladesh Liberation War 14, 243, 245,
    249, 253
Bangladeshi *Muktijuddho* films 14,
    243–256
Banneker, Benjamin 3
Bannerji, Kaushalya 175
Bartky, Sandra 305
basic human needs 136, 156, 188; South
    Africa 122

Be Girl 300
Beitz, Charles 298
Belleau, Jean-Philippe 13, 215–227
Beloved (Morrison) 7
Benedict, Ruth 80
Bengali people 243, 244, 247, 248–249,
    250–251, 253–254; Bengali Muslims
    244, 246, 251, 254
Bennett, Mary 203
Berlant, Lauren 264, 265
Bersani, Leo 281n16
Bhaskaran, Suparna 169
Bill of Rights, South Africa 114–115, 121
Birangona 248–249, 250, 252,
    253–255, 256
Black and Pink 176
Boas, Frank 80
Bobel, Chris 14, 297–311
bodily integrity, right to 22–23, 80, 94,
    117, 171, 172
body modification practices 22–23
Bolivia 67
Boosey, Robin 301–302
border patrol, US 12, 99, 103–104, 105,
    106, 107
Bourdieu, Pierre 113–114
Brazil 65, 67–69
Brexit 229
Broeck, S. 50
Brown, Wendy 267–268
Buck-Morss, S. 56, 57
Buddhism 4–5
Budhiraja, S. 171–172
Bunch, Charlotte 171
Burke, Timothy 305
burkha 248
Burn, Shawn Meghan 79
Bush (George W. Bush) administration,
    US 105, 106
Byrd, Jodi 60

California 101, 103, 104–105
cannibalism, in Haiti 218–219
capital, accumulation of 51, 53, 57, 287
CAR (Council for Aboriginal Rights)
    202, 203
Carlson, John 112
Carre, C.e.a. 91
Carter, Jimmy 70, 74
CEDAW (Convention on the
    Elimination of All Forms of
    Discrimination against Women) 11,
    40, 79, 81, 88, 89, 94, 148–149,
    153–154; GR no. 19 148, 149, 154;

GR no. 28 153–154; GR no. 35, and Mexico 12, 149, 154–160; overview of 82–83
Central America 65, 74–77
Césaire, Aimé 52
Chakrabarty, D. 58
Charles, Chrislene 319
Chavez, Vivian 322
checks and balances, South Africa 113
child abuse: South Africa 117–118, 121; *see also* abuse
childhood 266
children: education in refugee camps 13, 180–192; and Eudora Welty's queer love 262, 267, 273, 275; mental health of in refugee camps 181–182, 183; rights of 116, 117–118, 121, 182
Chile 72, 73, 75
Chinese migrants to US 102–103
Chomsky, Noam 331
Choo, H. 151
Chowdhury, Elora Halim 1–16, 14, 243–260, 333
cinema: human rights cinema 14, 143–144; national cinema 14, 143, 144–145
Citizen Initiative and Social Development INCIDE Social AC 158–159
citizens/citizenship 3, 4, 12, 13, 20, 25–28; South Africa 111, 120, 121; US, and the US-Mexican border 99, 102, 103, 104, 108
civil rights *see* first-generation rights (civil and political rights)
civil society 46; and UN institutions 34–35
Clastres, Pierre 217
Clements, John 2–3
close reading 199, 245, 262
closet 272
closeted 272–273, 275
Cmiel, Kenneth 70, 71
Cohen, Ilana 304
Cold War, and Latin America 65–78
Cole, David 332
Collins, Patricia Hill 150, 244, 250, 256
Colombia 14, 286, 288, 290–293; Constitution of 1991 14, 286, 291–292, 293; peace accords 292, 293
coloniality of power 285–286, 286–287, 293
colonized people, and human rights 3

Commission on Human Rights, UN 40, 132–133, 203
common humanity, and education 185–188
community councils, South Africa 118–119
compassionate empathy 314
Conadis (National Council for the development and inclusion of persons with disabilities), Mexico 157–158
Conavim (National Commission to prevent and eradicate violence against women), Mexico 157, 158
Conference on Environment and Development (Earth Summit), 1992, UN 133
Conference on Sustainable Development, UN 139
constitution: Australia 201, 202–203, 204; Colombia 14, 286, 291–292, 293; Haiti 218, 219; ILO 231; South Africa 12, 111–112, 113–115, 116, 117, 120–122; US 99, 103, 104, 106
Constitutional Court, South Africa 112, 113, 114, 120, 122
Constitutional Referendum, 1967, Australia 204
consuming femininity 305
Convention 107, ILO 203–204
Convention against Torture and Other Cruel, Inhuman or Degrading Treatment or Punishment, 1984, UN 40
Convention Concerning Indigenous and Tribal Peoples in Independent Countries, 1989, UN 41
Convention for the Safeguarding of Intangible Cultural Heritage, 2003, UN 41
Convention on the Elimination of All Forms of Discrimination against Women *see* CEDAW (Convention on the Elimination of All Forms of Discrimination against Women)
Convention on the Rights of Persons with Disabilities (CRPD), UN 40, 149, 155, 158
Convention on the Rights of the Child, UN 41, 83, 132, 182
Convention Relating to the Status of Refugees, 1951, UN 229
Cormier, R. 152
Correa, Sonia Onufer 172

Council for Aboriginal Rights (CAR)
202, 203
courts, South Africa 112–115, 118–119,
120, 122–123
creative arts 323–325
creative empathy 314
Crenshaw, K. 150, 152
critical consciousness 14, 314, 315, 334
critical discourse analysis 289;
feminist 298
critical health psychology 316
critical human rights 14, 44, 95,
287–288
cross-cultural legitimacy 20, 23, 24, 45
CRPD (Convention on the Rights of
Persons with Disabilities) 40, 149,
155, 158
"cruel optimism" 264
cruising 272–273
cultural diversity 21–24
cultural humility 318, 319
cultural identity inventory 318
cultural practices 21, 22–23, 27, 28,
80, 92
cultural relativism 44, 80, 113, 122
cultural rights *see* fourth generation
rights; second-generation rights
(economic, social and cultural rights)
cultural specificity 23, 81, 82, 87, 88, 90,
92, 268
cultures: dynamic nature of 80; and
Eudora Welty's queer love 262,
268–269; gendered nature of 80–81
Curiel, O. 286
customary law: South Africa 113, 115,
117, 118, 123; Sudan 85
Cyrus Cylinder 2–3

Daiya, Kavita 256
Dajani, Rana 191–192
Darrow, M. 135
Davis-Floyd, R. 317
Day, Ikyo 53
de-animation 55
Dean, Tim 272–273, 275
Decety, Jean 192
Declaration of Commitment on HIV/
AIDS 41
Declaration of the Rights of Indigenous
Peoples (UNDRIP) 198, 199, 200,
205–208, 209; Article 3 206; Article 46
(1) 206–207
Declaration of the Rights of Man and
the Citizen, France, 1789 11, 57

Declaration of the Rights of the Child,
1959, UN 182
Declaration on the Fundamental
Principles and Rights at Work,
1998, ILO 13, 230, 231
Declaration on the Right to
Development, UN 132
Declaration on the Right to Peace,
UNGA 285, 290
decolonial theory 11, 14, 50, 52–53, 285,
286, 292–293
decolonization 50, 56, 57, 60–61, 169,
190, 197, 288; and indigenous people
in Australia 197–198, 202, 205
Deleuze, Gilles 266
Democratic Rights Council 202
Den Ouden, Amy 333
Department of Homeland Security,
US 106
deportation of US citizens 104, 106–107
Derrida, Jacques 272, 273
desire, and Eudora Welty's queer love
264, 267, 273, 274, 276, 278
Deskaheh, Chief 200
determination in the last instance 50, 51
development: "girling" of 298–299; as a
human right 290. see also human
development
Devlin, Albert 275
DfG (Days for Girls) 297, 298
difference, and Eudora Welty's queer
love 262, 263, 269, 270, 271, 274,
275, 276
dignity, and menstruation 14, 297, 298,
299–301, 302–303, 304, 305
Diop, Abdoulaye 232, 236, 237
"dis/empowerment paradox" 111, 120
disability 12, 137, 141, 142, 148, 149,
150, 151, 152, 154–160
disciplinary power 58
disciplined embodiment 299
discourse analysis: critical 289; feminist
critical 298
discrimination 151, 315, 317; Australian
Aboriginal people 196, 207; disability
12, 60, 137, 148, 149, 155, 157–158;
gender 11, 12, 19, 40, 79, 82–83, 137,
148–149, 150, 153–154, 155, 157, 159;
migrant workers 235, 236, 237;
multiple 149, 155; racial/ethnic 36,
137, 142, 150; sexual orientation 166,
167, 168, 172, 173
displaced children, education of *see*
children, education in refugee camps

domestic law 25, 27, 28, 46
domestic violence: and migrant workers
in the Gulf region 234–235; *see also*
gender-based violence
domestic workers: female migrant
workers 234–235; ILO *Domestic
Workers Convention, 2011* 237
Dominican Republic 66, 67, 225, 319
Dorf, Julie 168
Dryden-Peterson, Sarah 185, 186
dual labor market 230
dualism 262, 271
DuGuid, Charles 202, 203
duty 24–25, 28, 29, 30; South Africa
115–116, 121

EcoFemme 300
economic and social rights 40, 41, 131,
132, 133, 135, 136; *see also*
second-generation rights (economic,
social and cultural rights)
ECOSOC (Economic and Social
Council), UN 35, 36
Edelman, Lee 61, 279n4
education: and common humanity
185–188; in refugee camps 13,
180–192; right to 313; *see also* human
rights education
Ekattor er Shongram (film) 255
El Jack, Amani 13–14, 228–242
El Salvador 75, 76
electoral observers, Haiti 220–224
elimination, settler colonial logics of
53, 59
empathy 314, 315, 334; and education in
refugee camps 186, 191, 192
empire, transit of 60
Enlightenment, European 52, 263
environmental rights 34; *see also* fourth
generation rights
equality: and the MDGs (Millennium
Development Goals) 137; and the
SDGs (Sustainable Development
Goals) 141–142
Eskiocak, Ozlem 188
ethnic discrimination 36, 137, 142, 150
ethnography 9, 86, 174, 326;
ethnographic methods 215; and
experiences of human rights work
in Haiti 217, 221, 226
EU (European Union), citizenship
rights 27
Europe, migration crisis 29, 30

European Commission of Human
Rights 42
European Convention on Human
Rights, 1953 42
European Court of Human Rights 42
exclusion, settler colonial logics of 53, 59
Exclusion Act 1882, US 103
experiences 26, 30

Fanon, Frantz 50, 60–61
Faulkner, William 262–263,
265–266, 274
FCAA (Federal Council for Aboriginal
Advancement) 197, 201, 203, 205
feeling, and Eudora Welty's queer love
266–267, 273, 276, 277–278
female adultery 267, 275
female genital cutting/mutilation (FGC/
M) 81, 82, 90–94
femininity 92, 116, 303, 305; and
Bangladeshi *Muktijuddho* film
244, 249, 251
feminism: and LGBTQ 170–171;
transnational 171, 176, 251
feminist critical discourse analysis 298
feminization, of vulnerability 246
Ferree, M. 151
FGC/M (female genital cutting/
mutilation) 81, 82, 90–94
fiction, and Eudora Welty's queer love
261, 265–267, 269–270, 272–273,
275–277, 278
Filipina female domestic workers
234–235
first-generation rights (civil and political
rights) 34, 37–40, 43, 44, 289, 290
First Protocol to the ICCPR 37, 39
Foucault, Michel 52, 55, 58, 305
Fouché, Rayvon 306
fourth generation rights (environment
and cultural) 34, 44
France 3, 43, 50, 56
freedom fighters, Bangladesh 243, 245,
246, 248, 249, 250, 251, 252, 253, 255
Freeman, M. 44, 46, 293
Freire, Paulo 312, 314, 334
French Revolution, 1789 3, 43, 50, 56
Fukuda-Parr, S. 137
fungibility 55
Furtado, Grace 14–15, 314, 325–326
future, the, and Eudora Welty's queer
love 263–264, 265, 268, 271, 275, 276,
277–278

Galtung, J. 289
Gangemi, Bryan 6, 331–334
gay men 167, 168, 169, 267, 272;
    see also LGBTQ
gay rights 167; *see also* LGBTQ
Gayen, Keberi 245
Gaza, refugee camps 13, 185, 187–189,
    190
GCC (Gulf Cooperation Council) states
    (Bahrain, Kuwait, Oman, Qatar, Saudi
    Arabia, United Arab Emirates),
    migrant workers 232–238
GCE (Global Citizenship Education)
    program, UNESCO 185–186, 189,
    190
Geertz, Clifford 217
gender: Eudora Welty's queer love 266,
    268, 269, 277; migrant workers
    234–235
gender-based violence 95, 235, 315,
    323–325; female domestic workers
    234–235; GR 35 and Mexico 12,
    148–149, 153, 154–160
gender discrimination 11, 12, 19, 40, 79,
    82–83, 137, 148–149, 150, 153–154,
    155, 157, 159
gender identity 165, 166–167, 168, 170,
    172, 173, 174, 177; *see also* LGBTQ
gender ideology, Bangladeshi
    Muktijuddho film 244, 250–251,
    253, 255
gender justice, Bangladeshi *Muktijuddho*
    film 14, 243–244, 245
General Act on Women's Access to a
    Life Free of Violence, 2007, Mexico
    157, 158
General Colonization Law 1824, US 100
Geneva Declaration on the Rights of the
    Child, 1924 182
Gibbs, Pearl 202
Gilson, Erinn Cunniff 251, 252, 254
girls, and development 298–299
Giroux, Henry 183–184
global citizenship: education in refugee
    camps 180, 186, 190; Global
    Citizenship Education (GCE)
    program, UNESCO 185–186, 189,
    190; human rights education for 314,
    315, 317, 320–321
Global Compact, UN 41
Global North 10, 79, 95, 140, 167, 169,
    175, 234, 238
Global South 11, 14, 140, 167, 169, 230,
    287; MHM project 297, 298, 300,

304–305, 306; women and
    gender-based violence 81–82, 87,
    91–92, 94, 95
Goldenberg, J.L. 305
Gosse, V. 76
Gottlieb, Laura 318
*Government of the Republic of South Africa
    v Grootboom* (2001 (1) SA 46 (CC)) 112
Gramsci, Antonio 51
Green, James 68, 69
Grinker, R.R. 81
Guadalupe Hidalgo, treaty of 102
Guatemala 67
Guerilla (film) 243, 245–250, 255, 256
Guiding Principles on Business and
    Human Rights, UN 41
Gulf Cooperation Council (GCC) states
    (Bahrain, Kuwait, Oman, Qatar, Saudi
    Arabia, United Arab Emirates),
    migrant workers 232–238
Gulf region, migrant workers 228,
    231—238

Hagen, Jamie J. 12–13, 165–179
Haiti: experiences of human rights work
    in 13, 216–226; Haitian Revolution
    50, 56–57; US occupation of 66
Halperin, David 279n5, 280n10
Hamid, Mohsin 181
Hamid, W. 88
Hancock, A. 150
Hankivsky, O. 152–153
Haque, Syed Shamsul 245–246
Harris, J. 230
Hartman, Saidiya 55
Hasratian, Avak 14, 261–284
"healing classrooms" process, IRC 183
health promotion, and UMass Boston
    312–315, 326; course organization
    316–319; Health Promotion Research
    Team 316, 318–319; students'
    personal narratives and testimonies
    319–326
Hegel, G.W.F. 51
hegemony 51
Henao Castro, Andrés Fabián 11, 50–64
heritage, and Eudora Welty's queer love
    265, 268, 275, 278
heteronormativity 167
High Commissioner for Human Rights,
    UN 37, 40
Hirschl, Ran 112–113
history: and Eudora Welty's queer love
    261, 263, 265, 277; of the "other" 52

HIV/AIDS 111
Hollibaugh, Amber 176
homonationalism 170
homophobia 167, 168, 170, 172, 175
homosexuality 86, 173, 175, 270, 272;
 see also LGBTQ
Hoppe, Trevor 280n10
hospitality 270, 272, 273, 275, 276
Hossain, Rubaiyat 252, 255
HRW (Human Rights Watch) 168, 235,
 236, 303
HRWG (Human Rights Working
 Group), UMass Boston 6–7, 331–334
Hulme, D. 13–136
human, the 19–20, 24, 25, 26, 27,
 28, 29, 30, 31, 52–53, 285–286,
 293; 287–288
human development 134, 136, 313–314,
 316; *see also* development
Human Development Index, UN 313
human rights: critical 14, 44, 95,
 287–288; critiques of 57–60; and
 cultural diversity 21–24; and Eudora
 Welty's queer love 261–262, 263,
 264–265, 267, 268, 272, 275, 276, 277,
 278; experiences of working in 13,
 215–226; history and development of
 1–5, 132–134; methodological
 'messiness' of 7–9; regional system of
 42–43, 79, 94; rise of global regime
 34–46; and state power 3–4
human rights advocacy 135, 168, 169,
 171, 200, 244, 313, 315
human rights cinema 14, 143–144
Human Rights Committee, UN 38,
 39, 40
Human Rights Council, UN 37, 40, 41,
 132–133, 172–173, 290
human rights discourse 1, 50, 80, 117,
 229, 261, 264, 267, 288, 320; context
 and history 10–12; in development
 campaigns 297, 299, 306; indigenous
 people in Australia 196, 197, 198, 202,
 204, 205, 206
human rights education 6, 188, 189,
 312, 313–315, 316, 320–321, 326,
 331–334
human rights legal instruments 19, 20,
 25, 30
human rights missions, Haiti 216–220
human rights violations 13, 19, 20, 21,
 22, 23–25, 27, 28, 29, 30, 31, 36–37
Human Rights Watch (HRW) 168, 235,
 236, 303

Human Rights Working Group
 (HRWG), UMass Boston 6–7,
 331–334
Hunt, L. 287–288
hygiene 297; menstrual 14, 299, 300, 302,
 303, 304, 307n6; racialized and
 gendered discourse 305; *see also*
 MHM (Menstrual Hygiene
 Management)
Hyndman, Jennifer 189
hypersexuality 255

IBPA (intersectionality-based policy
 analysis) 152–153
ICCPR (International Covenant on Civil
 and Political Rights) 37–38, 39–40, 79,
 83, 133, 137, 182
ICESCR (International Covenant on
 Economic, Social and Cultural Rights)
 37–38, 38–39, 40–41, 79, 131, 132,
 133, 137–138, 182
ICGLR (International Conference on the
 Great Lakes Region) protocol on the
 Prevention and Suppression of Sexual
 Violence against Women and
 Children, 2008 84
identity: and Eudora Welty's queer love
 265–266, 267, 271, 273; political 204;
 sexual 169, 267
identity politics 265, 320–321
IESOGI 173
IGLHRC (International Gay and Lesbian
 Human Rights Commission) 168
ILGA (International Lesbian, Gay,
 Trans, and Intersex Association) 168
ILO (International Labor Organization)
 13, 41, 203, 228, 230, 231, 232, 233,
 235, 236, 237; Convention 107
 203–204; Declaration on the
 Fundamental Principles and Rights at
 Work, 1998 13, 230, 231; *Domestic
 Workers Convention*, 2011 237
Immigration and Nationality Act,
 US 106
*Immigration and Naturalization Service v.
 Delgado* 104
Imperial Constitution of Dessalines,
 1804 11
India: LGBTQ 169, 175; partition
 244, 256
indigenous peoples, and social death
 53–54
indigenous rights 34, 44; Australia 13,
 196–209; *see also* third-generation

rights (solidarity rights); UNDRIP
  (Declaration of the Rights of
  Indigenous Peoples)
indigenous studies 50, 51, 52
individuality 262, 278; "burdened" 62n9
infibulation 92; *see also* FGC/M (female
  genital cutting/mutilation)
institutional account 24–25, 29, 30
Inter-American Commission on Human
  Rights 42
Inter-American Court of Human
  Rights 42
interactional account 24–25, 28, 29,
  30, 31
interdependency, and the SDGs
  (Sustainable Development Goals)
  143–144
International Civilian Mission to Haiti
  (MICIVIH) 216–220
International Conference on Population
  and Development, 1994, UN 133
International Conference on the Great
  Lakes Region (ICGLR) protocol on
  the Prevention and Suppression of
  Sexual Violence against Women and
  Children, 2008 84
International Convention for the
  Protection of All Persons from
  Enforced Disappearance, 2006 40
International Convention on the
  Protection of the Rights of All
  Migrant Workers and Members of
  Their Families, UN 228, 230
International Convention on the
  Protection of the Rights of All
  Migrant Workers and Their
  Families, 1990 41
International Covenant on Civil and
  Political Rights (ICCPR) 37–38, 39–40,
  79, 83, 133, 137, 182
International Covenant on Economic,
  Social and Cultural Rights (ICESCR)
  37–38, 38–39, 40–41, 79, 131, 132,
  133, 137–138, 182
International Gay and Lesbian Human
  Rights Commission (IGLHRC) 168
International Labor Organization *see*
  ILO (International Labor
  Organization)
international law 21–22, 25, 27, 35;
  challenges for 44–46
International Lesbian, Gay, Trans, and
  Intersex Association (ILGA) 168

International Organization for
  Migration 236
international organizations, and Haiti
  220, 222, 226
International Rescue Committee (IRC)
  182, 183
internationalism 11, 65–67, 69, 72–73,
  74–75, 76–77
intersectionality 89, 150–154, 176–177,
  313, 314, 316–317, 318, 325; gender
  and disability 12, 149, 154–160
intersectionality-based policy analysis
  (IBPA) 152–153
intersex 155, 166, 167, 172, 174; *see also*
  LGBTQ
Iran, Cyrus Cylinder 2–3
IRC (International Rescue Committee)
  182, 183
Islam, Morshedul 253
Israel, LGBTQ 170
Izméry, Antoine 220

Jackson, Holly 279
Jefferson, Thomas 3
Jiménez, Luis 11–12, 98–110
John, Maria 12, 13, 196–211
Johnston, Trevor 232, 236, 237
Jones, Camara 317
Jordan, refugee camps 190
Joseph, Mona 319
judicialisation of politics, South Africa
  112–113
Judisman, Clara 158–159
Jureidini, Ray 229
Justive, Nerson 319

Kafala system (migrant sponsorship)
  14, 228, 230, 231, 232, 233,
  234–237, 238
Kakuma refugee camp, Kenya 184–185
Kakutani, Michiko 181
Kenya, refugee camps 13, 184–185, 189
Keown, Damien 4
Kew, Darren 10, 34–49
kindness 14, 267, 270, 276
kinship 263
Klasing, Amanda 303–304
"Know Your Rights" workshop, UMass
  Boston 312, 313
Kuwait 236–237; *see also* GCC (Gulf
  Cooperation Council) states (Bahrain,
  Kuwait, Oman, Qatar, Saudi Arabia,
  United Arab Emirates)

labor, and land 53
Laclau, E. 51
Lamonthe, Diana 14–15, 314, 325–326
land, and labor 53
Land Act 1851, US 101
Latin America 11, 65–70; Amnesty
  International and the rise of human
  rights 70–78; colonial legacy 287
Lauren, Paul Gordon 19–20
law *see* customary law; domestic law;
  international law
"lawfare" 112
Le, Kien Trung 232, 236, 237
League of Nations 200
LeBlanc, Kim 187
legal consciousness 121
legal culture, South Africa 112–113
legal process, South Africa 114,
  118–120, 122, 123
Lemaitre Ripoll, J. 291
Lesbian Avengers 170–171
LGBT rights 168, 171
LGBTQ 12–13, 165, 176–177, 292;
  definitions and terminology 165–167;
  feminist organizing 170–171; local and
  national contexts 174–176; resistance
  to 170, 174; sexual rights 171–172;
  transnational organizing 167–170; and
  the UN 165, 172–174
liberal democracy 287
liberal peace 288–289, 290, 293
Linde, Makude 91
Lindsey, Treva 255
literary criticism 261–262, 264, 269,
  271, 272
local, the, and Eudora Welty's queer
  love 261, 268, 269
Lombardo, E. 152
Lorde, Audre 171
Louisiana 279n3, 281n14
love: Eudora Welty's queer love
  262, 267, 270, 271, 272, 275,
  276, 278
Lugones, Maria 314
lynching 101, 103, 250

MacNaughton, Gillian 12, 131–147
magistrates' courts, South Africa
  118–119, 120
Magna Carta, 1215 1
Maldonado-Torres, N. 287
Mantashe, Gwede 113
Manuel, G. 44
Marks, S. P. 43

marriage: Eudora Welty's queer love
  262, 264, 267, 268; same-sex 167, 170,
  174, 264, 267
Marriot, David 54
Marrs, Suzanne 280n12, 281n13
Marx, Karl 51, 53, 57–58
Marxism 50, 51, 59, 261
masculinity 92, 170; and Bangladeshi
  Muktijuddho film 244, 250, 253,
  254, 263
Mattei, Ugo 114
McCall, L. 151
McClennen, Sophia A. 268
McLeod, Don 203
McMahand, Donny 272
McWilliams, Sally 249
MDGs (Millennium Development
  Goals) 131, **134**, 134–138, 139–140,
  141, 143–144
Mead, Margaret 80
Meherjaan (film) 143, 252–253, 255, 256
melancholia 265
memorialization 246, 250, 254, 255,
  264, 272
memory, and Eudora Welty's queer love
  262, 263, 264
men who have sex with men (MSM)
  171, 264, 272, 280n8
menarche, celebration of 304
menstrual hygiene 14, 299, 300, 302, 303,
  304, 307n6; *see also* MHM (Menstrual
  Hygiene Management)
mental health, of children in refugee
  camps 181–182, 183
Mergens, Celeste 297
Merry, Sally 169
Mertus, Julie 168–169
Mexican Brown 103, 104
Mexican Revolution, 1910s 66, 103
Mexico: US war with, 1800s 66,
  100–101; violence, gender and
  disability study 12, 149–50, 156–160
MHM (Menstrual Hygiene
  Management) 14, 297–298, 305, 306;
  dignity discourses 299–304; and
  human rights 298–299
Michaels, Walter Benn 279n2
MICIVIH (International Civilian
  Mission to Haiti) 216–220
Mignolo, W. 45, 187–188
migrant workers 7–8; discrimination
  235, 236, 237; false dichotomy with
  refugees 229; Gulf region 13–14, 228,
  231–238; theories and praxis 228–231

migrants/migration 20; Asian migrants to US 102–103; and citizenship 26–27; to Europe 29, 30
Millennium Declaration 2000 41, 134, 142
Millennium Development Goals (MDGs) 131, **134**, 134–138, 139–140, 141, 143–144
minorities, sexual 168–169, 175, 177n2, 261, 264, 268, 272
minority rights 34; *see also* third-generation rights (solidarity rights)
Mississippi 265, 272, 273
Mnisi Weeks, Sindiso 12, 111–124
Mohammad, Kosar 14–15, 314, 317–318, 320
Mojola, Sanyu 305
monogamy 262
Mookherjee, Nayanika 250, 253–254, 255
moral concepts, thick and thin 22
moralism 270, 280n10
morality 21–22, 35
Morrison, Toni 7
Mouffe, C. 51
mourning 265
MSM (men who have sex with men) 171, 264, 272, 280n8
Muktijuddho films, Bangladesh 14, 243–256
Mullins, Greg A. 268
Muntarbhorn, Vitit 172, 173
Murphy, A.V. 251
Murphy, Kevin 272
Murray, Heather 232
Mutua, M. 45, 46, 293

Nader, Laura 114
Nagy, Sharon 234–235
narrative, and Bangladeshi *Muktijuddho* film 243, 248, 249, 250, 253, 254, 256
Nash, Jennifer 255, 256
national cinema 14, 143, 144–145
National Comprehensive Program to Prevent, Assist, Punish and Eradicate Violence against Women 2014–2018 (PIPASEVM), Mexico 157
National Democratic Alliance 83, 85–86
National Program for the Development and Inclusion of Persons with Disabilities 2014–2018, Mexico 157

National System for Integral Family Development (SNDIF), Mexico 156–157, 158
nationalism, Bangladesh 245, 249, 256
nationality, right to 27–28, 29
Native Americans 100, 102, 103
neglect 19, 25, 30
Neumeyer, Hannah 303–304
New Criticism 261–262
New Historicism 261
New Orleans 267, 273, 274
Nicaragua 66, 75
non-citizens 25–26, 29, 31, 59, 99, 154
non-discrimination: and the MDGs (Millennium Development Goals) 137; and the SDGs (Sustainable Development Goals) 141–142
Noonuccal, Oodgeroo 196, 204
North, Joseph 261–262, 269, 277
nostalgia 263, 265
nuclear weapons testing, Australia 200–201

OAS (Organization of American States) 42; electoral mission to Haiti 220–224
object of desire 264
O'Connor, Flannery 270
OHCHR 182, 183
Okihiro, Gary 3
Oliva, Nelson 320
Oman *see* GCC (Gulf Cooperation Council) states (Bahrain, Kuwait, Oman, Qatar, Saudi Arabia, United Arab Emirates)
"One Laptop per Child" (OLPC) initiative 306
Open Working Group (OWG) 139
Operation Wetback 104
optimism, and Eudora Welty's queer love 263, 264, 265
Organization of American States *see* OAS (Organization of American States)
Osiewicz, M. 181
otherness 256, 269, 272, 277
Otto, D. 44–45
OutRight Action International 167, 168, 174
overdetermination 50–52, 53, 60
overrepresentation 52
OWG (Open Working Group) 139
Oxfam 226

Pad for Pad 300
Pakistan, peacekeeping forces in Haiti 224–226
Palestine: LGBTQ 175; UNRWA (United Nations Relief and Works Agency) refugee camps 13, 185, 187–189
Paraguay 67
Parikh, Crystal 3–4
Paris Convention 1794 11
Parken, A. 152
participation: and the SDGs (Sustainable Development Goals): 138–139; South Africa 123
partition of the Indian subcontinent 244, 256
past, the, and Eudora Welty's queer love 262–266, 267, 268, 271, 273, 276, 277–278
patriarchy 57, 170, 172, 175, 176, 246, 249
Patterson, Orlando 53
peace: liberal 288–289, 290, 293; right to 14, 285–286, 288, 289–293
Perina, Mickaella 10, 19–33
Perkins, Charles 197
Permanent Forum on Indigenous Issues, UN 205, 209
Persian Gulf region see Gulf region
personal narratives and testimonies, UMass Boston students 319–326
persons of color, and human rights in the US 3–4
Pierre, Mardia 14–15, 315, 323–325
pinkwashing 170
Piore, M. 230
PIPASEVM (National Comprehensive Program to Prevent, Assist, Punish and Eradicate Violence against Women 2014–2018), Mexico 157
place, and Eudora Welty's queer love 262–267, 268, 269, 273–274, 275, 276, 277–278
Plata Diaz, Germán 331
PMA2020 300–301
Pogge, T. 24.25
political emancipation 57–58
political identities 204
political membership 26, 27–28, 29, 30
political parties 83, 85, 86, 89
political promises, South Africa 111, 112, 113
political rights see first-generation rights (civil and political rights)

politicization of the judiciary, South Africa 113
politics, judicialisation of in South Africa 112–113
politics of verification 59
Poslun, M. 44
poststructuralism 52
power, coloniality of 285–286, 286–287, 293
Pratt, Lloyd 262–263, 265, 271, 277
present, the, and Eudora Welty's queer love 262, 263, 264–265, 266, 268, 271, 273, 274, 275, 276, 277
Prilleltensky, I. 312, 316
primary health care 317
Priyobhashini, Ferdousi 253
Pro igualdad program, Mexico 159
promises, South Africa 111, 112, 113
Protocol to the African Charter on Human and People's Rights on the Rights of Women in Africa, 2003 11
Puar, Jasbir 170
pull factors 230
Puri, Jyoti 251
push factors 230

Qatar: migrant workers 233–234, 235–236, 237; see also GCC (Gulf Cooperation Council) states (Bahrain, Kuwait, Oman, Qatar, Saudi Arabia, United Arab Emirates)
queer 166, 167, 169, 170, 174, 176; see also LGBTQ
queer love, Eudora Welty's 14, 261–281
queer rights 268
queer theory 61, 166, 170, 171, 262–263, 269, 271, 278
Queers for Economic Justice 176
Quijano, A. 286–287

race, and Eudora Welty's queer love 266, 267
racial discrimination 36, 137, 142, 150
racialization 50, 51, 55, 250, 251, 286–287, 305, 306, 315, 325, 326
racism 175, 229, 251; Sudan 93, 94; UMass Boston education program 315, 316, 317, 319, 322–323; US 176
Raju, Zakir Hossain 244
Rancière, Jacques 58, 59
rape: Bangladeshi *Muktijuddho* film 248–249, 250, 252, 253–254; Sudan 83, 84–85; see also sexual assault; sexual violence

Ratana, T.W. 200
Reagan, Ronald 65, 74, 76
reckoning, ethical 14, 243, 256
recognition, and Bangladesh 243, 244, 245, 246, 254
reconciliation, and Bangladesh 243, 245, 255
Reda, Latife 229
reflexivity 226, 314, 315, 316–318, 319
refugee camps: education in 13, 180–192; Jordan 190; Kenya 13, 184–185, 189; Palestine 13, 185, 187–189; UNRWA (United Nations Relief and Works Agency) 185, 187–189
refugees 27, 28, 29, 30; false dichotomy with migrant workers 229
regional system of human rights 42–43, 79, 94
religiosity, and human rights 4–5
remittances by migrant workers 230, 231
representation 82, 90–94
research as a human right 312
Resolution 1325 on Women, Peace and Security, 2000 11
respect, South Africa 115–118, 119, 121
Restuccia, Frances 281n15
rhizome 266
Rich, Adrienne 171
Rich, R. 44
Richmond, O.P. 288, 289
right to a nationality 27–28, 29
right to bodily integrity 22–23, 80, 94, 117, 171, 172
right to have rights 29, 57–60, 98, 101
right to peace 14, 285–286, 288, 289–293
rights discourse, South Africa 12, 111, 117, 121, 122–123
Roafm Virginia 302–303
Röbblom, M. 152
Roberts, T.A. 305
Romo, Jésus 101
Roosevelt, Eleanor 36
Roosevelt, Franklin D. 132
Ross, A. 288, 289
Roux, C. 315
Roy, A. 288, 289
rule of law: Colombia 291; South Africa 114
ruling parties, South Africa 113
Russell-Einhorn, Malcolm 10, 34–49

Sahin, M. 297
Saikia, Yasmin 254–255
Salima campaign 93

same-sex marriage 167, 170, 174, 264, 267
San Francisco Conference, 1945 37
Sánchez Rodríguez, Ana María 12, 148–164
Satterthwaite, M.L. 142
Saudi Arabia 7, 235, 236–237; see also GCC (Gulf Cooperation Council) states (Bahrain, Kuwait, Oman, Qatar, Saudi Arabia, United Arab Emirates)
savages-victims-saviors (SVS) metaphor 45–46, 81, 82
Save the Children 182
scarification 22–23
Schachter, Oscar 298
Schmidt-Leukel, Perry 4–5
Schulman, Sarah 171
Schultheis Moore, Alexandra 268
SDGs (Sustainable Development Goals) 12, 89, 131, 138, 139–144, **140**, 298–299, 301; see also 2030 Agenda for Sustainable Development Goals
second-generation rights (economic, social and cultural rights) 34, 40–41, 43, 44
Security Council, UN 35, 37, 79
Sengupta, Arjun 133
sensibility 277
separation of powers, South Africa 113
Seshadri, Kalpana Rahita 280n11
settler colonialism 50, 51–52, 53, 54, 57, 59–61; logics of exclusion and elimination 53, 59
sexual assault: Sudan 84, 85; US-Mexico border 107; see also rape; sexual violence
sexual identity 169, 267
sexual minorities 168–169, 175, 177n2, 261, 264, 268, 272
sexual orientation 152, 154, 165–166, 167, 168, 170, 172–173, 174, 177, 292, 331; discrimination 166, 167, 168, 172, 173; see also LGBTQ
sexual rights 171–172; see also LGBTQ
sexual subjectivity 261
sexual violence 156, 325; Bangladesh 245,248,249,251,253,254; see also rape; sexual assault
sexuality, and Eudora Welty's queer love 14, 261, 264, 265, 266, 267, 268, 269, 272, 275, 276, 277, 278
Shalhoub-Kevorkian, Nadera 187–188
Shapiro, Ester 14–15, 312–334
Shingirai, A.A. 88

slavery 3, 7, 11, 51, 52, 53, 54–55, 58, 59, 100, 250, 255, 288; and the Haitian Revolution 56–57; and human rights 3; international prohibition of 22, 36, 38; and social death 51, 53–54

SNDIF (National System for Integral Family Development), Mexico 156–157, 158

social death 50, 51, 53–54, 60

social determinants of health 312, 313, 316, 318, 319, 326

social ecological theories 316, 317, 318

social enterprises, and menstrual hygiene 298, 299–300

social isolation of migrant workers 235–236

social justice 15, 72, 94, 153, 289, 292, 313, 322, 331, 333, 334

social rights 40, 41, 131, 132, 133, 135, 136; *see also* second-generation rights (economic, social and cultural rights)

socioeconomic transformation, South Africa 112

SOGI (sexual orientation and gender identity) 167; *see also* gender identity; LGBTQ; sexual orientation

solidarity: education of refugee children 185, 186, 189; Latin America 11, 65–68, 69, 70, 71, 72–73, 74, 75–77

solidarity rights *see* third-generation rights (solidarity rights)

Somali refugee camps 13

Sommer, M. 297

South Africa, rights discourse 12, 111–114, 120–124; context and custom 115–120; rights in the constitution 114–115

South Australian Aborigines Act 197

southern American literature 261, 270, 271; *see also* Welty, Eudora

Southern Border Communities Coalition 107

sovereignty 20, 27, 31, 35, 55, 82, 180, 198; Aboriginal communities, Australia 202, 204, 205, 207, 208, 209; Haiti 57

"space," in public policy 152

Spanish-American War 66

specificity 262, 265, 271, 275; cultural 23, 81, 82, 87, 88, 90, 92, 268

speculative fiction 180–181

speculative vision of the future 183, 185, 191

Spivak, Gayatri 89

Srikanth, Rajini 1–16, 13, 180–195, 280n7

statelessness/stateless persons 26, 28, 29, 30, 59, 155, 187

state power 66

states 3–4, 20, 22, 25, 26–27, 28–29, 30–31; sovereignty 20, 27, 31, 35, 55, 82, 180, 198

Steiner, C.B. 81

Stevens, J. 106

stigma, and menstruation 299, 302

stillness 262, 266, 275, 277

Stockton, Kathryn Bond 266, 267

strangers 20, 24–28; and Eudora Welty's queer love 265, 267, 268–269, 270, 272–276, 277, 278

Street, Jessie 197, 203

Striffler, Steve 11, 65–78

subaltern studies 51

Subz Pants and Pads 300

Sudan 81–82,83–95; refugees 13, 184–185

Sustainable Development Goals (SDGs) 12, 89, 131, 138, 139–144, **140**, 298–299, 301

Sustainable Health Enterprises 298

Suyemoto, Karen 333

SVS (savages-victims-saviors) metaphor 45–46, 81, 82

Syrian refugee camps 13

"technologies of passing" 304–305

temporality 266; *see also* time

Temporary People (Unnikrishnan) 7–8

Texas 100, 101, 104

Texas Rangers 101

thick moral concepts 22

thin moral concepts 22

third-generation rights (solidarity rights) 34, 43–44, 285

Thoreson, Ryan 174

time, queer 262–267

Todaro, M. 230

transformation, South Africa 111, 113, 122

transformative constitutionalism, South Africa 111, 122

Transforming our world: The 2030 agenda for sustainable development (UNGA) *see* 2030 Agenda for Sustainable Development Goals

transgender rights 321–322

transit of empire 60

transitional justice 121

transnational feminism 171, 176, 251
transnational migration *see* migrant
  workers; migrants/migration
transphobia 167, 168, 170
trauma: Bangladeshi *Muktijuddho* film
  243, 249, 252, 253; children 182,
  183, 190
Treatment Action Campaign, South
  Africa 111, 112
Trump administration, US 107

U Thant 2
UDHR (Universal Declaration of
  Human Rights), 1948, United Nations
  1, 3, 9, 10, 12, 19, 20, 22, 28, 29, 30,
  36, 37–38, 42, 68, 79, 80, 102, 131,
  132, 133, 142, 143, 196, 202, 203, 234,
  268, 287, 289, 298, 332; article 2 234;
  article 3 22; article 4 22; article 15 29
Uganda, refugee camps 185, 186
UMass Boston (University of
  Massachusetts Boston) 5–7; HRWG
  (Human Rights Working Group) 6,
  331–334
UMass Boston (University of
  Massachusetts Boston), Psychology
  403 Capstone/Gender, Culture and
  Health Promotion course 312–315,
  326; course organization 316–319;
  students' personal narratives and
  testimonies 319–326
UN (United Nations): CEDAW
  (Convention on the Elimination of All
  Forms of Discrimination against
  Women) 11, 12, 40, 79, 81, 88, 89, 94,
  148–149, 153–154, 154–160; Charter
  35, 36, 45, 132, 229, 289, 298;
  Commission on Human Rights 40,
  132–133, 203; Conference on
  Environment and Development (Earth
  Summit), 1992 133; Conference on
  Sustainable Development 139;
  Convention 13; Convention against
  Torture and Other Cruel, Inhuman or
  Degrading Treatment or Punishment,
  1984 40; Convention Concerning
  Indigenous and Tribal Peoples in
  Independent Countries, 1989 41;
  Convention for the Safeguarding of
  Intangible Cultural Heritage, 2003 41;
  Convention on the Rights of Persons
  with Disabilities, 2006 40, 149, 155,
  158; Convention on the Rights of the
  Child 41, 83, 132, 182; Convention

Relating to the Status of Refugees,
  1951 229; Cyrus Cylinder 2–3;
  Declaration of the Rights of
  Indigenous Peoples (UNDRIP) 198,
  199, 200, 205–208, 209; Declaration of
  the Rights of the Child, 1959 182;
  Declaration on the Right to
  Development 132; ECOSOC
  (Economic and Social Council) 35, 36;
  experiences of working with 220;
  General Assembly (UNGA) 26, 35,
  39, 40, 41, 132, 185, 286, 289, 290,
  292, 293; Global Compact 41;
  Guiding Principles on Business
  and Human Rights 41; High
  Commissioner for Human Rights 37,
  40; Human Development Index 313;
  Human Rights Committee 38, 39, 40;
  Human Rights Council 37, 40, 41,
  132–133, 172–173, 290; human rights
  development 132–134; human rights
  mission in Haiti 216–220; IESOGI
  173; International Conference on
  Population and Development, 1994
  133; International Convention on the
  Protection of the Rights of All
  Migrant Workers and Members of
  Their Families 228, 230; and LGBTQ
  165, 172–174; MICIVIH (International
  Civil Mission to Haiti) 216–220;
  Permanent Forum on Indigenous
  Issues 205, 209; Security Council 35,
  37, 79; World Conference for Social
  Development, 1995 133; World
  Conference on Education for All,
  1990 133; World Conference on
  Human Rights, 1993 45, 133–134, 171;
  World Conference on Women, 1995
  133, 171; World Food Summit,
  1996 133
UNDRIP (Declaration of the Rights of
  Indigenous Peoples) 198, 199, 200,
  205–208, 209; Article 3 206; Article 46
  (1) 206–207
UNESCO (United Nations Education,
  Scientific, and Cultural Organization),
  GCE education program 185–186,
  189, 190
UNGA (UN General Assembly) 26, 35,
  39, 40, 41, 132, 185, 286, 289, 290,
  292, 293
UNICEF 192, 299, 301
United Arab Emirates 236–237; migrant
  workers 7–8; *see also* GCC (Gulf

Cooperation Council) states (Bahrain, Kuwait, Oman, Qatar, Saudi Arabia, United Arab Emirates)
United States v. Brignoni-Ponce 104
United States v. Martinez Fuerte 104
Universal Declaration of Human Rights *see* UDHR (Universal Declaration of Human Rights), 1948, United Nations
universality 44–45; of the Haitian Revolution 50, 56–57; of human rights 21, 23, 24, 27, 29, 31, 81, 90, 92, 135, 137, 285, 287–288, 293, 301; of individuals 262, 265, 269, 271; and the MDGs (Millennium Development Goals) 136; and the SDGs (Sustainable Development Goals) 139–141
Unnikrishan, Deepak 7–8
UNRWA (United Nations Relief and Works Agency) refugee camps 185, 197–189
unsettling coloniality 57, 61
Uruguay 69
US: Bill of Rights 3; Declaration of Independence, 1776 1–2; healthcare 316–317; human rights and persons of color 3–4; LGBTQ 176; role in development of UN institutions 35–36, 46; solidarity with Latin America in the Cold War period 65–78; Supreme Court 104
US Border Patrol 103–104; 12,99,105,106,107
US-Mexico border 11–12, 98–100, 108–109; construction of modern border 102–105; establishment and aftermath of 100–102; post-9/11 era 99, 105–107

VAAL (Victorian Aborigines Advancement League) 201
Valdez, Fernando Andino 14–15, 314, 320–321
values, South Africa 113, 119, 121, 122
Vasak, Karel 43
verification, politics of 59
Verloo, M. 152
Veronese, G. 189–190
victimization 246, 252, 256
Victorian Aborigines Advancement League (VAAL) 201
Vienna Declaration 133, 137
Vienna Declaration and Programme of Action, 1993 45

Vietnam War 68, 74
Villegas, Adriana Rincón 10, 14, 34–49, 285–296
violence, gender-based 12, 95, 148–149, 153, 154–160, 235, 315, 323–325
voodoo 219, 224
Vostral, S.L. 304
vulnerability, and Bangladeshi *Muktijuddho* film 14, 243, 246, 251–252, 254, 256

Wagner, Ann-Christin 190
Wal, Matiop 184–185
Walby, S. 151
Walzer, Michael 22
Warner, Michael 280n10
water sanitation and hygiene/WASH 297, 303, 307n6
Water Sanitation Supply Coordinating Council 299
Waters, Tony 187
"We Love Reading" (WLR) program 191–192
Wellman, C. 43–44
"wellness as fairness" 312, 316, 322
Welty, Eudora 14, 261–281
West Bank, refugee camps 13, 185, 187–189
"Whatever" (Agamben) 271
Whitlam, Gough 204
WHO (World Health Organization) 301, 316
Wilderson, Frank 55, 58
Wilson, Emily 301–302
Winkler, Inga 142, 302–303
witchcraft, in Haiti 218–219
WLR ("We Love Reading") program 191–192
Wolfe, Patrick 53, 57
women: citizenship rights 29; in Colombia 291–292; discrimination 11, 12, 19, 40, 79, 82–83, 137, 148–149, 150, 153–154, 155, 157, 159; and human rights 79–88; as migrant workers 234–235; Sudan case studies 83–95
women who have sex with women (WSW) 171
women's rights 34, 44; LGBTQ 170–171, 176; South Africa 116, 119, 121; Sudan 83–95; *see also* CEDAW (Convention on the Elimination of All Forms of Discrimination against

Women); third-generation rights (solidarity rights)
Wong Kim Ark 103
Wood, Nick 14–15, 321–322
Woodman, Gordon 123
working in human rights 13, 215–226
World Conference for Social Development, 1995, UN 133
World Conference on Education for All, 1990, UN 133
World Conference on Human Rights, 1993, UN 45, 133–134, 171
World Conference on Women, 1995, UN 133, 171
World Council of Indigenous Peoples 209

World Food Summit, 1996, UN 133
World Health Organization (WHO) 301, 316
WSW (women who have sex with women) 171
Wynter, Sylvia 52, 60–61

Yamin, A.E. 137
Yeomans, Neville 112
Yogyakarta Principles 172, 173
Young, Andrew 68
Young, H. 152
Yousuff, Nasir Uddin 245, 249–250; *see also Guerilla* (film)
Yuval-Davis, N. 79–80

Žižek, Slavoj 56, 57